European Community Economics
Second Edition

European Community Economics
Second Edition

T. Hitiris
Senior Lecturer in Economics, University of York

St. Martin's Press
New York

First published in the United States of America in 1991

Printed in Great Britain

ISBN 0–312–06752–6 (cloth)   ISBN 0–312–06753–4 (paper)

Library of Congress Cataloging–in–Publication Data applied for.

Contents

Tables

Figures

From the preface to the first edition

This book is concerned with the objectives, successes and failures of economic policy in the European Community. It is designed for students and other persons interested in European integration who wish to acquire a reasonably comprehensive introduction to major economic policy issues of the European Community. In this it is assumed that the reader has no prior knowledge of economics beyond that taken in an introductory course on economic principles. In an attempt to evoke and maintain the reader's interest and make the book intelligible and self-contained, a conscious effort has been made to explain specialised terms and concepts within the text and to use only the necessary minimum of numerical data. For the same reasons, footnotes are not used and the number of references is kept very low. Chapter 1 presents an introductory exposition of the objectives, policies and effects of Regional Economic Associations. Chapter 2 surveys the institutional background of policy-making in the European Community. Chapters 3–11 deal with contemporary economic policies of the European Community. Clearly the coverage is selective, but it is hoped that it includes most areas of major economic activity in the Community.

A feature of the book is its emphasis on the economic analysis of public policy rather than the detailed description of European Community institutions. The chapters are integrated closely and conform to the following standard format:

1. Presentation of the problem.
2. Set of possible solutions.
3. The solution chosen by the EC.
4. Effects of the EC choice.
5. Evaluation and conclusions.

The book started to take shape a few years ago when I was asked to teach a one-term undergraduate course on the economics of the European Community at the University of York. In preparation for this course I had the opportunity to read a number of good books, collections of essays and articles dealing with European Integration and related issues. In contrast to their treatment of the subject, the approach followed here aims at a differentiated product which attempts to explain the origin of EC policies and their effects. In this, account is taken of the limits of power which the treaties conferred on the Community and of the constraints on the choice and exercise of Community economic policy that the governments of the member states have imposed. Novel features of the book are that: (a) it is concerned with positive economics, explaining what the EC policies are and why, rather than speculating on what they ought to be or dispersing unsolicited advice to policy-makers; (b) it aims at a balance between theory, policy and facts and follows an integrated and consistent treatment of the whole subject of policy-making in the context of European integration; (c) it includes the latest developments, and up-to-date information and policy decisions.

It should become clear from the following that this book is concerned primarily with economic policy-making in the European Community. But the reader should not forget the first President of the European Commission's dictum: 'Make no mistake about it. We are not in business; we are in politics' (Walter Hallstein in *Time Magazine*, 6 October 1961).

Theo Hitiris
York, October 1987

Preface to the second edition

As a result of the Single European Act and other political and economic developments in Europe and the world, the European Community (EC) has made more progress towards integration since 1986 than in any other similar time period during its thirty years of existence. After a slow start, implementation of the necessary measures for completion of a single market by the end of 1992 accelerated, and significant progress has already been made in expanding monetary integration, removing capital controls, enhancing labour mobility, liberalising road and air transport, harmonising technical standards and reducing tax diversification and customs formalities. Proposals are also under discussion concerning the Community's 'social charter', the rights of people in the enlarged market. The mutual openness of frontiers in the single market is such a basic step towards integration as to make a common political stand towards the rest of Europe and the world inevitable.

All these changes have prompted the rewriting of this book. As in the first edition, my objective is to examine the workings of the EC with emphasis on policy analysis. However, as a concession to the more advanced students and their counterparts in business, finance and government, there is an increased treatment of analytical issues which are considered necessary for thinking about problems of economic integration and interpreting economic policy. The section on the theoretical foundations of regional economic associations has been much enlarged, a new section on the measurement of the welfare effects in the single market has been added, and the introductory sections on the basic theory of economic policy have been extended. In each policy chapter the structure follows the guidelines set in the first edition: first a review of the problem confronting policy-makers, then identification of policy alternatives and their theoretical foundations, followed by an outline of EC policy and an assessment of its performance in the light of-the objectives set out in the Treaty and subsequent agreements. The presentation is biased in favour of the most important areas of the Community's economic activity which have also attracted most of the theoretical and political disputes. Although care has been taken to keep up with the available information concerning policy directions, initiatives and statistical evidence, the European Community's progress is nowadays of such speed that what is new at the time of writing this preface in the summer of 1990 may already have been overtaken by events by the time the book is printed.

Theo Hitiris
York
1990

Abbreviations

ACP	African, Caribbean and Pacific ocean countries: signatories of Lomé Convention.
BICEP	Bonus Incentive Commodity Export Programme.
CAP	Common Agricultural Policy
CCP	Common Commercial Policy.
CCT	Common customs tariff, also CET.
CFI	Court of First Instance.
c.i.f.	cost, insurance, freight.
CET	Common external tariff, also CCT.
CFP	Common Fisheries Policy.
CJEC	Court of Justice of the European Communities (also ECJ: European Court of Justice).
CMEA	Council of Mutual Economic Assistance, also referred to as Comecon.
COREPER	Committee of Permanent Representatives.
CTP	Common Trade Policy.
CTP	Common Transport Policy.
D-G	Directorate-General.
DISC	Domestic International Sales Corporation.
EAEC	European Atomic Energy Community, also referred to as Euratom.
EAGGF	European Agricultural Guidance and Guarantee Fund, also referred to as FEOGA.
EC	European Community, comprising EAEC, ECSC and EEC.
EC-6	The first six members of the EEC: Belgium (B), Germany FR (D), France (F), Italy (I), Luxembourg (L), Netherlands (NL) (from 1958).

EC-9	The first six members of the EEC *plus*: Denmark (DK), Ireland (IRL) and the United Kingdom (UK) (from 1973).
EC-10	The first nine members of the EEC *plus* Greece (GR) (from 1981).
EC-12	The twelve members of the EEC (from 1986).
ECB	European Central Bank; also ESCB and Eurofed.
Ecofin	Council of Economic and Finance Ministers.
ECSC	European Coal and Steel Community.
ECU	European Currency Unit (also ecu).
EDF	European Development Fund.
EEC	European Economic Community: there are twelve members: Belgium (B), Denmark (DK), Germany (D), Spain (E), France (F), Greece (GR), Ireland (IRL), Italy (I), Luxembourg (L), Netherlands (NL), Portugal (P) and the United Kingdom (UK).
EEIG	European Economic Interest Grouping.
EES	European Economic Space.
EFTA	European Free Trade Area.
EIB	European Investment Bank.
EMCF	European Monetary Cooperation Fund.
EMF	European Monetary Fund.
EMS	European Monetary System.
EMU(a)	European Monetary Union.
EMU(b)	Economic and Monetary Union.
EP	European Parliament.
ERDF	European Regional Development Fund.
ERM	Exchange Rate Mechanism.
ESC	Economic and Social Committee.
ESF	European Social Fund.
ESCB	European System of Central Banks; also ECB and Eurofed.
Esprit	European Strategic Programme for Research and Development in Information Technology.
ETUC	European Trades Union Confederation.
Euratom	European Atomic Energy Authority.
f.o.b.	free on board.
FTA	free trade area.
GATT	General Agreement on Tariffs and Trade.
GDP	gross domestic product.
GNP	gross national product.
GSP	Generalised System of Preferences.
IGC	inter-governmental conference.

IMP	Integrated Mediterranean Programmes.
LDC	less developed country.
MCA	Monetary Compensatory Amount.
MFA	Multi-Fibre Arrangement.
MFN	most-favoured-nation.
NCI	New Community Instrument.
NIC	newly industrialising countries.
REA	regional economic association.
SAP	Social Action Programme.
SEA	Single European Act.
SEM	Single European Market.
TAC	Total Allowable Catch.
UNCTAD	United Nations Conference on Trade and Development.
UNICE	Union of industries in the EC.
VAT	Value Added Tax.
VER	voluntary export restraint.
YTS	Youth Training Scheme.

1

Regional economic associations: objectives, policies and effects

1.1 Forms of economic associations

The term 'regional economic association' (REA) defines collectively the various forms of economic integration among independent states. The relevant literature distinguishes five forms of REAs as presented in Table 1.1. This classification is taxonomic, and does not represent the different stages of integration of actual economic associations which usually combine characteristics from two or more forms.

It is important to note that economic integration has an internal dynamic. The only stable levels of regional economic association are minimal (free-trade area) or maximal (complete integration), with of course no definite time setting for the completion of one or the other of these processes. Thus, a customs union would inexorably lead to higher forms of economic integration – provided, of course, that the members agree to it. The dynamics of integration arise from increasing openness and political and economic interdependence among the participating countries, both of which reduce their ability to follow an independent course or to diverge significantly from the performance of the group as a whole. Progressive interdependence generates positive and negative 'externalities' in the form of spillover effects and feedbacks from the exercise of economic policy in a country to other countries; hence, interdependence causes gains and losses to the members of the economic association. In an attempt to maximise the gains or minimise the losses, the members of the economic association either adopt 'cooperative' policies which lead them further into economic integration or, alternatively, they decide to adopt 'non-cooperative' policies and retrace their steps back to a looser, and stabler, form of international interdependence, the

1

Table 1.1 Forms of regional economic associations and their features.

Forms	Free trade among the members	Common external tariff	Free mobility of factors of production	Harmonisation of economic policy	Unification of economic policy
1. Free-trade area, FTA	*				
2. Customs union, CU	*	*			
3. Common market, CM	*	*	*		
4. Economic union, EU	*	*	*	*	
5. Complete economic integration, EI	*	*	*	*	*

free-trade area (FTA). In the latter case the need for 'policy compatibility', additional to that already required of countries engaged in international trade, is minimal and can be handled by existing inter-governmental channels of negotiation and consultation.

In REAs, forms more advanced than the FTA, gains may be derived from intergovernmental cooperation ranging from policy compatibility to full policy 'coordination' and 'harmonisation' of targets and instruments. These involve the imposition of constraints on policy objectives, and the adoption of rules which require new elaborate international agreements and ultimately the establishment of special supranational institutions for their administration (Johnson, 1968). The taxonomy in Table 1.1 shows distinctly that as openness increases and the degree of economic interdependence rises, intervention in the market in the general form of 'harmonisation' of policies, which are implemented jointly in pursuit of shared objectives, becomes more intensive. For example, beginning with customs unions, the abolition of restrictions on intra-union trade and the unification of national tariff schedules disturbs the motive of national tariff policy, that is the economic and social reasons on which each member country had based trade intervention prior to the establishment of the REA. Thus, not only are tariffs eliminated from the instruments of national policy, but also the targets of tariff policy are exposed by participation in the customs union. If these targets are incompatible with the aims of the REA, they will be completely abandoned or appropriately modified. In the latter case, new instruments have to be found for the continuation of the policy. Similarly, following the formation of a common market, free mobility of factors of production will alter the endowment of production resources available to a member country (and their prices), and thereby the pattern, the pace and the limits of that country's economic growth.

Consequently, coordination and harmonisation within REAs is a set of intervention policies, the need for which arises from market liberalisation and from the emerging divergence between the objectives pursued, in common by the economic union, and individually by each member state as a sovereign national economic unit. For example, if all the members of a customs union want a surplus in the balance of trade with their partners, not all of them can possibly succeed. Harmonisation in this case is an interventionist policy which attempts to make the conflicting targets of the participants compatible.

In general, if the main economic objective of countries participating in a customs union is to increase their own national welfare, it seems more likely that this would now have to be pursued within a framework of additional constraints imposed by the need for coordination and harmonisation of both targets and policies. Therefore, not all the participants in the union will succeed in fully realising their private objectives. Similarly, free trade in commodities, services and factors of production within an economic union gives rise to problems of adjustment and income transfers between the participating countries. Consequently, an economic union cannot be mutually beneficial for all of them without some kind of interventionary policy. In this case, harmonisation will aim at some sort of equality in the distribution of the costs and benefits arising to the members from market liberalisation and from the reallocation of resources, production and trade according to comparative advantage. But then harmonisation is another form of intervention which includes among its results the increase in the degree of interdependence among the participating states.

Interdependence rises with integration. Free-trade areas foster a linkage between the demand of a country and the supply of another via trade. Common markets establish more and closer interdependence via channels in the markets of commodities, services and factors of production. Hence, policies adopted by one country affect other countries in the common market. This calls for collective action, leading to a higher degree of integration by the elevation of the common market to an economic union, and this in turn would require more coordination which at a later stage would progressively lead to more integration (Hitiris, 1982). Consequently, our contention is that there are only two truly stable forms of REAs: (a) free-trade areas and (b) complete economic integration. All other forms of REAs simply constitute intermediate and temporary stages in the process of the voluntary integration of national states by piecemeal methods. These transitional forms of REAs for economic, political and other reasons are inherently unstable. These arguments do not imply that countries embarking upon some form of REA will necessarily end up integrated into some sort of federal or unitary state. In fact, examples of voluntary subjugation of independent states in a multi-state federation, i.e. an advanced form of integration, are rare. Historically, most of the existing federations or unifications of states have been formed after wars, by force, not by peaceful negotiations (e.g. the United States and Italy).

The progress towards integration depends on the willingness of the national authorities of the member states to confer real powers to the supranational authorities of the REA. In fact, integration is a process during which the power of the national authorities of the member countries to exercise independent national economic policy is progressively diminished, while at the same time the power of the central authority of the REA to design and implement common policies is rising. The 'surrender' of power and the 'loss of sovereignty' of the national authorities is very often strongly resisted. Hence, in practice and during a long period of transition, an economic union may appear to be rolling from crisis to crisis (as, for example, the EC). However, willingness among the members to accept compromise and to reach consensus usually leads to the survival of the association, but at a higher level of interdependence and integration. Alternatively, if the participating countries either are unwilling to accept further curbs in their economic and political independence, or if by their intransigence they fail to resolve their differences and conflicts, the complete dissolution of the REA must not be discounted. This is not a remote theoretical possibility, but a fact which is confirmed by the large number of failed attempts for economic integration.

An issue of critical importance for the success or failure of the REA is the nature of its objective, that is the purpose for which hitherto free, independent and self-governing states might willingly sacrifice a considerable part of their national sovereignty for the sake of integration with other countries of similar inclination. Associations between states aim in general at the realisation of a benefit. It is important to emphasise that this benefit may not be primarily of an economic nature even if the association of states is described by the term 'economic'. For example, some of the participants in the economic association, or all of them, may have strictly political, nationalistic, defence or other objectives. However, all economic associations invariably have positive and/or negative economic implications, and these economic implications should be subject to examination. Inevitably, this means that countries may proceed with the formation of a REA although the economic effects they expect to derive from it are positive but negligible, or even negative overall. On the other hand, even if the potential economic benefit for a country from participation in an economic union might be large, its membership in the union is not necessarily a foregone conclusion. Many countries value their independence and national identity more than the prospect that within an economic union they might become more prosperous.

In general the causes and the objectives of REAs between developed countries are different from those between developing countries.

Regional economic associations between developed countries

The essential requirements for a successful economic association between developed/industrial countries are: first, that the participating countries are more or less of comparable levels of economic development; and, second, that they are similar, but potentially complementary, in the structure of both their production and demand.

The formation of an economic association between developed economies aims at the realisation of this potential complementarity. The abolition of trade restrictions between the members brings about immediate general benefits to the participants, the so-called static economic effects of the association. They are the effects derived from increased competition and trade with the existing structure of production. In the longer term, rationalisation and competition within the enlarged market are expected to accelerate development and to increase welfare by the dynamic effects of economic integration which consist of the following:

1. Improvement in the allocation and utilisation of resources within and between the participating countries.
2. Specialisation according to comparative advantage.
3. Realisation of economies of scale in both production and demand.

The full extent of these benefits cannot be accomplished easily, if at all, by the efforts of one country on its own, especially if it happens to be economically 'small'. Obviously, substantial benefits would be derived from economic integration, if in addition to production exhibiting increasing returns to scale, markets had been oligopolistic before the formation of the economic union. Integration will open up the markets to increased competition leading to improved allocation of resources and specialisation according to comparative advantage leading to cost reductions. Increased competition and enlargement of the market may in turn stimulate research and development inducing innovation and technical change, more investment and faster economic growth.

Regional economic associations between developing countries

Developing countries on the whole are both actually and potentially similar. Therefore, economic associations between developing countries cannot aim at the maximisation of static welfare. On the contrary, developing countries form REAs in an attempt to foster growth and to bring about fundamental changes in the structure of their production and trade. By these means they attempt to fashion a regional trade mechanism which will help to orient their economies in the direction of regional specialisation. These aims are usually pursued by the following:

1. The pooling of scarce resources essential for economic growth, such as capital, skilled labour, foreign exchange, entrepreneurship, etc.
2. The avoidance of unnecessary and uneconomic duplication in capital investment, research expenditures and the application of modern technology.
3. The enlargement of the market for the purpose of generating production capable of realising economies of scale, and of developing at a later stage the potential for a competitive structure.

In general, it is argued that developing countries tend to form REAs because any objective of production for import substitution of any one of them can be satisfied at a lower cost by participation in a customs union than by unilateral action (Cooper and Massell, 1965).

The nature of these goals implies that developing countries are not attempting to (and in fact cannot) make short-term gains; they have instead a longer-term perspective for forming economic associations. Hence, the rationale of integration among developing countries is not based on the expectation of static benefits accruing from competition-induced changes in the existing pattern of trade, which necessarily reflects the existing underdeveloped pattern of their production. On the contrary, it is based on the dynamic effects, the expectation that integration will develop regional markets which in turn will shape a new developed structure of production capable of generating a greater volume and range of trade. Therefore, the success of a REA among developing countries must be judged in the longer term, after the development of a productive sector capable of responding to increases in inter-regional demand. An additional justification for the formation of economic associations among developing countries might be that regional cooperation may increase the group's bargaining power in its economic, and sometimes political, external relations.

However, with the prospect of deriving benefits after a long period of economic sacrifice, the economic associations among developing countries contain, in a sense, elements of self-destruction. They consist of a number of countries, each one of which aims at the same objective – acceleration of its own development – which it cannot easily achieve with its own resources. Therefore, in a 'zero-sum game' setting, they try to raise their individual shares out of the resources available for collective development. This process creates tension and leads to conflicts among the members of the economic association which are difficult to resolve and usually result in long periods of strife and inactivity. In these circumstances, the economic associations among developing countries very rarely survive long enough to reap actual economic benefits. Since the late 1950s, more than forty economic cooperation and association arrangements have been established between developing countries. Their experience has shown that most of them disintegrate prematurely in an atmosphere of hostility and recrimination, or otherwise they become inactive and continue to exist, but only on paper (e.g. East African Economic Community, Central American Common Market, Latin American Free Trade Area and many others).

1.2   Trade protection

As we have seen, each of the forms of REAs entails the abolition of trade restrictions on intra-regional trade between the members. Therefore it is reasonable to start with the study of the effects of instituting trade restrictions, and to follow with the effects of abolishing trade restrictions within a REA. In this section we examine (a) the instruments of commercial policy, (b) the effects of tariffs and (c) the differences between tariffs, quotas and subsidies.

Policy instruments

Theory shows that if certain conditions are satisfied, not only can every country benefit by engaging in international trade but also that free trade is the best welfare-maximising policy. However, because perhaps not all the necessary conditions are met in the real world or for a number of economic and non-economic reasons, most countries intervene in the market to protect their economy from foreign competition. The aim of the present section is to show the effects of different protective policies.

The commonest form of protection involves the levying of a tariff on imports. The tariff is a tax charged usually *ad valorem*, that is on the price of imports, but it may also take the alternative form of a specific duty per unit of imports. In general, tariff policy discriminates in favour of domestic production, and against foreign production of competitive commodities. Among the many instruments of similar policies we distinguish the following:

1. *Tax discrimination* in favour of the domestic producers. If the instrument is indirect taxes on commodities, this policy has effects equivalent to those of tariffs.
2. *Variable levy* which is a tariff adjusted to keep the domestic price of imports equal to some target level. Therefore, a fall in the price of imports results in an increase in the levy.
3. *Quotas* which are quantitative restrictions, limiting the total volume (or sometimes the total value) of imports allowed into a country per time period.
4. *Production subsidies* which reduce production costs and provide the domestic producers with advantages in the competition with foreign producers. In contrast to the policy of levying discriminatory taxes or tariffs which penalise the foreign suppliers (negative discrimination), subsidies reward the domestic suppliers (positive discrimination).
5. *State trading*: the state, which is a relatively large economic unit, does not necessarily obey the rules of the free market. On the contrary, the market outcome can be affected by government demand or supply: state purchases (public procurement) can affect market prices or may favour domestic suppliers, while state sales of inputs may be provided to domestic producers at favourable low prices.
6. *Exchange controls* represent a policy of administrative restrictions on transactions involving foreign exchange. Restricting the amount of foreign exchange available for imports in general, or imports of certain commodities, increases the price (in domestic currency) and reduces the volume of imports, providing the domestic producers of competing commodities with unfair advantages.
7. *Import prohibition* of certain commodities is sometimes used by government in an attempt to completely eliminate foreign competition from the domestic market.
8. *Other non-tariff barriers* to trade include mostly administrative red-tape and similar bureaucratic devices (such as the discriminatory enactment of sanitary and safety regulations, different standards, quality controls, buy-at-home campaigns, etc.), which discriminate against imports.

Effects of tariffs

For the partial equilibrium analysis of the effects of tariffs, consider the market for a commodity X in a small price-taking country operating under conditions of perfect competition in both commodity and factor markets. Throughout the analysis of tariff imposition and abolition we also assume the following:

1. Factors are available at given supplies, fully employed and mobile between industries within a country, but immobile between countries.
2. Transportation costs are ignored.
3. There are no distortions or trade impediments other than the policy-imposed tariffs. Hence money prices and costs represent real social values and costs.
4. The commodity X is homogeneous, but while domestic production and imports supply the market with perfect substitutes, i.e. identical units of the commodity, the domestic supply is given priority over imports. Hence imports, M, are always equal to the *excess demand*, that is the difference between the domestic demand, D, and the domestic supply, S.

$$M = D - S \qquad\qquad (1.1)$$

This case is illustrated in Figure 1.1, parts (a) and (b). In part (a), D is the domestic demand curve for his commodity, S is the domestic supply (the long-term marginal cost) curve, and W is the perfectly elastic world/foreign supply curve. In part (b), EH is the country's import demand curve. Under free international trade, equilibrium in the domestic market will be established at price P_w, which is the domestic as well as the world price of the commodity. Equilibrium is reached for the domestic producers at marginal cost = price, and for the domestic consumers at demand = price. Therefore, at market equilibrium domestic demand will be Q_4, domestic supply Q_1, and imports Q_1Q_4, as shown in Figure 1.1(a). The volume of imports is also illustrated in Figure 1.1(b) where $O'M = Q_1Q_4$. Consumers' expenditure on this commodity is the rectangular area $P_w \times Q_4$, which consists of $P_w \times Q_1$ consumers' expenditure on domestic production – hence, domestic producers' revenue – and $P_w \times (Q_1Q_4)$ consumers' expenditure on imports (which is equal to the area $g + y$ in Figure 1.1(b): for the equivalence between parts (a) and (b) of Figure 1.1 see the Appendix, section 1.4). Next, the government decides to restrict imports by levying a tariff on import price, e.g. because it wishes to increase the share of the domestic supply in the market, to save foreign exchange spent on imports, to raise tariff revenue, etc. In general, any restriction on imports will reduce welfare because it will cause the substitution of domestic production for imports, which are a cheaper source of supply, and it will raise the price of the commodity and force consumers to reduce their purchases. Formally, the *ad valorem* tariff at t per cent shifts the foreign

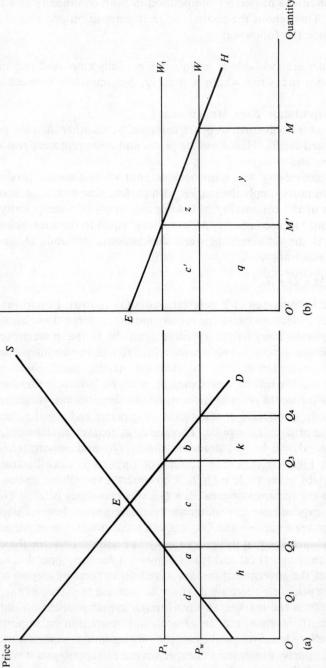

Figure 1.1 Effects of tariffs: (a) the domestic market; (b) imports.

supply curve upwards from W to W_t with the following effects:

1. *Price effects*: under the specified assumptions, domestic prices rise by the full percentage of the tariff. Thus, for world price remaining at P_w the domestic price, P_t, becomes

$$P_t = P_w(1 + t) \qquad (1.2)$$

   The policy of levying the tariff has created a distortion between domestic prices and free trade/international prices.

2. *Demand effect*: the increase in the price induces consumers to reduce their demand from Q_4 to Q_3. The utility value of this reduction is represented by the area $(b + k)$. The rectangular area k represents the social value of the reduction in demand, while the triangular area b represents the social waste stemming from consumption distortion after the levying of tariffs.

3. *Production effect:* higher market prices attract more domestic resources in the production of the commodity and thus domestic supply increases to Q_2. The area under the supply curve represents the opportunity cost of the factors that are employed in the production of the commodity. Increases in the price raise production by attracting factors which (under the full employment assumption) were before employed elsewhere in the economy. This process increases the area under the supply curve by $(h + a)$. However, the overall effect of the increases in production must be considered as welfare-reducing. The rectangular area h is equal to the world cost of producing the quantity Q_1Q_2, while the triangular area a represents the excess domestic cost of producing this quantity at home instead of importing it. Therefore area a should be counted as waste caused by the distorted effect of the tariff on relative prices.

4. *Import effect*: decrease in domestic demand and increase in domestic production imply that the residual between demand – supply, the excess demand which is identical to imports, will be reduced by precisely the sum of the demand and production effects. Thus, the reduction in the quantity of imports is $(Q_1Q_2 + Q_3Q_4)$, the tariff policy leaving only the quantity Q_2Q_3 to imports from foreign sources.

5. *Foreign exchange-saving effect*: reduction in the volume of imports under the constant import price P_w implies that expenditure on imports is also reduced. In Figure 1.1 this reduction at domestic currency valuation is equal to the area $(h + k)$. (As imports are paid for in foreign currency, the foreign exchange saving because of the tariff

is $(h + k)/r$, where r is the foreign exchange rate defined as the cost of one unit of foreign currency in terms of domestic currency.)

6. *Tariff revenue effect*: the levying of a non-prohibitive tariff yields revenue to the government equal to the tariff per unit of imports multiplied by the volume of imports, area c in Figure 1.1. Under our assumptions, the tariff is a tax on the domestic consumers of the imported commodity. Hence, the tariff revenue constitutes an income *transfer* from these consumers to the government of the country.

7. *Distribution effect*: the levying of the tariff has changed the total consumers' expenditure on the commodity from $(P_w \times Q_4)$ to $(P_t \times Q_3)$. This amount of expenditure exceeds what consumers would have paid for the same quantity of purchases under conditions of free trade by the area $(d + a + c)$. The latter area in fact is the increase in the price per unit of the commodity (i.e. the tariff per unit) *times* the total consumption of the commodity, that is $P_w \times t \times Q_3$. As we have seen, area c, the tariff revenue, is a transfer from the consumers to the government, while area a is a waste of domestic resources. The remaining area d is an increase in the total revenue over total cost which accrues to the domestic producers as profit. Consequently, area d is also an income transfer, but this time from the consumers to the producers. Therefore, as a result of the tariff policy and the consequent reallocation of expenditure between imports and domestic production and the redistribution of income, the consumers end up worse off, while the two other economic groups in the country, the producers and the government, benefit from the effects of trade restrictions.

8. *Welfare effects*: taking into consideration the costs incurred and the revenues received owing to the levying of the tariff, we end up with two items which cannot be accounted for. These therefore constitute a clear waste, that is a net loss for the whole economy. They are the triangular areas a and b, respectively the resource waste and the social waste of the distortive effects of the tariff. Hence, the sum $(a + b)$ is the total welfare cost of the tariff.

Tariffs in general foster production of domestic goods, but at a higher real cost than identical imported goods. The price of the domestically produced good is equal to cost at the margin, whereas the price of the competitive imported good is above cost by the amount of the tariff collected on the good. If the tariff is non-discriminatory between suppliers, it does not interfere with the source of imports which will be the lowest-cost foreign producer.

Tariffs, quotas and subsidies

Under the assumptions of perfect competition in the production, supply and demand of the commodity, quantitative restrictions have effects on prices and quantities identical to those of tariffs. Hence, in this case the quota and the tariff are *equivalent* because both produce the same import level and therefore an equal discrepancy between foreign and domestic prices. In Figure 1.1(a), a quota of Q_2Q_3 volume of imports is equivalent to the tariff of t per cent which produced the same level of imports. However, only if the government auctions import licences, is the equivalence between tariffs and quotas complete, with area c appropriated by the government as revenue from the sale of import licences under quotas or tax revenue under tariffs.

With tariffs and quotas having many effects, it is not always easy to pinpoint the exact reasons for their use in government policy. Nevertheless, owing to their relatively large negative welfare effects, we can state that in general what tariffs or quotas can do, other policy instruments can do much better. Assuming, for example, that the specific objective of the policy is to raise the share of domestic production in the market, the subsidy is a better policy instrument than the tariff. In Figure 1.1, the tariff of t per cent raised domestic production from Q_1 to Q_2. The same increase in production can be achieved by subsidising the domestic production at rate s per unit of output, where s is equal to the tariff charged per unit of imports, $s = (P_w \times t)$. The following results obtain under the subsidy policy:

1. Domestic prices remain unchanged at the level of world prices, P_w.
2. Demand remains at the free-trade level, Q_4.
3. Imports are reduced by the quantity Q_1Q_2 with saving of import expenditure equal to area h in domestic currency terms.
4. There is no tariff revenue for the government which instead incurs additional budgetary expenditure equal to the area sum $(d + a)$ for the financing of the subsidy.
5. There is no direct transfer from the consumers to the government and the producers. Of course, the budgetary cost of the subsidy is ultimately paid by the taxpayers (who are not exclusively the consumers of this commodity).
6. The welfare effect of this policy is still negative but restricted to the loss of only the triangular area a, which is the waste caused by the distortive effect of government intervention in the production side of the market.

If the objective of trade policy is export promotion rather than protection of the domestic import-competing industry, then an export subsidy would be a way to achieve it. A subsidy has the same effects as lowered costs and makes it possible for domestic firms to compete in international markets. However, the best policy is one that does not discriminate between home and foreign markets. Therefore, the best policy for both protecting the domestic industry and promoting exports is that of subsidies at the production stage.

In conclusion, other things being equal, protection by tariffs or quotas is an inferior policy for promoting domestic production. However, the comparison between tariffs, quotas and subsidies has also to be extended over the administrative costs of operating each policy. The sums allocated to subsidies have first to be collected by taxation and then distributed to producers according to some exact plan of intervention. In contrast, import duties are relatively inexpensive to collect, they perform the tasks assigned to subsidies equally well and provide the government with the added bonus of a revenue.

The tariff is both a tax on consumers and a subsidy to producers, without having to be actually collected and distributed. However, as an instrument of policy, tariffs are considered to be inflexible because every time a change in them is contemplated, the government has to ask the legislature for changes in the tariff law. Quotas are in general more adaptable, administratively more flexible (their modification usually involving simple procedural requirements) and more efficient for preventing the volume of imports from exceeding prespecified levels. But despite the valid theoretical objections against tariffs and quotas and the economists' preference for subsidies, both tariffs and quotas are still widely used instruments of government commercial policies.

1.3   Trade liberalisation

We have stated that, if certain conditions are met, and from the welfare point of view, free trade is the best policy. A customs union and other more advanced forms of REAs entail the abolition of barriers to trade among the member countries and the adoption of a common external tariff on trade with non-member countries. Therefore, if we assume that the partners in the customs union start from a non-optimal tariff-ridden situation, establishment of the customs union would combine a move towards free trade among the member countries with the retention or increase of impediments to trade against non-member countries. This is clearly a case of discriminating trade liberalisation by abolition of protection only on trade between the union partners. Elimination of one distortion in the presence of others or substitution of one distortion for another does not necessarily improve welfare. This is an example of the theory of *second best*, according to which if *all* the conditions for optimality (i.e. maximum welfare) cannot be made to hold simultaneously, there is no presumption that attainment of one of these conditions will necessarily increase welfare. The effect on welfare of a movement towards fulfilment of one of the optimum conditions will depend on the precise circumstances of the case. Consequently, customs union theory represents an application of second-best theory.

In general, formation of a regional economic association has both positive and negative trade and welfare repercussions upon the members of the association, the non-member countries and the world as a whole. Whether the overall effect of the formation of the REA is negative or positive cannot be accurately predicted. We illustrate this problem with a study of the short-term trade and welfare effects of tariff changes following the formation of a customs union. The following effects are considered:

1. Trade creation and trade diversion.
2. Terms of trade.
3. Economies of scale.

Trade creation and trade diversion

In Figure 1.2, parts (a) and (b) illustrate the markets of two price-taking countries, A and B, for a homogeneous commodity X which has no close substitutes or complements. The demand–supply curves are D_A and S_A in country A and D_B and S_B in country B. We assume that both countries face increasing production costs, but country B, for reasons relating to its production and demand conditions, is able to reach self-sufficiency, $S_B = D_B$, at a lower price than country A. For convenience we, in fact, assume that country B's market reaches equilibrium at the world supply price, P_w, so that B's industry does not need protection from foreign competition. However, country A, facing the low-price world supply W, protects its domestic industry by an *ad valorem* tariff of t per cent. Hence, in A the world supply curve shifts to W_t and the domestic price of the commodity is P_t. Therefore, the following situation exists in the markets of the two countries, before the formation of the customs union:

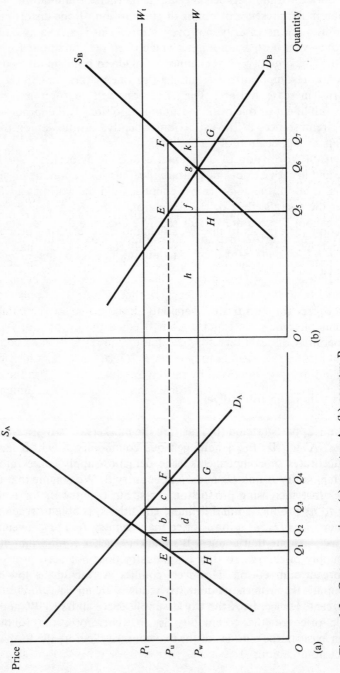

Figure 1.2 Customs union: (a) country A; (b) country B.

	Country A	Country B
Price	P_t	P_w
Demand	Q_3	Q_6
Supply	Q_2	Q_6
Imports	Q_2Q_3	nil

All other effects of tariffs occur in A as previously described.

Next, we assume that countries A and B form a customs union, retaining the tariff of t per cent as the common external tariff of the union. Hence, while the world supply W is subject to the tariff, the partners' supplies are not. Therefore, within the union B's producers are provided with a higher selling price and an expanded market where, up to a certain point, the only competition they face comes from the less efficient producers of country A. Consequently, B's producers increase production for exports to meet A's demand. But, at rising production costs and therefore prices, B's excess supply for exports originates, first, from increase in production and, second, from decrease in domestic demand. In Figure 1.2, this process will continue until equilibrium in the market of the customs union is reached, that is until the supply from A and B equals the demand of A and B. Equilibrium in the combined market implies that the exports from B equal the imports of A. This occurs at price P_u, and therefore the union requires to adopt a common external tariff at least equal to $t' = (P_w P_u / O P_w)$ per cent, which would eliminate foreign competition by raising the domestic price in the union to P_u. Consequently, after the formation of the customs union, the following situation is observed:

	Country A		Country B	
	Level	Change	Level	Change
Price	P_u	$-(P_t - P_u)$	P_u	$+(P_u - P_w)$
Demand	Q_4	$+Q_3Q_4$	Q_5	$-(Q_5Q_6)$
Supply	Q_1	$-Q_1Q_2$	Q_7	$+(Q_6Q_7)$
Imports	Q_1Q_4	$+(Q_1Q_2 + Q_3Q_4)$	nil	nil
Exports	nil	nil	Q_5Q_7	$+(Q_5Q_7)$

Disaggregation of A's imports, Q_1Q_4, is of particular importance. Country A's imports have undergone both a change of origin and an expansion. After formation of the customs union, all imports to A come from its union partner, country B, for two reasons. First, the substitution of imports from (a) country B for imports from the world, the quantity Q_2Q_3; and (b) country B for domestic production in A, the quantity Q_1Q_2. Second, the increase in domestic demand following the lowering of the price: the import quantity Q_3Q_4. The first two components of imports, Q_2Q_3 and Q_1Q_2, make up the *inter-country substitution effect* of the formation of the customs union. The third component of imports, Q_3Q_4, is the *inter-commodity substitution effect* which results from the reallocation of consumers' expenditure towards purchases of the commodity whose (relative) price has fallen by the abolition of the tariff.

The increase in imports was caused by (a) replacement of high-cost domestic production by partner production of the same good, Q_1Q_2, a *production effect*; and (b) increased demand for the good after the fall of its price, Q_3Q_4, a *consumption effect*. Therefore, the import expansion associated with these two events improves efficiency and has a positive welfare effect, the area $(a + c)$ which in the context of customs union theory is termed *trade creation*.

The change in the origin of imports was caused by the discriminating elimination of tariffs which led to the displacement of the lower-cost imports from the world, Q_2Q_3, by higher-cost imports from the partner country. This relocation of the supply of imports reduces efficiency and is detrimental for country A, causing a negative welfare effect, the area d, which is here termed *trade diversion*. Area b, which before the formation of the customs union was part of the government's tariff revenue, and area j which was a transfer from consumers to producers, remain now with the consumers. Therefore, country A's welfare effect of participation in the customs union is the gain from trade creation weighed against the loss of trade diversion, $(a + c - b)$. The net result can be positive, negative or even zero.

The overall welfare effect emerges in the comparison of 'before' vs. 'after' situations from the abolition of the tariff on the intra-union trade of a single commodity. With many commodities being traded, each one of the partners in the customs union will realise trade and welfare effects. The net outcome of these effects can be negative for certain countries and positive for others, with net welfare effect for the customs union as a whole negative or positive. These ambiguities arise from the second-best nature of customs unions where one set of distortions is replaced by another. Obviously, a non-preferential tariff reduction leads to pure trade creation, while a non-preferential tariff increase leads to pure trade diversion. Since customs unions involve preferential tariff changes, their net welfare effect depends on whether or not trade creation outweighs trade diversion.

The elimination of tariffs within a customs union affects each member's imports as well as exports. Import effects can be achieved by unilateral tariff reductions, but export effects require tariff reductions by others. Hence, one of the principal economic objectives of a country's participation in a customs union might be to increase its exports. Under conditions of full employment, the additional demand for exports, which is created by the abolition of tariffs, is met by diverting productive resources from other activities to the export-producting sector, where they will enjoy higher rewards. Hence, the gain for the export side should be measured by the excess reward which these resources obtain over and above the remunerations they received in their previous occupation. Figure 1.2(b), presents the effects of the formation of the customs union for the exporting country B. The increase in the price from P_w to P_u enables B's producers to hire more factors of production and expand their supply to Q_7. However, when the price of the commodity rises, the consumers in B cut down their consumption to Q_5. As a result of these changes, B's producers gain the area $(h + f + g)$, while B's consumers lose the area $(h + f)$. Under the assumptions employed in the construction of Figure 1.2(b), while area h is a transfer within country B from consumers to producers, area f is an outright loss for the consumers. However, B's producers gain the areas f and g from the consumers of country A as profit from exports. Therefore, B's net benefit from the customs union with country A is the export expansion Q_5Q_7 which is associated with a positive welfare effect for the economy equal to area g.

This net welfare benefit for B is associated with additional trade – exports in this case – and therefore it can be considered as trade creation. Alternatively, and more accurately, this benefit is a net profit (revenue – cost) for B's exporters, that is a rent identical to an income transfer from country A to country B. Country A would have been better off by purchasing its total imports, Q_1Q_4, from W at price P_w than from B at price P_u. Had country A done so, it would also have a tariff revenue, the area $EFGH$, which is now lost to B's exporters partly as profit, $(f + g)$, and partly as production cost, k, in excess of W's competitive supply price. Although in this case the customs union benefits only country B and makes A worse off, it may still be beneficial for both if B's gain is large enough that B has the potential to compensate A for its losses and itself remain better off (Kemp, 1969). Nevertheless, under the demand and supply conditions described, *ex post* and from a global welfare point of view, the customs union between A and B is trade diverting and cannot be justified on static economic-welfare considerations alone. Since joining a customs union is second best, there are always better policies available. However, as remarked earlier (Section 1.1), customs unions are not formed for economic reasons alone: non-economic motivations may be more important (Corden, 1984).

In the analysis above, as a result of the inter-country substitution effect, the partner country B displaced completely the outside world in the import market of country A. However, it is possible that the inter-country substitution is only partial. This will occur if the common external tariff is lower than that required to reserve the market exclusively for the internal supply of the union (tariff $t' < (P_w P_u / OP_w)$ in Figure 1.2). In this case, the union's combined supply falls short of the combined demand at the level of protection afforded by the common external tariff. Therefore, imports from W will continue after formation of the union, and the trade diversion effect will be lower. Country A will continue to import from W at price P_w, the domestic price will be $P_d = P_w(1 + t')$ and the government will collect a tariff revenue.

It is clear from the analysis above that the extent of the trade creation and trade diversion depends on the economic structure of the countries participating in the customs union. Thus, a high level of tariffs in trade between the prospective partners combined with high elasticities of demand and supply of the commodities traded between them before and after the formation of the customs union may raise welfare through substantial trade creation. Also, a low level of tariffs in trade with the outside world and low elasticities of demand for imports from non-participating countries may cause relatively low trade diversion. Clearly, if the customs union between two or more countries sets its common external tariff on non-member countries so as to preserve the same volume and composition of net trade with the rest of the world, trade diversion does not occur and the customs union is beneficial for the members without hurting the outside world. In essence, this means that a customs union can devise an appropriate external tariff schedule to eliminate all trade diversion (Kemp and Wan, 1976). Then the customs union benefits, because the only effect it experiences is trade creation by the liberalisation of intra-union trade. This is shown in Figure 1.3 where D_A and S_A are A's demand and supply curves. With an import tariff of t and export price of the supply from the rest of the world, W, of P_w, A's domestic price is $P_t = P_w(1 + t)$, domestic production Q_2, domestic demand Q_4 and imports Q_2Q_4 from W. After formation of the customs union its combined supply in A's market is the lateral sum of A's domestic supply and B's export supply, the curve $S_A + S_B$. The union adopts a common external tariff $t' < t$ which preserves the same volume of imports from the outside world. The price in A falls to $P_{t'} = P_w(1 + t')$, domestic demand rises to Q_5, domestic production falls to Q_1 and imports rise to Q_1Q_5. Total imports consist of imports Q_1Q_3 from the partner country B, and imports $Q_3Q_5 = Q_2Q_4$ from the rest of the world. The trade effect of the customs union after the lowering of the tariff is additional imports from the partner country B. Its

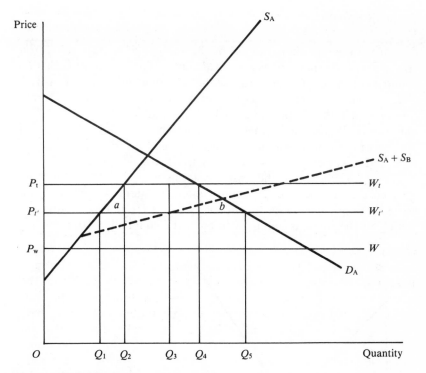

Figure 1.3 Trade-creating customs union.

export supply enters the market at the lower price $P_{t'}$ to meet A's increased demand and partly to displace more expensive domestic production, but without reducing imports from the outside world. The net welfare effect is a benefit from trade creation arising from inter-country (partner-to-partner) and intercommodity substitution, the consumption effect $(a + b)$.

In general, if two small countries A and B form a customs union, A exporting the commodity X to B for imports of the commodity Y under conditions of free trade, and before and after the union both countries also export the same products to the rest of the world for imports of commodity Z, which are subject to the common external tariff, then both countries will gain if (a) the commodities X and Y are net substitutes and (b) the commodity Z is neither a net complement nor a net substitute for X or Y (McMillan and McCann, 1981). Then, while trade between the two union partners expands, trade with the rest of the world is not affected.

Terms of trade

One of the obvious shortcomings of the analysis of welfare gains from customs union formation, as presented above, is the assumption that the countries of the union were so small that we could ignore terms-of-trade effects. In the real world, terms-of-trade effects of customs union formation may be rather important, for both the individual countries of the union in trade with each other and the union as a whole in trade with the rest of the world. An improvement in the terms of trade raises welfare, and a worsening in the terms of trade lowers welfare.

Figure 1.4 illustrates the case of terms-of-trade effects in trade between the members of a customs union. Country A's demand and domestic supply curves for a commodity X are D_A and S_A. Before formation of the customs union, A imports the commodity from country

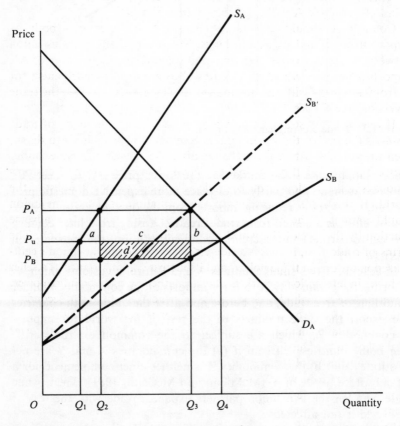

Figure 1.4 Terms of trade in a customs union. .

B, its future partner in the union, whose export supply curve S_B is less than perfectly elastic. Under protection by an *ad valorem* tariff of t per cent, B's supply curve shifts to S'_B. Then A's domestic price is P_A, total demand Q_3, domestic supply Q_2 and imports Q_2Q_3. The tariff revenue is $(c + d)$, appropriated by country A.

The crucial difference between this case and the previous one of perfectly elastic import supplies is that when A restricts its trade by a tariff, its domestic price does not rise by the full amount of the tariff: for P_u free-trade supply price from B, the price in A after the imposition of the tariff is $P_A < P_u(1 + t)$; B's export price falls to P_B. Consequently, part c of A's total tariff revenue is borne by its consumers and part d by B's producers. After formation of the customs union, A's tariff on imports from B is lifted and its domestic price falls to P_u. Demand rises to Q_4, domestic supply falls to Q_1, and imports from B expand to Q_1Q_4. Country A gains the trade-creation effect $(a + b)$ but loses the area d to its union partner B. Therefore, while the customs union as a whole gains, the country A will gain only if $(a + b) > d$.

Country A should experience terms-of-trade effects in both its imports from B and its exports to B. Moreover, if the customs union between A and B is trade-diverting, and the foreign supply curve of A's imports is not perfectly elastic, there will be a terms-of-trade benefit for A from any trade with the outside world which might survive the trade diversion (see Figure 3.1).

If one of the customs union's aims is to improve its terms of trade *vis-à-vis* the rest of the world and its economic size enables it to do so, then the volume of trade will change after the formation of the union. However, as a rule the principal objective of the formation of customs unions is not to exploit terms-of-trade advantages against the rest of the world. If this were the case, then the formation of a customs union would amount to the formation of a cartel, which may attract adverse reaction by the rest of the world and the possibility of retaliation. The terms-of-trade gain, if any, is a side-effect derived from the union's centralisation of foreign trade policy, and its increase in importance as a seller or buyer in international markets and strengthening of bargaining power. Nevertheless, though the terms-of-trade benefit might be a secondary objective, it is still of crucial importance for the customs union.

Assume that each member of the customs union is small, facing terms of trade with the outside world which it cannot affect. But when these small countries pool their economies, the customs union itself is sufficiently powerful in world markets to affect its terms of trade for the benefit of the participating countries. Figure 1.5 shows this case for a commodity X in a customs union formed by the countries A and B. Before formation of the union the combined total demand (that is, the

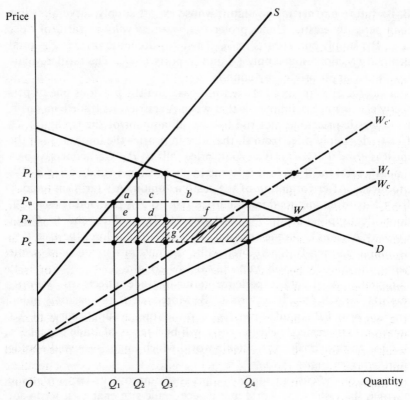

Figure 1.5 Customs union and terms of trade.

sum of the individual demands) of the two countries is D and their combined total domestic supply is S. Each one of them faced the foreign imports supply price P_w which it could not affect by its own action. On this import price each country levied a national *ad valorem* tariff giving average rate for both countries of t per cent. The tariff-inclusive price in the combined market is $P_t = P_w(1 + t)$, resulting in equilibrium demand Q_3, domestic supply Q_1 and imports $Q_1 Q_3$ from W. Tariff revenue is the area $(c + d)$, paid entirely by the consumers of the commodity in the two countries, A and B. After the customs union is formed, the two member countries together become a significant purchaser of the commodity X and have enough power to influence the price of their imports. The customs union now faces the less than perfectly elastic foreign supply W_c which, with the members' average tariff rate t as the customs union's common external tariff, shifts to $W_{c'}$. The union's domestic price falls to P_u, where $P_u < P_w(1 + t)$, and the import price falls to P_c. Total demand rises to Q_4, domestic supply falls to Q_1 and imports rise to Q_1Q_4. Tariff revenue is the area $(e + d + f + g)$ which is borne partly by the domestic consumers, $(e + d + f)$, and partly by the foreign producers, the shaded area g. Therefore, the customs union's welfare benefit consists of the trade-creation effect $(a + b)$ *plus* the terms-of-trade effect g. In the particular case of Figure 1.5, the terms-of-trade effect is much larger than the trade-creation effect.

Similar considerations apply to the case of terms-of-trade improvement in the exports of the customs union. Other things being equal, the less inelastic the foreign supply (demand) curve, the greater the improvement in the terms-of-trade. Similarly, the larger the customs union and the larger its economic (monopsonistic or monopolistic) power in world trade, the larger is the terms-of-trade effect. It can also be shown that, under conditions of imperfect competition, for a country or a customs union restricted trade may be superior to free trade and that there is an *optimum* tariff rate that maximises the welfare gain. This gain consists of the difference between the benefit from improved terms of trade *minus* the loss from reduction in the volume of trade. Notice also that for any terms-of-trade gain, the customs union imposes on the rest of the world a loss that exceeds the customs union's gain. The terms--of-trade effect is a transfer, an income redistribution and not a wealth-creating effect. Moreover, any terms-of-trade gain can be realised only if the rest of the world remains passive and does not retaliate by imposing its own tariffs. From a global point of view the optimum tariff is zero.

Economies of scale

The preceding analysis assumed increasing production costs in the countries forming the customs union, and constant or increasing production costs in the world markets. However, the integration of markets within a customs union may bring about cost reductions from exploitation of economies of scale. Internal economies of scale accrue to the firm as a result of its own expansion, while external economies of scale accrue to the firm as a result of expansion of the industry in which it is engaged. The analysis here concerns internal economies of scale. Although internal economies of scale can occur in every production activity, in a customs union they will be more probable in monopolistic industries which before the union operated in protected national markets, not sufficiently large to accommodate plants of the most efficient size. Economies of scale may also occur in a customs union by enlargement of the market for output which offers the opportunity of spreading initial costs over a larger volume of production. The cost reduction gains from internal economies of scale potentially may account for the major benefits of free trade within the customs union.

Figure 1.6 (a) and (b) depicts the case of a customs union between countries A and B when production of a commodity X is subject to internal economies of scale. The demand curves of the two countries are D_A and D_B. It is assumed that the world supply W is perfectly elastic at price P_w. Country A, which has no domestic production of this commodity, restricts its imports by a tariff of t per cent, so that its domestic tariff-inclusive price is P_{At} and the volume of imports/domestic demand is Q_1. Country B's average cost/supply curve is S_B, indicating that its domestic production enjoys internal economies of scale but at costs higher that those of world supply at any level of output. We have assumed that in the presence of increasing returns to scale, B's firm will follow an average-cost pricing policy; otherwise, a non-discriminatory marginal-cost pricing would result in losses. Prior to the formation of the customs union, country B protects its domestic production by a tariff rate at the level that exactly reserves the domestic market for the domestic supply, a 'made-to-measure tariff'. Hence B's domestic price P_{Bt} (= average cost, including normal profits), is equal to the tariff-inclusive import price, and domestic production is the market equilibrium output Q_3.

When the two countries form the customs union, country B's producers would be able to supply the entire market, if the partners in the customs union adopt as common external tariff the 'made-to-measure tariff' $t' = (P_w P_u / O P_w)$ per cent. Then, at customs union price P_u and combined demand curve $D_A + D_B$, the following will be observed:

	Country A	Country B
Price	P_u	P_u
Demand	Q_2	Q_4
Supply	–	Q_5
Imports	Q_2	–
Exports	–	$Q_4 Q_5$
Trade diversion	c	–
Trade creation	$a + b$	$d + g$

Country A's welfare effects of trade creation and trade diversion are the standard ones, as described in the preceding analysis. As a result of the formation of the customs union and expansion in demand, country B obtains its domestic supplies at lower cost of production. Hence the welfare gain $d + g$ is a cost-reduction or an economies-of-scale related welfare effect, which is similar but not identical to trade creation: it is

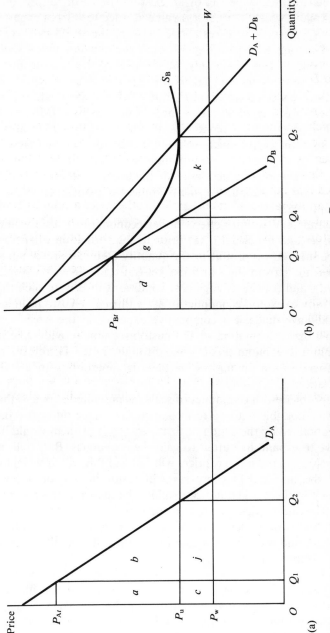

Figure 1.6 Economies of scale in a customs union: (a) country A; (b) country B.

not the welfare outcome of 'a movement to a cheaper source of supply but rather of the cheapening of an existing source of supply' (Corden, 1972). Area k, which is the excess value accrued to B from exporting the quantity Q_4Q_5 to A at prices above those of the world market, is also included among B's welfare gains from the customs union (Johnson, 1958b; Robson, 1987). Actually, at the level of the customs union k is a transfer from A to B equal to the tariff revenue which country A would have collected under tariff rate t' if it had bought its imports from the rest of the world rather than from B: $k = c + j$. Evidently, the possibility of exploiting economies of scale does not necessarily mean that each partner will be better off with the customs union than without; as shown in Figure 1.6, even though such economies of scale have reduced the cost of production inside the union, that cost is still higher than the cost of supplies formerly imported from outside the union (Johnson, 1962).

The trade and welfare effects under economies of scale would have been larger and beneficial if (a) prior to the formation of the customs union country A was producing the quantity Q_1 under protection instead of importing it from the world market (no trade diversion would have occurred), and (b) the average cost conditions in B were such that, the opportunity to exploit economies of scale through a customs union with A would have made it a competitive exporter in the world markets. In such a case, formation of the customs union provides the market for exploiting economies of scale through trade. Therefore, mutual trade liberalisation among the partners is superior to unilateral trade liberalisation.

One problem with economies of scale, as presented above, is that they are not compatible with perfect competition. Since internal economies can be obtained by the action of firms, each one of them would have an incentive to expand its output to gain the economies. But if all firms in the industry expand output, prices will fall and this will drive many firms out of the market. This process will result in one or a few firms remaining in the market and controlling the industry as a monopoly or cartel. This means that, if prior to the formation of the customs union production was undertaken in both countries, competition will strengthen, and production within the union will be limited to only one of the member countries.

The import and export effects as presented above and illustrated in Figures 1.1–1.6 are based on partial equilibrium static analysis and depend on a number of simplifying and restrictive assumptions:

1. First, that the countries concerned produce exactly the same com-

modity or perfect substitutes; if this is not the case, then the trade
and welfare effects, which depend on the degree of substitutability
between competing commodities, will be smaller.

2. Second, that market structure (perfect competition mostly) and cost
   conditions are as described; different assumptions about either or
   both may lead to different results.
3. Third, that the elimination of trade barriers, enlargement of the
   market and intensification of competition improve efficiency, but
   only through increasing the volume of trade, not through the
   import-competing and non-traded goods sectors.
4. Fourth, that the main issue concerning the customs union is the
   short-term reallocation of a given endowment of resources to
   different production activities and not the long-term growth and
   optimal allocation of productive factors.

These assumptions have to be relaxed when one considers the long-term
and dynamic effects of the formation of REAs.

Despite their shortcomings, the concepts and procedures so far
described have been used as the basis for measuring the static welfare
effects of actual or potential customs unions (see the appendix, Section
1.4, for an outline of basic methodology). The approach used is that of
partial equilibrium analysis which, in contrast to *general equilibrium
analysis*, has the drawback that it cannot account for spillover substitution effects between sectors which occur as relative prices change. In
addition to aggregation problems, which both methods share, problems
also arise in the partial equilibrium analysis from the probable violation
of certain crucial assumptions, as for example that factor supplies are
perfectly elastic and that factor prices remain constant while commodity
prices change. However, in practice general equilibrium analysis is
usually inapplicable, because either the statistical information or the
necessary techniques are not available. Partial equilibrium methods have
the advantage of simplicity of application. Moreover, when markets are
characterised by perfect competition and price changes are relatively
small, the partial and general equilibrium calculations are approximately
equal.

The estimates of the 'dead-weight loss' static welfare effects of actual
or potential customs unions are invariably small and unimpressive. Low
values of import demand elasticities, low tariff rates and relatively low
average propensities to import mean that the measures of the static trade
and welfare effects of tariff changes are necessarily very modest. But
even if they had been larger, they should not be considered crucial for
deciding whether a customs union ought to be formed. These effects are
static, occurring only once, and in any case static efficiency is not a good

predictor, of, nor a necessary precondition for, dynamic efficiency. As we have emphasised, most important are the dynamic effects which arise from intensification of competition and the opportunities offered by integration of the market. A large market can lead to a greater degree of specialisation leading to cost reductions from fuller utilisation of plant capacity, learning by doing, development of a pool of skilled labour and management, and in general from optimum allocation of resources and exploitation of economies of scale. However, the scale and dynamic effects of customs unions can be neither accurately estimated nor easily predicted.

1.4 Appendix: measurement of the trade and welfare effects of tariffs

Figure 1.1(b) illustrates the import side of the domestic market as described by equation (1.1). Since imports are allocated a residual share in the market, with domestic demand equal to domestic supply, as at point E, imports are nil. Free-trade imports Q_1Q_4 are exactly equal to imports M, and imports Q_2Q_3 under tariff protection exactly match imports M' in Figure 1.1, parts (a) and (b) respectively. Similarly, the areas under the demand and supply curves in Figure 1.1(a) exactly match the areas under the import demand curve in Figure 1.1(b), namely: $c = c'$, $z = a + b$ and $y = h + k$.

We have seen that the effects of tariffs are caused by their distortive increase in prices. The increase in the market price leads to two reactions of particular importance:

1. A decrease of the quantity demanded by the consumers.
2. An increase of the quantity supplied by the domestic producers.

The size of these effects obviously depends on the sensitivity of demand and supply to price changes, that is on the demand and supply price elasticities. Thus, from the definition of the price elasticity of demand

$$e_d = (dD/dP)(P/D) \tag{A.1}$$

where D = quantity demanded, P = price and d denotes a change, the effect of the change in price on the volume of demand is a decrease equal to

$$dD = e_d(dP/P)D \tag{A.2}$$

With reference to Figure 1.1, $dP = P_t - P_w$ and since the price increase is entirely due to the imposition of the tariff, $P_t = P_w(1 + t)$. Therefore

$(\mathrm{d}P/P) = (P_t - P_w)/P_w = t$, and the decrease in demand, equation (A.2), can now be written as

$$\mathrm{d}D = e_\mathrm{d}Dt \tag{A.3}$$

where, of course, $e_\mathrm{d} < 0$.

Similarly, from the definition of the price elasticity of supply

$$e_\mathrm{s} = (\mathrm{d}S/\mathrm{d}P)(S/P) \tag{A.4}$$

where S denotes the quantity of supply. After substitution we obtain that the supply effect of levying the tariff, is an increase in domestic supply equal to

$$\mathrm{d}S = e_\mathrm{s}St \tag{A.5}$$

where $e_\mathrm{s} > 0$.

As we have seen, the import effect of the tariff is equal to the sum of the reduction in demand and the increase in domestic supply, that is the demand and the supply effects. Hence the decrease in imports is:

$$\mathrm{d}M = \mathrm{d}D - \mathrm{d}S = (e_\mathrm{d}D - e_\mathrm{s}S)t \tag{A.6}$$

where $\mathrm{d}M = (M - M')$, the change in the quantity/volume of imports. However, from the definition of the price elasticity of the demand for imports

$$e_\mathrm{m} = (\mathrm{d}M/\mathrm{d}P)(P/M) \tag{A.7}$$

we obtain

$$\mathrm{d}M = e_\mathrm{m}Mt \tag{A.8}$$

where $e_\mathrm{m} < 0$.

Hence, under the specific assumptions we employed in the construction of Figure 1.1, from equations (A.6) and (A.8) we obtain the following relationship between the three price elasticities:

$$e_\mathrm{m}M = e_\mathrm{d}D - e_\mathrm{s}S \tag{A.9}$$

and

$$e_\mathrm{m} = e_\mathrm{d}(D/M) - e_\mathrm{s}(S/M) \tag{A.10}$$

Since it is relatively easy to derive estimates of price elasticities of demand and imports rather than of supply, in empirical measurements of the effects of tariff policies equation (A.8) is used more frequently than equations (A.3) and (A.5).

The welfare cost of the tariff is the sum of the areas a and b in Figure 1.1(a), or the equivalent area z in Figure 1.1(b). The measure of the latter area is

$$z = (\tfrac{1}{2})\,(\mathrm{d}MP_\mathrm{w}t) \tag{A.11}$$

or, substituting for $\mathrm{d}M$ from equation (A.8),

$$z = (\tfrac{1}{2})\,(e_\mathrm{m}MP_\mathrm{w}t^2) \tag{A.12}$$

The product MP_w is in fact the initial, or base-year, value of imports, V. Hence, the measure of the waste caused by the tariff is

$$z = (\tfrac{1}{2})\,(e_\mathrm{m}Vt^2) \tag{A.13}$$

The import contraction and the welfare loss which follow the imposition of the tariff are, of course, reversed to import expansion and welfare gain when the tariff is abolished. The percentage decrease in price, following the abolition of tariff t, is $(DP/P) = (P_t - P_\mathrm{w})/P_t = t/(1 + t)$. Therefore, the relevant formula of the increase in imports is

$$\mathrm{d}M = e_\mathrm{m}M't/(1 + t) \tag{A.14}$$

causing a rise in welfare equal to

$$z = (\tfrac{1}{2})\,(e_\mathrm{m}V't^2/(1 + t) \tag{A.15}$$

where $V' = M'P_\mathrm{w}$ is the value of the original volume of imports M' at price P_w.

Taking into consideration Figure 1.1 and the relevant equations for the estimation of demand, supply and import effects, we observe that in general the effects of the abolition of a tariff are greater (a) the larger the price elasticity of domestic demand, domestic supply and imports, (b) the higher the level of tariffs and (c) the larger the initial value of imports.

Further reading

Krauss (1973) and Pomfret (1986) are good guides to the customs unions literature. For standard classical treatments see Meade (1955) and Lipsey (1970). Since the analysis of customs unions is based on second-best considerations, the propositions derived from formal models depend crucially on the assumptions made. The three-commodity × three-country customs union models yield welfare results which differ from those of the three-country × two-commodity models: see McMillan and McCann (1981) and Lloyd (1982). One of the first attempts of systematic analysis of the theory of integration is Balassa (1961). Robson (1987) presents a concise analysis of theory and practice of international economic integration. Cooper and Massell (1965) developed the 'new theory' of customs unions between LDCs. See the same authors and Johnson (1965) for an explanation of customs union formation in terms of 'public goods'. On the welfare effects of trade, customs unions and trade policies see Corden (1984).

For methodology and results in estimating the welfare effects of customs unions see Johnson (1958b) and Winter (1987); for a general equilibrium approach to the measurement of welfare effects see Miller and Spencer (1977). The EC's calculations of welfare effects of the single market go beyond the 'dead-weight loss' approach and are presented in Chapter 3.

2

Structure of the European Community: objectives, policies and constraints

2.1 Approaches to integration

Economic and political integration is frequently identified with the reduction of the sovereign power of the member states and the increase of the power of the supranational central authority. Depending on the extent of transfer of power, there are many degrees of integration and different ways to reach it. Four approaches to integration have been discussed with reference to the European Community.

The *pluralist approach* advocates a form of loose association based on the sovereignty of nation-states which envisage integration as a 'pluralistic community of states' by the development of links of international cooperation. In this type of integration the national states aim at 'political union' in the form of inter-governmental cooperation at the level of heads of state or government, while 'the international organisation has no real will of its own and no power to create a new political entity apart from the wishes of its members' (Pentland, 1973, p. 51). This is the 'Europe *de patries*' vision of the European Community which advocates a minimum degree of integration for the attainment of certain limited economic and political objectives: trade liberalisation in an international environment of peace and security. The pluralist approach is sometimes recommended by the advocates of more advanced structures of international organisation as the first step towards some federal form of integration.

The *functionalist* school of thought argues that the technological, economic and social forces of the modern world create a highly complicated network of economic interrelationships between states and cause problems of international dimensions. Accordingly, maximisation of economic welfare transcends the boundaries of nation-states. The pressure of these economic problems and developments makes the need for international cooperation inevitable and ultimately leads to economic and political unity. Consequently, political integration follows in the steps of economic integration which comes about by market forces.

Functionalism had its advocates in the European Community. The assumption made is that the merger of markets and resources in the unified Europe will inevitably lead to some form of political integration. As one of the founding fathers of the Community has observed:

> it is difficult to believe that six countries can combine their resources, opportunities and capabilities to a greater degree, can integrate and dovetail their interests more and more, without one day setting up a political authority to crown this economic organisation. (Paul-Henri Spaak, quoted in Camps, 1965, p. 128)

Neofunctionalism argues that the need for economic and political integration comes about less through pressure from functional needs or technological change as such and more through the interaction of economic and political forces, that is interest groups which seek to exploit these pressures in pursuit of their gain. In this system, countries delegate certain of their shared duties and policies to common institutions which slowly develop to a decision-making authority. The end product of cooperation is a mixed system in which the common institutions and the national governments share responsibilities and shape the form of integration, the terminal point of which may be some variant of federation. The process of integration evolves around the 'spillover', or forward linkage, from customs union through common market and economic union. Alternatively, if the partners are not satisfied by the implications of integration, there will be a retraction of the scope or level of the process via 'spillback', or backward linkage.

In neofunctionalism, integration develops not through an economically determined process (as in the functionalist approach) but through the resolution of conflict among competing interest groups. In the light of neofunctionalism, the Community institutions – Commission, Council, Parliament, Court of Justice, etc., as explained in the following sections – constitute the beginnings of a supranational state. Integration is pursued by the 'Community method' which comprises *negative integration*, such as the elimination of internal barriers to trade, and *positive integration*, the inauguration of common policies such as the Common Agricultural Policy.

The *federalist* approach to integration involves the formation of a supranational authority to regulate the behaviour of the constituent states and assume many of their sovereign rights, duties and obligations. The division of economic, political and legal power between the member states and the federal government is decided by a 'constitutional conference'. For the functionalists and neofunctionalists federalism is the end stage of the dynamic process of integration and not a separate process of its own.

The federalist approach to European integration is supported by the 'pragmatists' who are seeking to integrate national states and the 'regionalists' who are seeking to decentralise them. Both groups argue that 'gradualism' has failed to produce anything resembling federalism and that the political and social conditions are ripe for convening an 'intergovernmental conference' to speed up the process of integration. For the functionalists federalism in Europe is probable but distant. For the neofunctionalists federalism is desirable and almost inevitable. For the pluralists federalism is undesirable and should never be allowed to happen.

In the following sections of this chapter we review the structure, objectives and policies of the European Community. As we will see, the Community has remained for a long time in a state of uncertainty. Although a more positive approach has been followed in recent years, it is still unclear where it will go, how and at what speed.

2.2 The European Community

The European Community (EC) comprises three communities: the European Coal and Steel Community (ECSC) established by the Treaty of Paris on 18 April 1951 but not fully implemented until February 1958; the European Atomic Energy Community (EAEC or Euratom) and the European Economic Community (EEC). The last two were established respectively by the Euratom Treaty and the Treaty of Rome, both signed in Rome on 25 March 1957. After ratification by the member states' national parliaments, they entered into force on 1 January 1958. The signatories of these treaties agreed, by a convention annexed to the Treaty of Rome, to establish common institutions (Assembly, Court of Justice and Economic and Social Committee) for all three Communities (EC, 1973a). By the 'Merger Treaty', signed in Brussels on 8 April 1965, the three communities agreed to create a single 'Council of the European Communities', a 'Commission of the European Communities' and an 'Audit Board'. This agreement came into force on 1 July 1967 and the established institutions, in the form that they are known today, began to operate on that date. The three communities were designated 'the European Community' by the Resolution of the European Parliament of 16 February 1978. Signatories of these treaties were the original EC members, the Six (EC-6): Belgium (B), Federal Republic of Germany (D), France (F), Italy (I), Luxembourg (L) and the Netherlands (NL). Under Article 237 of the Treaty of Rome 'any European State may apply to become a member of the Community'. In the same spirit, the signatories also called 'upon the other peoples of Europe who share their ideal to join in their efforts' (Preamble). The prerequisites for considering applications for entry are as follows:

1. The applicant state must be European.
2. It must be democratic (summit declaration October 1972, confirmed by the European Council 1978).
3. It must accept the political and economic objectives of the European Community (Articles 2 and 3).

The United Kingdom (UK), Irish Republic (IRL) and Denmark (DK) signed treaties of accession and joined the EC on 1 January 1973 (first enlargement, EC-9). Greece (GR) became an associate member of the EEC in 1962. When the political requirements for entry were met, and after lengthy negotiations, Greece joined the EC on 1 January 1981 (second enlargement, EC-10), and Portugal (P) and Spain (E) on 1 January 1986 (third enlargement, EC-12). The *Single European Act* has introduced the requirement that after 1992 new EC members must be approved by the European Parliament.

2.3 Community institutions

Under Article 4 of the Treaty of Rome and the 'Merger Treaty' the operation of the EC is entrusted to four principal bodies: the Council of Ministers, the Commission, the Court of Justice and the Assembly or European Parliament. The first two constitute the administrative branches of the EC, while the Court of Justice and the European Parliament are, respectively, the judicial and the legislative bodies of the Community. Among the auxiliary institutions are included the Court of Auditors, the Economic and Social Committee and the European Investment Bank.

The Council of Ministers is the principal decision-making body of the EC, and it is the only organisation which explicitly represents the Government of the member states. The Council takes the final decisions in response to proposals from the Commission, and after consulting the

European Parliament and the Economic and Social Committee (ESC). Each member country has one representative in the Council of Ministers. For major decisions the Council consists of the foreign ministers of the member countries but, depending on the subject under discussion, meetings of other ministers are held and are known by subject, e.g. the Agricultural Council and the Transport Council. The office of the President of the Council is held for a term of six months by each member state in turn, in alphabetical order. A new six-year alphabetical cycle began on 1 January 1987. After the first cycle, that is in 1993, each pair of countries will be inverted, in order to ensure that the presidency falls to every member state in the important first half of the year (when decisions about farm prices, etc., are taken).

Under the treaties the Council may take decisions by unanimity, simple majority or qualified majority. Where the Council is required to act by a qualified majority, the vote is weighted (ten each for Germany, France, Italy and the United Kingdom; eight for Spain; five each for Belgium, the Netherlands, Greece and Portugal; three each for Ireland and Denmark; and two for Luxembourg), giving a total of seventy-six. For a qualified majority fifty-four votes in favour are required. On matters regarded of particular importance for the member states, it has been the Council's normal practice to proceed only on the basis of unanimity. However, protracted disagreements on a number of issues finally led to the 'Luxembourg compromise' of 29 January 1966, whereby it was tacitly agreed that, despite the majority voting provisions of the Treaty of Rome, a member state could insist on a unanimous decision in the Council when its vital national interests are involved. In this way the right of national veto was introduced, which has been used by some countries in a number of cases.

The Single European Act (1985) added Articles 100a and 100b to the Treaty of Rome. Article 100a extends the original common market idea by liberalising capital and labour and stabilising the exchange rates, and Article 100b changed the existing system of voting. Accordingly, qualified majority replaced the requirement of unanimity for a number of issues associated with the objective of creating a single internal market, transport and research, such as (a) changes in customs duties (Article 28), (b) liberalisation in the trade of services (Article 59), (c) liberalisation of movements of capital (Article 70.1) and (d) the opening up of markets in the field of transport (Article 84). The Council meets about five times a month. A large part of the preparation for these meetings is carried out in COREPER which is the Committee of Permanent Representatives of the member states, that is ambassadors accredited to the EC (Noël, 1979).

The Treaty of Rome does not stipulate that the Heads of Government of the EC member states constitute a decision-making institution. However, during the 1960s occasional summit meetings became necessary. This has been interpreted by some observers as a declaration of power by the member states and as a manifestation of the pluralistic approach to European integration. The first two summits, at Paris and Bonn, were held in 1961, when leaders of the Six agreed to meet 'at regular intervals to exchange views, to concert their policies and to arrive at common positions in order to facilitate the political union of Europe'. The next summit meeting took place after an interval of six years on the occasion of the tenth anniversary of the Rome Treaty. Since the Paris summit of December 1974, the Community Heads of Government decided to meet on a regular basis three times a year 'and whenever necessary', with a view to solving outstanding problems and making more rapid progress on Community policy. Heads of State (France) or Government (all other members) and their foreign ministers and the president and one vice-president of the Commission meet as the *European Council*, which deals with major Community matters arising out of the treaties and with general economic and political cooperation. The presidency of the European Council rotates every six months in conformity with that of the Council of Ministers. The European Council, whose meetings usually last two days, does not normally take formal decisions. This function is instead delegated to a separate meeting of foreign ministers convened immediately after the summit. Since 1986, the European Council meetings are restricted to twice yearly.

The Commission has five main roles:

1. It acts as Community guardian and ensures that the provisions of the treaties and Community decisions are applied by the member states, with recourse, if necessary, to the Court of Justice.
2. It initiates policy, drafts the detailed measures needed for its implementation and steers legislative proposals through the European Parliament.
3. It acts as a mediator at meetings of the Council, frequently amending its own proposals in order to reach a compromise acceptable to all the member states.
4. It negotiates on behalf of the Community, for example in matters relating to international trade.
5. It has certain powers in administering Community rules, and limited power to legislate, mainly in the detailed implementation of the Common Agricultural Policy.

The Commission, which is based in Brussels, consists of seventeen members – two each from Germany, France, Italy, the United Kingdom

and Spain, and one from each of the other seven member countries –
who are nominated by the national governments of the member states
for a renewable four-year term of office. The Commission is headed by
the President and six Vice-Presidents who hold office for a two-year
renewable term. Decisions are made by majority vote. The Commission,
which is strictly independent of the national governments, heads an
administration organised as twenty-two Directorates-General, each
responsible to one of the Commissioners (EC, 1989a).

The Court of Justice of the European Communities (CJEC) deals
with the interpretation, application and development of Community
law. It comprises thirteen judges, one drawn from each member country
plus one from the larger states on a rota basis, and six advocates-
general, appointed for six-year renewable terms by agreement between
the member governments. However, the judges serve the Community in
their own capacity and do not represent the member states. The role of
the Court is to ensure that the law is observed in the interpretation and
application of the treaties and of the legislation deriving therefrom
(Articles 164–88). The Court has jurisdiction in disputes between
member states on Community matters, between member states and
Community institutions and in actions brought by individuals against
the Community. It also has the right to review the legality of Directives
or Regulations issued by the Council or the Commission. In general,
Community law in the fields covered by the Treaties forms a special,
autonomous legal system, independent of the legal systems of the
member states (EC, 1981a). Community law is not incorporated into any
national law but has direct applicability to the member states where it
takes precedence over national law. Consequently, any provision of
national law which conflicts with Community law is invalid. In general,
the nationals of each member state are governed by two legal systems,
national law and Community law, and therefore they are citizens of two
interdependent entities, the member state of their origin and the
European Community. Consequently, individual citizens of the member
states have the right to bring their government before the Court of
Justice if their rights under European laws are being infringed through
the application of national laws.

At the request of national courts, the Court of Justice gives 'preliminary rulings' on questions of interpretation of Community Treaties and
Community law. Under the Treaty (Article 189), the Community makes
use of five legal instruments:

1. *Regulations*, which are laws binding, and directly and uni-
    formly applicable in all member states, to those who are

parties to legal relationships under Community law (member states, citizens, firms, etc.), without any implementing national legislation.

2. *Directives*, which are EEC laws addressed to member states and binding as to the end, but the means of implementation are discretionary. In practice, national implementing legislation in the form deemed appropriate in each member state is necessary in most cases.

3. *Decisions*, which deal with specific problems and are binding entirely on those to whom they are addressed.

4 and 5. *Recommendations* and *opinions*, which have no binding force (they are not laws).

In contrast to the above, the term 'mutual recognition' refers to legislature acts which are national responsibilities but recognised and enforceable under EC law. Therefore, 'mutual recognition' is a decentralised form of legislation, typically applicable to standards and norms.

Since 1989, the Court of Justice has been assisted in its task by a supplementary institution, the Court of First Instance (CFI) which consists of twelve judges, one from each member state.

The Community, and its agent the Commission, does not have its own police force to see that Community rules are respected in the member states. Enforcement of the rules is left to the national governments and national law enforcement agencies (Louis, 1980). In addition, the Commission depends on individuals, companies, pressure groups and the governments of the member states to draw its attention to dubious practices or infringements of the law. The Commission will then take up the case with the member state in question or take the matter up with the Court of Justice.

The European Parliament (EP) 'which consists of representatives of the peoples of the states brought together in the Community, shall exercise the advisory and supervisory powers which are conferred upon this Treaty' (Article 137). Consequently, while the Council of Ministers represents the states, the European Parliament represents the people. Relative to the national parliaments of the member states, the European Parliament has rather limited powers. It can scrutinise, but not initiate legislation. Draft proposals from the Commission go to the Parliament for its opinion and suggestions, which are not binding but are in general incorporated in final proposals. Therefore, the Parliament has 'advisory and supervisory powers' and mostly acts as a *consultative* body on Community affairs, but has no general right to be involved in the decision-making process. However, it can amend the 'non-obligatory' expenditures of the Community budget and, under very specific conditions and by two-thirds majority, it may also enforce the resignation of the Commission (but not of individual Commissioners); but this has not yet happened. The European Parliament has, however, the power to set its own agenda to debate any issues it considers important. Hence through time it has gained influence in the field of policy-making and international relations beyond the limits formally allocated to it by the treaties. More recently, the European Parliament acquired the limited, but significant, power to reject or amend Council decisions pertaining to the unification of the EC market under the Single European Act. Under a newly instituted cooperation procedure with the Council, the Parliament has the right of 'second reading', that is of a chance to re-examine a proposed Directive after Council has reached a 'common position' and to reinstate amendments which it had put forward in its first reading. The move towards the single market, which raises the necessity for more common policies and institutions, suggests that the European Parliament should be endowed with additional powers, so that integration does not result in any weakening of democratic control. The most likely reform is an enhancement role for the European Parliament, which may include the right to initiate legislation, sack individual commissioners and ratify treaties, such as trade agreements and constitutional reforms.

The direction of the Parliament is in the hands of the President and twelve Vice-Presidents, elected every two and a half years. Much of the Parliament's work is done by specialist committees. The Parliament's

Table 2.1 Members of the European Parliament.

Country		Members
B	Belgium	24
DK	Denmark	16
D	Germany	81
E	Spain	60
F	France	81
GR	Greece	24
IRL	Ireland	15
I	Italy	81
L	Luxembourg	6
NL	Netherlands	25
P	Portugal	24
UK	United Kingdom	81[1]
Total		518

[1] Scotland 10, Wales 5, Northern Ireland 3, England 63

administrative seat is Luxembourg, but plenary sessions are now held in Strasbourg. The Parliamentary committees normally meet in Brussels. Since 1979, the Members of Parliament are elected by direct elections for a fixed term of five years. The member country representation in the European Parliament is presented in Table 2.1.

In addition to these four constitutional authorities there are a number of auxiliary institutions. The most important of these are the Court of Auditors, the Economic and Social Committee and the European Investment Bank.

The *Court of Auditors* has twelve members, one from each member state. It was set up by amendment treaty in 1975, on the initiative of the Parliament, to exercise control over the Community's expenditure and revenue.

The *Economic and Social Committee* (ESC) is made up of 189 members, representing employers, trade unions, farmers, the professions and 'representatives of the general interest'. They are appointed by the Council according to quotas allocated to each member state and from lists supplied by them. The members of the ESC serve in their personal capacity and are not bound by any mandatory instructions. The Committee is convened, at the request of the Council or the Commission, to be consulted in cases laid down by the Treaty or in any case where this is deemed appropriate, but it also has the power to undertake its own enquiries and to draw up opinions on all questions relating to the Community. The *Consultative Committee* carries out similar tasks for ECSC affairs.

The *European Investment Bank* (EIB) was set up as one of the institutions of the EEC Treaty (Articles 129–30) to promote economic and social integration. It operates independently as a public non-profit-making organisation. The Bank's task is to contribute to the balanced and stable development of the Community by making or guaranteeing loans for investment projects, principally in industry, energy and infrastructure. The EIB facilitates the financing of: (a) investment that contributes to the economic development of the less-developed regions of the Community; (b) projects which contribute to the economic integration of the Community or serve other Community objectives; (c) investment projects for modernising or converting undertakings or for developing new activities, particularly in energy saving, import diversification, transport and telecommunications.

The Bank does not normally contribute more than 40 per cent of the cost of any project. The Bank's resources consist of reserves, capital subscribed by member states and funds raised (i.e. borrowing) on capital markets inside and outside the Community. The EIB has received a mandate to administer New Community Instrument (NCI) loans for the account and at the risk of the Community. The NCI (or the Ortoli facility) was established in 1978 and has as its objectives the financing of investment projects which contribute to greater convergence and integration of the member states' economic policies and, through the dissemination of new technology and innovation, the reinforcement of the competitiveness of the Community economy. The EIB is also participating in the Integrated Mediterranean Programmes (IMP) and is responsible for Euratom project appraisals and loan management. By permission of the Board of Governors, the Bank may grant investment finance for projects in a country or group of countries under association or cooperation agreements with the Community. Most of the finance is in the form of loans at subsidised interest rates. Many countries have made use of this facility.

2.4 Objectives of the European Community

Table 2.2 presents economic statistics for each of the twelve member states of the EC. These statistics reveal substantial differences between the countries comprising the European Community, with reference to the following:

1. *Physical size* (area, population). The smallest member in both area and population is Luxembourg, the largest in area is France and the largest in population is Germany. The EC-12 make up a market of more than 324 million people, nearly a third more than the population of the United States which is four times larger in area than the EC. The unification of the two Germanies has added to the Community more than 16.5 million people.
2. *Structure of employment.* In every member the services sector predominates, while agriculture is the least significant sector of the economy. However, important differences in the structure of employment still exist, e.g. agriculture takes up 27.0 per cent of total employment in Greece and only 2.2 per cent in the United Kingdom.
3. *Economic size.* With GDP per head taken as a measure of the level of economic welfare and development, the least developed members (Portugal and Greece) reach only 45 per cent of the level of the most developed member (Luxembourg). In general, eight countries occupy places above, and the remaining four below, the EC-12 average level of GDP per head. The twelve economies together have a combined GDP accounting for over 27 per cent of global GDP

Table 2.2 Basic statistics of the Community.

Member Country	Area (1,000 sq.km)	Population (1,000s) 1988	Employment (per cent 1988) Agr.	Ind.	Serv.	GDP per head (1988)[1] PPP value	% on EC average	% on EC highest	Annual growth rate of GDP per head 1983–88	Gross value added by branch, 1987 Agr.	Ind.	Serv.	Member's share in EC GDP, 1988	Foreign trade per cent of GDP, 1988 Imports	Exports
B	30.5	9.902	2.7	28.2	69.1	15,971	101	83	2.1	2.3	31.9	65.8	3.1	60.8	58.7
DK	43.1	5.130	6.3	26.3	67.4	17,184	109	90	2.0	4.7	28.0	67.3	2.3	24.5	25.6
D	248.7	61.450	4.3	41.2	54.5	17,907	113	94	2.5	1.5	40.3	58.2	25.3	20.8	26.8
E	504.8	38.765	14.4	32.5	53.1	11,821	75	62	3.1	5.2	37.3	57.5	7.1	16.8	12.6
F	544.0	55.884	6.8	30.4	62.8	17,168	108	90	1.7	3.7	31.5	64.8	19.9	19.5	17.9
GR	132.0	10.004	27.0	28.0	45.0	8,619	54	45	1.8	15.8	28.6	55.6	1.0	23.9	10.4
IRL	68.9	3.538	15.4	27.8	56.8	10,304	65	54	2.8	9.7	36.8	53.5	0.8	47.6	57.4
I	301.3	57.452	9.9	32.6	57.5	16,422	104	86	2.8	4.1	34.1	61.8	17.4	16.6	15.5
L	2.6	375	3.4	31.6	65.0	19,130	121	100	3.7	2.2	30.6	67.2	0.1	–[2]	–[2]
NL	41.2	14.760	4.8	26.5	68.7	16,244	103	85	1.8	4.3	32.1	63.6	4.8	46.0	46.6
P	92.1	10.287	20.7	35.1	44.2	8,553	54	45	2.3	7.5	37.9	54.6	0.9	40.2	25.7
UK	244.1	57.065	2.2	29.4	68.4	16,994	107	89	3.4	1.2	36.7	62.1	17.3	23.7	17.7
EC-12	2253.3	324.611	7.4	32.7	59.9	15,828	100	83	2.5	3.1	35.5	61.4	100.0	23.0	22.5
GDR[3]	108.0	16.700	12.0	48.0	40.0	8,534	54	45							

[1] Current prices in ECUs.
[2] Luxembourg's trade figures included in Belgium's.
[3] GDR = East Germany, now united with West Germany, D.

Sources: Eurostat (1990) *Basic Statistics of the Community*, 27th ed., Luxembourg; EC (1990) *Europe without Frontiers*, European Documentation, periodical 2/1989, Luxembourg; EC Commission (1990) *The Agricultural Situation in the Community, 1989 Report*, Luxembourg.

(excluding the ex-eastern block countries). However, four of the twelve member countries (Germany, France, Italy and the United Kingdom) account for 80 per cent of the total Community GDP, one of them for more than a quarter of the total (Germany 25.3 per cent), while the other eight countries share the remaining 20 per cent.

4. *Composition of value added.* As with the structure of employment, the services sector predominates. But agriculture is still important for Greece (15.8 per cent), Ireland (9.7 per cent) and Portugal (7.5 per cent), while for four countries (Belgium, Germany, Luxembourg, United Kingdom) the value added contributed by this sector is below the EC-12 average (3.1 per cent).

5. *Openness to trade.* Here, the smaller, more developed countries are also the more open to trade. Belgium is the most, and Italy and Spain the least, open economies of the Community.

These statistics confirm that, in general, the twelve members of the EC do not constitute a homogeneous group. Consequently, diversity in their physical characteristics and in their economic structures, both of which may determine a diversity in interests and growth potential, mean that the search for common objectives and common policies within the Common Market is not an easy process.

The EC does not fit easily into any of the forms of regional economic associations which we discussed in the previous chapter. It is clearly something more than a customs union because it has certain sovereign rights conferred to it by the member states, and a government separate from national governments, the EC Commission. On the other hand, the EC is not a federal state because its sovereign rights are limited to specific areas and it lacks the right to create new powers. The Community is instead an organisation of independent national states which have renounced part of their sovereignty in favour of an association of states aspiring to economic integration.

The Commission is in effect the executive body of the Community. However, its executive powers are limited to clearly defined areas: the 'primary' powers conferred to it by the Treaties and the 'derived' powers devolved on it by the Council. In principle, it is the member states themselves that have to ensure that Community rules are applied in individual cases.

The Community has been given by the member states its own budgetary resources. Therefore it is unlike other international organisations, which are financed by subscriptions from their member states. But the Community budget, unlike the budgets of the constituent states, is relatively small and heavily concentrated on one particular sector, agriculture. With the exception of this sector, integration of economic policy within the EC is still minimal. There is a common commercial policy and the beginning of a common monetary system and fixed exchange rates. Tariffs have gone on intra-EC trade, while the few remaining impediments to the free trade of commodities and services and to the inter-country mobility of factors of production will be eliminated before 1993.

The Treaty of Rome specifically states that the objective of the EC is to 'promote throughout the Community a harmonious development of economic activities, a continuous and balanced expansion, an increase in stability, an accelerated raising of the standard of living and closer relations between the States belonging to it' (Article 2). These objectives will be achieved by the creation of a single internal market free of restrictions on the movement of goods; the abolition of obstacles to the free movement of persons, services and capital; the institution of a system ensuring that competition in the common market is not distorted; the approximation of laws as required for the proper functioning of the common market; and the approximation of indirect taxation in the interest of the common market. All these objectives will be realised by the application of two sets of policies, those taken in common at the level of the EC and those taken individually by the member states but in coordination with each other. With the establishment of the Common Market, common policies will be specifically inaugurated in commerce, agriculture and transport. Article 3 of the Treaty states that the customs duties and quantitative restrictions on intra-EC trade of commodities and services are to be abolished and common commercial policy to be established with a common customs tariff on imports from third countries. The six original members of the Community removed all internal quantitative restrictions and tariffs by July 1968. The three members of the first enlargement (Denmark, Ireland and the United Kingdom) did the same in July 1977. Greece followed in December 1985. The two latest members, Portugal and Spain, were required to remove immediately on entry all import quotas and to phase out all customs duties on trade with their Community partners by 1 January 1993. By this time, they will also have adopted the common external tariff, which is already in force in the other ten countries.

The free Community market will be completed by the elimination of technical obstacles to trade which result from disparities between the laws, regulations and administrative provisions of member countries. With the common external tariff this enlarged market is also transformed into a large trading power acting externally as a single unit. The Treaty provides that, in addition to commerce, two other sectors, agriculture and transport (which at the national level of the member countries are riddled with regulations and distortions), will come under common policies exercised at the level of the Community.

Within the Community, impediments to the free movement of factors of production, persons and capital will also be lifted. Direct barriers to the migration of workers and the self-employed have already been eliminated among the EC-10. The same rights will be fully applicable from 1993 for Spain and Portugal. Capital market liberalisation will also be completed by 1993. In this way the economic frontiers between the member states will be removed and enlargement of the market for commodities, services and factors of production will ensue, increasing the potential for improvement in the allocation of production and exchange.

Realisation of market efficiency will lead to the ultimate objective of the economic union, which is the increase in economic welfare and in the rate of growth of Community GDP for the benefit of its peoples. These aims are to be pursued within a system of external and internal stability (Articles 3 and 104), which should be taken to mean: (a) full employment of productive resources and stable prices in the short term, and (b) an accelerated growth rate along a stable growth path in the longer term. These objectives will be pursued, if possible, within an environment of free markets and perfect competition.

Competition can be interpreted in a number of ways: a broad definition would be that competition means freedom for firms to produce what and where they wish; for consumers to have a wider range of material choice and cultural enjoyment; for people to live and work where they desire. A more legalistic interpretation with reference to the EC would be that competition is the means to an end, and this end is explicitly specified: the Treaty of Rome declares that the contracting parties decided to create the EC

> determined to lay the foundations of an ever closer union among the peoples of Europe, resolved to ensure the economic and social progress of their countries by common action to eliminate the barriers which divide Europe, affirming as the essential objective of their efforts the constant improvement of the living and working conditions of their people. (EC, 1973a, Preamble)

It can also be argued that the ultimate objective of the EC is the economic and political unification of Europe and the establishment of a federation, the United States of Europe. But, if this is the aim of the EC, nowhere in the treaties is it spelled out in so many words. However, the Articles of the Treaty of Rome and of subsequent agreements and declarations of Heads of States, and the course the EC has hitherto followed, show clearly that the aim of the 'high contracting parties' is the realisation of 'an ever closer union among the European peoples' and therefore economic integration is a prime parallel route towards the 'desirable objective' of establishing a European Union. The Single European Act is a step towards this direction.

The Treaty provides that the common market shall be established within twelve years in three stages of four years each (Article 8). However, this objective was not achieved. Market segmentation on national boundary lines continued from different national standards, regulatory barriers to market entry and restrictions on the trade of commodities, services and factors of production, border formalities and discriminatory government procurement practices. A new date for the unification of the market was set by the Single European Act at the Luxembourg Summit (December 1985) for the end of 1992. The Act, which after ratification by the member states came into force on 1 July 1987, entails the simultaneous implementation of six policies:

1. The establishment of a large market without internal frontiers.
2. Economic and social cohesion leading to greater convergence.
3. A common policy for scientific and technological development.
4. The strengthening of the European Monetary System.
5. The emergence of a European social dimension.
6. Coordinated action relating to protection of the environment.

After a slow start, implementation of the (approximately 300) proposals contained in the Single European Act accelerated in 1988, and significant progress has already been made in removing capital controls, enhancing labour mobility, liberalising road transport, harmonising technical standards and reducing customs formalities.

The objective of the Single European Act is the foundation of the 'People's Europe'. The Act declares that 'the completion of the internal market will provide an indispensable base for increasing the prosperity of the Community as a whole', while its 'social dimension' specifies that it will seek to establish the rights of people in the enlarged market: 'all citizens, whatever their occupation, will have effective access to the direct benefits expected from the single market as a factor of economic growth, and as the most effective means of combating unemployment' (Rhodes Summit, 1988). Moreover, it also calls upon the EC members 'jointly to implement a European foreign policy and to transform relations as a whole amongst [the EC] states into a European Union' (EC, 1987b). The mutual openness of frontiers is such a basic step towards integration as to make a common stand towards the rest of the world inevitable. Evidently, the EC objectives are not only economic.

The Single European Act introduced important changes in the Community's strategy for integration. Firstly, it limited the requirement for harmonisation to the essential standards by systematic adoption of 'mutual recognition' of national norms and regulations. Secondly, it established a faster and more efficient decision-making process by extending the scope of qualified majority voting, which makes it much more difficult for an individual member state to block progress. Thirdly, it increased the role of the European Parliament in the integration process. Fourthly, it reaffirmed the Community's objectives, emphasising the need for economic and social cohesion for their realisation.

The new (or clearer) intentions and the directions which the EC proposes to follow have not been received with unanimous approval by the governments of the member states. The United Kingdom in particular, which considers 1992 as an additional step on the road to European Union, is at present against any further shift of power away from the national governments and towards the Community. The basic question is whether the EC should remain a *Europe of nations* in a 'pluralistic community', a loosely knit customs union confederation of independent sovereign states, or move towards a more harmonised quasi-federal 'European superstate'. Many fear that the EC is actually going federalist 'by stealth', adopting its own flag and a European anthem and attempting to create 'an identikit European personality' by a combination of politics and economics. For others 'Europeanness', defined in terms of a common culture rather than economic and political terms, does not need to be invented because it already exists, despite the different customs and national languages. There has also been growing concern about the lack of adequate democratic controls over the increasingly important decisions taken in Brussels, the so-called 'democratic deficit'. But while some members see the solution to this problem in strengthening the role of the European Parliament, others object to the power gained at the centre to the detriment of the national parliaments of sovereign member states.

The question is whether 1992 will inevitably lead to European political unification. Some think not; others believe that while unification may not be inevitable, it is desirable, and that the idea that Europe can be nothing more than a customs union is insular and absurd.

For a long period after its formation, the EC's main concern was to achieve a single market. But as this target seems to be approaching in 1993, its ambitions have broadened to include: economic and monetary union (EMU); special links with Western Europe's other economic club, the European Free Trade Area (EFTA); closer ties with the emerging democracies of Eastern Europe; and the integration of East Germany. Now, undaunted by the task of realising all these objectives, the member states have decided to convene an inter-governmental conference on political reform which will start work in December 1990 on rewriting the treaties that define the European Community and prepare the ground for 'political union'. At this stage of European integration 'political union' will have four main objectives: to strengthen the Community's capacity to take decisions, to make it more democratically responsible, to make its institutions more efficient and to outline a common foreign and security policy. Indeed, some member states have talked about the completion of European economic and monetary union by January 1993, and for parallel talks among the twelve member states on political union by the same date. But this has not been received approvingly by every member state. Thus, while France and Germany are talking about the imminent need for a 'quantum leap towards political union', the United Kingdom argues that, since political union means 'very different things for different countries', the single market is quite enough for the time being. 'The UK does not consider that the Single European Act prepared the basis for the Community to take on the role and functions of the nation states writ large' (Brooke, 1989, p. 35).

2.5   Policies and constraints

The economic interdependence among the members of the EC, which will be increased by the integration of the markets for goods, services and factors of production, leads to a progressively increasing need for consultation and coordination among the member states and, finally, for integration of national economic policies. Coordination of economic policies is here taken to mean joint and interdependent action, but without legal force, in pursuit of shared objectives.

Membership in an economic union entails for each participating country a weakening of autonomy in the design and exercise of national economic policies. It influences each member country's macroeconomic policy by both restricting its ability to pursue independent national economic policies and rendering each economy more sensitive to developments in the economies of the partner countries; and by lessening each member country's access to and efficacy of various economic instruments. Economic interdependence gives rise to policy externalities and, thereby, to policy conflict. The interdependencies between markets in different countries via trade of commodities and services, financial links and labour migration transmit the effects of policy-induced changes in one country to others. Within a customs union, the feedback of externalities on the economies of partner countries can be positive or negative. Obviously, positive externalities provide benefits and are welcome, while negative externalities are unwanted and have to be stopped by inter-country cooperation for policy coordination. In this case, independent national economic policy is unsustainable and, whenever attempted, it leads to inefficiencies.

Policy conflict can stem from incompatibility in economic policy among the partners in the customs union. Harmonisation of policies refers to the adoption of common rules and the application of consistent policies with a view to achieving greater uniformity across the members of the union. Harmonisation refers to adjustment of the members' policy targets and instruments in recognition of international economic interdependence. In general, the objectives of economic policy will be reached faster, and the possibility of negative externalities on fellow member countries will be reduced, when national instruments are adjusted to reach national and partner/Community targets. The greater the degree of interdependence among the partners, the greater the required degree of coordination of both objectives and instruments of policies. Effects of the coordination and harmonisation of policies will be that adjustments are speeded up, and that the likelihood of cyclical approaches to equilibrium or overshooting of the targets will be reduced. With closer cooperation among the partners of the economic union there will be considerable economies from efficient assignment of policy instruments. Hence the Community gains not only from the reduction or elimination of the negative externalities of economic policies, but also from the savings from and efficient allocation in the use of instruments.

Coordination of policies leaves national frontiers intact. Integration transforms the policies from national to common, applicable throughout the Community. However, since harmonisation does not imply the search for and adoption of optimum policies, it does not necessarily lead to a more efficient allocation of resources. In contrast to harmonisation, which is an imposed reconciliation of different systems of national policies, mutual recognition of norms and regulations introduces liberalisation in inter-state standards in a common market. Therefore, mutual recognition can lead to approximation by competition in the market, and hence to improved efficiency.

Procedure in the European Community is governed by the principle of 'subsidiarity', according to which national or even local governments should make policy whenever possible. The Community's writ applies only when national law cannot be enforced within open frontiers. In general, establishment of the European Community creates four types of effects on the powers of the national authorities:

1. It leaves them unchanged.
2. It modifies them – hence, the need for consultation and coordination among members.

3. It limits them, by binding constraints.
4. It abolishes them, by the introduction of common policies.

The constraints on the exercise of national economic policy, which are imposed by increasing interdependence, are well recognised by the Treaty of Rome which provides general principles for the regulation and coordination and harmonisation of national economic policies. Its aims are to enhance the effectiveness of measures taken at the national level, to emphasise the need for concerted action aiming at a speedier progress towards integration, and to diminish the possibility of incompatibility between the objectives of policies. Thus, the Treaty specifies that in pursuing their common aims 'Member states shall regard their conjunctural policies as a matter of common concern. They shall consult with each other and with the Commission on the measures to be taken in the light of the prevailing circumstances' (Article 103). Furthermore, it is stated that in their domestic policy 'each member state shall pursue the economic policy necessary to ensure the equilibrium of its overall balance of payments and to maintain confidence in its currency, while ensuring a high degree of employment and the stability of the level of prices' (Article 104).

Maintenance of balance-of-payments equilibrium requires coordinated application of economic policies and consistent patterns of economic development among the partners, particularly in regard to trends in productivity, nominal incomes and prices, monetary policy and capital markets. The policy instruments which each member may employ to achieve balanced trade with its partners include: fiscal, monetary and exchange rate policy, provided that 'each Member State shall treat its policy with regard to exchange rates as a matter of common interest' (Article 107); trade controls *vis-à-vis* non-member countries; mutual assistance 'recommended by the Community'; and, in the last resort and subject to Community approval, temporary 'protective measures' against other members, provided that 'such measures shall cause the least possible disturbance in the functioning of the common market' (Article 109).

The exchange rate is not included among the recommended instruments of policy. This is taken to mean that the Treaty assumes implicitly a commitment on the part of the members to maintain fixed exchange rates, that is the *de facto* establishment of an 'exchange rate union'. This implicit requirement is in accordance with the international system of exchange rates in operation at the time of signing the Treaty of Rome, which was that of fixed exchange rates. A system of fixed exchange rates (with increasing capital mobility) implies a direct linkage between the monetary policies of the member states; therefore, in principle, loss of autonomy in national monetary policy.

The Treaty does not deal only with macroeconomic policy coordination among the members. It also provides an outline for the free movement of factors of production, at a later stage of the integration process, for the purpose of achieving optimisation in resource allocation within the wider area of the Common Market: 'Freedom of movement for workers shall be secured within the Community' (Article 48); 'Member States shall ... progressively abolish as between themselves restrictions on the movement of capital' (Article 67). The free movement of factors of production may indirectly contribute towards the economic and political unification of the member states. Indeed, many reports and Summit declarations have set explicitly as a long-term objective of the Community the establishment of a European Union.

During the early stages of integration the member states of an economic association are functioning as independent economic units, but within an environment of added restrictions imposed by the need for intra-union policy coordination and harmonisation. The liberalisation of factor movements may entail the gravitation of productive factors from slow-growth areas to fast-growth areas, and this may in the short term cause economic imbalances and inequality unacceptable to some member states. Hence, after an initial push towards achieving a common market with free trade in commodities, the process of integration slackens. Reallocation of resources aiming at optimisation might become possible in the longer run, when aggregate concepts, such as Community welfare as opposed to national (or even private) welfare, become politically acceptable, and a central authority can have control over both growth policy and income distribution in the common market. But when this stage of integration is reached, the central authority of the common market is invested with powers beyond those conferred by the member states to an appointed Commission. It is an authority which should be accountable to voters from whom it receives the mandate to govern; in other words, it should be an elected government. Therefore, after a certain threshold, economic integration cannot be advanced further without a parallel move towards political unification. This will make decision-making more effective and increase democratic control. However, its implementation will require fundamental changes in the constitution, the EC treaties.

In the meantime, during the transitional or intermediate stages of integration, instead of an optimal allocation, the economic association may pursue a balanced allocation of resources as a means for balanced economic development. During this phase, the members tend to pursue 'convergence' in the form of closer approximation, or even equalisation, of economic performance. Convergence, which may require convergence or divergence in economic policies, is an objective which conflicts with the long-term optimal allocation of resources within the area of the common market by imposing constraints on the growth rate of income of individual member countries, and thus on aggregate Community income. Therefore, convergence is an inferior policy which can be justified as a temporary political expediency aiming at cohesion among the members until the conditions allow a faster move towards economic unification: 'In order to promote its harmonious development overall, the Community shall develop and pursue its actions leading to strengthening its economic and social cohesion' (EC 1985a, Single European Act).

In the EC both political and economic convergence have been advocated as prior requirements for faster progress towards integration and the long-term objective of establishing the European Union. The enlargement of the Community from the homogeneous group of EC-6 countries to the less homogeneous EC-9 countries made the realisation of the ultimate goal more remote. Notwithstanding the problems involved, the Heads of State of the Community countries reaffirmed at the Paris summit of December 1974 that the original objective of European Union has not changed. Following this summit, the Tindemans Report (EC Commission, 1976) stressed the need for a new impetus for accelerating the establishment of the European Union which would be based on the following principles:

1. A united front to the outside world.
2. The interdependence of the economic prosperity of the member states and a common economic and monetary policy.
3. The solidarity of the peoples of the Community and action through social and regional policies to lessen inequalities.
4. Action to help protect people's rights and to improve the quality of life.
5. The existence of institutions with the necessary powers to determine a common and all-inclusive political view with the efficiency needed for action and the legitimacy needed for democratic control.
6. A gradual, step-by-step approach, with priority given to objectives likely to succeed.

According to the Tindemans Report these principles were to be given practical application in the form of a 'two-tier' Community in which a core of the strongest members would press ahead with faster policy integration, while the other members would follow at a slower pace. But the heads of states, while endorsing most of the Report's recommendations, for reasons of political necessity required a united front, and so did not take any specific decisions upon its content. The enlargement of the

Community from nine to twelve member states has diluted further the homogeneity of the EC, and thus it has postponed the realisation of the ultimate goal, establishment of the European Union. With the same objective and two more enlargements which added more members unable or less enthusiastic to follow the pace of the stronger countries, revival of the Tindemans Report in the future is not excluded. Events within the EC and in the rest of Europe have already given rise to the idea of 'concentric circles': a core of EC members committed to closer economic and political integration, leading towards federalism; a second ring of members who would follow at a slower pace; a third circle of European countries developing closer ties with the EC, such as the members of EFTA; lastly, other associated members of the EC, including the countries of Eastern Europe.

We will understand EC policies better if we consider that they are not related solely to an economic objective defined in terms of private consumption-oriented concepts of welfare economics, but to a political one, that of establishing a single internal market. This entails costs in terms of traditional concepts of economics, but it may bring about benefits which in the longer term may prove to be much more important for the peoples of Europe. Subject to this caveat we can state that, in relation to the policy developments which we will examine in the following chapters, the main objectives of the European Community are *enlargement of the market*, and *changes in production structures* leading to improvement in efficiency through specialisation and economies of scale. The aim of Community policy is to generate the conditions that will improve the competitive structure of the market so that, with few but notable exceptions such as the Common Agricultural Policy (CAP), the market mechanism will provide solutions to economic problems. This is the leitmotiv of economic policies of the European Community.

Further reading

The treaties establishing the European Community are in EC (1973a). On the problems of policy-making in interdependent economies see Cooper (1969, 1985) and Bryant *et al.* (1989). For the objectives of the Community see EC Commission (1976), Tindemans Report, and EC Commission (1985a), the White Paper on the single market. The political approaches to integration are reviewed in Pentland (1973).

3

The single market

3.1   Introduction

The Treaty of Rome specified that its objectives will be reached 'by establishing a common market and progressively approximating the economic policies of member states'. However, the *common market* did not come about through the market forces, among other reasons because they were not allowed to operate. The economic climate of the 1970s – the recession following the oil shocks of 1973 and 1978, and the high rates of inflation and unemployment – led the member states to focus on domestic economic problems rather than on market liberalisation. Many observers then concluded that these were features of inactivity derived from advanced 'Eurosclerosis'. But improvement of the economic situation in the 1980s revitalised the process of economic integration, which also started to be seen as the means for sustaining the economic recovery so far achieved and for fostering further growth. It is through direct action, the passing of the Single European Act (EC, 1985a), that unification of the market will be completed in 1992, thirty five years after the Treaty of Rome was signed.

For the creation of the single market two elements are necessary: (a) elimination of barriers to trade of commodities, services and factors of production; and (b) a common rules system of competition. In this section we review the progress made towards the single market before enactment of the Single European Act. The basic rules of competition in the Community are described in Section 3.2. The estimates of the expected benefits of the single market are presented in Section 3.3. The nature and aims of Community policies are the subject of ensuing chapters of this book.

The liberalisation of EC commodity trade is pursued by removal of tariff and non-tariff barriers. In spite of the progress made, particularly with regard to the elimination of tariffs and quantitative restrictions on trade between the members and the adoption of a common tariff on external trade, many of the original non-tariff barriers remained effective, and some new ones sprung up. They comprised varying product regulations and standards – technical and safety standards, quality controls, health and environmental standards, and standards for consumer protection – and differences in indirect taxation that operate from one member state to another. As a result of the different regulations, standards and legal, fiscal and administrative barriers, the Community market remained fragmented along national lines, adding costs and distorting production and trade patterns. Attempts to liberalise the market have been many, but the member states failed to agree on a common approach to overcome national differences. The impediments to market integration persevered despite a long line of judgements of the European Court of Justice (since the 1978 *Cassis de Dijon* ruling against jurisdictional sovereignty and in favour of a supranational European Community) which have affirmed that in certain areas of international law national norms are automatically acceptable by all other member states on 'mutual recognition' grounds. Accordingly, products made and marketed according to the legal requirements of any member state should have been allowed to circulate freely in the rest of the Community.

The move from 'non-Europe' to a completely integrated 'Europe without frontiers' requires the implementation of a legal structure which will provide the conditions necessary for opening up the market. This objective is pursued by the following:

1. The complete elimination of technical differences that create barriers to the unification of the market.
2. The convergence of fiscal barriers, such as tax systems and tax rates, by harmonisation.
3. The mutual recognition of national standards, subject only to the harmonisation of essential health and safety requirements.

Despite provisions in the Treaty requiring the abolition, within a transitional period of twelve years, of restrictions preventing Community nationals from establishing and providing services in other member states (Articles 59–66), the free flow of services is still incomplete. This is due to general procrastinations and intransigence by some members to the opening up of national markets and the harmonisation of different national regulations concerning the supply of services, such as transport, insurance and banking services. Services account for more than 50 per cent of the value added to the Community economy. Therefore, the trade in services is as important in the single market as the trade in commodities.

The basic legislation for the free movement of labour and the professions is almost entirely complete. However, in practice certain obstacles (such as administrative procedures for the granting of residence permits, comparability and mutual recognition of qualifications, right of establishment of the self-employed) are still present and restrict the free mobility and residence of labour. A decision for the mutual recognition of higher education diplomas was taken in 1988, and a proposal for the mutual acceptance of vocational training qualifications for apprentices is under consideration.

Substantial progress had been made in the liberalisation of capital movements, but from time to time, owing to problems with their balance of payments, temporary derogations are permitted or re-introduced on the grounds of macroeconomic policy objectives (as provided by Articles 73 and 108 of the Treaty). The completion of the internal market and the drive towards Economic and Monetary Union (EMU) entail the complete liberalisation of capital markets. The free movement of capital also implies the development of a single market for financial services, commercial banking and insurance (in accordance with Article 61 of the Rome Treaty), and an integrated European stock market.

3.2 Competition rules

The EEC Treaty provides for the establishment of a Community-wide system of competition rules in the unified European market. The principal objective of the common competition policy is to harmonise the competition rules among the members so as to ensure the unification of the European market for the benefit of all – producers, traders, consumers and the economy in general. The common competition rules seek to prevent enterprises and governments from distorting trade by abusing their market power (EC, 1983a), and provide for action to be taken in cases of anti-competitive practices which are 'incompatible with the common market'.

The common competition rules do not annul the national competition legislation and policy which are the prerogative of national governments. However, the Community competition law has precedence over national anti-trust legislation but does not replace it automatically. Where the Commission finds that a discrepancy between the legislative or administrative provisions of a member state hinders competition in the Community by producing distortions which need to be eliminated, it consults the member state concerned. If an agreement is not reached, the Council issues the necessary directives and takes any other appropriate measures provided for in the Treaty for elimination of the distortion (Article 101). In general, the Treaty of Rome (Article 177) stipulates that the implementation and enforcement of Community law would be left to the national courts of the member states, while the Community Court of Justice (CJEC) would play a residual yet guiding role (Article 177). Competition rules in the form of regulations are directly enforced by the Commission.

The EEC Treaty contains the basic competition rules in Articles 85–94, which deal with infringement of the principles of competition by agreements among enterprises (85–91) and by state aid (92–4). The provisions of these Articles have been interpreted, clarified and extended by subsequent legislation and by rulings of the Court of Justice. The EEC competition rules do not apply to the coal and steel industry nor to the nuclear energy field, which are subject to the rules prescribed in the ECSC and Euratom Treaties respectively (EC, 1973a). National anti-trust laws exist at varying degrees in every country. The Community anti-trust law is concerned with the preservation of competition in trade between the members of the common market: free trade rules over any other consideration. The approach followed in the Treaty is to define first the prohibited agreements and then to provide for exemptions in certain specific circumstances.

Article 85 relates to agreements and practices between enterprises that by their restrictive nature are liable 'to affect trade between member states and have as their object or effect the prevention, restriction or distortion of competition within the common market'. In practice, 'trade between states' is widely interpreted and a variety of cases can fall within the EC rules. 'Restrictive practices' is a general term which refers to collusive arrangements between firms which ultimately aim at price fixing for the purpose of exploiting the market. These agreements may be horizontal, between firms at the same level of production, or vertical, between producers and dealers. Market exploitation does not necessarily mean that the firms involved aim exclusively at monopoly profit maximisation. It may well be that their intentions included some degree of market stability, defence of their market share and gaining competitive advantage over other, domestic or foreign, firms.

Article 87 has three parts: 87(1) contains the basic prohibitions; 87(2) declares the prohibited agreements null and void; and 87(3) describes the specific exemptions. The following agreements are specifically prohibited: price fixing, market sharing, restriction of production or technical development, discrimination, collective boycotts (market prevention) and tie-in clauses (when you purchase one good or service, you are obliged to buy another unrelated good or service). The list of restrictions referred to in the Article is illustrative only. Under certain conditions a number of other forms of collusive agreements for buying or selling goods or services, may be deemed incompatible with perfect competition, for example, joint purchasing, joint selling, exclusive distribution or purchasing, and so on. These prohibitions apply to vertical agreements between manufacturers and the retail sellers of their goods, as well as to horizontal agreements between producers of the same goods, and in principle cover all firms operating in the common market irrespective of whether they are established within it or outside it. The conditions for exemptions from these competition rules are specifically enumerated in Article 85(3). They are that (a) the agreement must contribute 'to improving the production or distribution of goods or to promoting technical or economic progress', and (b) allow 'consumers a fair share of the resulting benefit'. In addition to these specific conditions, Council Regulation 17 (1962) gave the Commission sole power to authorise exemptions from the ban on restrictive practices for agreements with economic benefit. If an agreement satisfies the conditions of Article 85(3), the Commission grants exemption either by an individual decision or by *block exemption*, that is by a regulation covering a whole category of similar agreements. Block exemption has been granted to the following types of agreement; of specialisation, exclusive distribution, exclusive purchasing, patent licensing, research and development and motor vehicle distribution.

Article 86 outlaws 'any abuse by one or more undertakings of a dominant position within the common market or in a substantial part thereof' in so far as they affect trade between member states. Dominant position here means concentration or monopoly power which enables the firm or firms (undertakings) to influence, by independent action as a buyer or seller, the outcome of the market. However, following the precedence of national legislation, the Article does not define what degree of concentration, that is what size of market share, constitutes dominant position, since this may vary from product to product. The emphasis is rather on the *abuse* of power in trade between member states. Dominant enterprises are prohibited from practising price or personal discrimination in the goods they purchase or sell in inter-state markets.

This is also the Article on which the Commission, following a Court of Justice decision, had until recently based its powers of control over mergers and acquisitions occasioning dominant positions. Certain forms of cooperation agreements between enterprises, which are considered beneficial for the consumers by improving production, distribution or technical progress, are deemed not to restrict competition and therefore they are exempted. Cross-border concentrations of Community interest, regardless of whether they are brought about by agreement or by take-overs, are also exempted. One major drawback of Article 86 as an instrument of merger control has been that it can only be activated after a merger has taken place; pre-emptive action by the Commission is not possible.

With regard to mergers, a common policy empowering the European Commission to block or authorise them was approved at the end of 1989, thus ending sixteen years of protracted negotiations. What finally convinced the EC partners to sign the agreement is the run-up to 1992 and the expectation of a boom in cross-frontier mergers as companies start to tackle the single market. Under the new regulation, which came into force on 21 September 1990, all mergers with a world-wide aggregate turnover each year of more than 5 billion ECUs need prior clearance by the Commission. Smaller mergers – or larger ones where each company has over two-thirds of its Community turnover in the same member state – must apply to the national monopolies and mergers authority for approval, but the Commission may intervene at the request of a member state involved. Large companies incorporated outside the EC, but generating at least 250 million ECU of their annual business in the Community, are also subject to the EC regulations, if a merger between them threatens to distort competition on the Community market. Special rules apply for banking, financial and insurance institutions. The agreed thresholds for intervention will apply for four years, after which they may be varied on the basis of qualified majority vote in the Council of Ministers. With the introduction of the new regulation, the Commission has effectively renounced all existing powers under the Treaty of Rome competition rules over mergers below 5 billion ECU, unless explicitly asked by national governments to intervene (*Bulletin EC*, Supplement 3, 1989).

National aids to industry are controlled by the Commission under Articles 92 and 93. As a rule, all government aid to business is forbidden under Article 92 of the Treaty: 'Save as otherwise provided in this Treaty, any aid granted by a Member State or through State resources in any form whatsoever which distorts or threatens to distort competition by favouring certain undertakings or the production of certain goods shall, in so far as it affects trade between Member States, be incompatible with the common market'. However, some types of aids, such as transparent development subsidies which are regionally specific, are exempted. Governments are obliged to notify the Commission of any plans to introduce new aid schemes or alter existing ones, and the Commission then decides whether or not these are acceptable under the Treaty. If the aid is found to be incompatible with the Treaty, the

Commission has the power to ask the member state to amend it or to abolish it. For example, credit facilities which aid exporters have been terminated under Community instigation. The Commission may authorise certain forms of aid, if it considers that any distortions of competition are offset by advantages to the Community. For example, the Commission has relaxed its application of the competition rules to state aid for companies which are engaged in research and high technology.

Little progress has been made in the field of public procurement mostly because of resistance to changes in the *status quo* by some member states which consider this function of the government to be an essential element of national sovereignty. Purchases of goods and services by national or local authorities and by public enterprises (energy supply, post and telecommunications, railways, etc.) cover a sizeable part of the GDP – more than 15 per cent of national economic activity in most member states – and are still marked by specifications which tend to direct them exclusively to domestic sources of supply. Despite general anti-discrimination provisions of the Treaty (Articles 7, 30, 34) and the publication of a number of Directives which specifically seek to terminate discriminatory practices in this field, at the moment less than 2 per cent of members' public contracts are placed outside the national frontiers. In the run-up to 1992, the Commission has presented proposals aiming to increase awareness of who is awarded the contracts for the provision of services to public bodies and enforcement of the current legislation to ensure that firms from all members of the Community have an equal chance in gaining a contract. But an attempt to include the sectors of water, transport, energy and telecommunications in the liberalisation of public purchasing contracts narrowly failed in 1989.

Articles 87–91 deal with procedures for implementation of the rules of competition. The competition rules of the EEC Treaty can be applied by national courts. However, running parallel to this possibility, the Commission is directly responsible for the application of the European legislation. The Commission is entrusted with powers, exercised independently of the Council of Ministers, to investigate, to declare restrictive arrangements by companies or government null and void, to order the parties to terminate them, and to impose fines and penalties (of up to 10 per cent of the firm's world-wide turnover) payable to the Community budget for infringement of the competition rules. However, the Commission can act only if the relevant agreement has a perceptible restrictive effect, actual or potential, on trade between member states. Restrictive agreements whose effects are purely domestic are a matter for the laws of the member states concerned. Anticompetitive behaviour can be investigated by the Commission on its own initiative. Alternatively, it can be brought to the attention of the Commission by interested parties by way of a complaint. Commission Decisions may be challenged at the Court of Justice which has the power to confirm, cancel, reduce or increases fines and penalty payments or to annul Commission Decisions (Article 173).

In practice, the competition law has developed through experience and Court rulings, which in general have tended to support the Commission's reasoning, with the implication that the Commission has lost very few cases. However, the Commission has been criticised for its preoccupation with excessively bureaucratic procedures which delay decisions for many years. The Court of First Instance (CFI) has been specifically established to relieve the Court of Justice of such cases as competition law, which involve complex facts needing lengthy examinations.

3.3 Benefits of the single market

The theoretical aspects of trade and welfare effects of trade liberalisation in a customs union and their measurement were discussed in Chapter 1. The drive towards the single market in the European Community entails much more than the elimination of tariffs and quantitative restrictions on trade between the member states. It also involves the abolition of all the barriers that prevent the establishment of the common market by constraining competition, efficiency and the optimal utilisation of resources. In this section we examine the nature of these barriers in the Community and present quantitative estimates of the economic effects of their abolition.

As we have seen, most tariffs and quantitative restrictions on trade between the member states have been eliminated. The next stage for completing the Single European Market (SEM) includes 'the abolition of barriers of all kinds, harmonisation of rules, approximation of legislation and tax structures, strengthening of monetary cooperation and the necessary flanking measures to encourage European firms to work together' (EC, 1985a). The Single European Act was followed by a detailed programme for attaining this objective, set forth by the Commission in a White Paper entitled 'Completing the internal market' (EC Commission, 1985a). This Paper listed 300 specific areas (subsequently reduced to 279) for action, aiming at the elimination of the remaining physical, technical and fiscal barriers of the internal market by the end of 1992. Two types of barriers were distinguished: tariff and non-tariff restrictions and market entry controls:

1. Cost-increasing tariff and non-tariff barriers on foreign and intra-EC trade:

(a) *Tariffs and quantitative restrictions.* Border taxes or subsidies still apply on trade of agricultural products (in the form of monetary compensatory amounts, MCAs). Production quotas have been reintroduced for steel and some agricultural commodities and national quotas on imports from outside the EC (e.g. on textiles from less developed countries and cars from Japan) are still prevalent. Market-sharing arrangements (e.g. road and air transport) have effects similar to those of trade restrictions.

(b) *Different norms and technical regulations* between the member states.

(c) *Border controls.* Customs formalities and other administrative burdens causing frontier delays, such as those arising from different tax rates and tax systems (VAT rates, excise taxes, etc.), application of MCAs, different health regulations for plant and animal products, different licensing qualifications, and so forth.

(d) *Market-distorting subsidies* at the Community and national levels. These are now kept under control by the Community's competition policy, but certain markets are still distorted by price controls and specific taxes.

2. Market entry restrictions:

(a) *Protectionist public procurement practices.* The public authorities in the EC countries have granted preferential treatment to domestic suppliers of goods and services. This is effected in a number of ways, including procedures through which bids are solicited and contracts are awarded.

(b) *Differing regulation of services.* The service industries, such as transportation (air, freight) and especially finance (banking, insurance, stock markets, etc.), have been subjected to regulation. Restrictions exist on the freedom to engage in certain service transactions, or to become established in certain service activities in other Community countries.

(c) *Controls on movement of capital.* Eight of the twelve EC countries have maintained some degree of control over capital movements to or from other member states.

(d) *Lack of a common legal framework for business.* Differing national laws and regulations introduce complications into cross-border business activity involving mergers, joint ventures, patents, copyrights, and so forth.

An important result of these barriers is that the European economy is segmented along national lines and many markets display weak competitiveness and oligopolistic structure. Evidence of this is seen in the substantial price differences between countries. Across countries in 1985, the average before-tax price variation from the EC mean price was 15.2 per cent for consumer goods and 12.4 per cent for capital equipment. Much wider were the price differences in the service sectors: 28 per cent in road and rail transport, 42 per cent in electrical repairs and 50 per cent in telephone and telegram services. These differences were sustained by the walls of barriers which prevented inter-state trade (EC, 1989b). Therefore, price convergence by free arbitrage across countries should lower the average price level. In general, completion of the internal market offers a large potential for rationalisation of production and distribution, leading to improvements in productivity, and reductions in cost and prices.

The elimination of the internal market barriers is expected to bring about cost reductions from the following:

1. Enhanced competition, leading to greater allocative efficiency.
2. Economies of scale, associated with the size of production units and enterprises.
3. Specialisation of production and trade according to comparative advantage.
4. Improved access to the flow of innovation, new processes and new products.

In turn, these cost reductions are expected to lead to the following:

1. Reallocation of production and trade within the large Community market.
2. Improved efficiency and increased output.
3. Increased competitiveness leading to improved performance in international trade.

The quantitative evaluation of these effects and of the overall economic gain of completing the internal market is complex and inexact. Moreover, the completion of the internal market is gradual and, as the necessary measures are implemented through time, some effects will occur instantly while others will be delayed. Consequently, any quantification would be subject to speculations about long-term economic conditions in the EC and the world and would depend on a number of assumptions concerning policy considerations. Therefore, all these estimates should be taken only as a rough approximation of orders of magnitude.

The quantitative estimates presented in the following are those made by the EC (1988b, 1988c). Two types of effects are distinguished:

1. *'Barrier removal' effects*: these are the *static* welfare effects derived from the elimination of price differences which are caused by tariff and non-tariff barriers, as listed above.
2. *'Integration' effects*: these are the *quasi-dynamic* effects of increased technical efficiency (or reduced 'X-inefficiency': the technical inefficiency that stems from a failure to maximise), erosion of oligopoly profits and improved consumer choice derived from improved market access leading to greater market integration and increased competition, as listed above.

The genuine dynamic effects, which are derived from technical progress and reallocation of production and employment in the integrated market and from specialisation according to comparative advantage, are not easily quantifiable and no attempt has been made to estimate them.

The static effects have been estimated by partial equilibrium analysis, separately for each barrier observed and for each economic sector. The sum of these effects is the total static effect of market liberalisation. A drawback of this technique is that it ignores the extent to which the barriers overlap and economic sectors are interconnected. Therefore, no account is taken of spillover and interactive effects between sectors which occur as barriers are eliminated and relative prices change. Use of the alternative approach of general equilibrium analysis, which could account for all these effects, is not possible.

The methodology of estimating the costs of tariff and non-tariff regulatory barriers is basically that of consumer and producer surplus as employed in the calculation of trade creation and trade diversion effects of customs unions (described in Chapter 1). The analysis is based on the following assumptions:

1. The supply curve is not perfectly elastic, so that in a single Community country an increased demand for imports increases their price.
2. Goods and services may be imported both from other Community countries and from the rest of the world (RW).
3. The completion of the internal market entails the removal of non-tariff barriers between the Community countries while the common external tariff (CET), inclusive of non-tariff barriers, remains intact against the rest of the world.

Figure 3.1 (adapted from Johnson, 1957, 1958a) illustrates the welfare effects of trade barriers removal for country Z, a member of the EC. Imports to Z come from both the Community and the rest of the world with (excess) supply curves *EC* and *RW*, respectively. Z's market

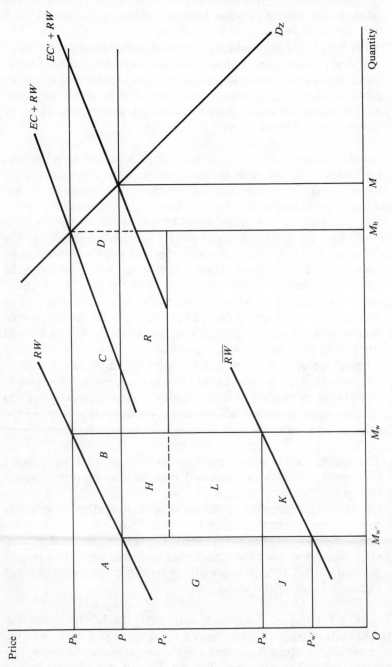

Figure 3.1 Trade and welfare effects of barrier removal.

demand curve is D_Z. Prior to the removal of trade barriers, equilibrium in country Z is reached at the point of intersection between its demand D_Z and the lateral sum of the two foreign supplies, $EC + RW$, at price P_b and quantity M_b. This quantity comprises imports OM_w from RW at price P_w and imports $M_w M_b$ from EC at price P_c. Since $P_w < P_c$, the Community EC is the least efficient producer. When the internal barriers are removed, the supply curve EC shifts to EC', prices in Z fall to P and total imports rise to M. The price fall in the market of Z, from P_b to P, depends on the cost equivalent of the removed barriers (the downward shift of EC), the elasticity of the demand curve D_Z and the elasticity of the supply schedules EC and RW. Total imports comprise imports $OM_{w'}$ from RW at price $P_{w'}$ and imports $M_{w'} M$ from EC at price P.

The increase in total imports, $M_b M$, is equal to the algebraic sum of the reduction of imports from RW *plus* the increase in imports from EC. Actually, the discriminating removal of trade barriers has caused a fall in the price and an increase in the volume of demand/imports for two reasons:

1. The *inter-country substitution effect*: imports from RW equal to $M_{w'} M_w$ have been replaced by imports from EC. Since RW is the most efficient producer, this effect is trade diversion.
2. The *inter-commodity substitution effect*: total imports have risen by $M_b M$, originated in EC. This effect is trade creation (see also Chapter 1, Section 1.3).

The welfare effects of these changes for country Z are as follows:

1. A consumer surplus gain of $(A + B + C + D)$.
2. A loss of tariff revenue of $(A + B + G + H + L) - (G + J)$. Since the foreign supply RW is not perfectly elastic, there is a terms-of-trade effect; the import supply price from RW falls and the tariff revenue is paid by both the domestic consumers and the foreign suppliers.

Therefore, the net welfare gain to country Z is given by the areas $(C + D - H - L + J)$. These areas may be interpreted as a terms-of-trade gain on imports from EC of $(C + D)$, a terms-of-trade gain on imports from RW of J and a trade diversion loss of $(H + L)$, from the displacement of imports $M_{w'} M_w$ from RW by an equal volume of more expensive imports from EC. Producers in the Community EC gain the areas $(H + R)$ from increase in the volume and price of their exports to Z. The suppliers of RW suffer the loss of the area $(J + K)$.

The removal of cost-increasing trade barriers and production and market distortions will have an impact effect and a delayed effect in the Community. The impact effect arises from reduction in economic rents (wages and profits) and improved efficiency after the abolition of protection. The delayed effects will arise from restructuring production, new investment and exploitation of economies of scale. The latter can be expected in every production activity, but they will be most probable and more significant in industries which currently operate in national markets which are imperfectly competitive and not large enough to accommodate plants of maximum efficiency scale. The effects will be more pronounced if in the union protection, different national standards and diverse technical specifications have contributed to the development of non-contested markets to the extent that exports cannot provide a sufficient outlet for reaching an efficient scale of production.

Figure 3.2 illustrates in broad outline the effects of eliminating cost-increasing trade barriers in the market of a Community country Z. The

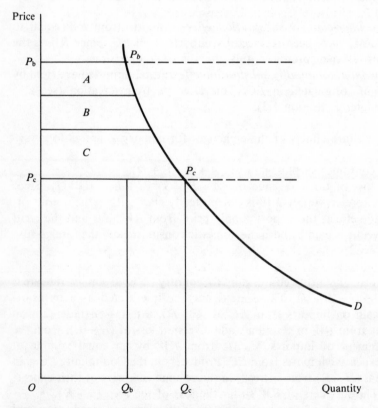

Figure 3.2 Effects of eliminating trade barriers.

country's demand is given by the curve D. The domestic supply is as competitive as the supply from other member countries, so that there are no comparative advantages between countries (EC, 1988b, p. 36). Before the removal of barriers the market price is P_b and the equilibrium quantity is Q_b. As barriers are eliminated, the direct costs on competitive imports (delays at frontiers, differing technical regulations, etc.) fall immediately and the foreign suppliers in Z's market reduce their prices. In order to remain competitive, the domestic suppliers respond by reducing excess profits or wages (area A) and by eliminating 'X-inefficiencies' (such as overhead costs, overmanning, excess inventories, etc., area B). As prices decline from P_b, demand also increases from Q_b. This increase in demand, in association with the development of a more competitive environment, induces more investment in new productive capacity by both domestic and foreign producers. In the longer term, restructuring of the industry by new investment and mergers provides the opportunity for a fuller exploitation of internal economies of scale and further reductions in costs and prices (area C). The price eventually falls to P_c with total demand increasing to Q_c.

At the aggregate level of the customs union as a whole, both internal and external economies of scale may have positive effects on total output. External economies of scale will come about at the level of the industry from technological spillovers which are expected to increase the productivity of one firm when the output of other firms rises. In general, integration of the market allows greater specialisation and efficiency leading to higher output. Competition in the integrated market will, of course, eliminate the less efficient firms and even industries, causing temporary wastage and unemployment. But this is an inevitable outcome of the optimal reallocation of resources within the area of the customs union, which in the longer run will benefit the economy by increasing output, employment and welfare.

The costs of customs formalities, different technical regulations, entry restrictions, public procurement and 'X-inefficiency' were estimated for the EC by industry case studies and market research. Estimates were also made of the effects of eliminating the remaining controls on capital flows and the integration of financial markets under the European Monetary System (EMS).

Finally, the total microeconomic impact of fully integrating the Community market was calculated by two methods under two different assumptions:

1. The price-convergence approach which takes no account of the response of production to a rising demand, stimulated by price reductions, or cost reductions derived from economies of scale. This

method provided an estimated maximum gain of 4.25 per cent of Community GDP.

2. The welfare-gains approach which, in addition to secondary demand effects, takes into account profit losses that might be suffered by some currently protected producers. This approach provided an estimated maximum gain of 6.5 per cent of GDP (Table 3.1).

The microeconomic partial-equilibrium estimates of direct and induced effects were supplemented by macroeconomic analysis, which focused on the repercussions of the single market on major components of the GDP. The quantitative evaluations at the macroeconomic level took into consideration intersectoral relationships and interdependencies, such as multipliers and accelerators, income distribution, price competitiveness, inflation mechanisms, capital accumulation, growth potential, etc. The effects were calculated under two different assumptions: first, that in the run to the single market, macroeconomic policy remains passive; and, second, that active macroeconomic policy would exploit the new opportunities as they emerge from liberalisation of the market. The abolition of the internal frontiers will, however, in the short term cause problems of adaptation to the dynamics of competition in the large market. Reallocation of production could mean the loss of employment in the short term as industry adjusts to the new conditions. But it is also expected that, as the restructuring process of production proceeds and real incomes rise, a substantial amount of new jobs will be created increasing total employment in the medium and long term. Taking all these changes into account, the aggregate results of estimations (Table 3.1) indicate a possible medium-term increase in GDP of 4.5 per cent and a decrease in the price level of 6 per cent, creating 1.75

Table 3.1 Effects of completion of the internal market in the medium/long term.

Microeconomic approach			Welfare gains as % of GDP: 4.25–6.5		
Macroeconomic approach	GDP as %	Prices as %	Employment (millions)	Public deficit (% on GDP)	External balance (% on GDP)
Passive policy[1]	4.5	−6	1.75	2.25	1
Active policy[1]	7	−4.5	5	0.5	−0.25

[1] Margin of error ±30 per cent.

Source: EC Commission (1988), 'The economics of 1992', Table 10.3.1, p. 167, *European Economy*, No. 35, Office for Official Publications of the EC, Luxembourg.

million new jobs in the medium to long term for the Community as a whole. However, if the market liberalisation measures were to be accompanied by the easing of macroeconomic constraints – improved public or external balances, reduced inflationary pressures – the GDP gain could be 7 per cent and an additional 5 million jobs created. Although these figures must be treated with caution, their order of magnitude should confirm that the effect from completion of the large internal market will be fairly sizeable in macroeconomic terms.

The study of the effects has assumed that the single market will be established before currency unification, but in an environment of monetary stability within the European Monetary System. The welfare benefits of effective currency unification, which are not included in the quantitative estimates, could potentially be very large (Goodhart, 1990). Against these optimistic expectations it can be argued that the programme's success requires faithful execution by the member states. If for any reason the necessary conditions for completion of the single market are not realised, then the actual outcome will fall short of the predicted one (Kay, 1989). For example, there is considerable doubt as to whether the governments of member states can overcome the lobbying by special interest groups and their own reluctance to sacrifice sovereignty in order to carry out the programme's objectives (Peck, 1989; Grossman, 1990).

In any case, since the estimates of the effects are not a prediction which can be verified *ex post*, the actual outcome of market integration can never be established precisely. What is certain is that a single market for the twelve member states of the Community will raise real incomes.

The gains from completion of the internal market are aggregate for the Community as a whole (and in fact they are based on data which are available only for Germany, France, Italy and the United Kingdom). The study offered no quantitative estimates of their distribution among the member countries. It is expected that proportionally larger gains will accrue to the countries which in the past protected their domestic market with relatively high barriers and hence developed industries dominated by small firms. Similarly, lower-wage countries will gain more than the high-wage ones. There is a possibility that, with the elimination of trade barriers, the low-wage southern countries of the Community may become attractive locations of production (Neven, 1990), if they can supply manpower possessing the necessary skills to match the productivity performance of the high-wage countries of the Community. Against this can be set the fact that the southern European countries are also the relatively most underdeveloped member states which in the short term may suffer large losses from adjustment to the new competitive environment of the single market. In general, consumers everywhere will benefit, but some producers will not. It is possible, of course, that some countries may end up as net losers.

Completion of the internal market by a one-off removal of barrier and institutional improvement will lead to a once-and-for-all static gain of a higher level of output and employment, spread over a number of years. This one-time efficiency gain will not necessarily affect the long-term rate of growth. The static benefit of market integration can potentially increase the rate of economic growth, by increasing the rate of capital accumulation, technical innovation and productivity. But the rate of growth and its determinants belong to the dynamic effects of economic integration and (as remarked earlier and in Chapter 1) static efficiency is neither a determinant nor a predictor of dynamic efficiency. Completion of the internal market will create the environment which will open up opportunities for reaching the dynamic effects of integration. Consequently, it is possible that in the single market an increase in static efficiency may exert a positive influence on savings and investment and therefore on the growth potential of the Community.

The next question concerns the effects of the single market on the rest of the world. If market integration yields the predicted improvements in economic performance, then rising EC income could lead to increased imports and thus to higher levels of economic activity in the rest of the world. But there is a caveat here: the benefits of 1992 will be a boost to world trade only if the EC becomes more open, so that the overall outcome of the single market is trade creation. Completion of the common market opens the possibility of combining widening competition within the EC with heightening protectionist barriers on foreign trade. Since the EC represents the largest trading power in the world, the initiative to set up the single European market has aroused fears abroad, and within Europe, that the intention of the Community is to turn itself into 'Fortress Europe'. This would occur if, with the elimination of border controls, the quantitative restrictions still maintained by individual members of the EC were to escalate and be adopted as the uniform set of protection at the level of the Community. Concerns about this possibility have intensified, particularly since some EC officials and published documents have espoused the principles of equivalent access or 'reciprocity' (EC Commission, 1985a). However, the Community has also stated that it 'will seek a greater liberalisation of international trade; the 1992 Europe will not be a fortress Europe but a partnership Europe'. This does not exclude the possibility that completion of the internal market may well entail the pre-existing degree of EC protection against foreign competition. Even if this were to be the case, increase in economic activity in the Community would provide opportunities for more foreign trade, therefore for sharing the benefits of market integration within and outside the European Community.

Further reading

The EC's approach to competition has been published in a number of reports, such as EC Commission (1989b). For a summary of official views on this subject see EC (1983a).

The EC's massive study of the 'Cost of non-Europe', EC Commission (1988b, 1988c) is a detailed multi-volume investigation of the effects of the single market. The results of this study are summarised in two general reports: Emerson *et al.* (1988) for the experts and Cecchini (1988) for the general reader. For a critical review of the EC approach and estimates of effects see Kay (1989) and Peck (1989). Two opposing views, potential vs. expected, on the Commission's estimates of effects are in Siebert (1990). For an overview of the probable gainers and losers among the EC countries see Neven (1990). Henderson (1989) examines the external repercussions of the single market.

4

The Community budget

4.1 Introduction

As we have seen, the EC objective is integration and enlargement of the market, with predominantly market-determined solutions to economic problems. The emphasis on the market mechanism does not mean that the EC completely abstains from application of economic policies. On the contrary, integration requires the active participation of the central authority in policy-making, particularly when the objective of a common policy is a Community target, and the process of integration involves costs or brings benefits which must be shared among the participating countries. One of the most important instruments of national economic policy is the budget. The budget is also a major instrument of economic policy in regional economic associations and in the EC. In the following we examine the principles governing budgetary policy and the structure and the objectives of the Community budget.

Government budget is the account of revenues received and expenditures incurred by the government in a period of a financial year. In general, the budget reflects the extent of government activity in the economy. Analysis of the structure of the budget is the study of the following:

1. The *origin* of government financial resources. Taxation is usually the most important source of government revenue. Taxes are levied directly on persons and firms and indirectly on expenditure.
2. The *destination* of these resources. This is determined by government expenditure on direct purchases of goods and services or for transfer payments directed to persons or firms.

3. The *effects* of the composition of revenues and expenditures and of the overall position of the budget, the budget surplus or deficit.

In any financial year, the government is not constrained in its spending by what it can earn. It can borrow from domestic or foreign sources and it can levy more taxes. Normally, the government has a real choice as to whether or not to balance its budget. This choice is based on the objectives of the government and on consideration of the benefits and costs of its policies. This brings into focus the question of the proper role of the government.

In general, three approaches to the question of the degree of government involvement in economic affairs can be discerned, which are based on concepts partly theoretical and partly ideological and political:

1. The minimum: government action is required only when the private sector cannot do the job. This is the traditional view about the neutrality of the state according to which a very limited number of tasks are assigned to it on the grounds that the state should refrain from any interference with the market economy.

2. The medium: the government must play an active role by means of interventionary economic policy. The view here is that the market mechanism is not always able to attain the community's social goals and state interference is indispensable. In particular, the market mechanism may not lead to an optimal allocation of the society's resources (the allocation problem) or it may fail to achieve a distribution of income satisfying some generally accepted standards of equity (the distribution problem). Similarly, the price mechanism may not ensure full employment with external and internal stability and a satisfactory rate of economic growth (the stabilisation problem). Accordingly, state interference for resolving these problems is, in many cases, not only acceptable but highly desirable.

3. The maximum: the government plays the main role, the socialist approach. The most active policy for the government occurs when the state owns the means of production and undertakes most of the functions which the private sector performs in market economies.

Under the first approach, the government is required to operate in the market economy only as a provider of *collective goods and services*, and to intervene only in case of *market failure*. The distinguishing characteristic of collective (or public) goods is the indivisibility of their services among persons: they are supplied to a group of people rather than on an individual basis and cannot be withheld from individuals who refuse to pay for them (the free-riders). Defence, law and order, foreign policy and environmental control are such goods. Market failure occurs when there is divergence between private and social costs or benefits, causing external economies or diseconomies. An example of external economies is education which benefits not only the individual but also the society in which the educated individual lives and works. An external diseconomy requiring government intervention is pollution. The government is also expected to intervene in the case of natural monopolies, such as the supply of public services (electricity, telephone, certain modes of public transport), when investment and operations may display large economies of scale.

A more active role for the government includes the exercise of fiscal and monetary policy to prevent depression and inflation, induce investment and growth, and redistribute income by welfare and social security policies. In contrast to the private sector, where decisions are made through the market mechanism, in the public sector decisions are reached through the political process.

In general, different budgetary measures (taxation and expenditure policies and the size of the budget surplus or deficit) have a different incidence on the economy as a whole and its constituent sectors (households and firms; production, consumption, investment, balance of payments, etc.). As a rule, there are certain commonly invoked criteria for organising a fiscal system, that is deciding the tax and expenditure structure. These criteria involve aspects of *equity* and *efficiency*. Fiscal equity, or fairness, is the principle of equal treatment for equally situated economic agents (individuals or firms) with respect to the allocation of burdens or the distribution of benefits (horizontal equity), and proper division of the budgetary burden according to ability to pay (vertical equity). Economic efficiency concerns the allocation of resources and the goal of optimality, and is based on the rule that the operations of the public sector should cause the least price distortion.

While some criteria raise no conflict-of-interest issues, others generate sharp differences of opinion among different social and economic groups. Consequently, the budget mirrors the ideology and the political, economic and social aims of the government in power. For the economists, the budget is the policy instrument which is used by the government to pursue fiscal policy objectives or expenditure objectives relating to: (a) the allocation of resources between public and private uses, consumption and investment, and geographic regions; (b) the distribution of income; (c) stabilisation; and (d) economic growth. Ultimately, these objectives constitute part of the more general target of the economic policy of the government, the improvement in social welfare.

In a federal system there exist public sectors in both the component states and the federal government. In principle, in a multi-level system of government (local, state, federal), each level should be allocated the functions that it can do best. The federal government is concerned with the provision of federal public goods and other policies which can be pursued more efficiently at the level of the central government rather than of the state (e.g. defence and foreign policy). However, in most federal structures some evening-up of fiscal capacity is envisaged with member-state autonomy over the degree of local taxation and public expenditure. Since the structure of a federation expresses the wishes of the constituent states, different federal structures require different types of fiscal federalism. This is manifested in federal budgets that are based on elaborate systems of constitutional rules regarding the origin of budgetary revenues and the destination of budgetary expenditures. The 'federal approach', which is a general characteristic of the budgets of existing federations (United States, Canada, Australia), is the active involvement of the central government in income redistribution policies by substantial income transfers from richer to poorer states or regions.

In general, the relative importance of the budget as an instrument of policy is to be found in the following:

1. The size of the budget: whether it is large or small in relation to a certain base reference, such as the national income.
2. The structure of the budget: the composition of its credit and debit sides.
3. The net position of the budget: whether the budget shows an overall surplus or a deficit.
4. The incidence of the budget: net transfers from the rest of the country to particular industries, regions or population groups.

4.2 General characteristics of the Community budget

Background

One of the basic aims of the Treaty of Rome is 'to establish the foundations for an ever closer union among the European peoples', that is an economic and political union rather than another international organisation. To reach this objective the member states must gradually confer to the Community certain of their functions and activities and the powers to operate them. These will be the common targets which will be pursued by common policies at costs shared by all the participants. The Treaty of Paris (1951) had provided the ECSC with its own budget, financed by a direct Community tax, a levy on coal and steel production, and by borrowing. Euratom also started with its own budget, financed by national contributions. In accordance with the terms of the Treaty of Rome, the EEC Commission was given an operational budget and the task of administering two funds, the Social Fund and the Agricultural fund. In 1967, following the 'Merger Treaty', the budgets of the three communities were brought together in a single general budget, the Community budget. However, some autonomy still remains with the ECSC and the European Development Fund (that provides aid to developing countries) which run separate operational budgets (Shackleton, 1990).

Initially, the budget consisted of financial resources made available, and expenditures allocated in accordance with decisions taken in common by the contracting parties. The budget was *specific*, the revenues consisted of fixed financial contributions made by the member states on an agreed scale, and the expenditures were directed to clearly specified activities (Articles 199–209), with the additional constraint that 'the revenue and expenditure shown in the budget shall be in balance' (Article 199). Hence, this budget was not substantially different from the budgets of other international organisations, which usually have more moderate aims than those of the European Community.

In order to pursue successfully the objective of economic integration by common policies, the government of the economic union must be provided with the power to choose what revenues to collect and how to spend them, that is to use its own budget. As in the case of a federation of states, community financing means the transfer of resources from the national to a common supranational level. In the EC, the target of this process is the provision of resources which would be used in operational activities geared to the integration of peoples and countries. Hence, the EC, although it is not a federation of states, has specific objectives in many ways similar to those of a federation, and these can be realised only if an adequate budget becomes available. But progress towards this direction has been very slow:

1. In 1970, in accordance with the provisions of the Treaty (Article 201), the Council decided to replace gradually the financial contributions of member states to the Community budget by revenues from appropriately allocated 'own resources' directly paid to the Community as of right. An advantage of this new system of financing the Community budget is that the Commission gained a certain degree of power by loosening its financial dependence on the member states which, however, cannot default on payment.

2. At the current phase of European integration the Community

budget is based on narrow foundations and continues to remain relatively insignificant in size. To a large extent, the EC budget is still functioning as 'public expenditure estimates', an account of revenues from specific resources and expenditures for specific purposes, in *ex post* balance as required by the Treaty.

3. But if the ultimate policy objective of the contracting parties is to establish a European political and economic union, the present small Community budget cannot function as an effective policy instrument. That role can be played only by a larger and more independent Community budget, which could progressively absorb many of the functions currently coming under the jurisdiction of the national budgets. Fiscal federalism implies the gradual shift of the responsibility for redistributive activities from the government of the member states to the federal government (Oates, 1972). However, fiscal federalism is not as yet one of the explicit objectives of the Community.

The Community budget thus perfectly reflects the present stage of economic integration in Europe. There is as yet no question about using this budget as an instrument for pursuing Community policies at large, other than those explicitly specified in the Treaty of Rome. Unemployment, inflation, low rate of growth and other macroeconomic problems at the level of the Community, some of which may result from the process of integration, have not as yet come to be regarded as shared problems and are not subject to consideration by Community budgetary policy. They are still considered as the prerogative and responsibility of the national governments of the member states and are pursued at the strictly national level. With the exception of monetary coordination within the EMS, there is still little direct cooperation in the area of macroeconomic policy within the EC, and not enough attention has been paid to whether the integration of policies would make them more effective and bring gains to the Community.

Budgetary procedure

The Community budget, which is denominated in ECUs, is drawn annually for a calendar year. Supplementary budgets are added during the year, whenever necessary. Since 1975, the Parliament and the Council are the 'budgetary authority', with the Commission responsible for executing the budget. Both the annual budget and the supplementary budgets are subject to the same procedures.

Three of the Community's decision-making institutions are involved in the preparation and adoption of the budget:

1. On the basis of estimates submitted to the Commission by five Community institutions (the Council, the Commission, the Parliament, the Court of Justice and the Economic and Social Committee), the Commission prepares the *preliminary* draft budget which it submits to the Council by 1 September.
2. The Council, acting by a qualified majority, prepares the *draft budget* which it forwards to the Parliament by 5 October.
3. The Parliament approves, amends or rejects the draft budget, which in the latter two cases is referred back to the Council for modifications.

The Parliament can, however, reject the draft budget *in toto* and ask for a new draft to be submitted. Final adoption of the budget is the prerogative of the President of the European Parliament. The Commission has the sole duty to implement the budget (Article 205) and is responsible to the European Parliament for ensuring that the budget is implemented as voted (Article 205a).

After the end of the budgetary year, a fourth Community institution, the Court of Auditors, scrutinises all Community revenue and expenditure, and decides whether financial management has been sound and regular. Finally, after the Parliament has examined the accounts, deliberated on the report of the Court of Auditors and considered the recommendations of the Council, it grants *parliamentary discharge*, confirming that the Commission's management of Community funds during the preceding year has been approved.

This is a simplified version of a procedure which is rather complex, and it frequently leads to delays in the approval of the budget beyond the required date for completion (usually December). The complications arise mostly from the treaties, because the texts laying down rules and regulations are not very clear. Most frequently problems emerge from the classification of expenditure as *compulsory* or *non-compulsory*. The Parliament has the power to determine only the non-compulsory expenditure, and only within prespecified limits. Compulsory expenditure is 'expenditure necessarily resulting from the Treaty or from acts adopted in accordance therewith' (Article 203). This definition is rather vague and has given rise to a number of demarcation disputes between the Council and the Parliament. Currently, about 75 per cent of the total expenditure is compulsory, such as expenditure for the Common Agricultural Policy. Expenditure on transport, regional development and social policy is non-compulsory.

The latest dispute between the Council and the Parliament, concerning the classification of expenditures, was resolved in July 1986. The point at issue was that in December 1985 the Parliament had added 1.9 per cent expenditure on the 1986 Budget without previous consultation with the Council, which objected to the increase and appealed to the European Court of Justice. The Court ruled that the Parliament was technically in the wrong and had exceeded its legitimate powers: namely, if there are 'important reasons', the Parliament can reject the entire budget, but it cannot, without Council approval, change the compulsory parts of the budget item by item. Nor can the Parliament raise the discretionary part of the budget above the 'maximum rate', a ceiling calculated annually by the Commission and set by the Council. The Court also confirmed that drafting the budget was a task in which the Council and Parliament were jointly, though not equally, involved.

4.3   The Community budget since 1980

In 1990 the Community budget was approximately 48,000 million ECUs (or nearly £34,500 million). It appears to be a very large sum, but actually it is just 1 per cent of the EC countries' GDP of the same year. In contrast, the national budgets of the member states currently take up

Table 4.1 Community budget allocation, 1980–90.

		1980–84	1985–9		1990
			Revenues (per cent)		
1. Customs duties, agricultural levies, sugar levy		45	40		39
2. VAT		55	60		61
			Expenditures (per cent)		
1. Agriculture		67.5	68.0		58.3
Guarantee	64.3		65.3	54.8	
Guidance	3.2		2.7	3.5	
2. Social policy		4.8	6.4		8.4
3. Regional policy		9.9	7.6		11.9
4. Industry, research, energy		3.1	2.6		3.5
5. Development aid		3.7	3.0		2.9
6. Administration		4.6	3.8		4.9
7. Reimbursements to members		5.5	5.6		1.8
8. Other policies and reserves		0.9	3.0		8.3

Note: Commitment appropriations for 1990.

Source: *Eurostat 1984* and *Bulletin EC*, No. 11, 1989, and other issues.

a large (and in some cases increasing) share of national GDP. For instance, the share of general government current receipts on GDP varies between 33.3 per cent in Portugal and 58 per cent in Denmark, with a weighted average for all the EC countries of 44 per cent. The Community budget is approximately equal to 4 per cent of the sum of budgets of the EC-12 countries (1990), which makes it almost equal to Greece's GDP. However, comparisons between the Community budget and the national budgets of the member states are not enlightening: the Community budget does not include expenditures for defence, education, health, etc., which account for most of national budgetary expenditures.

The average composition of the Community budget during the periods 1980–84, 1985–9 and the year 1990 (preliminary budget) are shown in Table 4.1. The analysis of its structure is as follows.

Revenues

1. Customs revenue from the application of the common customs tariff (CCT) on goods imported from third countries. The customs duties are collected at the point of entry in the Community which can be in a country other than the country of final destination or consumption of the imported commodity. It is therefore revenue from operating a Community policy, and it rightly goes to the Community purse.
2. Variable import levies on imports of agricultural products from third countries arising under the Common Agricultural Policy. Reasons similar to 1 above apply for directing this revenue to the Community rather than the treasury of the country collecting it. Agricultural levies are designed to offset the differences between the (usually much higher) Community price and the price of imports. The sugar levy, which is a charge on the production and storage of sugar and isoglucose of member states, is also included here.
3. The revenues collected from the 'traditional own resources', 1 and 2 above, are inadequate relative to the functions allocated to the Community budget and may also fluctuate from year to year. In the longer term their relative shares in the budget may further diminish as international trade is liberalised and more special agreements for free or freer trade are concluded between the EC and third countries. Consequently, the member states (in accordance with Article 201 of the EEC Treaty) decided to create an additional and more secure source of budgetary revenue by allocating to the Community

'own resources' a certain proportion of each member state's Value Added Tax (VAT) base calculated on a common basis.

The VAT yield has been chosen in preference to any other tax yield because (a) under the Sixth Directive of 17 May 1977, VAT is a tax paid by all the Community citizens and (b) as an indirect tax charged at the consumption stage, the VAT was supposed to reflect each member state's spending capacity, that is their ability to pay; but as we will see later, this is not so.

Expenditures

Expenditures from the Community budget are in the form of direct payments to recipients in individual member states or to countries outside the EC, such as agricultural intervention boards, government departments of member states, research establishments, private firms or foreign governments as aid, etc. Items 1–4 in Table 4.1 constitute the *allocated* budget expenditure, that is expenditure which can be attributed to individual member states. It accounts for more than 80 per cent of total expenditure. The *unallocated* expenditure goes either to recipients outside the Community, e.g. as aid to developing countries, or to research and administrative outlays at the headquarters. Another distinction of expenditures is drawn between *payment appropriations* (amounts which can be paid out in the year) and *commitment appropriations* (amounts which can be legally committed for payment over a number of years ahead).

The relative shares in total expenditure of the various economic sectors to a large extent reflect the relative growth of Community intervention, that is the areas of active Community (as opposed to national) policy. Thus the highest proportion of the Community budget is spent on agriculture. Expenditures under the Regional, Social and other Funds aim to improve the economic conditions either in disadvantaged regions or for disadvantaged categories of people. It is assumed that expenditure from these funds constitutes a supplement to, and not a substitute for, similar expenditures incurred by the national governments of the member states. The expenditure on energy, industry, transport, research and development aid has remained low.

The new members of the EC (Greece 1981, Spain and Portugal 1986) were covered by transitional arrangements for the first five years of their membership. During the transitional period they contributed to the budget as full members, but in return they received a refund equal to a progressively diminishing share of their contributions.

4.4   The budget as a source of problems among the partners

The allocation of payments to and receipts from the budget are different for each member state. Hence unintentionally the Community budget functions as an instrument of redistribution among the member states. The Community argues that the budgetary costs and benefits (the budgetary incidence) per country cannot be assessed accurately and are not a factual reflection of the costs and benefits of membership in the Community; provided gross injustices do not occur, they should not even be assessed. However, the budgetary incidence caused problems which for a long time continued to be a source of friction between the member states. The United Kingdom in particular argued repeatedly, since its accession to the Community, that it consistently contributed to the budget the most and benefited the least. The problem reached crisis level in the early 1980s.

Table 4.2 presents the distribution of the burden of the EC budget among the partners for 1980 and 1984, as calculated by the Community. The data show that in 1984 three of the members, Germany, France and the United Kingdom, were net contributors to the Budget, while all other countries were net recipients from the Budget. The United Kingdom's contribution to the Community budget has been regarded as particularly disproportionate to its position in the per capita income scale within the

Table 4.2 Net contributors ($-$) to, and net recipients ($+$) from the Community allocated budget, 1980 and 1984.

Member state	1980		1984 Before UK compensation		1984 After UK compensation		
	Total[1]	Per head[2]	Total[1]	Per head[2]	Total[1]	Per head[2]	GDP[3]
B	+237	+24	+343	+35	+294	+30	105
DK	+327	+64	+497	+98	+468	+92	116
D	−1,526	−25	−2,957	−48	−3,201	−52	115
F	+431	+8	−367	−7	−705	−13	109
GR	−	−	+988	+100	+965	+98	54
IRL	+650	+191	+926	+264	+913	+261	67
I	+737	+13	+1,691	+30	+1,468	+26	87
L	+206	+515	+282	+705	+278	+695	124
NL	+454	+32	+536	+37	+462	+32	101
UK	−1,512	−27	−1,938	−34	−938	−17	96

[1] Million ECUs.
[2] ECUs.
[3] Real GDP per head as a percentage of EC-10 average.

Sources: *Official Journal of the European Communities*, 1985; *Eurostat Review*, various issues.

EC (seventh from the top among the EC-10, in 1984; Table 4.2). The reasons for differential inequality in the impact of the budget are to be found in the narrowness of its structure which affects both the receipts from it and the contributions to it by member states.

Receipts from the budget

The EC budget is dominated by a few main items that account for the bulk of expenditure. First, agricultural policy expenditures through the European Agricultural Guidance and Guarantee Fund (EAGGF), which until the mid-1980s accounted for about two-thirds of the total budget. Second, expenditure by the 'structural funds', in particular the European Regional Development Fund (ERDF) and the European Social Fund (ESF), which accounted for about 10–15 per cent of the total. These expenditures had different distributional effects among the partners in the Community:

1. The *budgetary impact of the CAP*: a member state's production of agricultural output may exceed its own consumption. The surplus output is disposed of by:
    (a) exports to other member countries at current Community prices;
    (b) sale to Community agencies at support prices;
    (c) exports to the world markets at prices subsidised by the Community.
    As it can be seen in Table 4.1, the Agricultural Fund (EAGGF) has been using approximately 70 per cent of the total revenue of the budget. Hence, a substantial share of Community expenditure is directed towards member states with relatively large agricultural sectors, which are surplus producers and exporters of highly supported agricultural commodities (mostly cereals, dairy products and beef). On the other hand, member states with relatively small agricultural sectors, which are importers of agricultural products covered by the CAP, tend to be net contributors to the budget. Table 2.2 shows that Germany and the United Kingdom belong to the latter category of member countries, with share of agriculture in gross value added equal to 1.5 per cent and 1.2 per cent respectively (1987). The degree of self-sufficiency in key market-regulated agricultural products has, of course, little connection with the country's relative wealth. Consequently, the budgetary effect of the CAP between the member states does not reflect relative wealth. Denmark has one of the highest per capita incomes and is also one of the highest

beneficiaries of the CAP. Changing the budgetary impact of agriculture means reforming the CAP itself. Some progress towards this end has been achieved in recent years.

2. *Other budgetary expenditure*: the sums remaining after subtracting the CAP outlay for regional development, social assistance and other relevant expenditures are relatively small and thinly spread among the member states. Therefore, they are unable to counterbalance the impact of the CAP on the member countries. In other words, the CAP takes up too much money, creates imbalances and leaves too little to the other sectors. However, as the latest data show (Table 4.1), there has been a slight trend towards reducing the share of agriculture in the budget and increasing the expenditure on other sectors such as social and regional development.

Payments to the budget

The *revenues from customs duties and agricultural levies* depend on the level of imports from non-EC countries. The Netherlands and Belgium, which have large ports through which imports destined for other members of the EC arrive, may appear to be contributing high customs duty payments to the Community budget (the 'Rotterdam effect'), but some of the burden of the customs revenue collected by the Netherlands and Belgium will in fact be borne by consumers elsewhere in the Community.

The level of agricultural levies is not necessarily related to the level of GDP. Thus countries with a relatively small agricultural sector, who are net importers of food from outside the Community, both contribute more to the budget and receive less out of it than members with relatively large agricultural sectors. The problem with the United Kingdom's contribution to the Community budget arises from the fact that the United Kingdom is both a relatively small producer and a major importer (for historical reasons, mostly from outside the EC) of agricultural products. Since accession in 1973, the pattern of UK trade is changing direction with the proportion of imports from non-EC countries declining rather rapidly. Nevertheless, the United Kingdom continues to have a relatively large share of its trade with non-member countries (see Table 8.1).

The *VAT contribution* is standardised for all members of the Community and is neither directly related to actual national VAT revenue nor proportional to the level of GDP and the ability to pay. Consumption expenditure on goods and services is subject to VAT, and in poorer countries is a higher proportion of disposable income than in richer countries. But investment and exports are not subject to VAT (see Chapter 5) and are relatively higher in richer countries. Therefore, the VAT-based contribution to the EC budget does not reflect relative prosperity and is probably regressive (Strasser, 1981). In other words, relative to the level of per capita income, some of the poorer member countries are required by the existing arrangements to contribute more to the Community budget than the better-off countries.

The national incidence of the EC budget caused a number of problems and crises, which led to a settlement but only after a long period of acrimonious altercations.

The UK budget rebate

The basic problems of the impact of the Community budget on the United Kingdom were debated even before accession in 1972 (HM Treasury, 1982). When the United Kingdom joined the Community, it accepted the existing system of budgetary finances, but it was agreed that during a transitional period its contributions to budgetary costs would rise gradually from 8.64 per cent in 1973 to 18.92 per cent in 1977. It became, however, obvious from early on that under the existing system of Community finances the United Kingdom's contribution to the Community budget would be rising despite its low growth performance. Hence, the special arrangements governing the UK contributions were extended for two more years with the understanding that from 1980 the United Kingdom would be fully subject to the Community budgetary system. Moreover, at the insistence of the UK government, the Dublin Summit (1975) reached agreement on a correction mechanism designed to limit the gross contribution of countries in situations similar to that of the United Kingdom. However, when soon after the agreement it became clear that the correction mechanism was inadequate and that in 1980 and subsequent years the United Kingdom, a relatively poor member of the Community (see Table 4.2), would be the biggest net contributor to the budget, the UK government demanded a large cut to its contribution. When after repeated complaints this failed to materialise, the United Kingdom finally claimed that a case of 'unacceptable situations' had arisen and that 'the very survival of the Community would demand that the institutions find an equitable solution' (in accordance with supporting documents of the Treaty of Accession).

In an attempt to reach agreement the Community decided to link the budget debate with the setting of agricultural support prices. As a way of reducing expenditure on the CAP, the Commission proposed that production targets be set for every agricultural sector. Once these targets were reached, producers would be required to contribute to the expenses or the intervention guarantee could be reduced. Although this device (which is known as the 'co-responsibility levy') was selectively applied, the problems of budgetary finances and the diverse budgetary impact on the members were not resolved. After repeated negotiations, the principle of compensating the United Kingdom for excess payments was accepted in 1980, when it was agreed that the United Kingdom would get back a fixed refund, approximately equal to two-thirds of its own contribution. But since the contributions of the members were governed by the 'own resources' provision of the Treaty and were 'mandatory', the refunds to the United Kingdom were granted on a temporary *ad hoc* basis (for the years 1980–84), partly by direct payments to the British Treasury and partly in the form of 'extra EC spending on approved projects'. A new agreement reached at the Fontainebleau summit in June 1984 cut the United Kingdom's budgetary contribution by 66 per cent of the difference between its share of VAT payments and its percentage share of Community expenditure. The Fontainebleau agreement attempted to settle once and for all the problem of budgetary imbalance between the member countries on a longer-term basis by stating explicitly that 'any Member State sustaining a budgetary burden which is excessive in relation to its relative prosperity may benefit from a correction at the appropriate time'.

The data in Table 4.2 show that in 1984, despite the refund, the United Kingdom remained a net contributor to the EC budget, the second largest after Germany. The Community insists that the budget is

Table 4.3 Member states' budgetary contributions to own resources and receipts from allocated expenditure, 1985 and 1987.

Country	1985		1987	
	Payments	Receipts	Payments	Receipts
B	5.0	4.3	4.8	3.2
DK	2.4	3.7	2.4	3.7
D	28.2	17.0	26.5	14.7
E	–	–	4.8	6.4
F	20.4	21.9	20.7	21.9
GR	1.5	6.9	1.0	6.1
IRL	1.1	6.3	1.0	4.7
I	13.9	18.1	14.7	17.1
L	0.2	0.03	0.2	–
NL	7.2	9.0	6.7	9.4
P	–	–	1.0	2.4
UK	19.5	12.6	16.2	10.1
Unallocated	0.6	0.17	–	0.3

Source: Court of Auditors (1986 and 1988) *Annual Report Concerning the Financial Years* 1985 and 1988.

formulated on the premise that overall burdens and benefits cannot be precisely estimated. Bearing this in mind, the published data still show (Table 4.3, for the years 1985 and 1987) that Germany and the United Kingdom continue to remain the largest net contributors to the Community budget.

Budgetary crises

The 1970 agreement to assign a new source of finance to Community 'own resources' set a ceiling for members' contribution of 1 per cent of the VAT base. But delays in the introduction of the VAT in some EC countries meant that the replacement of all member states' financial contributions by VAT payments was not completed before 1980. In the meantime, budgetary expenditures kept rising and, after two years of operating the new system, the ceiling of 1 per cent was reached, with the implication that the Community had exhausted its finances before fulfilling its legal obligations. A new ceiling of 1.4 per cent was set at the Fontainebleau summit, and came into force on 1 January 1986. The new agreement provided that, under certain conditions, by a new unanimous decision of the Council and after ratification by the member states in accordance with national procedures, the ceiling could be raised to 1.6 per cent from 1 January 1988. However, with expenditure exceeding revenue, the financial crisis continued. Hence by inter-governmental agreement the Community's budgetary resources were temporarily increased further to an implicit level of 2.2 per cent of VAT revenues.

In an attempt to solve the budget's financial crisis on a longer-term basis the Fontainebleau agreement introduced 'budgetary discipline', a check procedure on the growth of budget expenditure. Accordingly, the Council early on in the financial year has to establish in collaboration with the Commission a 'reference framework' setting the maximum level of expenditure which it considered it must adopt to finance Community policies during the following financial year. An additional constraint was also imposed, that the net expenditure relating to agriculture, calculated on a three-yearly basis, should increase less than the rate of growth of the own resources base. The Commission was required to observe these limits when making its initial (draft) budget proposals. If ministers agreed to any measures which threaten to result in the budgetary limit being exceeded, the Commission had the power to suspend it (EC, 1984a, 1986). However, this mechanism for reducing the growth of expenditure had not taken into consideration events which were outside the Community's control and had detrimental effects on the budget.

In the first half of 1986 the dollar fell by approximately 11 per cent and thus the ECU appreciated, increasing the cost of EC export subsidies. Moreover, the limits set by the budget proved ineffective to stop agricultural support prices from rising, and CAP guarantee expenditures continued to expand. As a consequence, the sums allocated to agriculture were rapidly depleted, exports ceased and the Community was forced to hold on to its food mountains with associated increases in storage expenditure. On the 'own resources' side, customs revenues and import levies declined as the value of imports fell because of a substantial fall in the price of oil, while at the same time, owing to a general decline in economic activity, the VAT 'take' was not rising sufficiently to make up the difference. Thus the Community faced another budgetary crisis. The Commission came up with a temporary solution involving the introduction of 'creative accounting', that is of deferring payments until the next year, when it was hoped that the situation might have improved. But this device did not work as expected and half way through the financial year the budget came apart and the Commission requested more emergency funds. These became available by intergovernmental agreements, and thus the final outcome was a budget much larger than the draft budget which the Council rejected a few months earlier as being excessive. Nevertheless, in September 1986 the Commission released figures showing that the Community budget, agreed only two months earlier, was unworkable.

Without having yet solved the budgetary problem for 1986, the budget ministers prepared the European Community's 1987 draft budget. In an attempt to safeguard funds for compulsory spending on farm support, the draft budget included cuts in non-compulsory expenditure, such as development aid, food aid, spending on transport and funds for agricultural improvements. As we have seen, current compulsory expenditure on agriculture is such a dominant factor of the EC that the Community budget is built for the sole purpose of serving it first; all other needs have to wait.

At the beginning of 1987 the Commission came up with the proposal that the Community budget should rise by 30 per cent from its current level by the end of 1992. To ensure that the farm policy does not swallow up the extra funds, the Commission proposed that the size of the budget should determine the extent of agricultural spending. This would involve the introduction of 'budgetary stabilisers', that is of set limits for the guarantee section of expenditure on agriculture determined by the size of existing stocks of output and current prices in the markets of the Community. The expectation was that the overall farm budget would increase by no more than the natural, annual increase in Community revenue, which was estimated to be about 2 per cent in real terms.

By June 1987 the Community finances reached a new crisis. The Commission's original plans to effect large savings through CAP price support curbs and other measures were all but destroyed by the determination of member states' governments to preach austerity, but secure the best deal for their own agricultural sectors. The net result was that the Community once again ran out of money. With no realistic alternative in sight, the Commission estimated that either the VAT contribution should be raised from 1.4 to 1.9 per cent or the Community would be unable to meet its commitments and a new large deficit would occur. At the same time the Parliament made it known that it would no longer be prepared to put up with creative accounting measures designed to delay the Community's day of reckoning.

With the Community staggering from one financial crisis to another, it is remarkable that the day of reckoning had been postponed eight times in as many years. The repeated crises helped, inadvertently, to produce a widespread consensus for a long overdue budgetary reform. It became very clear that the Community was in urgent need of a saner and fairer budget system to enable it to meet its Treaty obligations regarding common policies and to remain on the road to European integration. The need for reform finally reached consensus.

4.5   Evaluation and reform

Where a federal level of government has over the years acquired wide powers of raising taxes and spending, complex patterns of equalisation both of revenues and of expenditures may make sense. However, the Community budget is at the moment relatively small and questions about its impact seem to be out of proportion: the UK contribution to the Community is about 0.3 per cent of UK public expenditure.

Nevertheless, the Community budget is structurally unsound. By having a narrow base of both revenue and expenditure, it gives rise to net positions of the member states that are highly sensitive to yearly changes in economic conditions.

When a member country is a net contributor to the budget, a transfer of resources takes place from this country's taxpayers to the beneficiaries of Community policies in other member countries which are net recipients of budgetary policies. Net contributions and net receipts provide a measure of budgetary transfers within the Community. However, there are limits in what these figures represent. Budgetary transfers should not be confused with the cost and benefits of membership in the Community. Community policies have many and varied economic effects, and the budgetary accounts provide a partial and highly distorted view of what is actually happening. In general, net budgetary transfers do not, by definition, take account of costs and benefits outside the budget and therefore they cannot become the basis for measuring the costs and benefits of economic integration. They are effects of a certain activity at the Community level, but there are many other activities which do not involve the budget. These activities must be considered for an evaluation of total costs and benefits. Some of the missing elements for the completion of the picture are as follows:

1. Gains and losses for individuals from operating the Common Agricultural Policy regarding the increase in the prices of agricultural commodities within the EC. Consumers pay more for their food than they would in the absence of the CAP, while farmers receive higher prices for their market sales than they would otherwise. These private sector payments and receipts are not passing through the EC budget and remain unrecorded.

2. Gains and losses from operating the customs union, that is from intra-community free trade in manufacturing commodities, services and factors of production. These gains or losses accrue to economic agents, firms or individuals within the Community, and arise from the enlargement of the market, the intensification of competition, the realisation of economies of scale, and the protection of the market from foreign competition by the common external tariff (CET). This sort of economic activity belongs to the private sector and is therefore not counted when the net budgetary impact on the member countries is evaluated.

3. Even those costs and benefits that accrue through the budget may misrepresent reality. Gross contributions collected in a member state may not accurately reflect the burden on the taxpayers of that state. The attribution of customs duties and levies to a country whose ports act as entrepôts for onward movement of imported commodities to other member countries inside the Community is clearly incorrect. Similarly, gross receipts paid to residents of a member country, such as MCAs, may not accurately reflect the benefits to citizens of that state, if cross-border exchange has taken place.

4. It is important to recognise that for most policies undertaken in common there is a substitution effect between Community and national expenditure. Community spending is frequently complementary to national spending: what is spent by the Community often represents saving for the national budgets. Therefore it is important to estimate whether the benefit from spending in common outweighs that from spending individually at the national level. There is no doubt that for the largest part of the budgetary expenditure (e.g. for agriculture or research) this is indeed the case. However, this should not be of crucial importance since a

common general budget which is oriented towards policies, and not individual issues, entails allocational inequalities in both costs and benefits.

These considerations do not exclude the possibility that certain member countries are significant net losers from the overall operation of the Community. However, the concept of net contributors to, and net beneficiaries from, the budget during the process of integration should be considered as of little consequence – except if it gives rise to 'unacceptable situations' which may threaten the existence of the Community. Progress towards integration and equality of contributions and benefits are incompatible. The problem is related to the links between budgetary revenue and expenditure. There are two general principles: one is that a *specific tax source* should be made available for a specific form of expenditure. This principle is usually associated with the notion of equality between costs and benefits, the *fair return* argument.

The other principle is that of a *common pool of funds* from which community expenditure is financed. This principle is usually associated with the 'ability to pay'. Clearly, neither of these principles is strictly applicable to the Community budget. However, the notion that each member should receive from the budget an amount equal to that which it contributed, so that the net position of every participant is balanced at nought, undermines the concept and aims of integration. Even in unitary national states each region and each individual do not receive from the budget an amount equal to their contribution. If this was the case, then the distributional aims of the national budget would disappear. Although, as the UK government has argued, 'the EC is not a mechanism for redistributing wealth, it is a common enterprise for producing it', by agreement this is to be achieved by market integration which may make some member countries more wealthy by making others poorer. Integration has first to be attained, and this requires certain expenditures to be undertaken in common. But this does not imply that these expenditures must be contributed in accordance with current receipts from the budget.

The Community's target of 'harmonious development of economic activity' suggests that the Community budget has an important role to play in the process of integration. Nevertheless, problems with the Community budget do exist, because, although at this stage of integration it is small, it certainly has inter-state income redistribution effects which cannot be ignored: the net budgetary transfers to the least developed smaller members, Greece, Ireland and Portugal, amount currently (1989) to approximately 5 per cent of their GDP. Harmonious development does not, of course, mean equality of performance. However, *convergence at a higher level of performance* might be a requirement for harmonious development, competition on equal terms and balance in the spatial distribution of costs and benefits. This is a very important target for the EC which should become the objective of a larger and more ambitious Community budget with national contributions based closer to progressivity and the ability to pay.

Towards this end, further budgetary reforms were undertaken in conjunction with changes in the CAP in preparation for 1992. The Commission pointed out that the resources available under the present system of finance are inadequate for meeting the objectives of the single market, even after the intended raising of the ceiling on the Community's share of VAT from 1.4 to 1.6 per cent. The Commission therefore proposed a reform of EC finances based on the introduction of a further source of revenue which would augment the Community's own resources. The basis of this supplementary resource would be provided by the difference between the gross national product (GNP) of each country and the VAT assessment. It is expected that in this way the members' contributions will be related to their ability to pay. The Community's share of VAT could then be reduced to 1 per cent. Therefore, the origin of own resources entered in the EC budget will be as follows:

1. Agricultural levies and sugar and isoglucose duties.
2. Customs duties.
3. The application of a rate of 1.4 per cent to the VAT which is determined in a uniform manner according to Community rules; the assessment base for VAT should not exceed 55 per cent of the gross GNP at market prices of each member state, measured in a uniform way on the basis of a Commission Directive; in this way, high-consumption, low-income member states would not be unreasonably overcharged.
4. The application of a rate based on the difference between each member state's GNP and its harmonised VAT base for an overall ceiling of 1.4 per cent of GNP maximum, to be reached gradually by 1992.

The new arrangements provided that the conclusions of the Fontainebleau Council on the correction of budgetary imbalances remain applicable. Compensation to the United Kingdom will be financed on the basis of a GNP scale.

The reorganisation of the system, which will increase the volume of finances by about 15 per cent annually in real terms, has been supplemented by measures to instil greater budgetary discipline and therefore it will be linked to reforms of Community policies, in particular, the following:

1. New guidelines for agricultural expenditure, binding on the member states, that the rate of increase in guarantee expenditure on agriculture must not exceed 74 per cent of the rate of increase in Community gross national product.
2. A legal binding limit on agricultural production covered by the Common Agricultural Policy.
3. Annual expenditure stabilisers on a product-by-product basis, the implementation of which will be supervised by the Commission. Consequently, the proportion of farm spending in the budget is expected to decline from 66 to 56 per cent by 1992, with a guaranteed rise in the share of the structural funds (Regional Fund, Social Fund and guidance section of the European Agricultural Guidance and Guarantee Fund) to over a quarter of the budget.

The new system of Community finances was approved by Council with the addition of an amendment introduced by the Parliament, that the own resources paid by each member state should reflect the 'relative wealth and income of the citizens' rather than its 'ability to contribute'. The Parliament also asked the Commission to submit a proposal for the introduction of a new levy in the form of a Community tax to replace one or more national taxes. Finally, the European Parliament, the Council and the Commission signed an inter-institutional agreement (July 1989) setting out for each of the years 1988 to 1992 detailed financial perspectives representing annual expenditure ceilings and budgetary discipline. The Commission was also asked to present before the end of 1991 a report on the application of the new budgetary system and the amendments which need to be made to it in the light of experience (EC, 1988b). Barring surprises, the budget problem has been solved until 1992. The European Council has not decided what the Community budget should be like after 1992.

The new system started for the 1989 budget, and the Commission stated that 'for the first time in several years, the Community will have a budget based on an amount of available own resources sufficient to finance all its political, economic and social objectives' (*Bulletin EC*, 6, 1989). On the expenditure side, the situation was also eased by the strengthening of the dollar which pushed world agricultural prices up and thereby reduced demands on the Community budget. The new budget revealed also the implementation of structural changes with a significant increase in non-compulsory expenditures (+ 20 per cent) and virtually no growth in compulsory expenditures.

The move towards completion of the single market by the end of 1992 and the progressive implementation of Economic and Monetary Union require the national budgets of the member states to come under a progressively stronger Community influence. The demarcation line between Community and national policy is based on the principle of 'subsidiarity' — that only those activities which can be 'best' (more efficiently) done at Community level should be taken from national or regional responsibility. Since the Community has at present a narrow range of policy functions, for the foreseeable future the national budgets will continue to be the main instruments for the exercise of policy, and the member states will continue to be the main providers of important public goods, such as national defence, education, justice, etc. After 1992, enhancement of competition in the unified market and the move towards monetary integration are expected to have profound effects on certain regions, population groups and even member states. Hence the EC budget will be called to play a more substantial role in the allocation of the costs and benefits of the common market because, first, this will be required for upward convergence, cohesion and growth in the whole of the Community, and, second, the member states, in the pursuit of common policies, will tie some of their policy instruments (such as interest rates, exchange rates and monetary policy in general) which they would otherwise have used to alleviate the adverse effects of market integration on regions and groups of people in their national economies. Therefore, the EC budget will evolve along fiscal federation lines.

The Community budget will continue to be concerned with redistribution issues arising from the operation of common policies. What will be required for solving problems created by the single market and the effects of common policies is a high-powered centralised mechanism for budgetary redistribution of resources from rich to poor areas and from low unemployment to high unemployment regions. This would mean the extension of Community budgetary policy beyond the limited potential of coordination between the member states, with explicit rules on borrowing limits, spending and taxation. Otherwise, what the Community attempts to do with monetary integration, the member states could undo with national budgetary policies. This could happen if, without the restraint imposed by stability considerations of the national currency, member states overborrow and overspend by uncoordinated public expenditure policies.

Further reading

Strasser (1981) presents the most detailed and authoritative account of EC finances. For the early problems of the budget see Wallace (1980).

The United Kingdom's budgetary problem is described in HM Treasury (1988). The implications of the Fontainebleau Agreement are in Denton (1984). Shackleton (1990) gives a good account of the latest reforms and their implications. For information on current EC finances and the budget consult the monthly *Bulletin of the European Communities*.

5

Tax harmonisation

5.1 The problem

Abolition of trade barriers among the members of the customs union does not necessarily imply that a common perfectly competitive market has been completed. Impediments to the smooth functioning of the competitive markets for commodities, services and factors of production are still many. Differences among the tax systems of the members of the customs union are one of the most important of these impediments and one of the most difficult to remove. This has also been the case in the EC; hence we discuss the problems of tax harmonisation rather extensively.

The nature of tax harmonisation

Tax systems may differ between countries in a number of ways associated with (a) what is taxed – the tax base; (b) by how much it is taxed – the tax rate; (c) by what particular kind of tax is taxed – the tax type. Furthermore, even if the tax base, rate and type are the same, tax compliance and tax enforcement may differ across countries.

Tax harmonisation attempts to make different tax systems compatible with one another and with the objectives of the economic union. The aim of tax harmonisation is 'to encourage the interplay of competition in such a way that integration and economic growth ... may be achieved simultaneously and gradually' (EC Commission, 1963, the Neumark Report, p. 188). The scale of compatibility ranges from nil to perfect and exactly what degree of compatibility/tax harmonisation is ideal for a particular economic union will depend on the degree of integration the members are aiming at. In a free-trade area, where only tariffs among the members are abolished, the required tax harmonisation is minimal. But even fully independent states may choose to coordinate their tax systems, for reasons relating to tax avoidance, double taxation, etc. In a regional economic association aiming at complete economic and political integration, complete tax harmonisation may become inevitable, and this means that ultimately the members will have to adopt a unified tax system.

Approaches to tax harmonisation

In general, two approaches to tax harmonisation in economic unions have received much attention: the equalisation approach and the differentials approach.

The equalisation approach advocates 'standardisation', that is uniformity of tax base and equalisation of tax rates among the members of the union. Standardisation can be reached with or without actual unification of the tax system under a single fiscal policy authority. The equalisation approach is supported primarily for two reasons:

1. It accords with the aims of the economic union designated simply as 'enhancing competition on equal terms'.
2. It is the favourite of those who consider tax harmonisation as one of the means for moving forward with economic and later political integration, where equalisation of rates and uniformity of taxes are regarded as necessary.

The problem of tax harmonisation under the equalisation approach consists of selecting the set of taxes and tax rates which will direct the economic union towards achieving its objective. This objective is economic integration and maximisation of welfare for the economic union as a whole (Dosser, 1967).

The *differentials approach* is based on the principle that the tax system of each country functions as an instrument of policy for attaining major economic objectives. Therefore, it is argued that the same principle should apply at the scale of the economic union, with the proviso that the externalities of each country's tax system on other countries should be minimised by close coordination among the members. Under the assumption that the sum of the members' welfare adds up to the welfare of the economic union, the problem of the differentials approach is to select for each participant the set of taxes and tax rates which optimises its own welfare. This principle is based on the presumption that private (member's) benefit and social (economic union's) benefit coincide.

A variant of the differentials approach maintains that imposed tax harmonisation is an unnecessary interference with the price system. What an economic union should aim at instead is *tax competition*, based on the recognition that states have differences in: (a) preferences for one tax over another; (b) perceptions on the role of taxation; (c) acceptability and feasibility of various taxes; and (d) preferences for public sector size. Consequently, taxation should be based on residence, which in an economic union depends on subjective choice. Then, like participants in the market-place, governments will have to compete for scarce resources, tax revenues. This will restrain the growth of public expenditure, promote efficiency in the public sector and lead to the necessary convergence of tax systems through harmonisation by market process.

It should be obvious from the above discussion that tax harmonisation encompasses in general both the equalisation and the differentials approaches. Tax harmonisation ranges between the one extreme of *zero change* in taxes and tax rates and the other extreme of *unification of taxes and complete equalisation of rates*, with all the variations in between. The differentials approach covers most of the cases, while the equalisation approach occupies only the upper limit of this range.

Effects of tax harmonisation

In general, changes in a tax system, implemented either within an economic union through tax harmonisation or individually by a national state through tax reform, alter a number of economic variables and have welfare implications. Tax changes and their effects take place within the framework of 'second best' conditions. In theory, even under these conditions a tax system designed on the basis of optimal tax rules would lead to efficiency. However, in practice tax changes are implemented for a number of economic and political reasons, regardless of optimality. Since 'second best' conditions prevail, it cannot be decided on *a priori* considerations whether tax changes will lead to an improvement or a deterioration in social welfare.

Taxes are used by governments as instruments of budgetary, social and economic policy. With changes in taxes and tax rates consequent upon tax harmonisation there will be effects on both the instruments and the objectives of economic policies. Hence tax harmonisation would have effects on tax revenues, and this may imply the requirement for public expenditure harmonisation. In general, tax harmonisation is multidimensional, affecting all the functions of the tax system, such as allocation of resources, economic stabilisation, economic growth, income distribution, balance of payments and tax revenue. Every government's policies relate to these functions, but different governments have different sets of objectives and therefore different priorities and rankings of these functions. Tax harmonisation affects both the functions of the tax system and the order of their priority.

The equalisation approach gives precedence to the common goals of the economic union, placing them over and above the goals of the individual members. Uniformity of tax rates between countries or even agreement for a closer alignment of rates will severely restrict the member states' capacity to manipulate these rates for short-term economic policy purposes. Moves towards a uniform tax system, with common tax rates, imply that the members have considered and endorsed the transfer of the necessary power for policy-making from themselves to the authority of the economic union. In other words, the members would adopt tax harmonisation in the form of tax equalisation, only if they have already decided that the ultimate objective of the economic union is economic (and political) integration, and that a common tax system is a direct way towards that goal. Equalisation provides a common tax system, just as in the case of a single national state. If at any time departures from uniformity might be deemed necessary, they would not be pursued by tax policy; they will be taken care of by other policies, such as public expenditure or regional policy.

Under the differentials approach the presumption is that for the time being the economic association will not move towards full integration and, more specifically, that fiscal policy will remain in the domain of each member state. Tax harmonisation in this case is akin to tax coordination and is not free of complications. The members have to decide the degree of economic integration they aim at, before deciding the exact form of tax harmonisation they require. For example, they may have to consider the following:

1. Whose welfare they attempt to improve by tax harmonisation. Conflicts may arise between individual members and the economic union as a whole with regard to diverse objectives, the ranking of tax functions, the effects of harmonisation, the degree of coordination imposed by the adopted system, the effects on the distribution of income among the partners and so on.
2. Whether the tax system will be used to restrain or to enhance intra-union factor mobility. With factor mobility, the framework of the REA is that of a common market, without it of a customs union.
3. Whether there will be a general harmonisation of the whole tax

system or a partial harmonisation of those taxes whose effects impinge on the functions of the economic union.

4. Whether the harmonisation will be introduced gradually or at once.
5. Whether the harmonisation will be constrained by *tax neutrality*, that is whether it will leave the tax revenue and the allocation of resources in the private sector undisturbed.

Trade and taxation

Changes of indirect taxes affect relative prices and therefore the terms of trade within an economy and between it and other countries, so that the pattern and the volume of trade may also be affected. Changes in the terms of trade imply redistribution of income between (a) the citizens of the country, (b) the country and its partners in the economic union and (c) the economic union and the outside world. The effects are similar to those derived from changes in tariff structures. Consequently, changes in relative domestic/foreign prices originating from tax changes give rise to welfare effects, the trade creation and trade diversion effects of tax harmonisation.

Regarding traded commodities, indirect taxes are levied according to the *origin* or *destination* principles of taxation. Under the origin principle, taxes are levied at the production stage and the tax revenue accrues to the country of production. Therefore exports from a low-tax country to a high-tax country enjoy an artifical comparative advantage. Under the destination principle, which is used in international trade worldwide, taxes are levied at the consumption stage and the tax revenue accrues to the country of consumption. Therefore under the destination principle, countries make border tax adjustments, that is they levy taxes on imports and refund taxes on exports. Countries can gain an unfair advantage by taxing imported products at rates higher than those levied on similar domestic products, and by refunding taxes on exports at levels higher than those actually paid. This amounts to imposing disguised customs duties on imports and subsidising exports, hence it is specifically forbidden in common markets (EEC Treaty Articles 95 and 96).

The destination principle of taxation, which (barring unfair practices) treats imported and home-produced goods alike, does not lead to distortions of international competition and in general does not upset comparative costs (Musgrave, 1969). Therefore, under conditions of perfect competition production will be located in the country with the lowest cost ex-tax. The origin principle would have had similar or equivalent effects only if all trading countries taxed the same commodities and services (same tax base) by a general tax (common tax rate), which could be different between countries. Then the differences in tax rates would be counterbalanced by changes in price and the exchange rate, leaving the pattern of production and trade undisturbed. However, the necessary conditions for the equivalence of the destination and origin principles are never met in practice, hence 'this tenet may be of interest to the theory of tax harmonisation, [but] it is of no interest to the real world' (Cnossen and Shoup, 1987, p. 69).

In practice, it is usual for countries forming economic unions to adopt initially the destination system of taxation. But later, a desire to eliminate border controls may induce consideration of a change to the *restricted origin principle*, whereby the origin principle applies on internal trade while the destination principle remains in force for trade with the outside world. In general, the change from one principle to another will have effects on tax revenues, hence on the budget, and probably on allocative efficiency, that is on the location of production and on the inter-commodity substitution in consumption within the common market.

5.2   Introduction to Community tax harmonisation

The tax systems of the six signatories of the Treaty of Rome differed substantially in a number of ways: sales taxes were in the form of Value Added Tax (VAT), cumulative turnover tax and taxes on gross value. Excise taxes were applied to different goods in different countries, at different rates and mode of evaluation. Different systems of corporation taxation had different implications on capital mobility and investment. The personal income tax system differed among the contracting states in rates, allowances, administrative procedures, compliance and enforcement. Furthermore, the social security obligations and the social benefits to individuals were also diverse. In general, the tax systems of the Six were greatly heterogeneous, reflecting important differences in the members' economic and social structures and policy objectives.

The Treaty of Rome specifies that harmonising 'the legislation ... concerning turnover taxes, excise duties and other forms of indirect taxation' (Article 99) is a principal objective of the EC, and that laws in general – including tax law – should be approximated (Articles 100–102). Details about what tax harmonisation and approximation of tax laws would involve are not provided in the Treaty. The missing details are usually filled by specially constituted Study Committees and Working Parties of experts. Their proposals and recommendations are published in the form of Reports which, when they are approved, are issued as Directives binding on the member states.

The EC has defined tax harmonisation as the process by which the tax systems of the member states are aligned with each other so that tax considerations no longer influence the inter-country mobility of commodities and factors of production within the Community. Consequently, aspects of optimum taxation are not relevant. The Commission has indeed insisted that tax harmonisation 'is not an attempt to design an ideal fiscal system for the Community, but a blueprint for abolition of fiscal frontiers' (EC Commission, 1987a). Actually, tax harmonisation in the EC has aimed at two objectives: competition on equal terms among the EC partners, implying the abolition of tax frontiers, and acceleration of the process of integration and unification of the market. The following quotation from general guidelines issued by a member of the Commission presents an early official view of the objectives of tax harmonisation in the EC very clearly:

> We want to carry tax harmonisation as far as is required by the objectives of the Common Market. We must harmonise where this is necessary to eliminate tax frontiers and avoid distortions of competition; we must harmonise in order to facilitate mergers across the internal frontiers of the Community and to help build up a European capital market. We must also harmonise as a part of the work to be done before we can arrive at a common economic policy, and quite simply with a view to achieving the aims of a number of common policies in various sectors of our activity. (Vice-President of the Commission Haferkamp, quoted in Schneider, 1973)

In practice tax harmonisation has proved more difficult than envisaged. The complexity of the problem and the widely held principle of 'no taxation without representation', which makes tax sovereignty one of the fundamental components of national sovereignty, meant that little could be achieved, and at a very slow pace. For the same reasons, most of the measures adopted so far or proposed for the future are confined to the harmonisation of tax structures and bases of assessment under strict neutrality. Proposals for the approximation of tax rates have been made but with little success: decisions on tax rates are still regarded as a sensitive issue which must remain with the national authorities of the member states.

Table 5.1 presents the structure of taxation in the EC countries, that is the relative tax burden as revealed by the ratio of tax revenue on GDP (the effective tax rate), the share of sales taxes on GDP and the contribution of different taxes to total tax revenue. The data show considerable differences between the EC countries in both the burden of taxation and

Table 5.1 Relative size and composition of receipts of general government.

Country	Taxes % on GDP[1]		Taxes % in total receipts[2]			
	Total	Vat and excise	Goods and services	Income and profits	Property and other	Social contributions
B	45.7	11.5	24.0	40.4	2.0	33.6
DK	60.3	19.4	35.4	56.2	4.8	3.6
D	44.6	12.2	25.2	34.5	3.1	37.2
E	37.2	10.2	32.0	25.2	3.8	39.1
F	49.0	14.7	29.4	18.2	7.7	44.7
GR	35.6	16.5	45.4	17.5	2.8	34.2
IRL	44.6	17.9	44.1	36.1	3.9	15.7
I	40.2	10.1	24.6	37.9	2.7	34.8
L	55.1	16.0	24.5	43.2	6.2	26.2
NL	54.4	13.0	26.0	27.7	3.9	42.5
P	35.5	16.0	48.0	21.2	2.8	28.1
UK	39.5	16.4	30.9	38.5	12.9	17.9
EC	43.5	13.2	32.5	33.0	4.7	29.8

[1] 1988.
[2] 1986.

Sources: Eurostat (1989) *Basic Statistics of the Community*, 26th ed.; OECD (1988) *Revenue Statistics of the OECD Member Countries 1965–87*, OECD, Paris.

the composition of tax revenues. This is the situation at present, despite many years of economic cooperation and after many attempts at tax harmonisation. These attempts and their results are examined in the following with reference to certain basic taxes.

5.3 Indirect taxes

Indirect taxes enter the final prices of goods and services on which they are imposed. Therefore, under similar production-cost conditions, different principles and levels of taxation will be reflected in different price levels.

Tax harmonisation in the Community has followed a pragmatic approach: the objective of harmonisation is not to design an optimal tax system for achieving efficiency but to facilitate integration by the approximation of members' existing tax systems. Consequently, the harmonisation of indirect taxes in the Community involves a three-stage process: (a) fiscal neutrality in intra-Community trade; (b) simplification of administrative procedure in this trade; and (c) with a view to the longer term, creation of a single market by the abolition of fiscal frontiers.

In the following we examine the nature of indirect tax harmonisation in the Community and the role and limitations of indirect taxation in the integrated market.

Sales taxes

While the first moves for trade liberalisation among the members of the Community had started, the Commission appointed a group of experts, the Neumark Committee, to review the fiscal systems of the member states and to recommend methods for harmonising them. The Neumark Committee issued its report in 1962 recommending the introduction of a common sales tax, the Valued Added Tax, VAT. This tax was chosen as the common sales tax because it had been shown to have a number of advantages over the traditional forms of sales taxes (turnover, single stage, etc.). For instance, it may provide more neutrality as regards saving, investment and work decisions, particularly if the tax base is wide and there is a single rate of tax. VAT is neutral between production by a vertically integrated enterprise and production by several independent firms. In contrast, a multi-stage cascade tax levies a lesser tax burden on production undertaken within the same enterprise and therefore it encourages the vertical integration of firms. Moreover, under the destination principle of international taxation, VAT facilitates exact refunding of taxes on exports, therefore tax rebating on exports is accurate and cannot be used as a disguise for granting export subsidies. On the other hand, VAT may involve heavy administrative costs for both the tax authorities and the taxpayers. For this reason exemptions are usually granted to small firms as a means of reducing administrative costs relative to revenue.

It is important to emphasise that VAT is a method of taxation and not a new kind of tax. Its base is the 'value added'; taxes are levied piecemeal stage by stage and double taxation is prevented, so that the tax collected in relation to final product price will be precisely equivalent to that obtained by a single-stage tax levied on the same aggregate base with the same *ad valorem* rate. The calculation of VAT is usually based on the indirect or invoice method: the tax is applied to total sales of the firm, but the tax already paid on input purchases is subsequently subtracted. This procedure, which is also known as the 'tax credit' method, introduces into the tax system a self-policing operation which helps tax collection.

The Neumark Committee dealt also with the question of the jurisdictional principle of taxation on internationally traded goods and services. The report proposed that the Community should adopt the *restricted origin principle* which would promote integration by facilitating the abolition of fiscal frontiers between member countries. This recommendation was based on the experience of federal states which has shown that a common system of indirect taxation, combined with the origin principle, could make a positive contribution to the creation of a single market. This in turn would mean that, in the longer term, without internal border controls and without preliminary harmonisation of rates, competition among the members of the economic union would necessarily bring about a tendency towards tax-rate equalisation. Sufficiently close tax rates will ensure that the operation of the common market is not affected through distortions of trade, diversion of trade and effects on competition (EC Commission, 1987a).

The Community accepted the Neumark Committee's proposals for the introduction of VAT. It decided, however, that for as long as the process of building up the common market is in progress, it should continue to apply the destination principle of taxation. The preference for the destination principle arose from the need to avoid distortions in competition, and to reassure the member states by allocating indirect tax revenues to the country levying the tax. However, the Community emphasised that as a long-term solution, it formally adheres to the introduction of the origin principle and the abolition of border controls (EC, 1967).

Since 1969, six Directives have been issued, setting up VAT as the common sales tax of the Six, and of all new members joining the Community at a later date. Tax harmonisation at the ongoing phase of integration in the EC meant only that a common sales tax structure was to be adopted, but no attempt was made to impose on the members a common VAT rate. Acting on the axiom that fundamental changes in the tax field impinge on the prerogative of national parliaments, sales tax harmonisation in the Community was based on the operational principle of structural uniformity first and rate equalisation later. The sixth Directive of 1977, on the uniform basis of assessment for VAT, aimed at closer structural harmonisation, with the introduction of a common list of taxable activities and exemptions, including a common lower limit of exempted transactions, the tax threshold. With regard to international trade formalities, an important simplification was made by the replacement of a plethora of national customs papers by two, and later by a single common administrative document.

It is usually assumed that a general flat rate consumption tax is regressive, and that tax rate differentiation can change it into a progressive one. Therefore, in some countries goods holding a relatively large share in the budget of low-income consumers (food, clothing, etc.) are taxed at a lower rate, luxury goods at a higher rate. These operational principles are also observed in the countries of the Community. Table 5.2

Table 5.2 VAT rates in the Community (per cent).

Country	Standard[1]	Reduced[1]	Increased[1]
B	19	1, 6 and 17	25 and 33
DK	22	–	–
D	14	7	–
E	12	6	33
F	18.6	5.5 and 7	25
GR	18	4 and 8	36
I	18	2 and 9	38
IRL	25	0 and 10	–
L	12	3 and 6	–
NL	20	6	–
P	16	8	30
UK	15	0	–

[1] Rates applicable in April 1990.

Sources: EC (1989) *Europe Without Frontiers – Completing the Internal Market*. European Documentation, 2; EC (1988) *The Economics of 1992*, European Economy, No. 35; OECD (1990) *Economic Surveys*, OECD, Paris.

presents the VAT rates of the EC member states. It can be seen that considerable differences exist as regards the number of rates and their levels: there is a single rate in Denmark and four rates in three other countries; 12 per cent standard rate in Luxembourg and Spain, and 25 per cent in Ireland. Differences also exist with regard to what products are wholly or in part *zero rated* (that is, subject to reduced or zero rate of VAT on output, but receiving credit for tax paid on inputs). Certain broad categories of VAT exemptions are: agricultural and food products; pharmaceutical and medical products; and in some countries fabrics, clothing and footwear. Owing to different exemptions, the VAT coverage of private consumption is only 35 per cent in Ireland and 44 per cent in the United Kingdom, whereas in most of the other member states it is about 90 per cent. Therefore, a uniform base has not as yet been reached (EC, 1980).

Excise taxes

Positive measures to harmonise the structure of excise taxes have still to be approved by the Community. The exception is the excise tax on cigarettes which has been partly harmonised since 1978.

Excise duties are specific, single-stage taxes levied on certain products which are characterised by their relatively large share in consumers' expenditure (up to a fifth) and small price elasticity of demand. Excises are levied mainly for revenue-raising reasons, but sometimes also in order to discourage the consumption of harmful products for public health reasons, e.g. of tobacco and spirits. The yield of these taxes depends on their specific tax rate and the taxable quantity. Therefore, only an increase of the quantity purchased or the tax rate will increase the tax revenue, which does not automatically keep pace with changes in prices.

The systems of operating and enforcing excise duties in the EC countries exhibit considerable diversity. Some countries operate controls based on strict production supervision and distribution through a network of bonded warehouses, while others affix tax stamps on the product itself at the production stage. The tax rate varies from country to country, but in general it is very high. Expressed as a percentage on retail price, the average rate among the EC countries reaches 69 per cent on cigarettes and 52 per cent on petrol. But the deviations of national rates from the average are wide; for example, in absolute terms the highest basic rate of excise duty on alcohol in Denmark is almost forty times the lowest rate in Italy. High rates mean that excise taxes have a high incidence on prices and, in general, a wide economic impact. Therefore differences among the members with regard to structure, rates and administration of excise taxes have serious effects on competition. The significant divergence between the excise duty systems in the EC countries has been maintained by strict frontier controls that insulate domestic markets from duty systems abroad.

In assessing the proposals for harmonisation of excise taxes, the most important consideration is the revenue effect. In some members of the Community, excise taxes contribute more than 25 per cent of the total receipts from taxes and social contributions. Further complications arise from the fact that in certain countries some commodities, which are subject to excise duties, were traded by state monopolies (e.g. tobacco in France and Italy) and some other (such as mineral oils, tobacco, alcohol) are inputs to further processes whose output is subject to different systems of taxation.

The harmonisation of excise duties in an economic union aims at the abolition of distortions to competition and the elimination of fiscal frontiers. The first steps for a common policy concern the coverage of excise duties, that is which excise duties are to be retained and harmonised. Traditionally three broad groups of commodities are subject to excise taxes in most countries: hydrocarbon oils, manufactured tobacco and alcoholic beverages. In the EC countries, as in many other countries most of the revenue from excise duties is collected from 'the big five': tobacco products, beer, spirits, mineral oils and wine (but wine was not taxed in Greece and Italy, while only sparkling wine was taxed in Germany, and only imported wine in Luxembourg). However, a variety of other commodities has been subject to excise taxes in different countries (e.g. sugar in Belgium, spices in France, coffee in Germany, matches in Italy, and even cars in Denmark). Besides the tax base, there is also variation in the administration of excises and tax rates. Among the EC countries the heaviest taxation is to be found in Denmark, Ireland and the United Kingdom.

Over the years the Commission put forward a number of proposals, mostly concerning the harmonisation of tax structures rather than tax rates. However, despite the many attempts, very little has been achieved. The failure is officially attributed to the budgetary impact of excise tax harmonisation which for certain countries is estimated to be substantial. But actually the basic reasons for slow progress are those found in every attempt to introduce common policies: the conflict between national priorities and Community targets. At the moment, only the excise on cigarettes is partly harmonised. After a long period of deliberations, the member states agreed on a compromise system of tax structure for cigarettes, which are now subject to a tax partly specific (a fixed sum per unit) and partly *ad valorem* (a percentage on retail price). Since 1978 the specific duty must not be less than 5 per cent or more than 55 per cent of the total tax burden on cigarettes, the remainder being an *ad valorem* tax. At a later stage of harmonisation, the specific element of the tax is

Table 5.3 Excise duties in the Community (ECU).

Country	Beer	Wine	Pure alcohol	Petrol	Cigarettes ECU + %
B	10	33	1,252	261	2.5 + 66.4
DK	56	157	3,499	473	77.5 + 39.3
D	7	20	1,174	256	27.3 + 43.8
E	3	0	309	254	0.7 + 51.9
F	3	3	1,149	369	1.3 + 71.1
GR	10	0	48	349	0.6 + 60.4
I	17	0	230	557	1.8 + 68.6
IRL	82	279	2,722	362	48.9 + 33.6
L	5	13	842	209	1.7 + 63.6
NL	20	33	1,298	340	26.0 + 35.7
P	9	0	248	352	2.2 + 64.8
UK	49	154	2,483	271	42.8 + 34.0

Notes: Taxes applicable at 1 April 1987
For beer, wine, Pure alcohol: ECU/hundred litre
    Petrol: ECU/1,000 l
    Cigarettes: ECU/1,000 *plus ad valorem* %.

Source: EC (1988) *The Economics of 1992*, European Economy, No. 35.

to be narrowed to a band of 10–30 per cent. At the moment the actual rates of tax vary significantly from country to country (see Table 5.3). The excises on other tobacco products are not harmonised. An attempt to harmonise the excise duties on alcoholic drinks failed in 1981. Subsequently, the Commission judged that certain countries use their excises to discriminate against imports, and has taken a number of cases to the Court of Justice. Although the Court's ruling has in general favoured the Commission, neither the offending nor the offended states returned to the negotiating table.

Indirect taxation in the single market

The decisive stage in the process for completing indirect tax harmonisation in the Community started with the latest move towards unification of the market. The Single European Act, which introduced certain amendments to the Treaty of Rome, changed Article 99 to a commitment to harmonise indirect taxes to the extent necessary to ensure a free internal market by the end of 1992 (EC, 1989c). A free internal market 'without internal frontiers in which the free movement of goods, persons, services and capital is ensured' can begin with the abolition of fiscal frontiers, that is when trade taxes are eliminated and indirect taxes among the members are brought more closely into line. The Community's White Paper states that 'a true internal, or unified, market would not require border tax adjustments, whether or not these occurred at frontier posts' (EC Commission, 1985a).

It has been argued by outside observers, and is supported by certain members, that in the EC frontier obstacles can be eliminated without aligning tax rates. However, this argument seems to express more unwillingness to move forward with the integration of the market than a realistic proposal for establishing a single internal market. It is true that in the United States different states apply different sales taxes without having border controls, but the evidence suggests that tax differences of about 5 per cent is as much as can be sustained without causing large-scale tax-dodging. In other words, in an economic union tax harmonisation is indispensable, but this does not necessarily imply the complete equalisation of tax rates. On the basis of this argument, the Commission presented in July 1987 a proposal for the harmonisation of indirect taxes in the interest of achieving one unified market throughout the twelve member countries by the end of 1992. These proposals are based on the principle of fiscal equality for all products and revenue allocation to the consuming country. Under the destination system of taxation with differential tax rates between countries this requires the following:

1. Tax collection by the country of final consumption of the taxable item. At present, this is effected by border-tax adjustments: tax rebating on exports and tax levying on imports. However, when frontier controls are abolished, exports would bear the exporting country's taxes, and the necessary tax adjustments would be made later by the tax authorities of the importing country. Therefore, the system would involve a substantial tax revenue redistribution between member states.
2. Establishment of a clearing mechanism for the allocation of tax revenues to different countries according to the value they add to traded goods.
3. A considerable approximation of tax rates as a precondition for the abolition of frontier controls without distortion of competition.

On the last point, it must be noted that VAT applied according to the credit method, as in the EC, does not distort the conditions of competition between the various member states even if tax rates are different, since the ultimate tax burden is determined by the rate applied to the final consumer. Nevertheless, in an attempt to end 'tax discrepancies and trade distortions', the Commission prepared a plan for 'VAT approximation' on the basis of a dual-rate system, the normal or standard rate and the reduced rate. The Commission suggested that a degree of flexibility should be introduced to the system by allowing the actual rates of VAT in the member states to deviate no more than three points around the central rates. Therefore, the maximum permitted deviation of VAT rates between member states will be no more than six percentage points, approximately equal to that of the US system. In practical terms this means that the approximation of the rates will be achieved by squeezing all the currently operational VAT rates in the Community within two bands, a 4–9 per cent reduced rate for necessities and a 14–20 per cent standard rate for other goods and services.

The Commission recommended the abolition of the zero rates as a precaution against intra-EC trade distortions, but it accepted that member governments should be able to apply to the Council of Ministers for derogations for politically sensitive items, provided that they do not compromise the integrity of the internal market (EC Commission, 1988a).

As regards excise duties, the Commission intends uniformity throughout the Community in structure, rates and administration as a precondition for the abolition of frontier controls. The Commission has proposed that only the three principal excises should remain after 1992 (alcohol, tobacco and mineral oils) and that duty rates should be uniform, levied at the national currency equivalent of a uniform ECU level. The new rates would be approximately equal to the average of current national rates. However, if monetary integration has not progressed, exchange rate movements will give rise to divergences between countries, which will cause tax-induced opportunistic cross-border trade. Problems also arise with the administrative system to be chosen in association with the allocation of tax revenue to the country of consumption.

The Council considered these proposals and decided that they would cause difficulty for certain countries, in particular those with very high (Denmark) or very low (Luxembourg) indirect tax rates, and those that rely for their revenues on a very heavy indirect tax system (Ireland). Problems would also arise from the proposed uniformity of excise duties, which will have far from negligible consequences on consumption, social habits, health policy and tax revenues. As usual, certain member countries also protested against the proposed harmonisation, arguing that it would impose unwarranted constraints on their fiscal sovereignty: 'Tax approximation is inappropriate. Tax structures in different member states reflect differing economies and different social and political priorities. They cannot be suddenly "averaged"' (Brooke, 1989, p. 36). Hence, taking account of the politics of compromise, the Commission presented revised plans which include the following:

1. The introduction of a transitional period until the end of 1992, during which member countries would be expected to take progressive measures towards reducing tax discrepancies. Hence tax harmonisation is now replaced by tax approximation.
2. On VAT, the proposed standard rate band of 14–20 per cent would be replaced by a minimum rate of 15 per cent without any upper limit being set. The reduced rate would remain at 4–9 per cent, but with the possibility of maintaining zero rating for 'a very limited number of products currently subject to the reduced rate'. The proposed clearing house mechanism for settling tax transfer accounts between the member states would be replaced by a system of balancing payments based on macroeconomic statistics. But at a more recent meeting, finance ministers have decided to postpone until 1996, at the earliest, the introduction of a common VAT system that would allow Europe to be a single market. During the transitional period the VAT system will continue to be applied on the destination principle, hence zero rating for exports will continue. This system is to be reviewed before the end of 1996 with a view to introducing 'a definitive system involving payment of VAT in the country of origin'.

3. On excise duties, the attempt to achieve equalisation has been abandoned for the foreseeable future. Instead, the emphasis will be on reducing disparities between neighbouring states.

Since changes in Community taxation law require unanimous agreement of all the twelve governments, it is anticipated that some modified form of the Commission's plan will probably be accepted, but not without a long period of protracted negotiations. Consequently, as regards indirect taxation, the degree of market integration by the end of 1992 will be much smaller than previously anticipated.

The Community's proposals for tax harmonisation based on uniformity of tax structure and approximation of tax rates have not gone unchallenged. The most radical opposition argues in favour of introducing a uniform tax system but allowing tax competition to shape the tax rates of the member countries within the single market. This option is based on the grounds that in a unified tax system the downward pressure on domestic tax levels would deter governments from increasing public expenditure and would promote greater efficiency in the public sector (Cnossen, 1987).

Elimination of fiscal frontiers implies that the degree of interdependence between the member states will rise. Consequently, in choosing a particular rate of indirect tax, a country would have to consider the rates chosen by its neighbours. Member states setting indirect tax rates below those of adjacent states impose costly 'externalities' on their neighbours who could retaliate by cutting their tax rates. However unbridled tax rate competition is likely to cause drastic reductions in the tax revenues of certain member countries, thus reducing their ability to exercise budgetary policy and threatening the process of European integration. Therefore, an appropriate policy might be to set a statutory lower limit to member states' rates of tax (Pearson and Smith, 1988). Adoption of this approach would result in business pressure to reduce tax rates in the high-tax countries, inducing indirect tax harmonisation by limited tax competition.

5.4   Corporate taxes

The corporation tax affects the incentive to invest, the riskiness of investment and the volume of business saving and hence the supply of investment funds. Differences in corporation taxation between countries create tax arbitrage opportunities which can influence the international mobility of capital. In turn, if capital is induced to move between countries by tax motivations and not by financial and investment considerations, there will be distortive effects on allocative efficiency and on the distribution of tax revenues between states. The situation is more complex if companies registered in one country have subsidiaries in other countries and thus are subject to different tax jurisdictions. In principle, foreign-owned companies should not be discriminated in favour or against in matters of taxation. However, this is what frequently happens as the means to induce domestic or to attract foreign investment.

Economic efficiency therefore requires taxation to be *neutral* with regard to a company's decision on where to invest and the nationality of the company. Similar considerations would apply to taxing shareholders: any shareholder should face the same tax rate regardless of which country he invests in, and shareholders from different countries should face the same tax rate if they invest in the same country. However, this is not always the case in practice and economic inefficiencies do occur. Harmonisation is required because of different corporation tax systems and different tax rates. Corporate tax harmonisation aims at integration of the capital markets and therefore at optimisation in the allocation of capital and investment. In a common market with harmonised corporation taxes, capital will gravitate where the rate of return is highest.

At the moment, among the EC partners there are considerable differences in the corporation tax. The most important of these concern the following:

1. The scope of the tax, that is the liability to corporation tax. All limited companies are subject to the corporation tax, but sole proprietors are not usually liable to it. In the case of partnerships, the situation varies from one member state to another.
2. The basis of assessment, that is the regulations and extent of exemptions, incentives, etc.
3. The tax rate.
4. The system of taxation. Depending on the extent to which corporation income tax and shareholders' personal income tax are integrated, there are four systems of corporate taxation:
   (a) The complete separation of corporate and personal income tax (the 'classical' system). The corporation is viewed as a separate entity, distinct from its shareholders, and is taxed on its own capacity. Therefore, the distributed corporate income is taxed twice, first as income of the corporation and then again as shareholders' personal income (dividends).
   (b) The split rate or two-rate system. A lower tax rate applies on corporate distributions than on retained profits.

(c) The tax credit or partial imputation system. This system is designed to avoid the double taxation on dividends by imputing part of the corporate profit tax to the personal tax liability of shareholders.

(d) The full integration system. In contrast to (a), the corporation is not seen as a separate entity but as a partnership of shareholders. In essence, under this scheme corporation tax does not exist, but instead the shareholders are taxed under the personal income tax liability. Therefore, this system is an extension of system (c) with full imputation of corporate profit tax to shareholders' personal income tax.

Most of the EC states operate system (c) at the moment. This system formed in the 1970s the basis of a proposed directive by the Commission for approximation of company tax structures across the EC. However, this directive was rejected by the European Parliament on the reasonable argument that harmonisation of the rate structure is incomplete if there is no harmonisation of the tax base.

Differences among the member states that apply the partial imputation system exist in the following:

1. The rates of imputation between corporations and shareholders. Currently, these rates range between 100 per cent in Germany (i.e. full imputation) to 15 per cent in Denmark.
2. The tax rates themselves, which range from 56 per cent in Germany to 35 per cent in the United Kingdom and 10 per cent (for some manufacturing activities) in Ireland.
3. The basis of assessment for corporation tax and the definition of taxable profits. In particular, the member states differ on points of law about how they define and treat the concepts of depreciation, capital gains and losses, reserves and provisions, the valuation of assets and liabilities, stocks, taxation under inflation, etc., all of which contribute to the determination of taxable net income.

Another issue of contention is the question of incentives provided by the corporation tax. These incentives are introduced with the aim to encourage investment in a nation-wide scale or in certain less-developed or problem areas (e.g. of high unemployment) and sectors (e.g. energy conservation). Incentives take various forms (accelerated depreciation, tax relief on investment, tax exemptions on profits, tax concessions on modernisation, etc.) and differ in degree from one country to another. An outcome of these differences is that the capital markets of the

Community are compartmentalised and, therefore, the allocation of resources within the greater area of the common market is suboptimal. Harmonisation of the corporation tax is the first step towards restoring optimality.

The first proposals concerning the harmonisation of the corporation tax in the Community came from the Neumark Committee (1962) which suggested a split rate system, with taxation of retained profits at one rate and of distributed profits at a lower rate. Distributed profits would also be subject to personal taxation. However, the member states did not accept this proposal. A second committee chaired by Van den Tempel (1970) recommended in its report the separate system with a single common rate. But this recommendation too did not find favour with the Commission which instead published its first Draft Directive, 1975, recommending the imputation system of corporation tax and a common system of withholding tax on dividends. The proposal provided that member states would have similar, but not identical, corporate tax rates ranging between a lower limit of 45 per cent and an upper limit of 55 per cent. What the effect of harmonisation along these lines and rates would be for each member state cannot be easily assessed. In general, harmonisation of the corporation tax will affect (a) the use of corporation tax as an instrument for national policy, (b) the ratio of distributed over undistributed profits, (c) budgetary revenues and (d) capital flows among the EC countries and between the EC and the outside world.

However, these Community proposals, which were made at a time of serious economic recession in the world and the EC economies, have not been met with support for immediate implementation, particularly among the member countries which would have to raise their rates. Hence, the proposals have not as yet resulted in significant action. The completion of the internal market, capital market liberalisation and absence of significant harmonisation of national tax systems would provide corporations with opportunities for international tax avoidance through purely financial transactions. Multinational and Europe-wide corporations will be best suited to take advantage of tax arbitrage and tax loopholes within and probably without the Community. Continuation of large differences in tax systems and tax rates between the member states causes distortion and economic inefficiency. In the longer run, it may also cause competitive tax rate reductions between the member states which would either erode their corporate tax bases or induce them to reintroduce capital controls to the detriment of European integration. Therefore, new proposals are expected to be made by the Commission on the direct taxation of companies with a view to completion of the internal market and promotion of cooperation between companies in different member states (EC Commission, 1989e).

The principle of competition on equal terms would suggest that corporate tax harmonisation is desirable and it should start by harmonisation of the tax base. Then, after instituting a statutory minimum corporate tax rate, harmonisation can be left to the market process.

5.5 Other taxes

Personal income tax

The Community members have not included the personal income tax among the taxes intended for harmonisation. In effect, it is tacitly agreed that at the moment the harmonisation process should not directly impinge upon this tax which should remain within the sphere of national sovereignty. Although the comparison of income taxes is complicated by progression in the rates, the apparent differences between the EC countries are very significant, the top rate of personal tax ranging from 72 per cent in the Netherlands to 40 per cent in the United Kingdom. Personal tax rates may influence personal international saving and investment decisions and, indirectly, the location of corporation headquarters.

Social security

Personal income taxes and social security contributions and benefits affect the take-home pay and the social insurance of labour. Hence, they are among the factors affecting production costs and prices, as well as the mobility of labour between occupations and countries. Therefore, as in the case of capital and the harmonisation of the corporation tax, there should be a move for the harmonisation of taxes and benefits relating to labour. However, with the exception of certain agreements relating to social policy (see Chapter 10), nothing else has happened in this field.

Taxation of savings

At the moment, withholding tax rates on private savings varies among the EC states between zero and 51 per cent. Intra-European mobility of capital in the single market means that differences in national taxes on savings will trigger large tax-driven and destabilising flows of funds within the Community. Hence the Commission early in 1989 proposed a maximum 15 per cent withholding tax on savings and bond income for all residents of the Community. The rate chosen is intended to be low enough to discourage tax evasion within the EC or flight of capital to tax havens outside the Community. However, this proposal was unacceptable to countries which are international banking centres, such as the United Kingdom and Luxembourg. Under conditions of free mobility of capital and no harmonisation, capital will flow to take advantage of tax differences and the relative efficiency of financial markets. This means that, in the longer run, competition will drive the withholding tax on savings to zero in every member state of the Community.

Further reading

Economic analysis of sales tax harmonisation in economic (or tax) unions usually deals with the equivalence of different principles of taxation, mostly the destination vs. the restricted origin principles, in general equilibrium terms and under very restrictive assumptions: see Berglas (1981). For indirect tax harmonisation in the EC see Gammie and Robinson (1989) and Cnossen (1987); and for corporate taxation Devereux and Pearson (1990). For a market-based harmonisation proposal see HM Treasury (1988) and Brooke (1989).

6

Monetary integration

6.1 Principles: economics and politics

The term *Economic and Monetary Union* (EMU) is usually defined as: the free and unrestricted movement of commodities, services and factors of production; the existence of a common currency; and centralisation of economic policy. Therefore, monetary integration is an essential element of an EMU.

Monetary integration has two components: exchange rate union and capital market union. Exchange rate union is an area within which the exchange rates of the member countries bear a permanently fixed relationship to each other. Capital market union is an area within which capital can move absolutely freely. The process of monetary integration usually entails the following stages:

1. The total and *irreversible* convertibility of currencies.
2. The elimination of margins of fluctuations in exchange rates.
3. The *irrevocable* fixing of parity rates.
4. The complete liberation of capital movements among the members.

Successful completion of these steps ultimately leads to integration of the financial and monetary sectors of the participating countries. Then, the establishment of a common central bank, which would issue a common currency and exercise common monetary policy, is only a formality.

The rationale behind monetary integration in an economic union is based on the advantages of a common currency. These include the following:

1. The informational advantage of using a common standard or numeraire.
2. The efficiency of a single money as a unit of account and store of value.
3. Lower transaction costs in international trade.
4. The elimination of exchange rate risk.

Monetary integration is a prerequisite for attaining optimal resource allocation within the area of an economic union. The progressive integration of members' markets for commodities, services and factors of production increases economic interdependence and makes monetary integration almost indispensable. The allocation of savings and investment within the enlarged market may improve as capital controls are removed and competition in the financial sector is enhanced, owing to higher real rates of returns to savers, smaller interest rate spreads between borrowers and lenders, a lower cost of capital to firms, and better hedging opportunities against risks.

As the national economies of the member states in an economic union through trade and factor movement (capital and labour) become increasingly more open and more interdependent, two problems may arise:

1. Monetary and fiscal measures taken by a member country to regulate its own economic activity have spillover effects on other member countries.
2. Member countries find that it becomes progressively more difficult to cope with economic problems of their own, some of which arise from participation in the union but are no longer subject to treatment by the traditional instruments of national economic policy.

A crucial problem for every country participating in an economic union is how to reach and maintain balance-of-payments equilibrium. For example, a country may face deficits in its balance of payments with its union partners, but be prevented from using protective policies or exchange controls in intra-union trade. In principle, a given position in the balance of payments can be maintained under capital mobility, if the trend in nominal prices follows a similar pattern in the country and its trade partners. This in turn requires all the members to have similar rates of growth of income and productivity. If this condition is not met, then policy intervention for balance-of-payments equilibrium is necessary in one of the following three forms: (a) an exchange rate adjustment; (b) a reduction in real incomes; (c) a compensatory movement in the capital account. However, in an economic union aiming at free trade in commodities, services and factors of production the price level must not diverge between countries; consequently, the exchange rates must remain stable as a *de facto* introduction of a single currency. Therefore, the best solution to this problem is that the member countries ensure real consistency in their development objectives (inflation rate, growth, productivity, etc.) and apply consistent policies to pursue it.

When the members of the economic union pursue consistent monetary policies, they necessarily have to impose constraints on other policies, some of which also have to become compatible between the members of the union. The question now is whether monetary integration precedes or follows the integration of fiscal policies. Three different answers have been provided. The federalists argue that fiscal integration comes first and prepares the ground for the ensuing monetary integration. The neofunctionalists emphasise the political role of monetary integration and advocate its immediate implementation so that fiscal, economic and political unification become inevitable and are instituted next by necessity. Finally, the pluralists argue that monetary integration does not require fiscal integration, since monetary and fiscal policies can in principle be exercised separately. For similar reasons fiscal integration does not have to follow in the steps of monetary integration, since the governments of the member states can finance national budget deficits without recourse to monetary policy, by borrowing in the integrated capital market.

It can be argued, however, that within the economic union the exercise of national fiscal policy is impaired, but at the same time it has spillover effects on the other countries of union. Monetary integration creates pressures for fiscal policy harmonisation in both spending and taxation. Therefore, initially some degree of fiscal harmonisation is necessary. At a later stage of the process of monetary integration, fiscal as well as monetary policy should be subject to centralised control. If exchange rates are fixed and interest rates are the same in every member state, a fiscal expansion in one country would lead to a rise in prices everywhere. Hence, some of the costs of financial expansion in one country would be passed forward to other members of the union via balance-of-payments changes. Fiscal centralisation does not mean the complete substitution of a federal fiscal policy for members' national tax and public expenditure policy. Even in federal states, such as the United States, quite a sizeable proportion of total taxation is levied at the state and local level. Needless to say, for those who see economic integration as the means for moving towards political federation, fiscal integration is absolutely essential and it is irrelevant whether it precedes or follows monetary unification.

The enhanced mobility of factors of production within the economic union may make the move towards monetary integration indispensable. Free factor movement (capital and labour) may lead to economic imbalance between the members of the economic union. Capital would be much more likely to gravitate to the relatively faster growing areas of the economic union. Sooner or later, labour will follow the same way, migrating where the opportunities for employment and higher wages are present. As a result of these migrations the relatively less developed areas of the economic union will become more impoverished. Imbalance and inequality in sharing the benefits and costs of membership are liable to pose a threat to the cohesion of the economic union and the attempt for economic and political integration. If political unification is to be achieved, then inequalities and imbalances among the participants must be reduced to a minimum by application of appropriate measures, such as common monetary and fiscal policies. For these reasons the central authority of the economic union is endowed by the members with the necessary economic and political power to enable it to deal with these inter-state problems.

Monetary integration has immense political and institutional implications. Two of what are generally regarded as the prerogative functions of the government of every independent state – domestic monetary policy and control over the exchange rate – are surrendered to the central monetary authority of the economic union which takes responsibility for the general running of economic policy. To be able to do so successfully, the authority is also given the necessary instruments of economic policy which thus cease to be at the disposal of the national governments of the member states. Thus, at the national level, governments lose all direct monetary autonomy and the use of the exchange rate as instruments of national policy.

The transfer of the instruments of economic policy and the authority to use them requires the prior establishment of an appropriate central executive empowered to rule above the strictly national level. This entails the need to provide the central monetary authority with a certain degree of political power, a sizeable central budget and either an integrated system of money supply institutions or a central bank. In most cases the commitment to monetary integration implies explicitly integration of economic policy, a common pool of foreign exchange reserves and establishment of a central monetary institution of the economic union. Any lesser arrangement will not ensure the permanence of exchange rate parities within the union and will disrupt the process of integration by problems such as currency speculation, balance-of-payments disequilibria and the need for devaluations, etc.

In conclusion, monetary unification cannot proceed without a parallel move towards central fiscal/budgetary unification. This will enable the executive of the economic union to cope with problems concerning the coordination of economic policy at the level of the union, problems of regional inequality and fair sharing between the members of the costs and benefits of integration. Hence, the executive of the union must be endowed with economic as well as political power. This implies that economic and monetary integration can proceed only if the members of the economic union have a strong commitment towards political unification.

6.2 Inflation, unemployment and optimum currency areas

Monetary integration cannot be established in a vacuum, even if the will for political unification is very strong. Certain conditions must be met if monetary integration is to be a benefit rather than a burden. A premature drive towards monetary integration may in fact defeat the move towards political unity and undermine the process of economic integration. Historically, the debate about the conditions necessary for efficient monetary integration started with the theory of *optimum currency areas* under the implicit assumption of the existence of a trade-off between inflation and unemployment.

If the objectives of economic policy are conflicting, it is necessary to accept a trade-off between them. A trade-off relationship is portrayed by the 'Phillips curve' which shows that high inflation is associated with low unemployment, and vice versa. The rationale claimed for this relationship is that in periods of rising demand and employment, labour markets tighten, higher wages are demanded and acceded and prices drift upwards. If this trade-off does really exist, it means that countries can freely choose the rate of inflation and the level of unemployment which would best serve their national economic objectives. If money wages can rise but they are not allowed to fall, then the exchange rate can be used to alter real wages. Therefore, when countries tie their exchange rates in a currency union, they will be forced away from their preferred combinations of inflation/unemployment, will lose the use of the exchange rate as a policy instrument, and some would end up with more inflation than they wanted and others with more unemployment (Corden, 1979). Consequently, currency unification would be advocated only for countries which meet certain specific conditions, such as that they are in long-term monetary stability and pursue similar economic objectives.

The theory of optimum currency areas attempts to define which countries or regions would combine optimally in a currency union and whether a common currency offers to some group of countries more advantages than either a world-wide fixed or flexible exchange rates system (Mundell, 1961; Kenen, 1969; Grubel, 1970). The decision to form a common currency area is usually based on criteria for attaining optimality with reference to the fixed target 'price stability' (implicitly, under the inflation/unemployment trade-off) and a single criterion is selected to decide the suitability of countries for membership. Consequently, depending on the criteria adopted, different conclusions may be reached. Therefore, not all the theories of optimum currency areas arrive at the same policy recommendations or advocate the same country membership.

The conditions stated in the literature as necessary for moving successfully to monetary integration are usually based on a single facet of the economies involved or on an evaluation of costs and benefits arising from currency unification. The characteristics most frequently mentioned as necessary are as follows:

1. *High degree of factor mobility* so that factor movement will displace the exchange rate in adjusting real wages and unemployment. Thus, with a common currency and uniform wages in the economic union, shifts in demand will be accommodated by the migration of labour from low- to high-employment regions. In general, capital is more mobile than labour, and it is doubtful whether in practice inter-regional labour mobility within a monetary union will be high enough to play the role previously held by the exchange rate.

2. *Openness to trade.* In this case, prices are determined internationally and the exchange rate is a relatively inefficient instrument for changing real wages. Monetary integration is thus recommended primarily for stabilisation reasons: countries trading extensively with one another would benefit from forming a common currency area. This recommendation is based on two preconditions, that:
   (a) the countries trade more with one another and less with the outside world;
   (b) the instability they may suffer is caused by their participation in international trade.

3. *Low diversification.* The more an economy is diversified in its production and demand, the more independent it is of external influences, and thus the less vulnerable to exogenous fluctuations in income and prices. Hence, monetary integration is recommended if

it will result in greater diversification of the economic union. In this context increased diversification is identified with a wide-ranging import-competing industry able to reduce the dependence of the economic union on foreign trade.

4. *Other*. Within the inflation/unemployment domain, a number of other criteria have been suggested such as similarity in inflation rates, similarity in general economic policy attitudes and financial market unification.

5. *Benefits vs. costs*. This approach is based on the overall evaluation of the benefits and costs of monetary integration for the members (Ishiyama, 1975). The benefits include the facts that a common currency is conducive to allocation efficiency and economic integration, that speculative capital flows are completely eliminated within the area of the economic union and, finally, that there is a positive saving of exchange reserves.

Among the costs are:

(a) the loss of autonomy in national monetary policy of the members;

(b) the constraints imposed upon the national fiscal policy of the members;

(c) the possibility of worsening the existing unemployment/inflation relationships, at least in some member countries;

(d) the possibility of increases in regional disparities.

To these pros and cons every member in an economic union attaches its own subjective weights. Complete agreement is not always easy, hence the move towards monetary integration is very slow and difficult.

In general, the incentive for monetary integration in an 'optimum currency area' comes from the potential improvements of efficiency in resource allocation by the use of a single currency in inter-regional trade. But, in this respect, the theories of optimum currency areas are of little use for the formulation of policy in an economic union because, first, theoretical developments and recent experience have shown that the trade-off between unemployment and inflation is only temporary; and, second, in economic unions, such as the EC, the issue of monetary unification goes beyond optimum currency areas. If two or more countries form an economic union and their ultimate objective is to integrate the market for goods, services and factors of production and to proceed with some form of political unification, there are not many valid arguments against establishing a monetary union. It is possible that initially some countries which meet the criteria for participation in an optimum currency area and ought to join, are not members of the economic union, while other countries which should not be included in the currency area, are members of the economic union. However, if economic integration proceeds in stages, as in the EC, then, through time, most of the requirements for the formation of an optimum currency area are gradually fulfilled. For example, as economic interdependence between the members increases, both openness to trade and factor mobility tend to rise within the economic union. In general, if the ultimate goal of the contracting parties is economic unification, market integration without monetary integration is not conceivable. What would the United States be like with fifty different currencies and state monetary policies?

6.3 National monetary policy and international monetary integration

Monetary integration is a process usually implemented in stages. During the progress towards monetary integration, national monetary policies continue to function but under increasing constraints. Therefore, it is of interest to examine the objectives and the functions of national monetary policy during the transition from relative independence to full membership in a monetary union.

While fiscal and monetary policies may affect the levels of employment, output and prices, it is usually argued on grounds of efficiency that monetary policy should be used to combat inflation, whereas fiscal policy is more appropriate for combating recession.

Inflation is caused by supply and/or demand factors. According to the quantity theory of money and the monetarist doctrine, the demand for money is stable and therefore the sole cause of inflation is expansion of money supply:

$$MV = YP$$

where M = stock of money, V = velocity of circulation, Y = real income and P = index of price level. The velocity of circulation V is assumed to be constant over time, while prices and wages are assumed to be (perfectly) flexible. Therefore, an increase in M initially causes changes in other variables, such as the velocity of circulation V and the real income Y. But cash balances and real income will eventually return to their long-term equilibrium level. Ultimately, only prices will absorb the increase in the supply of money: the price level will rise. This leads to the conclusion that over the medium term there is a positive association between inflation and monetary growth. From this emerges the proposition that in the medium term countries can control inflation by controlling the growth of money supply. Therefore, a solution to the problem of inflation, which was strongly advocated in the 1970s, is to formulate targets for money stock growth which would guide macroeconomic policy and control inflation. But how the controls on monetary growth operate depends on whether the international monetary system is that of flexible or fixed exchange rates.

In a system of flexible exchange rates, countries allow their exchange rates to float, and fix the growth of money supply (by money supply targets or interest rate policy) to control their inflation rate. However, the application of monetary controls to combat inflation brings about fluctuations in the exchange rate. Subsequently, these fluctuations alter the relative competitiveness of countries via changes in the relative prices of traded commodities. These price changes are purely monetary and therefore are not caused by productivity improvements. In other words, the monetary sector induces fluctuations which may produce damaging effects to the real sector of the economy.

An important component of this analysis is that under floating exchange rates, each country assumes that it can alter its exchange rate by a change in its money stock, taking its trading partner's monetary policy as given. However, monetary policy in one country has spillover effects on other countries. These effects are unwanted and countries try to limit them by counter-policies of their own. Alternatively, countries recognise their interdependence and cooperate by concluding inter-national agreements to coordinate monetary policy and manage exchange rates. Therefore, agreement on international exchange rate management implies a shift of national monetary policy from a domestic target, the rate of inflation, to an external target, the exchange rate. Consequently, in a system of flexible exchange rates, money supply is limited as an instrument for control of domestic inflation.

Under fixed exchange rates and free capital markets, within an economic union or world-wide, countries allow the money stock to adjust to the exchange rate and the interest rate. Consequently, when the exchange rates are permanently fixed, every country completely loses the possibility of control over inflation by money supply. The money stock is determined by the demand for money at the common interest rate. Therefore, the member countries have to accept, in the long run, the rate of inflation of the union. If a country does not do so, but deliberately chooses to have a higher rate of inflation than other members, its exports become less competitive and its imports more competitive, leading to a balance-of-trade deficit and lower domestic output and employment. The ensuing recession is expected to put downward pressure on the rate of inflation. But until this happens, the country is exporting inflation to its partners in the fixed exchange rates group via its trade deficit, that is by directing its expanded demand for imports and its supply of exports to its union partners. In contrast, member countries with relatively low inflation rates will experience balance-of-trade surpluses and export-led growth. The system leads to asymmetries because the deficit countries are under pressure to correct their economic policies by adopting tight monetary and fiscal policies and, as a last resort, devaluation, while the surplus countries are not. This introduces to the system a deflationary bias.

However, the system's deflationary bias is not a solution to the problem of inflation. In general, under fixed exchange rates a need exists for a mechanism to regulate the common inflation rate of the participants in the union. In the gold standard system such a mechanism was provided by the limits in the supply of gold. In the Bretton Woods system of fixed exchange rates, the supply of dollars, on which the system was based, was in effect the inflation control mechanism. In the case of monetary integration in economic unions the problem can be solved by the 'nth currency' as an instrument for combating inflation. According to this approach, if $n - 1$ countries employ national monetary policy to keep the exchange rates fixed, the nth country has no influence on its exchange rate. Therefore its monetary policy is a surplus policy instrument. Then, by agreement between the partners, the nth country's surplus instrument can be used as a 'nominal anchor': the countries in the union fix their exchange rate against the nth currency and manage their money stocks in support of the fixed exchange rates system, thus effectively losing their monetary sovereignty. Then, the nth currency can be employed to pursue a common inflation target in the union, or an exchange rate target of the union *vis-à-vis* a third currency, as the means for maintaining the competitiveness of the currency union in international markets. Naturally, a necessary condition for guiding the economic union towards monetary integration is that the member states should agree on a common inflation rate or exchange rate target. However, this may cause problems for the weaker and less competitive regions within the single market, which may become permanently depressed as a result of being forced to choose lower rates of inflation than they would otherwise. One possible solution to the regional problem of a currency union would be to establish a common regional policy able to cope with the short-term problems of adaptation to market integration.

6.4 The moves for monetary integration

More than three decades after the establishment of the EC the creation of Economic and Monetary Union still remains 'a desirable objective', a common target worth pursuing but without an agreed date for its completion. In this section we will examine the causes, objectives and first attempts for monetary integration in the European Community.

Treaty provisions

The Treaty of Rome declares that the aims of the Community would be pursued 'by establishing a Common Market and progressively approximating the economic policies of Member States' (Article 2). However, while for the creation of the common market there is a detailed timetable of action, the approximation of members' economic policy remained unspecified. This omission probably reflects the prevailing ideas at the time of signing the Treaty, that free trade between the member countries would lead progressively to greater functional interdependence, hence approximation of economic policy will follow automatically. Consequently, it was expected that the free movement of goods, services and factors of production and, in general, competition on equal terms will inevitably lead to monetary integration. However, if a system of fixed exchange rates in support of market integration and common policies is not introduced by design, it does not necessarily follow that it will emerge automatically by the introduction of common policies. Market integration and common policies cannot be sustained for long enough if the exchange rates between the partners are freely flexible or if they are fixed but change at will by competing devaluations among the participating countries.

If the members maintain in their trade relations flexible exchange rates, then the target of common prices is undermined by changes in currency parities which impede the unification of the market, create uncertainty and may lead to trade contraction. Therefore, flexible exchange rates are not conducive to economic integration. In contrast, a fixed exchange rate system requires the member countries to give priority to Community targets and to constrain their national objectives by the common pursuit of maintaining the agreed parity of the exchange rates. Ultimately, fixed parities among the currencies in the economic union cannot be sustained unless the trend in nominal prices and productivities follows the same pattern in all participating countries, and monetary policies converge. This requires coordination of members' economic policies, of monetary targets and instruments in particular, for convergence of both policies and economic performance.

The Treaty of Rome did not deal with the requirement for monetary integration for two reasons:

1. In the 1950s, when the Treaty of Rome was signed, the EC countries were experiencing similar growth performance, low rates of inflation and satisfactory trends in productivity improvements. The six EC members also had favourable trade balances and adequate foreign reserves.
2. The international monetary system in operation was that of US dollar-based, fixed, periodically adjustable exchange rates. If the exchange rates system is fixed and is expected to remain so, then the world is effectively on a common currency standard.

This system adequately served the EC's attempts for consolidation of its common policies and for progress towards completion of the common market. However, in the late 1960s and early 1970s increasing pressure on the dollar (arising from the global financial and strategic commitments of the United States) and general exogenous shocks and disturbances in world markets (such as oil embargoes) caused divergences in inflation rates which in turn induced frequent exchange rate changes by devaluations and revaluation. Finally, the fixed exchange rates system collapsed and, in an attempt to insulate domestic policy from external constraints, many countries floated their currencies. Allegedly, floating exchange rates induce the isolation of national markets leading to the development of national price systems. If this is so, then they also operate against international market integration.

Meanwhile, the EC had already started to pursue common objectives by coordination of national economic policies at the level of the member states and by common policies at the level of the Community. The most important of the latter was the CAP which aimed at common prices in a single Community market for agricultural products. However, the ongoing exchange rates' turbulence of the international markets had repercussions on EC member states, which were forced to change their priorities by resorting to the use of policies selected on purely domestic considerations rather than their international obligations within the common market. For example, in 1969 France devalued the franc by 11.1 per cent, and soon after Germany revalued the Deutschmark by 9.29 per cent, thus changing the intra-Community parity rates (and the common agricultural prices) by more than 20 per cent.

These developments had an impact on economic performance and inflation rates which in the EC started to diverge significantly between the member countries. These problems confirmed that the foundations of the common market − free trade in goods, services and factors of production; competition on equal terms; coordination of policy and targets; and common policies for common objectives − could not be sustained without the support of a fixed exchange rate among the

Community partners. Under this externally imposed pressure the EC started to consider how to proceed towards closer economic and monetary cooperation.

Plans for monetary integration

The first concrete proposal for monetary integration (the Barre Plan, 1969) called for tighter consultation between member states on matters of economic policy, coordination of monetary policy and mutual assistance among the members of the EC during periods of financial crisis. Most important was the proclamation of the EC heads of states at the Hague Summit in December 1969, that the intention of the Community was to proceed gradually towards the establishment of Economic and Monetary Union (EMU). In this way monetary integration officially became a Community target. Since then, arguments have started to appear for and against this objective.

The arguments against monetary integration in the EC are both political and economic.

The *political argument* is that a full monetary union implies the transfer of control of monetary policy from the members' national monetary authorities to the Monetary Authority, established for this purpose, of the EC. But, since it is considered politically inappropriate to give such control to a supranational appointed, not elected, authority, prior to monetary integration, some form of political integration is required. Political integration involves the transfer of hitherto national power to the executive of the EC and it can be accomplished only at the expense of national sovereignty. Even a simple agreement among the member states to fix the exchange rates entails loss of economic sovereignty. Monetary union, even in its simplest form, reduces national monetary autonomy, imposes constraints on the use of instruments and erodes the ability of national governments to exercise national economic policy.

This argument is correct and, as we have seen, it implies that economic and political unification should be pursued simultaneously. Nevertheless, countries can proceed with economic and monetary unification before moving forward with political unification, if (a) the advantages from it exceed the disadvantages, and (b) it is used as the spearhead for political unification.

The *economic argument* is that commitment to irrevocably fixed exchange rates, and later complete monetary integration, deprives the participating countries of national control over monetary policy which is an instrument for economic stabilisation. Therefore, monetary integration imposes on the members a costly constraint which weakens economic independence and diminishes the ability of governments to exercise economic policy.

The counter-argument here is that, first, there are enough instruments left to the government for the exercise of economic policy; and, second, the high degree of economic interdependence within an economic union makes money supply and the exchange rate inefficient instruments of national economic policy. Hence, the commitment to irrevocably fixed exchange rates simply sanctions a situation which *de facto* exists already.

With the international monetary conditions worsening, agreement was finally reached in the EC that some steps for restoring monetary stability in the Community had to be taken. Disputes then followed regarding what degree of monetary integration was necessary and how it would be implemented. A number of different routes were suggested:

1. *Instantaneous integration.* The most radical method advocates the overnight establishment of the monetary union by:
   (a) immediate setting up of a central bank;
   (b) pooling of the members' reserves of gold and foreign exchange;
   (c) direct replacement of national monies by a common currency.

   The participating states still have their own budgets, levy taxes, borrow and lend, just as in a federal system.

   The great advantage of this method is that it avoids the problems of a transitional period, but it is not politically feasible. It is strongly opposed by national monetary authorities and governments, which by losing power become subordinate to the monetary authority of the economic union. Moreover, the less prosperous members of the Community argued that they will suffer most from this procedure because they will be forced to adjust their performance to the lower inflation rates of the prosperous members, with effects on their rate of unemployment and general internal balance.

2. *Currency competition.* Under this method all capital controls in the member states are abolished and all national currencies are accepted as legal tender. Free competition between currencies guarantees that eventually one of them will be established by market selection as the currency of the EC. Thus monetary union will be accomplished by market forces.

   The problem here is that the country whose currency will be adopted as the common currency gains, while all other countries lose. Besides the political prestige, the economic gain consists of the *seigniorage*, that is the rent which accrues to a country when its national currency is held by foreigners. Seigniorage in effect is the benefit derived from issuing non-interest bearing debt.

3. *Parallel currency* will be issued by the EC to compete with the national currencies and it should possess a purchasing-power guarantee to become stronger and stabler than any national currency. Since it will not be the currency of any particular state, national rivalries are avoided and the economic benefit from seigniorage will accrue to the union as a whole. If the parallel currency offers a stabler store of value and unit of account than the national currencies, then currency substitution will take place spontaneously in the market.

The parallel currency proposal contended that the new currency would succeed in displacing all national currencies of the member states by maintaining a constant purchasing power in terms of a basket of goods.

4. *Monetary union by steps.* Exchange rate margins will be narrowed gradually and at a later stage reserves will be pooled. Finally a central bank will be established. This method has the drawback of relying on successive negotiations for defining and implementing each stage in the sequence of steps. If the political will towards monetary integration is at any stage weak, the process will be halted.

The Hague Summit of 1969 finally decided that the Community should proceed towards economic and monetary integration by *gradualism*, the stepwise procedure. Although all the members agreed in principle, differences emerged as to whether the Economic component precedes or follows the Monetary component of the Union. The 'economist' group of countries (Germany, the Netherlands) supported the view that before attempting monetary unification, it is necessary to reach convergence of economic performance. This should be pursued by setting consistent common targets and coordinating national economic policies to meet them. After convergence is achieved, it will be easier to fix the exchange rates and establish the European Monetary Authority. The 'monetarist' group of countries (France, Belgium, Luxembourg) argued instead that the first step towards monetary integration should involve the narrowing of exchange rate fluctuations. Commitment to this objective would inevitably impose on the members the need for discipline and cooperation in policy and economic performance. Thus, convergence does not precede but follows the establishment of the European Monetary Authority.

The Werner Report and the 'snake'

These issues were considered by the Werner Committee which published its Report in 1970. The Werner Report (1970) recommended the establishment of the European Monetary Union (EMU) in stages by 1980, with rigidly fixed exchange rates, perfect convertibility of EC currencies, complete freedom of capital movements, and creation of a Community Central Bank. The Council meeting of February 1971 accepted the substance of the Report's recommendations and attempted to reconcile the different views regarding some issues which were judged to impinge on national sovereignty. It was thus decided that the first stage should involve the narrowing of exchange rate fluctuation margins, coordination of monetary policies, and the setting up of a European Exchange Stabilisation Fund to provide credit facilities for policies of monetary stability.

But new problems with the US dollar in the international markets led to the postponement of the implementation of the agreement. At the same time the turbulent international monetary situation convinced the member states that time was running out and steps should be taken towards closer monetary cooperation for the purpose of insulating the Community from the effects of volatile international exchange rate markets. Hence in 1971 the EC countries took the first positive step towards monetary integration by establishing, within the still-existing international fixed exchange rate system the 'European Band' or the 'snake'. This was a variant of the adjustable-peg exchange rates system, combining adherence to the international agreements with partial implementation of the Werner Plan. At the centre of the 'Band' remained the US dollar, with margins of permissible fluctuations set at 2.25 per cent either side of the central dollar rate for each of the participating currencies (except the Italian lira which was allowed ±6 per cent margins), giving a 4.5 per cent maximum of intra-EC exchange rate fluctuations between any pair of currencies. Thus, the Community currencies could float together around the dollar at a quasi-fixed relationship between them. The agreement provided for the system to be run and supervised by the European Monetary Cooperation Fund (EMCF) and for the margins of fluctuations to be adhered to by coordinated monetary policy and concerted action of the members' central banks. However, as a last resort, the participating countries were allowed to withdraw from the system, temporarily or permanently, if this was at any time deemed necessary.

The narrowing of exchange rates fluctuations was rapidly achieved. In addition to the Six, the United Kingdom, Ireland and Denmark also joined the scheme in anticipation of their imminent entry (1972) to the Community. Two other currencies, the Swedish krona and the Norwegian krone, also became associated from the outset. However, a few weeks after joining, the United Kingdom abandoned the 'snake' when sterling came under pressure, and within days Ireland was forced to follow suit. Thus the attempt to resume progress towards monetary union was undermined right from the beginning. Subsequently, the oil crisis of 1973–4 affected some Community countries more than others and forced them to give priority to national rather then common policy problems. Thus the currencies in the Band came repeatedly under pressure, the market exchange rates changed frequently and for some of the participants made the 'snake' unworkable. The lira was withdrawn in 1973 and the Swedish krone and Norwegian krona in 1977. France abandoned the Band in January 1974, rejoined it in July 1975, and left it again in August 1977. Under these conditions, progress towards monetary integration halted and it soon became clear that establishment of the EMU along the lines and the timetable proposed by the Werner Plan was not feasible.

It is important to realise that the Werner Plan advocated the gradual establishment of monetary union within the framework of the fixed exchange rates system, which it was believed would somehow survive the financial crisis. However, in March 1973 the fixed exchange rate system collapsed, and nothing was put in its place. Countries started to pursue domestic objectives by expansionary monetary policies, intervening in the foreign exchange market and, in general, following policies without consideration to their international repercussions. Hence, national policies, economic performances and rates of inflation started to diverge extensively. From 1973, the differences in inflation and unemployment rates between the members of the Community became so large as to be incompatible with exchange rate stability. The European 'snake' suffered under the onslaught of internal and external events: from April 1972 to March 1979, the 'fixed' parities of the system were altered thirty-one times, while the Band was abandoned and rejoined by committed participants eighteen times. By the end of 1977 only the Deutschmark, the Dutch guilder, the Belgian franc and the Danish krona remained in the 'snake'.

The European Monetary System

Meanwhile, the international monetary system adopted after the collapse of the fixed exchange rates was that of floating rates. This development, together with the ensuing uncertainties about the stability of exchange rates, the danger of increasing problems over operation of the common market and halting progress towards integration, convinced the EC authorities that both for political and economic reasons they should institute their own system of fixed exchange rates as a first step towards monetary integration. Consequently, a new agreement was reached at the Council meetings in Bremen (July 1978) and Brussels (December 1978) and the new scheme for monetary cooperation, now called the European Monetary System (EMS), was launched on 13 May 1979. The European Council declared that the objective of the EMS was 'closer monetary cooperation leading to a zone of monetary stability in Europe', 'as a fundamental component of a more comprehensive strategy aimed at lasting growth with stability, a progressive return to full employment, the harmonisation of living standards and the lessening of regional disparities in the Community'.

The new system fixed its own central rates independently of the US dollar. The permissible margins of fluctuations for the participating currencies were set at ±2.25 per cent around the central rates, except for Italy's lira which was allowed ±6 per cent margins. The United Kingdom and Ireland were also offered the wider band of margins; but, while the United Kingdom decided to stay outside the exchange rate mechanism (ERM) of the system, Ireland opted for the 2.25 per cent margins. As we will see later on, the United Kingdom finally joined the ERM in October 1990 at the ±6 per cent margins. Of the new members of the Community, Spain (EC member since 1986) joined the system in June 1989 at the ±6 per cent margins, while Greece (EC member since 1981) and Portugal (EC member since 1986) decided to remain provisionally outside the ERM.

It must be emphasised that the EMS agreement had economic and political origins and objectives. A common monetary system, through its effects on real variables in the markets of the interdependent economies and as a technical initiative in the monetary field for realisation of the general objectives of integration, goes beyond monetary and exchange rate arrangements. The EMS would not have been launched without the political commitment to the idea of a united Europe held by France and Germany and their desire to regain momentum to this end. It was also an attempt both to revive the process towards politico-economic integration after the 1971–8 stagnation and to establish a limited area of monetary stability in the turbulence that followed the demise of the international fixed exchange rate system.

6.5 The European Monetary System

Mechanism

The institutional arrangements of the EMS include three activities:

1. The exchange rate mechanism (ERM).
2. Credit facilities to help defend these pegged rates.
3. Establishment of the European Monetary Cooperation Fund (EMCF) which would ultimately be replaced by the European Monetary Fund (EMF).

These three activities of the EMS are described in the following.

The exchange rate mechanism

The EMS is based on an exchange rate mechanism of fixed, though adjustable, exchange rates. All members of the EMS may join the ERM. This obliges them to peg their exchange rates within certain bands. The members of the EC which do not participate in ERM are associate members of the EMS and take part in discussions on the functions and development of the system.

In practice there are two methods of pegging arrangements: the *parity grid*, which ties every currency to every other in a system of mutually agreed and consistent rates; and the *basket*, which ties every currency to a common currency unit. Under the parity grid, whenever a currency deviates from the agreed rate, all other exchange rates would also diverge. Hence, in this case all countries will respond, i.e. mutually assist the re-establishment of the agreed parity. Under the basket, a currency can diverge without effect on the parity of other currencies.

The EMS is based on a hybrid system, a basket with some features of the parity grid. The central rates of the parity grid are defined in terms of the *European Currency Unit*, the ECU. The ECU is a weighted basket of specific amounts of all the EC currencies. The weights of each currency in the basket are determined collectively by precise criteria based on the relative economic strength of each member country in the Community, such as each country's shares in EC GNP and intra-EC trade. The composition of the basket is re-examined every five years or on request, if the weight of any component currency has changed by more than 25 per cent. The current composition of the ECU and the weights of each currency are shown in Table 6.1.

The ECU is assigned four functions: it serves as (a) the denominator (numeraire) for the exchange rate mechanism; (b) the basis for a

Table 6.1   The ECU basket: weights, currency units and central rates[1].

National currency		Weight	Units	Central rate for 1 ECU
Belgian/Lux. franc	BFR/LFR	0.0790	3.431	42.4032
Danish krone	DKR	0.0245	0.1976	7.84195
Deutschmark	DM	0.3010	0.6242	2.05586
Dutch guilder	HFL	0.0940	0.2198	2.31643
French franc	FF	0.1900	1.332	6.89509
Greek drachma	DR	0.0080	1.44	205.311[2]
Italian lira	LIT	0.1015	151.8	1,538.24
Irish pound	IRL	0.0110	0.008552	0.767417
Portuguese escudo	ESC	0.0080	1.393	178.735[2]
Spanish peseta	PTA	0.0530	6.885	133.631
UK pound	UKL	0.1300	0.08784	0.696904

[1] Weights and units from 21 September 1989; central rates from 8 October 1990.
[2] Notional rate.

Source: *Bank of England Quarterly Bulletin*, **30**, No. 4, 1990.

divergence indicator; (c) the denominator for operations in both the intervention and credit mechanisms; and (d) the means of settlement between monetary authorities of the European Community.

As the standard of value of the ERM, the ECU is defined in relation to each currency, the *ECU central rate of exchange*. These central rates are used to establish a grid of implicit bilateral exchange rates around which permissive fluctuation margins of ±2.25 per cent (or, exceptionally for some countries, 6 per cent) are set.

The ECU also functions as the indicator of divergence. This indicator is a kind of early-warning system based on the spread observed between a currency's market rate in ECUs and its central rate. It flashes when a currency crosses its 'thresholds of divergence' (TD) which are fixed at 75 per cent of the maximum spread of divergence allowed for each currency: TD = 0.75 × 2.25 × 1 *minus* the weight of the currency in the ECU basket. Therefore, the larger the weight of a currency, the narrower is its 'threshold of divergence'. When a currency activates the early-warning system by crossing its TD, there is a 'presumption' that the country concerned will take remedial policy action (changes in interest rates, other changes in domestic economic policy) and, if necessary, unlimited intervention in the foreign exchange market (sales or purchases of currency by the central bank) to keep it within the permitted band of fluctuation. However, when a currency reaches its trigger point against another member's currency, it is expected that both countries will intervene to restore parity: the country of the weak currency borrows from the country with the strong currency as required. As a last resort, if market pressures become too great and the policies required to maintain exchange rates within the bands become unsustainable, adjustments of a more general nature are implemented by *realignment*, that is by mutually agreed devaluations/revaluations of the central rates. Realignments are also implemented when the trade balances and/or differences in inflation rates between the partners show the parities to be broadly out of line. Hence the EMS is not a system of irrevocably fixed exchange rates, but of managed exchange rates subject to periodic changes by collective decision and a common procedure.

Credit facilities

As a denominator of operations the ECU is the currency used for intervention by the monetary authorities of the member states, that is for buying or selling foreign exchange with the aim of influencing their national currency's market exchange rate. Credit facilities for these operations are provided by the EMS through the EMCF and are expressed in ECUs. To facilitate compulsory intervention, ERM participants created a 'very short-term financial facility' consisting of a reciprocal cash credit among their central banks. In addition, all EC members also have access to the following credit sources:

1. The 'short-term monetary support' which is a quasi-automatic facility that provides short-term (up to 75 days, but renewable for three months) finance for temporary balance-of-payments deficits. Under this facility each member is assigned a creditor quota that determines the extent of support it is expected to provide and a debtor quota that specifies the amount of assistance it can obtain.
2. *Medium-term financial assistance* for member states which are experiencing, or are seriously threatened with, difficulties in their balance of current payments or capital movements.
3. *Long-term mutual financial assistance* (up to 5 years).

Since 1985, central banks requiring intra-marginal (that is before the divergence thresholds have been reached) intervention funds can acquire dollars or Community currencies against their net creditor positions in ECUs with the EMCF, and repay in ECUs. It has also been decided that the official ECU may be held as reserve currency by non-EC countries.

The European Monetary Cooperation Fund

This fund is the central monetary institution of the Community. Its membership comprises the countries in the ERM of the EMS, and its board consists of the Governors of all the Community's central banks. The EMCF is essentially a bookkeeping operation. It issues ECUs to central banks in exchange for deposits by them of 20 per cent of their gold and dollar reserves in the form of a three-month revolving swaps, that is of combinations of a spot purchase (or sale) of a currency and a forward sale (or purchase) of the same currency at a fixed rate. Consequently, the ECUs issued are entirely matched by a counterpart deposit of gold and dollar reserves which do not actually change hands; they remain with the central banks of the member states which continue to manage them and earn interest on them. A drawback of this system is that the amount of ECUs created is determined by external factors (the value of dollars and gold) largely beyond the Community's control.

The everyday running of the EMS is currently assigned to the EMCF in consultation with member states' committees, such as the Monetary Committee and the Committee of EC Central Bank Governors. Final decisions are taken by the Council of Economic and Finance Ministers (Ecofin). The EMS agreement provided that the EMCF would be replaced by the EMF which, vested with institutional autonomy, would be developed as the central bank of the Community, administering a common monetary sector and holding the members' deposits on a permanent basis.

In response to changes in the economic and financial environment, the EMS mechanism has been extended and strengthened on two occasions (Palermo 1985 and Basle/Nyborg 1987). For similar reasons and in an attempt to edify the EMS, the European Council decided in 1985 to enshrine it in the EEC Treaty by a new Article 102A. This made the EMS and the ECU an essential part of the EC Treaty to be used as instruments for the progressive realisation of Economic and Monetary Union. Moreover, at the Luxembourg Conference in February 1986 the member states added in the Preamble of the revised Treaties (Single European Act) that Economic and Monetary Union is a long-term objective of integration in the Community and that the EMS is a stage towards achieving that goal.

Despite these innovations, many problems remained unresolved. First, not all members of the EC are full members of the EMS. Second, the convergence of fiscal policies had been insufficient, and this is reflected in the large and persistent budget deficits in certain member countries. Third, the EMS, being focused on rather short-term exchange stability, did not seem to be subject to a built-in evolutionary process which would transform it into the EMU. Moreover, as remarked earlier, the EMS system of pegged exchange rates at agreed values is maintained by the separate national central banks of the member states by coordinating domestic monetary policy appropriately. This system is successful for as long as the national central banks shape their policies solely with an external target objective, that of keeping the exchange rates of their currencies at the agreed level. However, if at any time pressures to use monetary policy for domestic purposes become irresistible, the exchange rate will become unstable. This may lead to periodic crises which, if they are major, may even cause the eventual collapse of the pegged exchange rate system. This is exactly what happened to the 'snake', the previous European exchange rate system. Consequently, a truly unified European currency would require the replacement of the decentralised system of national central banks by the central bank of the European Community and the introduction of a common currency. Wider acceptance of the need for a common currency within the Single European Market may provide the necessary impetus for closer economic and political integration leading to the European Economic and Monetary Union (EMU).

Performance

When the EMS was introduced, many observers found a variety of defects with it and predicted its imminent collapse. This was based, among other reasons, on the following arguments:

1. Nominal exchange rate rigidity will amplify the real exchange rate movements and increase the pressure for protection as a result of costs and prices in different member countries getting 'out of line'.
2. The asymmetry in the burden of exchange rate adjustment, which in effect requires only the weak currency countries to adjust, would force them to abandon the fixed exchange rates arrangement.
3. The availability of credit facilities would encourage diverging countries to postpone adjustment and this in turn could cause massive destabilising speculation.

However, the EMS surprised many by surviving a number of crises, and is still going strong.

For an assessment of the EMS we must examine whether the objectives set by the EC at the time of launching the system have been approached. Convergence of economic and financial policy among the members and establishment of a zone of monetary 'internal and external stability' are the two immediate objectives, while a third objective, that of creating Economic and Monetary Union in Europe, is the most important but also the most distant one. 'Internal and external stability' seems to have meant a reduction in the overall inflation level and in the differentials between member countries with a stabler/less volatile exchange rate. Therefore, the progress towards achieving these goals can be studied by examining the effects of the EMS on two related issues: exchange rate stability and convergence of economic policy and performance.

The performance of the EMS has been evaluated by comparing the *exchange rate volatility* between the participating currencies before and after the establishment of the system, and between them and currencies outside the system. Reported statistical findings confirm that, despite the unstable international monetary environment, relative stability of the currencies participating in the ERM of the EMS has been achieved: there is strong evidence of reduced intra-ERM exchange volatility after March 1979, and signs of increased volatility in dollar and (to a slightly lesser extent) sterling rates (Artis and Taylor, 1988). Moreover, the stability of the ERM exchange rates does not seem to have been reached at the cost of higher volatility of short-term interest rates, which in fact shows some evidence of reduction after 1979. These conclusions hold for both *nominal* exchange rates, which are the formal objective of the 'zone of monetary stability', and *real* exchange rates, regardless of the measure of variability chosen (International Monetary Fund, 1983; Artis, 1987). In general, the EMS 'has made a positive contribution to exchange rate stability' (EC Commission, 1984a) by successfully anchoring nominal exchange rates without causing intra-trade disturbances and misalignments in real exchange rates.

Convergence includes both the convergence of economic policy (money supply growth) and performance (inflation rates) among the members of the Community as well as the coordination of members' policies *vis-à-vis* third countries.

At the time of launching the EMS many observers argued that the system's fixed exchange rates would undermine the participating countries' ability to pursue domestic monetary targets in their anti-inflationary policies. Actually, the EMS has no direct mechanism for a common policy in pursuit of low inflation. Anti-inflationary policy is an outcome of the requirement that countries participating in the EMS are committed to operate coordinated and converging monetary policies. The evidence suggests that during the EMS years, monetary growth has been significantly lower than during the period of floating rates and that 'the EMS has not laid the ground for a looser monetary policy but rather provided a framework in which anti-inflationary policies could be pursued more effectively' (International Monetary Fund, 1986). In fact, average inflation in the ERM countries has fallen steadily from a peak of 11.6 per cent in 1980 to 2.3 per cent in 1986 (Russo and Tullio, 1988). Although price stability cannot be exclusively attributed to the existence of the EMS, the fact is that inflation in the member countries has been sharply reduced and convergence of inflation rates among the EMS members has occurred. Undoubtedly, the credibility of anti-inflation policy of the system increased by virtue of the close links between the monetary policies of the member states, France and Germany in particular. The EMS has so far succeeded not only in stabilising currencies but also in converging inflation rates towards Germany's low level. Germany provided the 'nominal anchor' for the EMS by ignoring the exchange rate of the Deutschmark against the other currencies in the ERM and regulating its money supply to control the German inflation rate. The other members of the system used their money supplies to maintain the fixed exchange rates against the Deutschmark, and allowed their inflation rates to follow that of Germany. This explains the asymmetry of the exchange rate adjustment mechanism in the EMS which was accepted by the participants as a solution to the problem of inflation (in the nth currency setting, see Section 6.3).

In conclusion, the experience of the first decade of the system suggests that the pessimistic predictions about its inflationary nature have not been borne out, nor can it be argued that participation in the EMS has actually reduced the ability of countries to pursue domestic anti-inflationary policies.

The EMS has also helped to decrease the frequency of simultaneous movements between the EC currencies and the dollar, thus asserting the independence and identity of European monetary policy. The unprecedented swings in the value of the dollar in the 1980s did not cause a symmetric response of the European currencies. This has been achieved mostly by the relatively strong performance of the Deutschmark in the world financial markets and the weight it carries in the EMS; hence by the implicit acceptance of German monetary leadership within the EMS and coordination of other members' monetary policy with that of Germany (Giavazzi and Pagano, 1986). Formally, as in the case of an inflation target, a target relationship between the EMS currencies and the dollar can be pursued on the basis of the *nth currency redundancy problem*. As remarked earlier (Section 6.3), if $n - 1$ countries employ monetary policy to keep the exchange rates fixed, the nth country does not need to do so. Then, by agreement between the partners, the nth country's redundant instrument (in this case the DM) can be employed to pursue an exchange rate target *vis-à-vis* a third currency (in this case the US dollar).

Another question concerns the operation of the EMS mechanism, in particular whether the divergence indicator has worked in practice as a reliable early warning signal of potential strains in the system. Critics have pointed out that under certain circumstances two currencies in the EMS could reach their intervention limits against one another well before the divergence alarm starts flashing. However, in practice the authorities recognised that there is no unique standard against which the deviations of all currencies can be measured and therefore did not rely exclusively on the divergence indicator for initiating policy changes. Despite this shortcoming, some observers argue that the divergence indicator provisions of the EMS have contributed positively to the stability of the system and the convergence of members' monetary policy by forcing 'monetary discipline', that is by inducing the participants to undertake action in time on their own initiative and at their own discretion (Melitz, 1988).

In conclusion, clearly the EMS has not yet completely achieved its objectives, but it has led to a significant degree of policy approximation and closer cooperation between the central banks of the members. However, this policy approximation has been almost exclusively concentrated in the field of direct monetary policy with as yet very little coordination in other policies, such as public deficit management which has a direct influence on monetary developments. Hence, the exchange rates in the EMS have tended to diverge, and this is one of the reasons for the frequency of realignments of the central rates (twelve since 1979 and in some cases by a wide margin). Nevertheless, timely and mutually agreed realignments have offered the opportunity for a thorough examination of the operation of the system and provided it with the flexibility which made it adapt to changing economic conditions, both domestic and international.

The ECU is used officially by the Community and all its institutions. However, a development which had not been envisaged at the time of the introduction of the EMS is the growth of markets in private ECUs, that is ECU-denominated financial instruments outside the context of the EMS. Although this was not much in evidence during the first years of the EMS, it took off in 1981. It is now a leading international loan currency, ranked fifth in international bond issues, with a 6 per cent market share. The comparatively high intra-EMS exchange rate stability and the fact that the ECU bond market is unique in that it lacks a clear-cut domestic counterpart, might explain why investors have turned to the ECU as a hedging against exchange rate risks. Since the ECU is a weighted average of all the EC currencies, each member currency can deviate less against the ECU ($\pm 2.25\%$) than against each other ($\pm 4.50\%$). Hence, as a hedge against currency risks, the ECU is preferable to any of its constituent currencies. Another benefit of using ECUs is that as a common currency it simplifies exchange and treasury management transactions. A practical step towards the greater use of the ECU in financial markets was taken in the summer of 1988, when the UK government offered to tender Treasury bills denominated and payable in ECUs.

6.6   The single market and European Monetary Union

The EMS provisions did not require capital market liberalisation, which is an integral part of an economic and monetary union. Controls hinder capital from flowing freely to the market of the highest yield and therefore they are obstacles to the optimal allocation of resources. Some ERM member states (France and Italy) retained considerable exchange and capital controls throughout the first ten EMS years. Indeed, many observers believe that the relative stability of the EMS can be attributed partly to the protection afforded by these controls rather than by the convergence of economic policies (Artis, 1988). According to this argument, capital controls shielded weak currencies from speculative attacks and isolated domestic interest rates from fluctuations in international markets. This narrowed the margin of domestic interest rate fluctuations and caused the need for constant monitoring of performance, with intervention in the form of realignments which kept the system on the right path. Once controls are lifted in a fixed exchange rate system, a large outflow of capital may lead to a sharp increase in domestic interest rates. Hence, with free capital mobility, domestic interest rates should become as volatile as those of open capital markets – and that would put the EMS under strain.

Further progress towards the EMU requires full integration of the financial markets. The question is whether the EMS will survive the removal of exchange controls. If in the course of financial integration the EMS system of fixed but adjustable parities does come under speculative pressure, then it would survive by either allowing greater exchange rate flexibility or removing flexibility altogether by adopting irrevocably fixed rates.

The counter-argument to all these is that, in general, there is no evidence that exchange controls are effective in the long run. Moreover, when exchange rates are completely and irrevocably fixed, the member countries have to accept the interest rate of the economic union. Departures from the common interest rate are short-lived and cannot serve any long-term objective. In the case of the EMS, Germany has been the interest rate setter, and the other members have followed. The controls play no role in this. When the EMS was set up in 1979, all members apart from Germany and the Netherlands had capital controls. Most of these controls had gone by 1988, with no undue difficulties to the countries concerned or to the EMS.

The Single European Act (EC, 1985a), which envisages the creation by 1992 of a large internal market comprising all the Community countries, has led to the formulation of the Delors plan which foresees two stages for advancing monetary integration. In the first stage, the aim is to achieve effective liberalisation of capital transactions most directly necessary for the proper functioning of the internal market. This came into effect on 1 March 1987 and concerns an unconditional liberalisation of capital movements most directly affecting the cross-border exchange of goods and non-financial services. The second stage involves the deregulation of all financial markets and the establishment of a single financial area, through the implementation of directives on banking, securities and insurance services. Following this recommendation, on a proposal from the Commission the Council adopted a Directive on the abolition of all remaining capital controls and complete liberalisation of capital movements by mid-1990.

France and Italy responded by abolishing their exchange controls well before the set deadline. Italy, which since the 'snake' had been allowed 6 per cent fluctuation margins around the central rate, also decided to adopt the narrower ±2.25 margins from January 1990. Four member states (Greece, Ireland, Portugal and Spain) were allowed the use of a derogation to maintain certain restrictions until 1992. The agreement is a precondition for the liberalisation of financial services within the single Community market by 1992 and the setting up of a common regulatory structure for financial institutions. It is expected that similar liberalisation measures will be adopted concerning capital movements occurring between EC and non-EC countries. Provided monetary policy in the EC remains a 'matter for common concern' and convergence in economic policy and performance continues unabated, 'the EMS should be able to function smoothly even after the liberalisation or abolition of capital controls' (Gros and Thygesen, 1988).

Another important step towards monetary integration was taken at the Hanover summit (June 1988), when the European Council set a special committee under the chairmanship of J. Delors, President of the European Commission, 'to study and propose concrete stages leading towards Economic and Monetary Union'. The Delors Report (EC Commission, 1989a) linked completion of the single market to a single currency, coordination of all macroeconomic policies and 'binding rules for budgetary policies'. As explained earlier, a certain degree of fiscal policy centralisation is considered essential because, if exchange rates between members are fixed and interest rates are the same in every member country, a fiscal expansion in one country would lead to a rise in prices in other countries and, under certain conditions, in the Community as a whole.

The report proposed three stages of transition towards EMU. During the first stage, all member states would participate in the ERM on equal terms (that is with ±2.25 fluctuation margins around the central rates), as full members of the EMS, and would endeavour to improve their economic policy coordination and convergence. All the impediments to the private use of the ECU would also be removed. During this stage, the existing committee of central bank governors will be allocated the task of making non-binding recommendations on how member central banks should conduct monetary policy, foreign market intervention and banking supervision. A new system for coordinating macroeconomic policy will include a twice-yearly review by the council of EC finance ministers of the general economic situation. This council will set objectives and make policy recommendations.

In the second stage, the member states would set guidelines for common economic objectives and precise rules on national budgetary deficits. They will also consider the setting up of a European System of Central Banks (ESCB) as an autonomous Community institution consisting of the national central banks of the member states ranged around a common central institution. Although throughout stage two ultimate responsibility for policy decisions would remain with national authorities, the federal structure of the ESCB would prepare the ground for moving gradually from national to common monetary policy and narrower fluctuation margins in exchange rates.

The final stage would begin with the introduction of irrevocably fixed exchange rates, common management by the ESCB of the pooled official reserves of the member states and binding guidelines on the exercise of monetary and budgetary policies. From then on the Community would act as a single entity in international policy measures. The formality of a central bank would follow, which would decide on any exchange rate and currency market intervention in third currencies and manage all the official reserves. Finally a single Community currency would be established. The report admits that monetary union will involve a transfer of power to the Community at the cost of national sovereignty, but argues that the gain will be greater economic opportunities for all the member countries. In any case the experience gained from operating the EMS shows that, as the economies of the member states become progressively more interdependent, sovereignty over monetary matters is something which can only be exercised fully at the level of the Community.

The Delors Report was considered by the European Council at the Madrid Summit in June 1989. The leaders of the twelve member states agreed that the first stage for establishing the EMU should start on 1 July 1990. This will be followed by an inter-governmental conference (IGC) by the end of 1990 to consider the EC Treaty changes needed to set up a federal banking system along lines suggested by the Delors Committee. The agreement was hailed by many observers as launching the EC definitely on the 'irreversible process' leading to a single European currency and to full EMU. The Community finance ministers also approved a set of regulations, the Second Banking Directive, to govern banking in the unified European markets after 1992. However, no explicit commitment was taken to proceed to the subsequent two stages and no date was set for the completion of the EMU.

The Strasbourg Summit in December 1989 confirmed that the inter-governmental conference to discuss the EMU will open in December 1990. Subsequently the EC central bank governors agreed to make their committee the forerunner of the European central banking system 'with price stability as a policy objective of all member central banks'. At a later stage, a common monetary policy will be fixed by the European central bank, but managed on its behalf by national central banks. The European central bank is envisaged as an independent central monetary institution which, free from political pressure, will pursue effective anti-inflation policies. Control of inflation will be the means for gaining and maintaining competitiveness in international trade. This decision has been seen as one of the most important steps towards the creation of the EMU with the central banks of the member states determined to take a much larger role in the framing of economic policy across Europe.

6.7 The United Kingdom and the European Monetary System

As a member of the EC, the United Kingdom was automatically an associate member of the EMS. But successive UK governments declined to make the country a full member of the EMS by locking sterling into the ERM, contending that 'the time is not ripe' because sterling was either overvalued or undervalued or even that, unlike the ERM currencies, sterling is a 'petro-currency' subject to the gyrations of oil prices. Finally, the United Kingdom joined the ERM in October 1990, eleven years after the launching of the EMS.

Throughout these years, the issue concerning the United Kingdom's full membership in the EMS has been associated with the question whether the UK government can effectively pursue domestic anti-inflationary policy, while subordinating domestic monetary policy to the requirements of exchange rate policy within the EMS. The UK governments since 1979 have declared that their prime objective is the permanent reduction in the rate of inflation. According to the monetarist dogma which they embraced, control of the rate of inflation requires control of money supply growth in a regime of flexible exchange rates. This would permit currency values to be determined in the foreign exchange market and allow each country to pursue a monetary growth target and to choose its own level of inflation. The price one has to pay for this freedom of choice includes high instability of financial markets, that is of exchange rates and interest rates.

This argument would have been a convincing reason for remaining outside the ERM if the UK economy had had a better record of reducing inflation than the countries in the ERM. However, the evidence shows that participation in the ERM has not proved inconsistent with a price stability target and adherence to domestic monetary targets. Actually, the average growth rates of monetary aggregates in the ERM countries have fallen; inflation rates have slowed down and inflation differentials narrowed; and nominal as well as real interest rates have converged (Padoa-Schioppa, 1985). Moreover, while the average rate of inflation of the ERM members was falling, that of the UK was the highest among the main industrialised countries. Similarly, the wage increases in the United Kingdom were running at an annual rate three times higher than the rate in France and Germany. In addition to these problems, the fluctuations in interest rates and exchange rates experienced by the United Kingdom have been particularly severe. For example, when the United Kingdom introduced tight monetary policy in 1980 to control inflation (the 'medium term financial strategy'), sterling over-appreciated against other currencies, reaching $2.45. This appreciation reduced inflation inside the United Kingdom, by making import prices (in pounds) much lower. But it also made export prices much higher, thus reducing the United Kingdom's competitiveness and causing a dramatic fall in employment and output of industries producing exportables. But when the United States adopted tight monetary policy and expansionary fiscal policy from 1981, the US dollar appreciated against other currencies and the pound plummeted to $1.04 in 1985, threatening the resurgence in domestic inflation and the spillover of US inflation by increased US imports.

The UK government's objections to these arguments were that the EMS discipline has worked for the ERM countries only because their capital markets were still protected by explicit (France, Italy) or implicit (Germany) controls on international capital flows, while the United Kingdom's capital market had been completely liberalised. Accordingly, the United Kingdom was crucially different from the other EMS members. Therefore, if it were to become a member of the ERM, a higher underlying rate of inflation would not have been contained by the EMS exchange rate discipline.

However, the differences in relative monetary performance between the United Kingdom and the EMS member states can be explained by a different set of arguments:

1. One of the basic objectives of the EMS and the countries particip-

ating in it is to curb inflation; this objective has on the whole been met by the sharp reduction of inflation rates in the ERM countries.

2. The EMS is not a system of rigidly fixed exchange rates. Full membership of the system provides the members with sufficient exchange rate flexibility (around the agreed central rates) to exercise adequate control over their money supply.

3. In an economic union and, in general, in an integrated world market the independence of national monetary policy is severely curtailed under both floating and fixed exchange rates; therefore the basic monetarist propositions are subject to qualifications.

In an increasingly integrated world, interdependence is also increasing irrespective of the exchange rate regime (Swoboda, 1983; see also Section 6.3). Economic interdependence causes substantial spillover effects from one country to another to the extent that the demand and supply of money transgress national frontiers. Therefore, it cannot any more be assumed that the demand for money is stable or that the increase in money supply is determined by the domestic supply of money. In the integrated world markets, the demand for money takes the form of a diversified portfolio of different currencies which together with the growth of the world money supply determine the rate of inflation. Hence, the proposition that inflation will be reduced if the ratio of domestic money to a stable domestic demand for money is reduced, is a necessary but not a sufficient condition. What is required is international monetary cooperation which has not as yet been re-established. The EMS aims at, and has already made some progress towards, international monetary cooperation by establishing 'a zone of [relative] monetary stability in Europe'. Similarly, the argument that by participating in the EMS countries lose the power to use monetary policy 'to alter the competitive relationship between one country's products and others' (Minford, 1990a) has no validity within an economic union. If every member country behaves in this way, the economic union is redundant and the outcome is trade war with sure losses for all.

The wide fluctuations in exchange rates induced a change in attitudes which were formalised by the Plaza agreement on exchange rates (1985), following which there was a shift from domestic inflation targets towards exchange rate management. In the United Kingdom this took the form of an increase in money growth rates at the same time as the focus of policy was switched towards interest and exchange rates. Although the UK government had refused to put sterling in the ERM, in 1987 and early 1988 the pound followed the movements of the DM so closely that it became a *de facto* full member of the EMS. The assumption made at that time was that, after abandoning the money stock targets, a policy of shadowing the DM rather than joining the EMS provided an anchor against domestic inflation combined with flexibility in monetary and fiscal policy. The link between sterling and the DM was maintained by increasing interest rates when the pound was falling, and decreasing them when the pound was rising. However, the combination of a strong pound and low interest rates obviously has different effects on domestic demand from that of a weak pound and high interest rates.

In 1985 the monetary controls on the economy were relaxed and deregulation of the financial markets led to a credit boom that encouraged expansion of demand. Further increases in demand were also induced by successive cuts in income tax rates. However, supply was in no shape to respond and when in early 1988 sterling kept appreciating against the DM while domestic credit and money supply kept rising fast, the alternatives left to the UK authorities were either to maintain currency stability by reducing interest rates, which might increase the rate of inflation, or to contain the rise in inflation by increasing interest rates and allowing sterling to rise further. Confirming that its first priority was to fight inflation, the UK government chose the second alternative by uncapping the pound from the DM and increasing interest rates by ten successive steps during 1988 which pushed the pound up. Such a diversion of monetary policy from exchange rate to domestic price targets would not have been possible under full membership in the EMS.

When the links with the DM were broken, the United Kingdom's monetary policy was left anchorless. The adopted policy would in the short term reduce the rate of inflation. However, its effects on the foreign trade sector were detrimental: UK imports rose at twice the pace of exports and the balance-of-payments deficit reached record levels. Whether any currency can remain strong under these conditions is ultimately decided by the financial markets. However, if in the longer term the effect of a strong pound and high interest rates is to reduce investment and to push up wages and prices, the international competitiveness of the UK economy will decline.

Critics of the government's policies argued that, arising from international interdependence, which is particularly strong and rising between the EC members, the UK 'sovereignty' over domestic monetary policy is already small and declining. Therefore, monetary policies which are based on the strong assumption of 'independence and sovereignty' cannot be very successful. For example, when in September 1989 Germany raised its interest rate, the United Kingdom followed suit, increasing its interest rate within an hour and by the same amount, thus proving that, despite the UK government's insistence that money matters are a vital part of a nation's sovereign rights, there is no monetary independence in interdependent economies.

All these do not necessarily mean, although it is frequently argued, that the situation would have been radically different and much better, if the United Kingdom had formally joined the EMS at an earlier date. The EMS should not be seen as a universal panacea: if there are structural problems in the UK economy causing instability and inflation, they will not be solved by participation in the ERM. In general, membership of the EMS must be seen as an integral part of the process of economic integration which may or may not confer short-term benefits.

Another argument against sterling's entry in the ERM was based on the observation that, under fixed exchange rates and free capital mobility in the EMS, capital will flood into the currencies offering the highest interest rates, which are the currencies of the high-inflation countries. However, when the fight against inflation would have dictated a rise in interest rates, participation in the EMS forces the high-inflation countries to cut interest rates in order to prevent their currencies from breaching their upper limits. In other words, the fixed exchange rates of the EMS exert pressure on nominal interest rates between countries to converge. In the case of the United Kingdom, where inflation is relatively high, this convergence of interest rates to levels prevailing in low-inflation countries could be inappropriate for domestic anti-inflationary policy. A low interest rate may cause acceleration of UK's monetary growth with further inflationary implications. Outside the ERM, this problem can be countered by interest rate increases as well as currency appreciation (Walters, 1990). Therefore, it was argued that for as long as the inflation rate in the United Kingdom remained much higher than that of its partners in the EC, the United Kingdom should not join the ERM. This argument was based on the monetarist assumption that the interest rate is the main (or even the only) policy instrument for combating inflation. The counter-argument is that a combination of monetary and fiscal policy may be proved more effective under the circumstances prevailing in the EC. In any case, the experience of the ERM countries shows that, under relatively free capital mobility, the divergence in national interest rates has been substantial.

Although the UK government eloquently protected its sovereignty on monetary matters, it officially accepted the Delors Report at the Madrid Summit and agreed to join the exchange rate mechanism of the EMS if certain conditions were met. The conditions were that (a) the United Kingdom should have made substantial progress in reducing inflation; (b) the European internal market should be completed; (c) EC competition policies should be strengthened by the abolition of state subsidies and protectionist measures; and (d) all the EC countries should liberalise all capital movements and financial services. Given the timetable for abolition of exchange controls in Portugal and Greece, the latter condition was interpreted by some observers as an attempt by the UK government to keep sterling out of the EMS at least until the mid-1990s. However, recent developments proved that, for UK domestic economic and political reasons, this was not to be the case. After redefining the Madrid conditions to mean 'reasonable expectations of' a substantial fall in UK inflation and of progress in the process of market liberalisation in the rest of the EC, the United Kingdom joined the ERM, but at the ±6 per cent margins 'for an initial period'. It also signed the proposed statutes for an independent European Central Bank (November, 1990) but only after entering a strongly worded note of 'general reservation', that the United Kingdom did not accept the case either for a single currency or for a European monetary authority.

While the question was about the speed of implementing the EMU, the United Kingdom produced its own plans for a loose monetary integration based on the competing currencies and parallel currencies proposals which the EC partners considered and rejected long ago as inflationary and impractical. The latest UK attempt for blocking EMU yielded a plan for parallel circulation of national currencies along with a 'hard ECU', which 'would appeal to tourists and business travellers' and in the very long run, 'if peoples and governments so choose', it could develop into a single currency. However, this plan of $n + 1$ currencies attracted no support from other member states which have already decided that 'monetary union implies nothing less than a single currency, a single, independent central bank and a single, EC-wide, monetary policy' (*The Times*, 26 June 1990).

Sterling's entry in the ERM has eliminated one of the obstacles towards EMU. It has also provided the EMS with greater monetary cohesion which in turn could make it gain more influence over financial markets for a wider agreement on European and international monetary cooperation. However, the United Kingdom still remains the most sceptical among the EC countries about the benefits of EMU and the most reluctant to give up its sovereignty over monetary matters in exchange for a common monetary policy and a single currency run by administrators. However, the United Kingdom realises that if it would continue its objections against EMU, those countries committed to monetary union will push ahead with the process leading to eventual merger of their monetary policies, and this would probably be the first step towards the *de facto* creation of a two-speed Europe, in which the enthusiasts make faster progress towards integration, while the rest are left behind. Obviously, the members of the second tier cannot expect to have much influence in the development of the economic union. Hence, the possibility is that, despite its justifiable hesitations, in the end the United Kingdom will help formulate the right plan for moving together all the participants in the EC towards EMU.

Further reading

The studies in Giavazzi *et al.* (1988) are an excellent source of analysis and information about monetary integration and the EMS. For the performance of the EMS see Artis (1987, 1988), Artis and Taylor (1988) and Minford (1990b). For the Commission's views on monetary unification and the ECU see EC Commission (1975a) and EC (1987a). For EMU see the Delors Report, EC Commission (1989a). Three informative articles on EMU, ERM and EMS are Wickens (1990), and Zis (1988, 1989).

The benefits from the EC's move to a common currency and the problems of the United Kingdom's participation in the ERM are discussed in Goodhart (1990). For the United Kingdom's alternative proposals to the EMS see HM Treasury (1989) and Minford (1990a, 1990b). For the latest UK parallel currencies proposal see *The Economist*, volume 315 (7660), 23 June 1990. Professor A. Walters is a critic of the EMS, who argues that, under fixed exchange rates and free capital mobility, the ensuing common interest rate would be too low in the high-inflation countries, thereby causing excessive monetary growth which would prevent inflation from falling: see Walters (1988, 1990). Notice that this problem would not arise under EMU and a common inflation rate.

7

Agriculture

7.1 Introduction

Agriculture has historically been considered special for economic, social and strategic reasons. As a result of this, in almost every industrial country and in many less developed countries governments intervene in the agricultural sector, in an attempt to modify its course and regulate the production and trade of agricultural commodities. The justification of government intervention is based on the principle that an institutional structure rather than the free market will move the agricultural sector towards preferred directions. The specific objectives of government intervention are usually four:

1. The desire to maintain a certain degree of self-sufficiency in agricultural products, particularly food, because of the risk of interruption or curtailment of foreign supplies, e.g. in the case of war.
2. The saving of foreign exchange arising from the availability of domestic supply rather than imports of agricultural products for domestic consumption and exports.
3. The stabilisation of prices at reasonable levels, for both the consumer and the producer, as the means for reducing hardship and uncertainty, and for encouraging investment and growth in the agricultural sector.
4. The desire to improve efficiency and productivity in the agricultural sector as the means for raising the level and the rate of growth of agricultural incomes.

The last two of these reasons are loosely based on the assumed existence of market failures and, in developed economies, are frequently used as the dominant excuse for government intervention in agriculture. Furthermore, government assistance to agriculture is often justified on the assertion that farming is not only riskier than other enterprises, but mechanisms for hedging that risk are limited in conventional private markets. A more recent excuse for intervention in agriculture is an awareness of another form of market failure associated with the conservation of resources and environmental issues. There often exists a divergence between the interest of societies at large and farmers in terms of land use and water resources, pollution, erosion and common property problems.

However, more often than not, the reasons for supporting the agricultural sector are based on political, economic and social criteria, both domestic and international. It is commonly argued that in most developed countries the agricultural support policies are frequently a reflection of vested interests and rent-seeking behaviour, the outcome of the relative power of sectoral lobbies and the influence of special and political constituencies rather than purely economic considerations. Although this may be so, in this section we will mostly review the economic rationale for agricultural policy, beginning with an examination of the structure of the agricultural sector and the markets for its inputs and outputs.

7.2 Problems of the agricultural sector

A general characteristic of the agricultural sector is that the markets for its output, free from intervention, possess most of the features of the competitive market model; namely, the number of firms is large, entry of new firms in the industry is unrestricted and the output of each commodity is on the whole homogeneous. However, as with most markets, information about the future quantity and prices of output and production techniques is imperfect. But these problems are made more complicated in agriculture than in other sectors by certain features of the short- and long-term demand and supply, in both the markets for agricultural commodities and factors of production. Furthermore, agriculture can be both an economic and a social problem. Although some farm enterprises are big agro-businesses, even in developed countries farms are typically small family units in which all or most labour is supplied by the family and the proprietor is the sole supplier of risk capital. Since the farmer generally lives on the farm, farming is a way of life rather than a modern business, and in some respects at the periphery, for example, (e.g. hill or island farming) it is not very different from subsistence agriculture.

All these characteristics of the agricultural sector in a way make government intervention in agriculture almost inevitable.

The most obvious manifestation of the peculiarities of the agricultural sector is that agricultural incomes are on the whole relatively low and fluctuate widely, and their rate of growth lags behind the national average. Specifically, for these reasons government intervention is often defended on considerations of *relative* national welfare, that is on the premise that the market mechanism does not on its own lead to a 'fair' distribution of national income between agriculture and the other sectors of the economy. Moreover, it is not only that there is an income gap between agriculture and the other sectors of the economy, but also that, in the absence of any positive policy, the process of economic growth tends to make this gap wider. In the following we examine: (a) the determination of prices and quantities in the markets for agricultural products; and (b) the characteristics of factor markets of the agricultural sector.

Determination of prices

The supply of agricultural products is characterised by short-term fluctuations and long-term trends which operate against the share of the sector in the production and distribution of national income. The reasons for this phenomenon are that, relative to other sectors of the economy such as manufacturing, the prices of agricultural products are flexible and the quantities of output can vary widely from year to year between gluts and shortages. Moreover in the longer term, technical progress brings about cost reductions which, owing to the competitive structure of the sector and contrary to the experience of other industries, are passed on to the consumer in the form of lower prices.

Short-term fluctuations in production are caused by the crucial dependence of agriculture on natural conditions such as the soil, climate and weather; on the incidence of pests and diseases affecting both crops and animals; and on biological constraints which result in the concentration of the flow of output into certain years or seasons within a year. Since in agriculture the output of many subsectors is frequently the input to other subsectors (e.g. cereals as animal feed), generalised fluctuations in the volume of agricultural output are not uncommon. Moreover, the relatively long time-lag between committing resources to production and gathering the output, a process which once started is not easily reversed, also means that the supply of agricultural products is in the short term unresponsive to changes in market conditions. Fluctuations in the short-term supply are therefore common and unpredictable.

In the longer term, modern agriculture is characterised by rapid technical and economic change, both of which tend to increase factor productivity. Rapid technical innovation in agriculture tends to increase the use of capital, to limit the need for more land and to decrease the use of manpower. Economic improvement occurs from the move towards more optimal plant size and the realisation of economies of scale, specialisation and cost-reducing advances in organisation and management. These developments also tend to accelerate the rate of substitution of capital for manpower and thus to decrease the utilisation of labour per unit of output. Hence in the longer run more is produced with less factor input and therefore the cost per unit of output is falling over time. It is alleged that in agriculture the competitive character of the markets implies that these cost reductions do not in general lead to higher profits per unit of output or to higher rewards to factors of production, but to lower prices for the consumer. This is in sharp contrast to manufacturing industry, where the presumed oligopolistic structure of markets for both commodities and factors of production ensures that technical innovation does not so much lead to lower consumer prices but rather to higher factor rewards.

On the other side of the market, the demand for agricultural products is characterised by low price and income elasticities. Consequently, as the economy grows and national income rises, expenditure on food is allocated a declining share.

Low-price elasticity of demand means that a fall in the price of a commodity at a given level of income will induce an increase in the quantity bought but proportionally smaller than the fall in the price. Therefore, producers' revenue from the sale of output will fall. Low-income elasticity of demand means that, at given commodity prices, as per capita incomes rise with economic growth, the demand shifts increasingly against the purchases of staples (i.e. resource-based products), so that the share of consumers' spending on purchases of these products, food in particular, falls – this is known as *Engel's Law*. Therefore, if productivity grows at the same rate in all sectors of the economy, the growth of income will cause the demand to shift against food in favour of luxuries, or, in general, against agricultural products in favour of manufactures. Consequently, the price of agricultural products falls and that of manufactures rises. These features of the demand, in association with the problems of the supply side of the market, tend to affect the agricultural sector adversely relative to other sectors of the economy. Rapid technical progress leading to relatively fast growth in the production and supply of agricultural products, combined with a declining demand, depresses agricultural prices and exacerbates the difference between the incomes of the agricultural sector and the rest of the economy. Agricultural incomes thus lag behind the rate of growth of national income without prospects of ever catching up. Fluctuating production, depressed product prices and increasing costs may also be the cause of farm income instability.

Factor market problems

Yield and price uncertainties imply that the agricultural industry is in the short term a relatively risky activity, and in the long term it is relatively unrewarding. Since many agricultural products are perishable, it is difficult and costly to build up stocks as a buffer against erratic short-term fluctuations of the supply. In the longer run, any solution to the problems of agriculture would involve the implementation of structural changes which would shift resources – surplus manpower in particular – from agriculture to activities which offer higher rewards. Typically, agricultural development is characterised by resource substitution, capital replacing both labour and land, leading to rising productivity. Ideally, this reallocation of resources should be initiated by market forces and be continued until the rewards of each factor are equalised between different uses. But, although following economic growth emigration of resources from agriculture occurs, its pace is frequently slow and uncoordinated, so that the differentials of factor rewards between sectors persist and widen. The slow mobility of factors of production employed in agriculture is caused by both economic and social reasons. An important economic reason is the high degree of *specificity* of the land, capital and labour that are engaged in the production of agricultural products. This means that these factors are not instantaneously and costlessly adaptable to other uses; structural changes take time and money.

Additional problems arise because the transfer of factors of production from agriculture to other sectors is almost always characterised not only by occupational limitations but also by the necessity for geographic mobility. This requirement gives rise to the social causes of relative factor immobility. Farmers in particular will reluctantly abandon their 'way of life', independence and abode in search for new employment and higher rewards, most probably in an urban environment. They prefer instead to continue living on the land in their traditional ways, frequently reacting to the fall in revenues by attempting to increase their productivity. More often than not, this form of individual behaviour may collectively lead the sector to yet more increases in supply, falling prices and further erosion of the agricultural incomes.

7.3   Policies

The preceding discussion shows that the agricultural sector may be subject to certain distinctive types of market failure. If this is the case, then the aim of government policy should be to restore the operations of the free market as the means of achieving optimal allocation of resources. Still, for a number of strategic, political, economic and social reasons governments intervene in agriculture in order to enable the sector to meet an adequate level of production for a target level of national self-sufficiency in output, with the added restriction that the factors engaged in agriculture receive renumerations comparable to those of other sectors in the economy. This objective is usually pursued by policies of direct intervention in the markets for factors of production and commodities, which attempt to stabilise prices and minimise unwarranted fluctuations in output. Policies for achieving this objective are many, hence the government has to choose the one it considers most appropriate under the prevailing circumstances.

Optimality requires that each policy instrument is assigned to the target on which it has the greatest impact. But as we have seen, governments in general use agricultural policy to pursue a number of different objectives, some economic and others social and political. Consequently, in the abstract, there is no single policy which is superior or more effective than any other under all circumstances. Depending on the particular problem in hand, the nature of the target in the short and the long run, and other economic, social and political constraints, governments apply to their agricultural sectors not one but a combination of policy instruments to achieve a number of objectives. In general, government intervention broadly takes into consideration the interests of both the consumers and the producers of agricultural commodities. However, in the field of pressure group politics, especially of developed economies, the farmers' lobby is relatively smaller, more homogeneous, better organised and more vociferous and powerful than the consumers' group, and it usually wins.

The policies available to governments differ in effectiveness and implications, particularly with regard to income distribution and resource allocation. The latter as a rule is affected negatively, that is in directions other than those which the free market would have dictated. This is frequently justified as a *temporary expediency* within a spectrum of objectives among which 'efficiency' is not ranked high in the government's list of priorities. The effects on income distribution are associated with the financing of the policy and other indirect costs. As a rule, policies which raise the market price of the protected commodity directly affect (i.e. are paid for by) the consumer of that commodity, while policies which do not raise the commodity's market price involve budgetary transfers and are paid for by the taxpayer. The two groups, consumers and taxpayers, are not necessarily identical. Significant differences may also exist in the cost of implementation and administration of the different policies.

Two general groups of policies can be distinguished: price stabilisation policies and income support policies.

Price stabilisation policies

These policies attempt to stabilise prices, usually at a relatively high level, by eliminating unwarranted price fluctuations caused by the interaction of variable supplies with an inelastic demand. They take the form of price controls and quantity controls. Their cost is mainly borne by consumers.

Price controls are policies directly applied on market prices for the purpose of changing them, or preventing them from changing by market forces. They include the following types:

1. Price fixing, which can be sustained only if the government eliminates from the market any disequilibrium tendencies by buying-in for stock all excess supplies, and selling-out (from stock or imports) all excess demands. A budgetary cost is incurred in stockpiling.
2. Tariffs and levies on imports, which raise domestic prices if the country is a net importer of the relevant commodity. Restrictive sanitary requirements have similar effects on the volume of imports. An alternative policy is to define a threshold or minimum import price – and hence a domestic price – by the imposition of a variable levy on import price.

Quantity controls are policies which alter directly the quantity of supply in the market as the means for changing market prices. They take the following form:

1. Building up of stocks as a buffer between production and consumption, at budgetary cost. The stocks are augmented when, relative to demand, supply is plentiful and reduced when supplies are scarce, so that short-term price fluctuations are minimised. This policy applies to commodities with inelastic demand and variable supply, provided they can be stored without undue deterioration or prohibitive cost.

2. Quota controls on imports, which reduce the supply and raise prices as in the case of tariffs.
3. Supply controls, such as the destruction of part of the available output as the means for reducing the quantity entering the market and thus eliminating the pressure on prices to fall.
4. Production controls, such as acreage quotas, licensing and diversion, etc., as an attempt to reduce the supply of output at the production stage and thus raise commodity prices.
5. Export subsidies, which can be included here as an indirect measure for controlling the residual quantity of output remaining available for supply in the domestic market. The subsidy is an inducement to export so that the residual supply for the domestic market is reduced and the domestic price rises. This policy affects both the taxpayer, who carries the burden of financing the subsidy, and the domestic consumer, who pays higher prices.

Income support policies

These policies have a budgetary cost and are divided into those that are indirect and those that are direct.

Indirect income support policies raise the price producers receive for their output as the means for increasing their revenue and income, leaving the domestic market price unaffected. They take the following forms:

1. Subsidies at the production stage (input subsidies) or at the output stage. The latter are fixed payments per unit or unit price of output. Subsidies reduce marginal cost of production to increase producer income.
2. Deficiency payments. The state makes up the difference between a guarantee price and the average price received by the producers from selling their output in the unprotected domestic market.

Direct income support policies are lump sum transfers related to or independent of the volume, price, revenue or income of agricultural activity. Naturally, this policy is the most effective for reaching a target level of income for the agricultural population but, while it leaves the domestic prices of agricultural commodities unaffected, it may carry high administrative costs.

In addition to the above short- to medium-term policies the government may operate long-term policies for changes in the structure and productivity of the agricultural sector, e.g. by investment on physical infrastructure, research and development. Expenditure on rural roads and other public works, land reclamation, conservation and environmental programmes are included in this category of government policy. If spending on these activities diverts resources away from competitive industries, the effects would be lasting and detrimental. Exchange rate policies in support of agricultural markets also have detrimental long-term effects on the national economy. In general, undervalued, overvalued and multiple exchange rates distort comparative advantage, do not produce a sustainable balance-of-payments outcome, and have harmful effects on the national economy.

Effects of government policies

If the economy is operating efficiently and the government intervenes in the agricultural sector, then the outcome is distortive and has income redistribution and factor misallocation effects with negative implications for national welfare. By restricting imports and promoting exports of agricultural products, government policies adversely affect the production and exchange of other trading sectors in the economy and the country's international comparative advantage. The reason for this is that the growth of the agricultural sector and agriculture-related industries is assisted at the expense of other traded goods sectors.

The problem is quite different if, to start with, the economy is not operating efficiently and the objective of government policy is to eliminate existing distortions affecting the agricultural sector. If this is the case, then the question is not whether government intervention is necessary, but which particular policy is the best for restoring optimality. Similar considerations apply if the objective of the policy is a more specific one. For example, if society's objective is to increase incomes or employment in the agricultural sector, then direct income supplements or employment subsidies are the most efficient policies to adopt. However, if there is a disparity between farm and non-farm incomes arising from misallocation of resources which allow the retention in agriculture of excess labour, then policies designed to raise farmers' incomes will not improve the allocation of resources. If agriculture is competitive, while manufacturing industry is oligopolistic and protected from international competition by trade barriers, then attempting to correct the misallocation of resources by price or income support policies in the agricultural sector will be a misguided exercise which most probably will not improve the situation. The problem of operating in a suboptimal world is that if all the conditions for maximum efficiency are not met simultaneously, then fulfilment of some of these conditions will not necessarily increase welfare – another case of the general theory of second best (as discussed in Chapter 1).

7.4 The Common Agricultural Policy

Principles

A recurrent theme in our analysis is that the main objective of the EC is the enlargement of the market, preferably in its free form, with market-determined solutions to economic problems. However, the market is the means to an end, and departures from market-determined solutions are not excluded *a priori*. For example, if the structure of the market is imperfect or if the prices of commodities and factors of production adjust sluggishly to changing market conditions, then intervention may be required to eliminate distortions or to assist the operation of the market mechanism. Nevertheless, the principle of competition on equal terms, which common markets adopt, implies that whenever intervention is deemed necessary, it must be general. That is, the interventionist policy must be applied equally to each member state. This means that the national agricultural policies existing in the member states prior to the formation of the EC had to be dismantled and to be replaced by a Common Agricultural Policy (CAP). Unequal relative size and level of development of the agricultural sector in each member state, different natural environment and different social, political and economic objectives meant that the countries that formed the EC pursued in the past different, but strongly interventionist, national agricultural policies. The presence of these policies later determined the principles, the structure and, to a large extent, the flaws of the CAP.

Nature and government policies shaped in turn the structure of agricultural production and prices in each country, in such a way that the members' agricultural sectors collectively were a markedly heterogeneous group. Therefore, when the EC countries decided to tackle in common the agricultural problem by establishing a Community agricultural policy, they embarked on a task of immense economic and social implications. Despite the difficulties which this has caused from the very start of the Community and the many problems which still remain unresolved, many observers argue that on the whole the EC has succeeded in establishing the most fully fledged Community policy, but at a substantial cost.

The Common Agricultural Policy in a way still reflects a balance of interests and a compromise among the original six Community members, all of which were developed and predominantly industrial countries, but continued to have vested social and economic interests in their relatively small agricultural sectors.

The main objectives of the Common Agricultural Policy are defined in the EEC Treaty (Article 39) as follows:

(a) To increase agricultural productivity by promoting technical progress and by ensuring the rational development of agricultural production and the optimum utilisation of the factors of production, in particular labour;
(b) thus to ensure a fair standard of living for the agricultural community, in particular by increasing the individual earnings of persons engaged in agriculture;
(c) to stabilise markets;
(d) to assure the availability of supplies;
(e) to ensure that supplies reach the consumers at reasonable prices

The particular policies by which these objectives would be attained are also outlined in broad terms in the Treaty (Articles 40–47), but it was left to the institutions of the Community, following prescribed procedures, to work out the details. For these purposes a conference of agricultural ministries and farmers' organisations was held at Stressa in 1958 which passed a number of resolutions dealing with the principles for a common agricultural policy in the Community. The CAP has been based on these principles ever since.

In general, since its inception the CAP was constructed upon three principles which guide every policy: the single market, Community preference and financial solidarity.

A single market means the free movement of agricultural produce within the Community. This requires the abolition of every distortion on competition (such as barriers to trade, subsidies, etc.) at the member country level. The unification of the market for agricultural products implies central administration regulations, policies and market organisation, resulting in common prices. Community policy is that these prices are to be administered in such a way that the objective of the EC is achieved: they should provide the farmers with remunerations at levels comparable to those enjoyed by other sectors of the economy.

Community preference within an integrated domestic market means protection from external influences, such as competitive imports and price fluctuations in the world markets. Protection is necessary because conditions in the Community differ greatly from those in the large exporting countries outside Europe and Community costs are on the whole high, and because Community prices are regulated as instruments of policy for the attainment of specified targets. Hence, Community prices are generally higher than the prices of the competitive market, which in any case are often distorted by government intervention. Since the aim of the CAP is not self-sufficiency and world market prices are policy-determined, the principle of Community preference also extends to embrace policies for export promotion. *Financial solidarity* means sharing the cost of the CAP among the member states and centralisation of the necessary funding. This task was allocated to a specially established community organisation, the European Agricultural Guidance and Guarantee Fund (EAGGF). The 'guarantee' section of the Fund finances the intervention policies of the CAP, while the 'guidance' section administers funds intended for policies of structural reform.

During the operation of the CAP, more objectives have emerged, reflecting inadequacies of the existing policies or new trends in public affairs. Thus, in recent years more emphasis has been given to problems of regional inequalities in the agricultural sectors of the member states and to concern about the relationship between agriculture, conservationism and environmental protection (*Bulletin EC*, Supplement 4, 1983b). These new issues affect the nature of policies dealing with agriculture in the EC by introducing additional constraints in the implementation of the CAP.

Method

The CAP covers all the quantitatively important agricultural products of the EC. The actual policy mechanism varies to some extent from product to product. However, we can study most of its important characteristics in the organisation of the market for cereals which, since the inception of the CAP, has been regarded as 'the model'. Cereals occupy a central role in the agricultural sector of the Community, first, as a quantitatively important final product of the sector, and second, as an input to further processes within the sector, e.g. as food for livestock.

The policy and its implications are presented in the following with the help of a diagram which is based on oversimplified assumptions, but at the same time draws attention to the most essential aspects of the problem. In Figure 7.1 the EC supply curve of cereals is upward sloping, indicating increasing costs of production, while the world supply of cereals is low-priced and perfectly elastic. After taking into consideration local price differentials arising from transportation costs and storage, the EC Council of Ministers of Agriculture fixes annually a *target price* P_t (known as the 'guide price' for beef, veal and wine, and as the 'norm price' for tobacco). This is the maximum, or the upper limit, of the price, for a standard quality of produce, which is desirable or 'optimum' for the realisation of the CAP objectives. The target price,

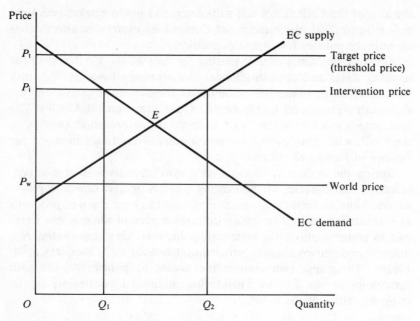

Figure 7.1 Common Agricultural Policy.

which is well above the world price, P_w, and the equilibrium market price, E, of the closed economy, is set on an annual basis for each commodity in the 'zone of greatest deficit' between production and demand. Consequently, at the target price there will be excess domestic supply and threat of competition from imports, both of which will tend to reduce market prices and so to undermine the policy objective of the Community. Hence, both these threats are dealt with by the policy.

The permissive minimum, or lower limit, of market price fluctuation is the *intervention price*, P_i (known as the 'basic price' for pigmeat) at which the Community halts the downward pressure of domestic supply on prices by purchasing the excess quantity on offer. Therefore, the CAP fixes a band of permissive price fluctuations which provides the producer with absolute certainty that the lowest price he can expect to receive for selling his output is the intervention price, P_i. The CAP's 'institutional' prices are fixed annually by the Council of Ministers on the basis of proposals by the Commission.

Since the market prices are allowed to fluctuate only within the range established by the target and the intervention prices, foreign trade is assigned only a supportive role. Thus, the lowest internal price for imports from any non-member country is the *threshold price* (known as the 'reference price' for fruits, vegetables, wine and fishery products, and as the 'sluice-gate price' for pork, eggs and poultry meat), which is fixed at or just above the target price. The lowest import price on offer (inclusive of transport, storage and incidental costs) is raised to the level of the threshold price by the imposition of the appropriate *levy* $P_t - P_w$, which is calculated on a daily basis and then applies equally to all imports regardless of source and cost of supply. Thus the levy is variable and operates as an equalising tariff, whose variation depends on the difference between minimum current international prices and domestic target prices. However, if for any reason the EC domestic prices tend to rise above the target price, imports become competitive, enter the market and keep domestic prices steady at the threshold price. In this way the consumer is guaranteed that prices will never exceed the threshold price.

By fixing producer prices above the market equilibrium price the CAP induces excess supply. The organisation of the CAP stipulates that the quantities bought by the intervention agencies are to be used as buffer stock for maintaining the market price within the permissible limits of fluctuation. Stocks in excess of this requirement are usually disposed of by sale either in the domestic market at reduced prices for specific purposes, or abroad at world prices as EC exports. In an attempt to encourage direct exports of the excess supply (and to save on storage costs), the policy provides export *refunds* or *restitutions* which compensate the exporters of both basic commodities and processed products derived from them for the difference between world and Community market prices. Hence, at a given world price P_w, the compensation/subsidy per unit of exports varies within the range of $(P_i - P_w)$ minimum and $(P_t - P_w)$ maximum. If for any reason world prices rise above the threshold price, the domestic producers will tend to export their output rather than sell it to the EC intervention agencies. The CAP provides that in this case the export refund is to be converted into an export levy, thus ensuring that domestic supplies reach first the EC consumer at a reasonable price (the threshold price P_t) and only surpluses are exported. Theoretically at least, Community preference extends to cover both producers and consumers.

Market organisation similar to that described for cereals applies to approximately 70 per cent of the EC agricultural production (dairy products, meat, sugar, fruits, table wine, etc.). Another 25 per cent of agricultural production (eggs, poultry, flowers, etc.) are covered by a looser organisation confined to external protection without substantial support measures for the internal market. A few other commodities whose production is limited geographically and quantitatively, or for which international agreements prevent extensive protection, get production subsidies (durum wheat, olive oil, tobacco, etc.). They cover approximately 2.5 per cent of total EC agricultural production. Finally, for certain specific products covering less than 1 per cent of the total agricultural output the CAP provides flat subsidies per hectare or per volume of output.

Common prices policy and common trading policy are the two principal features of the common market in agricultural products which the EC is implementing through the CAP. The third essential function of the CAP is to shape the future of agriculture within the Community by a common structural policy. As we have seen, structural diversity was, and still is, one of the main characteristics of European agriculture. This is noticeable at the level of member states, but it becomes more pronounced in comparisons at the EC inter-regional level. Under conditions of structural diversity such as that still existing in the Community, a uniform prices and trading policy would take little account of regional disparities. This may lead to the exacerbation of structural differences and the slowing down of the rate of economic growth of the integrated sector. These problems can be solved only by more direct intervention, undertaken by the appropriate EC organisation, which will aim at the restructuring of the agricultural sector at the level of the Community for the purpose of increasing efficiency and attaining optimality. This function of the CAP has been assigned to the guidance section of the EAGGF with the following specific objectives:

1. The implementation of technical progress.
2. The modernisation of farms.
3. The rationalisation of production.
4. The improved processing and marketing of agricultural products.

These tasks are pursued by the allocation of capital investments, the provision of grants and aid for agricultural development, and the dissemination of knowledge and information among the agricultural populations. The EAGGF also provides assistance for the relocation of labour migrating from agriculture to other sectors of the economy by financing retraining and related costs.

Special features: agri-monetary issues

The Community's common support prices for agricultural products, and the free trade in these products among the member states which still maintain different national currencies (see Chapter 6), mean that a common system of price setting had to be devised. After the introduction of the EMS in 1979, the common or 'institutional' prices of agricultural products are denominated in the European Currency Unit, the ECU. For the operation of the CAP, these common prices are next converted into national currency units in each member state. Under a system of fixed exchange rates, prices expressed in accounting units will be converted into national currency units of the individual member state by using the market exchange rate. Problems arise when the exchange rate parities are changed. If prices are to remain common, a country with an appreciating currency would have to reduce its agricultural prices; while a country with a depreciating currency would have to raise its prices.

In the 1960s exchange rate parities did periodically change by policy adjustments. They changed more frequently since the early 1970s, when the international fixed exchange rates system was replaced by a system of flexible exchange rates. Changes in the value of the market exchange rate would not have implications on the CAP common price policy, if the new market exchange rate is used in the conversions of accounting prices into commercial prices. However, the general price level, agricultural revenues and farmers' incomes would be affected. Devaluation of a currency raises the support prices in terms of that currency; revaluation has the converse effect. For this reason countries whose currency by either design or the market depreciated or appreciated were reluctant to apply immediately the same change to the exchange rate used for converting agricultural prices from accounting into national currency units. This problem first appeared in 1969, after the French franc was devalued by 11.1 per cent and within two months the Deutschmark was revalued by 9.29 per cent. In order to protect its 'consumers' from the resulting price rise, France was given permission by the Community to carry out a phased devaluation of its exchange rate for agricultural products over a period of two years. Conversely, when Germany revalued, in order to protect its 'farmers' it followed a similar course of action, introducing a phased revaluation of the DM for agriculture over three years. Thus a disparity was introduced between the market (and in the EMS, the central) exchange rate and the exchange rate applied to agriculture which came to be known as the *representative* or *green* rate.

With the frequent parity changes under the flexible exchange rates system and the currency realignments within the EMS, the divergence between central and green rates has persisted, thus becoming a permanent feature of the CAP. Meanwhile, the inequality between the two exchange rates is driving a wedge between the prices of the same agricultural product in the markets of different members which thus ceased to be 'common'. In this way, market prices no longer reflect actual economic conditions or planned structural changes. Instead, their divergence may give rise to distortive intra-EC trade flows which clearly have to be stopped. The following example shows why.

Assume that 1ECU = DM2 = FF4 and that 1 tonne of wheat is set by the CAP at 200ECU, that is DM400 in Germany and FF800 in France. Now, for reasons unrelated to agriculture, Germany revalues the DM by 50 per cent so that the new central exchange rates become 1ECU = DM1 = FF4. If this new exchange rate is to be applied to agricultural prices, 1 tonne of wheat will be valued at 200ECU = DM200 = FF800, and the German farmers will lose 50 per cent of their revenue per tonne of wheat sold, and this will be unacceptable to Germany. Hence, by common consent the old exchange rate is retained as the 'green' rate for agricultural prices and the German farmers continue to receive DM400 per tonne of wheat. However, the difference between the green rate and the market rate induces French producers to export wheat to Germany, sell it for DM400 per tonne, convert Deutschmarks into French francs at the central/market rate, and thus receive FF1,600 per tonne instead of FF800, which they would have received by selling their wheat in France. In general, the producers of every member country would try to sell their output in the German market (or to the EC intervention agency located in Germany) and pocket the profit.

Consequently, the divergence between the central/market rate and the green rate causes price differences which can give rise to trade flows unjustified by economic necessity. These trade flows would drain the funds available to the CAP and even threaten its existence. The solution is to stop these distortive trade flows by offsetting the differences between the green and the central exchange rates. This is effected by the imposition of Monetary Compensatory Amounts (MCAs) which are price equalising border taxes or refunds.

The MCAs are calculated on the percentage difference between the green rate and the market rate, and are applied as follows:

1. For members with a strong currency the green rate is below the market rate and the MCA is a levy on imports and a subsidy on exports:

   Positive MCA = market rate − green rate > 0

   The positive MCA is favourable to the consumer.

2. For members with a weak currency the green rate is above the market rate and the MCA is a levy on exports and a subsidy on imports:

   Negative MCA = market rate − Green rate < 0.

   The negative MCA is favourable to the producer.

Positive MCAs can be eliminated by revaluation. However, since revaluation involves a reduction in farmers' prices in terms of national currencies, countries with positive MCAs are reluctant to revalue. Elimination of negative MCAs is rather more acceptable to governments because it raises farm prices. In our example above, French producers attempting to export wheat to Germany would have to pay MCA/levy equal to FF800 so that the incentive to export for reasons of currency-induced speculation will be eliminated. Similarly, the German producer who will only receive for his sale of wheat in France the equivalent of DM200, will now get an additional DM200 per tonne of exports as MCA/subsidy.

The MCA as a levy is paid to the Community budget, while as a subsidy is paid from the Community budget. By this system the principle of common agriculture prices is preserved at the border and trade in agricultural products remains undistorted by the dual exchange rates. However, the prices of identical agricultural commodities, when they are converted to national prices at the central exchange rate, are not uniform throughout the EC. The MCA system creates national rather than EC prices and policies.

Another complication arises because the green rate is used for converting final goods prices only, while the prices of most of the inputs to agricultural production from outside the sector (machinery, fertilisers etc.) are expressed in prices for which the relevant exchange rate is the market rate. This has implications on the costs of production, giving rise to cost differentials between the members of the EC and thus potentially affecting the allocation of production and the flow of trade.

The MCA system has been justified on the ground that it adds stability to prices and farmers' incomes in periods of widely fluctuating exchange rates. As temporary measures, the MCAs can be defended for as long as adjustments are made to a new exchange rate. But owing to their high cost and with budgetary crises in sight, the Community decided to eliminate the MCAs by attacking the reasons of their development. From April 1987 changes in central rates under the EMS can no longer lead to the creation of positive MCAs, so that exchange rate realignments can only increase prices. The new arrangement is implemented by defining a new 'green' ECU, tied to the strongest currency within the Community, and applying a corrective coefficient (equal to the highest percentage revaluation resulting from the realignment) to the EMS central rates, respecting the ±2.25 per cent fluctuation margins. Negative MCAs are then introduced for all member states except for the one whose currency has appreciated most. These negative MCAs, which will be larger for countries with weak currencies, will be dismantled, on proposal from the Commission, as and when the economic situation in the various member states permits it. In effect the new regulations mean that the MCAs are calculated with reference to the Deutchmark, which is the strongest currency in the EMS, and are all negative. Appreciations of the Deutschmark will not cause positive MCAs for Germany. The system of MCAs has meant that strong-currency countries had an unduly high level of prices and of protection whereas weak-currency countries had below-average price levels for their agricultural commodities. At present this applies especially to Greece which experiences a price level for agricultural produce more than 30 per cent below the EC average (1990).

With the surge towards the single market, the Council and the Commission declared their intention to start dismantling the negative MCAs by four-stage adaptation of the green rates to be completed by 1992. Following the new arrangements, negative MCAs have already been reduced (by devaluation of the green currencies) by more than one-half.

In conclusion, green exchange rates and MCAs should be seen only as temporary measures attempting to mend a problem which requires rather more radical solutions. But persistent price distortions arising from persistent differences between the central and the green exchange rates have distortive effects on production and competition, on structural change and the allocation and utilisation of resources, and therefore on economic growth. Therefore, the MCAs make a mockery of the CAP's common price policy, and the sooner they are dismantled, the better. Both green rates and MCAs will be eradicated as the EC moves closer to monetary integration and the single market.

7.5 European Community agriculture under the Common Agriculture Policy

We must now examine the main features of agriculture in the Community for the purpose of evaluating the state of EC agriculture under the CAP and the cost-effectiveness of operating the CAP.

The CAP has had successes and failures which in a way have contributed to the present shape of EC agriculture. However, it is important to emphasise that not everything good or bad with EC agriculture can indisputably be attributed solely to the operation of the CAP. There are many other factors that influence economic developments and it is not always easy to disentangle the complexity of real situations for the purpose of ascribing specific outcomes to specific causes. A policy may aim at, or have spillover effects upon, many objectives. But frequently a number of policies are applied simultaneously to achieve a number of different (and sometimes contradictory) primary targets, and so cause and effect cannot be easily identified. Finally, changes in the constraints and in the general economic environment within which the policy is applied mean that both the effects and the targets of policy are not fixed but variable.

Three issues are examined in this section: trends, efficiency and reform of the Common Agricultural Policy.

Trends in Community agriculture

As we have seen the EEC Treaty specifies five main objectives of the Common Agricultural Policy (Article 39). It is therefore opportune to examine the trends in EC agriculture under five relevant headings, presenting arguments and statistics both in favour and against particular aspects and features, as they emerged during the operation of the CAP. The discussion is primarily concerned with the EC-9, since for most of the time under consideration Greece, Portugal and Spain were not members of the Community.

Structure and productivity

The importance of the agricultural sector as a contributor to the Community's gross value added and as an employer of factors of production is relatively small and declining (Table 7.1). Despite increases in the volume of production (Table 7.2), the share of agriculture in the Community's GDP, at market prices, accounted for by agriculture was halved between 1960 and 1980, from about 7 per cent to 3.4 per cent for the EC-9. A similar trend has been observed after 1980 within and outside the EC, and is of course due to both the relative contraction of agriculture and the expansion of other sectors of the economy. For all twelve members of the Community the contribution of agriculture to GDP was 3.8 per cent in 1983 and 3.2 per cent in 1987. The utilised agricultural area has also been contracting in most of the member states.

The workforce employed in agriculture has also declined at the drastic rate of nearly 4.0 per cent a year during 1960–75 and 2.5 per cent a year during 1975–85, reducing the manpower to half of what it was in 1960. In the Community of twelve, only 7.4 per cent of the total labour force is now (1988) employed in the agricultural sector (see Table 2.2).

The share of agriculture in total gross fixed capital formation remained relatively stable at 4.0 per cent, suggesting tendencies towards higher capital intensity. But while over the period 1960–80 the gross value-added of agriculture was increasing at a rate of just 7 per cent a year, the economy as a whole was growing much faster, at the rate of

Table 7.1 Structural changes in Community agriculture (per cent).

		B	DK	D	E	F	GR	IRL	I	L	NL	P	UK	EC	
Agriculture/GDP, at factor cost.	1968	4.9	7.7	4.4	—	7.5	—	18.8	9.9	4.6	6.9	—	—	—	
	1978	2.7	5.4	2.5	—	4.8	—	17.3	7.8	3.1	4.5	2.3	4.0	3.8	EC-12
	1983	2.6	4.7	1.8	5.9	4.0	15.5	10.7	6.4	3.1	4.4	6.5	2.1	3.2	EC-12
	1987	2.2	4.0	1.5	5.2	3.5	15.6	10.3	4.5	2.4	4.1	6.4	1.7	3.4	EC-11
Decrease in employment	1970–80	4.3	2.8	4.4	4.9	3.9	2.3	3.0	2.9	4.2	1.7	—	1.8		
	1980–88	1.4	2.1	2.7	3.2	3.2	0.4	2.8	4.2	4.3	+2.0	2.9	1.5	2.8	EC-12
Decrease in utilised area	1968–73	0.7	0.2	0.4	—	0.5	0.0	2.1	0.4	1.2	0.4	—	0.7	—	
	1973–83	0.8	0.4	1.0	—	0.3	1.7	0.1	0.4	0.5	0.2	—	0.2	—	
	1980–87	0.4	0.5	0.7	0.1	0.3	+0.1	0.1	0.3	0.3	0.1	0.0	0.2	0.2	
Labour productivity increase	1968–73	8.5	3.7	7.9	—	7.7	—	4.9	4.9	2.5	—	—	—	—	
	1973–83	3.9	4.6	5.5	—	3.9	—	6.1	4.9	6.1	5.8	—	5.3	4.7	
	1980–87	4.3	4.5	2.7	5.2	5.2	1.0	5.2	5.8	5.2	6.7	4.0	1.9	4.3	EC-12
Average size of agricultural holding, hectares	1985	16.7	31.0	16.9	—	29.2	5.7	22.7	8.0	31.5	16.7	—	69.4	17.4	EC-10

Sources: EC Commission *The Agricultural Situation in the Community*, Annual Report, various issues; Eurostat (1989) *Basic Statistics of the Community*, 26th ed., Luxembourg; EC Commission (1990) *The Agricultural Situation in the Community*, 1989 Report, Brussels.

Table 7.2 Agricultural production, prices and incomes.

Year	Volume of final production	Production of farm inputs	Farm gate prices: input prices	Net real value added in the sector	Farm labour income	Net value per person
1975	88.2	106.6	106.2	115	112	103
1976	88.4	100.6	108.8	116	110	105
1977	91.1	99.8	106.3	111	107	104
1978	95.7	99.8	107.6	112	105	107
1979	98.7	98.3	107.6	112	105	107
1980	100.6	100.0	98.7	97	100	97
1981	100.6	104.8	96.6	97	97	99
1982	105.7	104.4	97.3	104	95	109
1983	105.3	103.3	95.3	97	94	104
1984	109.1	106.4	93.2	100	91	109
1985	107.3	104.1	93.4	92	89	103
1986	109.7	106.1	95.9	90	87	104

Note: The average for 1979–81 = 100.

Source: EC Commission (1988) *The Agricultural Situation in the Community*, 1987 Report, Brussels.

10.5 per cent annually. Over the period under review, the average labour productivity growth in the Community was about 4 per cent a year, while in agriculture it was more than 6 per cent.

The data confirm that over a relatively long time period the agricultural sector of the Community is experiencing a rapid increase in productivity, mostly because of the restructuring of the agricultural sector towards larger farm sizes and the fast pace of mechanisation. However, more has to be done for the realisation of growth rates and levels of development in agriculture comparable to those of other sectors of the Community's economy. Despite the progress, the Community's relative productivity ratio between agriculture and the other sectors of the economy is only 0.5. The problems of the agricultural sector have become more acute after the accession of Greece, Portugal and Spain which have relatively large labour-intensive agricultural sectors and low labour productivity.

Standards of living

The second objective of the CAP is to ensure a fair standard of living for the agricultural community, in particular by increasing the earnings of persons employed in agriculture. This objective is pursued mainly by producer price support in the form of high administrative prices for agricultural products. The outcome of this policy is not an unqualified success. Agricultural prices have declined relative to the general price level in EC economies, and in recent years relative productivity gains have not been large enough to prevent farm incomes from deteriorating. Incomes from agricultural employment have increased less rapidly than other incomes in the economy. In fact, while output per head rose (Table 7.2), incomes in agriculture for the Community as a whole fell throughout the 1975–86 period, reaching in 1984 a level equal to 91 per cent of the 1979–81 income level. Table 7.3 shows that, relative to the EC average, some countries have done rather well (Ireland, Luxembourg) while others have experienced net income reductions (Italy, United Kingdom). In general the observed performance of farm incomes in the Community is in direct contradiction with the intended objectives of the CAP. Two explanations of this paradox are offered: it is argued that, first, most incomes in the economy experienced recent stagnation or decline, and that without the support of the CAP, the fall in farm incomes would have been worse; and, second, the price support policy is not an efficient method for improving incomes.

Another drawback of the income objective and the policy instrument by which it is pursued is that it has negative side-effects on other objectives of the CAP. For example, administered prices at levels above those which the free market would have determined tend to distort the mobility of factors of production, to delay the out-movement of labour and to impede the improvement in the allocation of resources between sectors. Prices above those of the competitive market would tend to attract rather than to release resources from agriculture to other industries. Therefore, price support policies delay the improvement of labour

Table 7.3 Farm incomes.

Country	Index A[1]	Index B[2]
B	9.3	9.5
DK	29.0	72.9
D	4.4	0.0
E	28.3	29.9
F	1.2	− 1.1
GR	15.4	11.5
IRL	27.8	45.5
I	− 6.5	− 10.1
L	45.4	44.2
NL	21.0	26.8
UK	− 0.4	− 4.7
EC-11	6.9	5.1

[1] Index A = net value added at factor cost per annual work unit.
[2] Index B = net income of the farmer and his family from agriculture per annual work unit. Both indices: average 1979–80–81 to average 1986–7–8.

Source: EC Commission (1990) *The Agricultural Situation in the Community*, 1989 Report, Brussels.

productivity and efficiency in production. Moreover, when farm prices keep rising, input prices may also rise with the implication that, along with incomes, profits may be squeezed. Low profitability means that capital investment may decline, while land values rise and agrochemical and machinery industries realise higher profits, although they are not those whom the CAP is meant to support. This implies that the target of better living standards for the agricultural population can only be approached and maintained if the prices of the sector's final products keep rising well ahead of the increase in input prices. This process inevitably leads to spiral increases of prices and costs (see Table 7.5) which, besides their inflationary effects, do not ensure that in the end the living standards of the agricultural population will actually improve. The data in Table 7.2 confirm that in recent years farm input prices were consistently above those of output prices.

The agricultural price support policy increases the costs not only of the agricultural sector but also of other sectors of the economy that compete in the same markets for factors of production and other inputs. Therefore under certain conditions, higher prices for agricultural products may raise the general level of wages and prices, and reduce the international competitiveness of a country. Hence, besides the distribution of national income, the agricultural price support policy may also affect the aggregate price level and other macroeconomic variables.

Another defect of the price support policy for raising living standards is that the actual size of farm incomes would now depend on the volume of production. Hence the policy provides a strong incentive to the big farmers (and other entrepreneurs in general who take advantage of the certainty of high prices and the opportunity to make a profit by investing in agriculture) to produce as much as possible, irrespective of market demand, which in any case under this sort of policy is irrelevant. A consequence of the price support policy and the dependence of incomes on the volume of output is that higher support prices benefit disproportionately the large producers who in general are not those in dire need of better living standards: it is estimated that 75 per cent of CAP support for farmers goes to the richest 25 per cent. At the same time, the Community accumulates mountains of surplus output which can only be sold at prices vastly lower than the costs of production.

A policy for fair standards of living for the agricultural community does not imply that these standards of living will converge or that farmers' incomes will be equalised throughout the Community. In fact, a characteristic of EC agriculture is the marked disparities in farm incomes between the member countries. Thus the richest 'average' farmer (the Netherlands) has an income two and a half times higher than the Community average and is more than five times better off than the poorest farmer (Greece). Among the reasons for this are the productivity of the farm (fertility of land), the average size of agricultural holdings (Table 7.1) and the actual price support received by the farmer.

Market stability

An indicator of market stability should be the stability of market prices. However, the prices of agricultural products are themselves administered as the instruments by which the EC is pursuing its objective of increase in agricultural incomes. Therefore, in the EC the prices of agricultural products should reveal three tendencies: (a) relatively high levels, (b) relatively high rates of increase, associated with both the CAP price support system and the attempt to reach the target of higher farm incomes and (c) relatively low fluctuations, associated with the market stability objective of the CAP.

The annual rates of increase in common support prices for the period 1973–90 (in ECU terms) are presented in Table 7.4. During 1973–84 the intervention prices rose by approximately 7 per cent annually. After 1984, with problems in the financing of the Community budget, they started falling (by 0.2 per cent annually), a trend that will probably continue. Table 7.5 presents price increases of inputs and outputs of the agricultural sector and of the consumer price index during the period

Table 7.4 Increases in the intervention prices of agricultural products, 1973–90.

Year	% increase
1973–4	6.7
1974–5	13.5
1975–6	9.6
1976–7	6.5
1977–8	3.5
1978–9	7.0
1979–80	1.0
1980–1	4.5
1981–2	9.1
1982–3	10.1
1983–4	4.1
1984–5	− 0.5
1985–6	0.1
1986–7	− 0.3
1987–8	− 0.2
1988–9	− 0.1
1989–90	− 0.3

Note: Common prices in ECU weighted by agricultural production.

Sources: *Bulletin EC*, various issues; EC Commission (1990) *The Agricultural Situation in the Community*, 1989 Report, Brussels.

Table 7.5 Price increases in the Community, 1980–87[1].

Member state	Agricultural sector Commodity output	Input goods Consumption	Investment	Consumer price index
B	20.9	22.1	56.2	44.5
DK	23.6	28.6	63.8	57.8
D	−5.6	0.2	25.1	21.0
E	75.4	99.4	89.7	101.9
F	40.2	48.5	71.1	67.3
GR	215.7	207.9	242.1	266.1
IRL	40.8	35.2	68.4	91.0
I	68.7	61.8	116.0	111.0
L	39.3	25.1	40.3	42.7
NL	5.0	−4.0	25.9	22.5
P	−[2]	−[2]	−[2]	247.2
UK	27.8	32.9	54.5	52.4
EC	50.3	45.5	81.2	64.3

[1] Based on nominal indices, 1980 = 100.
[2] Not available and excluded from EC total.

Source: Eurostat (1989) *Basic Statistics of the Community*, 26th ed., Luxembourg.

1980–87. The data show emphatically that, in comparison with the Community's inflation rate as reflected in the consumer price index, · the price increases in agricultural commodities can be considered as moderate. In the majority of the Community member states the price increases of inputs (goods and services both directly consumed and contributing to investment) in the agricultural sector were significantly higher than the increase in the price of agricultural output. Hence, with higher input costs and higher consumer prices than the prices of the agricultural output, most farmers' welfare has certainly declined over the period under consideration.

An implication of the policy of administered prices is that the Community prices of agricultural products are definitely more stable than the world prices. Thus in the Community, price fluctuation is no longer a matter of concern. However, stability has been attained at a cost, the relatively high levels of prices. For reasons of policy, the Community domestic prices of agricultural commodities are higher, in many cases significantly higher, than the world prices. But the Community's level of common prices reveals nothing about relative welfare, whether the farmers outside the EC are better or worse than the Community farmers or whether they experience declining standards of living comparable to those suffered by farmers within the Community. It is of some importance that these price differences between Community and world prices have occurred at a time of plentiful supplies, when food continues to take up a small and shrinking share out of the consumer's income. Nevertheless, the simple comparison between EC and world prices should be regarded as unreliable evidence for the case against the CAP because the Community's prices of agricultural commodities are high by design. Also the world prices (which are not the domestic prices of any particular country but the offer prices of exports, i.e. low-priced surpluses of countries which in all probability in their domestic markets follow price support policies) are low, among other reasons, because the EC first, is no longer a market participant as a buyer of these products, and, second, is a market participant as a seller of its own surpluses. What the world prices would have been in the absence of the CAP cannot be guessed easily. It is, however, certain that if the Community had been a more important buyer in the world markets for agricultural products, the world export prices would have been much higher than they are today.

However, the EC has come under attack by agricultural producers from other countries who attribute three major effects to the CAP:

1. First, that pricing policies and protection in the EC have led to excessive production, reducing imports and expanding exports. With growing world production and no corresponding increase in world demand, the rising farm output of the EC and its subsidies to exports have depressed world prices.
2. Second the EC variable import and export levies have tended to insulate the EC markets from external price fluctuations, thereby amplifying the variability of world commodity prices.
3. Third, depressed prices and price instability in world markets cause farmers in third countries to contract output, thereby lowering their incomes.

Although it may be true that the CAP has exerted downward pressure on the prices of certain commodities (particularly cereals and dairy products) and that it may have been a significant destabilising factor in world markets, it is not necessarily true that both world producers and consumers of agricultural products would have been better off without the CAP. In any case, since the EC is not unique in protecting its agriculture, abolition of the CAP would not necessarily mean free international trade in agricultural commodities.

Some of the effects of the CAP on the world market for agricultural products, for which the EC is a producer and exporter, are illustrated in Figure 7.2. The world demand (EC + rest of the world) for agricultural products is D_W and the world supply is S_R. Equilibrium is attained at E, with price P_W. The EC demand and supply schedules are D_{EC} and

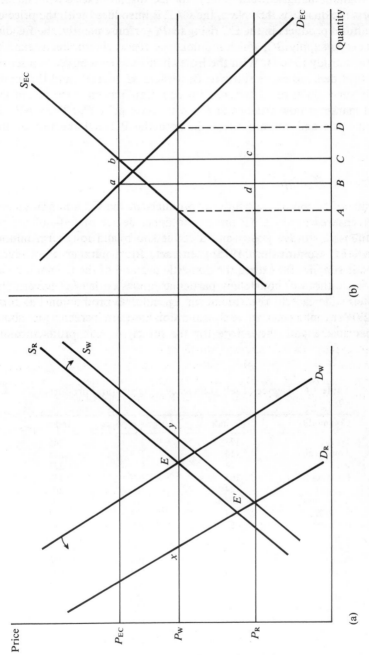

Figure 7.2   The markets for agricultural output: (a) the world market; (b) the EC market.

S_{EC}. Without an agricultural policy, the EC displays excess demand and imports the quantity AD. Next, the CAP is introduced with the price of agricultural products in the EC rising to P_{EC}. Consequently, the EC displays excess supply BC, which it unloads to the world market as exports at total subsidy ($abcd$). With the EC switching from a buyer to a seller, the world demand curve shifts to D_R (where $xE = AD$), and the world supply curve shifts to S_W (where $Ey = ab$). Equilibrium in the rest of the world market is now attained at E', with lower price P_R. The CAP has caused trade and welfare effects in both the EC and the rest of the world.

Availability of supplies

Security of supply of agricultural products in the Community (Table 7.6) is ensured by the CAP through a higher degree of self-sufficiency, 'an intensive storage policy and a stable short- and long-term import policy' (EC Commission, 1975b). In fact, for a number of products domestic supplies far exceed the domestic demand of the Community as a whole, without of course any particular effects on market prices. The long-term increase in the volume of agricultural production has been 1.5–2.0 per cent a year, while consumption has been increasing by about 0.5 per cent a year. Therefore for the principal farm products more

Table 7.6 Degree of self-sufficiency in agricultural products, 1987–8.

Commodity	EC-12: index[1]	Largest producer	Index[1]
Wheat	123	F	246
Total grain	114	F	218
Rice	74	I	223
Potatoes	103	NL	152
Sugar	124	B	202
Vegetables	106	NL	207
Fresh fruit	84	GR	144
Citrus fruit	67	E	214
Wine	103	E	122
Cheese	–	IRL	433
Butter	–	IRL	224
Beef	106	IRL	692
Veal	112	NL	594
Pork	103	DK	338
Poultry meat	106	NL	209
Total meat	102	DK	295

[1] For index = 100 demand equals supply, that is self-sufficiency.

Sources: Eurostat (1990) *Basic Statistics of the Community*, 27th ed., Luxembourg.

than self-sufficiency has been achieved and the Community has to rely increasingly on exports for the disposal of excess production.

Characteristic of the EC agriculture is that the demand/supply relationship is not uniform throughout the Community. The geographic dispersion of the member countries and the degree of their specialisation in production means that, for the same agricultural commodity, some of them produce surpluses and others experience deficits. For the Community as a whole, problems, of course, arise from the overall surpluses and deficits in farm products. Despite the increase in agricultural production and the mountains and lakes of unsold stocks, the Community remains the world's largest importer of food.

Reasonable prices for the consumer

Consumer prices are on the whole much higher than producer prices (farm prices at the farm gate) and there is no close correlation between the two prices. The increase in consumer prices in the EC over the last few years lagged behind the inflation rate. Between 1973 and 1980 the prices of agricultural products rose by 7.4 per cent annually against an 11.2 per cent increase in the general price index; and between 1980 and 1987, the prices of agricultural output rose by 50.3 per cent, while the consumer price index rose by 64.3 per cent (EC averages, Table 7.5). Table 7.7 presents the indices of producers' and consumers' (food) prices for 1988 based on 1980 = 100. The data show that, in general, producer prices fell behind consumer prices in every member state, in many cases by a very wide margin. What is most important is that in real terms producer prices (deflated) were in 1988 much lower than they were in 1980. An implication of this is that during the period 1980–88, although the prices of agricultural commodities within the Community did rise, those who produced them were neither solely responsible for the price increases nor did they manage to maintain in real terms the produce prices they enjoyed back in 1980. Since farmers' revenues from selling their output depend on the volume and price of commodities, lower prices do not necessarily mean that farmers' incomes have actually fallen. For many farmers quantities may have risen and, besides the price support mechanism, needy farmers may have received transfer payments from other funds.

As remarked earlier, world market prices for most agricultural products are well below those of the EC. Hence, the consumer has on the one hand gained from price stability and availability of plentiful supplies, but on the other hand he has lost from having to pay very high prices. Moreover, as the poor in the population spend a relatively high proportion of their disposable income on food and the CAP's price

Table 7.7 Producers' and consumers' prices of agricultural products, 1988.

Member state	Producers' prices Nominal (1)	Deflated (2)	Consumers' prices Food (3)	Difference (3) – (1)
B	121.1	82.8	142.8	21.7
DK	126.5	76.7	159.0	32.5
D	94.4	77.1	113.5	19.1
E	181.7	85.8	217.5	35.8
F	140.5	81.8	171.6	31.1
GR	359.0	86.4	404.0	45.0
IRL	154.5	79.2	170.5	16.0
I	172.4	77.8	203.7	31.3
L	142.2	98.3	146.5	4.3
NL	106.5	86.2	113.3	6.8
P	$-^1$	$-^1$	379.3	$-^1$
UK	128.5	80.4	146.8	18.3
EC	154.9	80.9	173.2	18.3

Note: 1980 = 100
^{1} not available.

Source: Eurostat (1990) *Basic Statistics of the Community*, 27th ed., Luxembourg.

support mechanism keeps food prices high, the poorer people and the poorer members of the Community are paying a large share of the burden of the CAP. For example, the proportion of income going to the consumption of food is in Greece, Ireland and Portugal twice as much as the EC average (food expenditure/consumption expenditure: 0.40 vs. 0.21). Therefore, the CAP causes massive transfers of income from consumers to producers of food within countries and, through trade, between EC countries. Since the CAP has failed to concentrate on poor farmers, the problem here is not only that the poor people of Europe are paying the costs of the CAP disproportionately, but that those who benefit from the policy are the richest farmers of the Community.

Efficiency of the Common Agricultural Policy

Domestic considerations

The main policy of the CAP, price support, was adopted not because it is considered to be the most efficient for achieving the set objectives, but because it is regarded as less interventionist than other policies, such as subsidies, and therefore politically more acceptable by the public. As we have seen, most objectives of the CAP, to a large extent, have been reached. However, the same or better results could have been achieved

Table 7.8 Budgetary expenditure on EAGGF, 1976–90.

Budget shares	1976–80	1981–5	1986–90
Guarantee	72.7	64.1	61.3
Guidance	3.1	2.8	3.0
Total EAGGF	75.8	66.9	64.3

Source: EC *Bulletin EC*, various issues.

by a less expensive and more rational policy. A disadvantage of the current CAP policy is that the impressive increase in agricultural output has led to a spectacular increase in Community expenditure on price support. Table 7.8 shows that on the basis of five-year averages the CAP share of budgetary expenditure has been reduced over the last fifteen years from 75.8 to 64.3 per cent. However, since the budget has risen at a faster rate than prices, the CAP takes a slightly smaller slice from a much larger pie. Agriculture still uses more than three-fifths of the total Community budget, 95 per cent of it on current price support and only 5 per cent on restructuring the sector. The EAGGF funds have been increasing in the last fifteen years approximately twice as fast as the rate of growth of Community GDP. The public costs of protection of the agricultural markets seem to increase inexorably, thus limiting the funds available for other competing purposes. Hence, since the mid-1970s mounting criticism has been directed against the CAP which has been blamed because of the following:

1. It has kept prices above world prices.
2. It has caused significant financial expenditures which required financial transfers between members.
3. It has led to substantial intra-Community income redistribution from consumers in one member country to producers in another.
4. It has generated surpluses of some commodities.

The surpluses of skimmed milk powder and butter are particularly notorious. These surpluses, besides the initial costs of accumulation and storage, cause new problems by being disposed of within the Community or as exports at prices vastly below costs. For example, the export price of skimmed milk powder is three times lower than the support price.

From the beginnings of the CAP until the early 1980s the EAGGF expenditure was dominated by the support provided to producers of the northern member countries. The 'northern commodities' were produced 'too much', receiving 'above-average protection' and consumed 'too

Table 7.9 Allocation of EAGGF expenditure: guarantee section (ratios per cent).

Commodity	1980	1983	1985	1987	1989	1990
Dairy products	42.1	27.7	30.1	22.6	17.4	15.8
Cereals	15.3	16.0	11.9	18.4	14.6	15.8
Meat and eggs	14.2	14.6	17.6	13.2	15.7	13.9
Sub-total	71.6	58.3	59.6	54.2	47.7	45.5
Other products	25.8	38.6	39.4	43.1	51.0	54.0
MCAs	2.6	3.1	1.0	2.7	1.3	0.5

Sources: *Eurostat Review*, various issues; EC Commission (1988 and 1989) *The Agricultural Situation in the Community*, 1987 and 1988 Report, Brussels.

little'. However, after the accession of the new Mediterranean members, their products started to receive an increasing share of financial support and the allocation of EAGGF funds between products changed significantly. Greece, Portugal and Spain were brought under the CAP agricultural systems with production structures in many respects more diverse and deficient than those of the other nine members. With the addition of new members the agricultural output of the Community rose with a sharp shift in focus away from the northern producers and commodities to Mediterranean producers and commodities: the Community's production of olive oil has been raised by half, wine by a quarter, citrus fruits by three-quarters and fresh vegetables by more than a third. Table 7.9 presents the distribution of EAGGF expenditure since 1980. The first three groups of products (dairy products, cereals and meat), which are typically northern, absorbed until 1980 more than 70 per cent of the EAGGF budget. After 1980, their share of support started to decline, reaching less than 50 per cent of the total by 1989. The share of 'other products' was doubled in less than ten years.

International implications.

During the period of operating the CAP the European Community has changed overall from a net importer to a net exporter of food and agricultural products. This turnaround has been the outcome of massive support policies and not of any market-inspired shift in comparative advantage. The EC is currently the largest exporter of meat and dairy products in the world, a net exporter of wheat since 1974, and overall the second largest exporter of temperate zone agricultural products. In its trading capacity the EC has been accused of using protectionism as an instrument for social policy in support of farmers, and of adding to the instability of world markets by purchasing agricultural products abroad only when domestic supplies are short and selling its surpluses on world markets at subsidised prices. Export subsidies provided under the CAP enable the Community to unload much of its surplus farm produce in other countries, squeezing out more efficient producers (see Figure 7.2). Community exports of surplus dairy products and cereals especially depress world prices and lead to competition with other producers for gaining and holding export markets. These operations cause financial problems to the Community itself and to its major trading partners and the less developed countries (LDCs) and complicate international relations within and outside the EC.

It has been calculated that, besides the restrictive import policies and the export subsidies, the domestic aids of the CAP meant that in recent years about 60 per cent of the value added by agriculture in the Community comes from transfers from elsewhere in the economy (Stoeckel, 1985). The massive intervention in favour of one economic sector changes relative prices and through them the allocation of resources in directions different from those reached by a free and efficient market mechanism. Production, specialisation and trade are thus determined by the comparative strength of policies and not by comparative advantage.

As we have seen in Section 7.3 above, in an environment of efficient markets, interventionist policies create distortions that cause negative welfare effects. However, if distortions are already present in the market, one of the reasons interventionist policies are probably applied is to restore allocative efficiency. But it remains questionable, first, whether the correction of generalised distortions is feasible by intervening in one sector only; and, second, whether the chosen policies are 'best' under the prevailing circumstances. In the EC, intervention in agriculture is probably concerned not so much with the preservation of a surplus-producing economic sector but with the long-term objective of structural adjustment under the constraint of a 'fair income' for the farmers. The problem is that for one or another reason (general economic recession, accession of new members with underdeveloped agricultural sectors, etc.) and for a long period excessive resources have been directed towards agriculture. The principal reason for this is not that agriculture continues to attract excess resources owing to price distortions caused by the CAP, but that labour and other resources are leaving agriculture too slowly, owing to their immobility. Cessation or drastic reduction of support would undoubtedly speed up the adjustments, but at considerable economic hardship for farmers in the short run. Hence radical solutions are ruled out for social reasons and, most importantly, for their domestic and intra-EC political implications.

All these changes in the structure of production and trade of the EC agricultural sector raise questions regarding the effects of the CAP on Community and world welfare. Lowering the level of agricultural support will certainly decrease the quantity and the rewards of resources employed in agriculture and the volume and price of production. The European Community is not, of course, the only offender, but along with the United States (which is by far the most important net exporter of agricultural produce in the world), it is one of the largest offenders in world agricultural trade. Practically all industrial countries pursue agricultural policies leading, to a greater or lesser degree, to distortions in resource allocation at domestic and world-wide level. Certain industrial countries (such as Sweden, Norway, Austria, Switzerland and Japan) claim that, although the support they provide to their agriculture is higher than in the United States or the EC, they do not export their produce and therefore their responsibilities for the problems in world agricultural trade is limited. Of course, problems are caused from both active participation in the export side and absence from the import side of world agricultural trade. This has created a strong feeling among the traditional agricultural exporters (Australia, New Zealand, Canada) who resent the aggressive encouragement of agricultural production and the unloading of surpluses in the world markets. In many instances during recent years international disputes regarding agricultural subsidies and countervailing duties (particularly between the EC and the United States) have ended in open trade warfare which led to demands for liberalisation of the trade in agricultural products under the auspices of the General Agreement on Tariffs and Trade (GATT). A first step towards this direction was the GATT declaration of the Uruguay Round of negotiations (1986–90) which talked of the urgent need to bring more discipline and predictability to world agricultural trade, to deal with distortions and surpluses and to achieve 'a fair and market-oriented agricultural system'. Positive results will be reached by reducing import barriers, improving world competition by disciplining the use of all direct and indirect subsidies and other measures affecting agricultural trade, 'including the phased reduction of their negative effects and dealing with their causes'. This last phrase was included at the insistence of the Community which put forward a proposal for the gradual liberalisation of agricultural trade 'to the extent necessary to re-establish balanced markets and a more market-oriented agricultural trading system', and the replacement of production support by income support. Implementation of this proposal will require 'tariffication', that is conversion of all protective measures, including the Community's variable levies, to equivalent tariffs which will put restrictions on a comparable basis for the application of reductions.

With particular reference to EC agriculture, the question is not whether the world and the Community would have been better off without the CAP, but whether: (a) the objectives of the CAP are too ambitious and unrealistic, therefore they should be replaced by some other set of objectives; and (b) there is a different set of policies which could achieve the (current or revised) objectives of the CAP more efficiently than the policies currently pursued.

Although the latest round of GATT negotiations have reached promising conclusions (see Chapter 8), free trade in agricultural commodities is not yet an option, therefore estimates of the effects of completely abolishing the CAP are meaningless. Reform of the CAP is, however, a realistic possibility.

Attempts to reform the Common Agricultural Policy

The CAP has replaced the national agricultural policies of the member countries, has achieved certain of its objectives and, to some extent, has unified the EC market for agricultural commodities. However, independent observers, the member states and the Community agree that the CAP is far from perfect and that it is in urgent need of reform. Given the current problems in the Community associated with over-supply and budgetary expenditure on open-ended price guarantees, the incentives the CAP offered to Community farmers in the past are unlikely to remain at the same level in the future. Two general types of reforms have been proposed:

1. Modifications in the existing structure of the CAP which would leave administered prices to meet the target of income support, but reduce production surpluses and budgetary expenditure.
2. Replacement of the price support mechanism as the principal instrument of the CAP by other methods, such as direct income payments.

Economic theory would consider the second type of proposals as the most efficient method for achieving the CAP objective of 'a fair standard of living for the agricultural community'. However, since farmers tend to regard high prices as a right but direct income payments as socially demeaning charity, social and political considerations may prove such schemes to be non-feasible.

At least the Commission cannot be accused of not trying to change the CAP. However, it is the Council, that is the representatives of the member states, that takes decisions. The first attempt for reform was unsuccessful. The Mansholt Plan (1968), which concluded that the twin objectives, of stabilising production at the level of demand while ensuring farmers an adequate income, could not be met, proposed a radical restructuring of the CAP based on 'reasonable incomes, reasonable prices and increased productivity', followed by agricultural trade liberalisation in line with the EEC Treaty. The Plan recommended the lowering of prices so as to eliminate surplus production and reorganisation in large production units for the realisation of scale economies; reasonable incomes for the producers through the market process; and a fairly liberal trade regime in agricultural products. However, political opposition to the Plan, arising from diverse interests among the members, and the concurrent early problems of the forthcoming economic recession meant that the proposed reforms were not accepted.

A second major attempt for reform was presented by the Commission in 'Guidelines for European Agriculture' (EC, 1981b). This plan aimed specifically at reduction in production by keeping prices down, with the long-term objective to bring prices in line with world prices. The Community recognised that the CAP required structural changes to help it fulfil its aims at a time of changing world economic conditions, fully aware of the fact that when financial resources are scarce 'it is neither economically sensible nor financially possible to give producers a full guarantee for products in structural surplus'. Subsequently, on the basis of these guidelines, 'guarantee thresholds' were introduced for a number of products, with entitlement to full CAP benefits limited to prespecified levels of output. When these levels were exceeded, the policy varied from product to product; either: (a) the target and intervention prices were reduced; (b) aid paid under the market regulation was limited; (c) the producers participated in the cost of disposing surplus output by means of a 'co-responsibility' levy; or (d) production quotas applied at the national or the enterprise level.

However, these measures did not solve the fundamental problem of the sector which is 'how to reconcile the social objectives of the CAP with real market conditions' (*Bulletin EC* **3**, 1984). Production continued to exceed the level of self-sufficiency with long-term growth for most products at least three to four times higher than the annual rate of increase of their intra-EC consumption, while the markets for agricultural exports proved to be unreliable long-term outlets for surpluses.

The crisis reached a peak in 1984 when, after the failure to bring production under control, the budgetary funds were exhausted and the CAP was threatened with imminent financial collapse. After protracted negotiations a solution was announced at the Agricultural Council of 31 March 1984. The Council's policy guidelines were later enhanced by parallel measures at the budgetary level which were taken at the Fontainebleau European Council. With reference to the CAP, the

Agreement included the following:

1. A more realistic policy on prices which were to rise by less than the rate of inflation. It was estimated that in most member countries improvements in productivity would keep farmers' incomes rising.
2. Gradual elimination of the MCAs and adoption of new arrangements whereby parity changes in the EMS would no longer entail the creation of green rates.
3. Control of milk production through quotas.

The milk sector attracted special attention because its output continued to rise by 3.5 per cent per year, while the consumption remained stagnant. Price support and subsidised exports meant that milk products in all forms were taking up more than a quarter of the total EAGGF expenditure. The new policy set national production quotas calculated on the basis of previous deliveries, thus ignoring the demand side of the market. The national quotas were allocated by each member state to its regions and producers with re-trading prohibited. In addition, the co-responsibility levy was raised with quota overruns attracting a 'super levy' of 75 per cent for individual quotas and 100 per cent for collective quotas. However, a loophole in the system and the unwillingness of the member states to comply with the spirit of the agreement allowed farmers in one region to balance surplus output against under-production in other regions of the same country and thus to reduce the punitive 'super levy' on over-producers. Taking advantage of this, over-production in England and Wales in 1985 was balanced against short-falls in Scotland, so that English farmers paid no more than a token levy.

However, the system of quotas, which later became tradeable, did not constitute a permanent solution to the problems of the CAP. One reason for this was that quota restrictions covered only the production of milk, while cereals, which were taking up the second largest share of the CAP budget, were not subject to quota restrictions. Another reason was that quotas were set well above the level of self-sufficiency and surpluses continued to accumulate. Thus, despite the restrictions, milk production in 1985 soared to more than a million tonnes above the official quota, and butter stores topped 1.4 million tonnes. In July 1985 the Commission published one more Green Paper, *Perspectives for the CAP* (EC Commission, 1985b), reviewing the shortcomings of the CAP and recommending appropriate measures to overcome them. For the first time in the history of the CAP, this document also stressed the links between agriculture and protection of the environment. Under the pressure of increasing production and financial shortages, the EC took at the end of

1986 the first significant steps towards reforming the CAP. The Council adopted a two-pronged strategy to reduce surplus production and lower the budget costs of the CAP:

1. Support was limited to certain eligible quantities and qualities with producer co-responsibility for the cost of disposing surplus output.
2. The size of the budget would determine the extent of agricultural spending which should grow 'no faster' than the Community's income.

In the meantime it became obvious that the latest enlargement to include Greece and the expected accession of Portugal and Spain tended to exacerbate the already wide differences in farm structures and incomes between the various regions of the Community. Under the pressure of unresolved and newly instituted problems, the mechanism of the CAP was in urgent need of radical reform. Adjustments on the same general principles that applied in the past were no longer financially affordable. Without reform, the CAP, which in the past was considered to be the main instrument for economic integration, could become a burden and a threat to European unity. The financial crises had also confirmed that, in principle, the direction of any new reform should necessarily be 'in accordance with market conditions prevailing in each sector ... [so that] budgetary intervention can be cost-effective' (EC, 1981a).

The problems of the CAP continued in 1987, when by the middle of the year the Council failed to secure agreement on lower farm prices and policy reforms. This threatened once again to deepen the Community's financial crisis, with farm spending set to overshoot the 1987 budget by more than 15 per cent. Behind all these problems remained the fact that the CAP's pricing mechanism encourages farmers to overproduce, while the institutional framework of both the Community budget and the CAP induce national governments to encourage such overproduction. Commodity prices continued to be fixed in response to political as much as economic pressures, and governments of member states preached austerity by cuts in agricultural expenditures, but at the same time they did not stop their attempts to secure the best deal for their own farming interests. The Community's competitors in the world markets of agricultural products also claimed with some justification that all the proposed or implemented reforms had been initiated by budgetary pressures rather than by any sincere wish for market liberalisation and efficient use of resources.

After bitter arguments, European Heads of State agreed at the Brussels European Council (1988) on a formula for funding the EC budget until 1992 (see Chapter 4). The size of the budget will determine spending on the CAP, which is supposed to decrease. This will be pursued by the introduction of additional measures aiming at the reduction of production surpluses by tightening the support policies and assigning a larger role to market forces. This will be applied by strict budgetary discipline and complementary measures, such as 'production stabilisers' to adapt supply to demand and 'automatic price adjustments' to farmers based on production levels and overall ceilings on spending per product. Annual support prices will be set at levels consistent with the limits laid down by budgetary outlines. It is also expected that farmers will be induced by market conditions and the effects of policy to switch to production of more saleable crops.

These measures are combined with a payment to farmers to cut production by 'land set-aside', reducing the area of land under cultivation. Farmers' participation in the latter scheme is voluntary. One problem here is that farmers may set aside their least productive land, while intensifying production on the remaining land. Hence, in the longer run the effect on the volume of production would be minimal. In addition to these measures the Community will also provide direct aid for early retirement, income support to soften the impact of the new policies and compensatory payments to designated 'less favoured areas' with natural disadvantages or where the proportion of the labour force working in agriculture is well above average. Measures will also be instituted at the regional level for preservation of rural societies, the economy of which is in decline and might deteriorate further by the adjustment of European agriculture to actual circumstances on the markets.

The move towards the single market requires reorganisation of Community finances which are interlinked with reforms in the CAP. The Commission is aiming to achieve a cut in the budget resources directed to agriculture from the present 64.5 to 56 per cent by 1992, and to 50 per cent by the mid 1990s. This target will be pursued by 'a restrictive price policy, more flexibility in guarantees and intervention mechanisms, a greater degree of producer co-responsibility, including resource to quota systems' and support of 'producers who have opted to go for quality'. Assuming that the objectives of the CAP remained the same, these reforms may necessitate the creation of a new supplementary mechanism at Community level for supporting farm incomes. Finally, the agri-monetary system of monetary compensatory amounts would have to be checked and later, with progress towards closer monetary integration, be completely eliminated.

The Community at last has made determined efforts to bring agricultural expenditure under control. These stop short of completely liberalising the agricultural markets or opening them unilaterally to international competition. Its position is that in the longer term phased liberalisation of agricultural trade will be possible on a multilateral basis (EC Commission, 1988h).

7.6 The Common Fisheries Policy

After protracted negotiations, which started in 1966, the Community introduced a Common Fisheries Policy (CFP) in January 1983. The policy aims to ensure 'optimal exploitation of the biological resources of the Community Zone' by improved efficiency in both the structure and marketing of the sector and 'equitable exploitation of these limited resources between member states'. In particular, the objectives of the policy are as follows:

1. *On the structural side*:
   (a) the rational use of resources;
   (b) the elimination of discrimination among nationals of the EC member states employed in the industry;
   (c) the conservation of resources.
2. *On the marketing side*:
   (a) secure employment in the industry, particularly of certain coastal regions traditionally specialising in fishing;
   (b) a fair income for those employed in the industry;
   (c) improvement in marketing and marketing standards;
   (d) adequate supply adjusted to market requirements;
   (e) reasonable prices for the consumer.

The necessity for a CFP was enforced by developments in the international field which took place during the 1970s, when many countries introduced 200-mile (320 km) exclusive fishery zones. The decision to establish a CFP is based on Article 38 of the Treaty of Rome, which deals with agriculture. This Article was subsequently interpreted to include 'the products of the soil, of stockfarming and of fisheries and products of first stage processing directly related to these products'. Hence, the objectives of the CAP (Articles 38–47) apply also to the case of the CFP. The methods for achieving the objectives of the CFP are broadly similar to those of the CAP. Particularly for the fishing industry, the instruments of the policy are as follows:

1. *Access arrangements* which determine exactly where fishermen may fish. These also provide 12-mile (19 km) national fisheries zones

for each member country, with limited access for other member countries, and a 200-mile exclusive Community zone with members' quotas of catches. A number of third countries have signed agreements for reciprocal fishing and trade arrangements (Norway, Sweden, Canada, etc.).

2. *Marketing arrangements* which are designed to promote 'rational disposal' of fishery products and to bring some degree of stability in the industry and the incomes of those employed in it.

3. *Quotas* (total allowable catches, *TACs*), technical conservation measures (minimum size, minimum mesh size, etc.) and surveillance. These are instruments of policies which aim at the preservation of stocks. The Commission has established a special unit whose specific task is to oversee member states' efforts at enforcement of the CFP regulations (such as mesh size, minimum landing size, closed areas and closed season areas). However, each member country is responsible for policing the waters under its nominal jurisdiction and for ensuring that the provisions of the CFP are adhered to.

4. *Structural policies* which aim at the contraction of the industry which suffers from over-capacity, a better allocation of resources, increased productivity and long-term development. Structural expenditures are financed by the EAGGF.

As in the case of the CAP, for the CFP a target price and a guide price are established annually at the start of each fishing season. A withdrawal price also applies. However, the withdrawals are limited to a maximum of 20 per cent of the permitted annual catch, so that a degree of response, a kind of co-responsibility, is left to the supply. The CFP also provides export refunds and import duties, but the Community is on the whole a net importer of fisheries products. Contrary to the case of the CAP which is based on guaranteed prices designed to ensure farmers a fair income, the CFP helps to stabilise the market and to shelter fishermen from falling prices. But it does not attempt to regulate the upper bound of price fluctuations, so that fishermen benefit from the peaks of prices and are protected from the troughs.

The Mediterranean member countries are covered by the CFP as regards market organisation, structural change and financial matters. The Community has also proposed measures regarding inshore fishing and the conservation of resources. However, there are no 200-mile zones, quotas or TACs established as yet.

The entry of Portugal and Spain has radically altered the structure of the fisheries industry in the Community by: (a) doubling the manpower employed in the industry; (b) increasing the fishing capacity by 75 per cent; (c) increasing the production of the industry for human consumption by 45 per cent; and (d) increasing the consumption of fish by 43 per cent. Both Portugal and Spain have accepted the CFP in its entirety. However, transitional arrangements apply to both fish trade between the EC and the new members and limited access to Community waters. Portugal will become a full member of the CFP by 1995, while Spain will become one no earlier than 2002. For these two countries fisheries are of greater economic and social importance than in the other ten countries of the EC. The contributions of fisheries to GNP is 0.12 per cent for the ten members of the Community, while it is 0.90 per cent for Spain and 1.6 per cent for Portugal.

With every year the European Commission, on advice from a panel of national scientists, redoubles its insistence that stocks are being over-fished and that TACs must be reduced further. Where governments are forced to accept that stocks are depleted, they will still attempt to win as big a quota as possible of the TACs for their national fleets. In recent years, a fierce dispute between Spain and the United Kingdom served to highlight an apparently insoluble contradiction in the present structure of the CFP. This was over 'quota hopping' and related to Spanish fishing enterprises setting up companies in south-west England to catch fish allocated to the United Kingdom under its quota. This problem was temporarily stopped by the United Kingdom, which unilaterally passed an Act which provided for nationality, residence and domicile rules to stamp out 'hopping' by foreign fishing firms newly established in the United Kingdom. However, on appeal to the European Court of Justice, it was ruled that the imposition of the nationality, residence and domicile links of the UK Act contravened the free-trade principles of the EC Treaty. Therefore, to the outrage of some members of parliament in the United Kingdom, the Act was suspended. The Single European Act provides for all business and workers – including fishermen – to practise their trade anywhere in the single market of the Community.

Further reading

Every single publication about the CAP, including those published by the EC, is critical of the policy. The documents EC (1983b, 1983c, 1987b) present official proposals for reform. For reviews of the CAP, criticisms and proposals for reform see: Buckwell *et al.* (1982), Fennell (1985), Harvey and Thomson (1985), Josling (1979) and Marsh and Swanney (1980). A comprehensive survey of the costs of the CAP on the EC and its adverse effects on international trading relations is

Rosenblatt *et al.* (1988). The effects of the CAP among the member countries are also discussed in Morris (1980) and Rollo and Warwick (1979). An important contribution to the modelling of agricultural policy and measuring the effects of the CAP is Stoekel (1985). Ritson and Tangermann (1979) and Strauss (1983) consider the mechanism and effects of MCAs. The common fisheries policy is discussed in EC (1985b) and Shackleton (1982).

8

Trade policies

8.1 Trade and protection

International trade increases world efficiency by specialisation in production and exchange according to comparative advantage. Under conditions of perfect competition, constant returns to scale and absence of externalities, and given technology, these gains from efficiency are maximised with free trade. However, either because not all the required conditions are satisfied or for non-economic reasons, departures from free trade occur frequently. In developed industrial countries, traditional arguments for interventionist trade policies are based on the following:

1. The need to preserve or encourage mature industries, such as steel and shipbuilding.
2. The need to promote and secure sectors strategic for growth, such as high-technology industries.
3. The need to accommodate the special characteristics of disadvantaged sectors, such as agriculture.
4. The need to protect sectors important for national security and defence.

Non-traditional arguments for protection include the following:

1. Persistent trade imbalances leading to macroeconomic problems.
2. Protection of labour and the high social and budgetary cost of unemployment.
3. Exchange rate changes causing exchange rate instability.

4. 'Unfair' trade practices of other countries.
5. Strategic trade policy: if international markets are imperfect with excess returns or externalities that create a divergence between private and social benefits, protection could be justified on the proposition that strategic trade policy can shift the terms of international competition to the domestic industry's advantage.

An issue of contention is the income distribution implications of trade policies and the relative power of different groups in the society (farmers, trade unions, industrialists, consumers, etc.) to influence the process of making trade policy. Protection and liberalisation do not benefit or harm all the residents of a country to the same extent, so there is always some group with vested interests in protection or anti-protection. In general, while consumers are made better off by trade liberalisation and producers by protection, free trade brings about a net collective benefit to the society as a whole (see Chapter 1, Section 1.3). However, if the costs of protection are diffused over a large and diverse group, such as the consumers, while the benefits are concentrated on a relatively small but well organised group that can exert political pressure, such as the producers or labour unions, protection may be introduced despite its adverse net effects on the society as a whole. Trade restrictions might also be defended on the grounds that they redistribute income in favour of some disadvantaged group. It is unlikely, however, that trade policy is the best tool for dealing with the problem of income inequality.

Protection takes the direct form of tariffs on imports or non-tariff measures, such as quantitative restrictions, subsidies, government procurement practices and technical barriers to trade. A system of multiple exchange rates (e.g. with high rates on imports and low rates on exports) can have effects similar to those of a system of tariffs on imports and subsidies on exports. In a wider sense, a whole range of interventionist government policies, such as grants and loans for industrial development, promotion of research and development (R & D), regional subsidisation, public procurements and preferential allocation of defence contracts, have wide implications on foreign trade and are undertaken at least in part for their trade protection and domestic production promotion effects. In general, industrial and trade structures and policies are intertwined, and different industry structures give rise to different trade policy incentives and instruments.

Successive rounds of trade liberalisation measures undertaken since the early post-war years at world-wide scale under the auspices of the General Agreement on Tariffs and Trade (GATT) have diminished the importance of tariffs and quantitative restrictions, particularly on manufactured goods. However, the rise of unemployment and slow growth in industrial countries during the 1970s and 1980s and, probably, shifts in competitiveness and comparative advantage have been met by a proliferation of non-tariff trade barriers in the form of quantitative restrictions, subsidisation and discriminatory administrative measures, which have collectively become known as the 'new protectionism'. The most widespread of these new measures of protection are trade-limitation agreements, either informal 'orderly marketing arrangements' (OMAs) or formal 'voluntary export restraints' (VERs). Both measures are quantitative restrictions on exports of a product, agreed bilaterally at government or industry level, between an exporter and an importer. Voluntary export restraints, which here will be used to designate any export restraint arrangement, are usually negotiated for a specific period, are administered by the exporting country and frequently raise the price that the exporters charge, thus improving their terms of trade. Hence VERs reduce export volumes but may increase the total value received by the exporters. Consequently, exporters enter into such agreements because they may gain or because they face a threat that, otherwise, they would be subject to more stringent limitations.

From the trade-restricting country's point of view, the advantages of VERs over tariffs are that they are 'opaque', therefore politically less damaging to the government than tariffs, and 'voluntary', therefore only implicit violations of a country's international obligations. A major disadvantage of VERs is that usually they are bilateral, hence discriminatory between exporters. Therefore, in contrast to non-discriminatory tariffs on imports, VERs may cause trade diversion.

Figure 8.1 illustrates the operation of a VER in the market of a commodity X. With domestic demand D, domestic supply S and perfectly elastic import supply from a country W, in the absence of trade restrictions the market will reach equilibrium at the international price P_w. The domestic supply of output will be Q_1, imports $Q_1 Q_2$ and domestic demand Q_2. Suppose now that the country's authorities decide that the domestic production of X should rise from Q_1 to V_1, so that more labour will be employed in this industry. This objective is pursued by restricting the volume of imports in the domestic market by negotiating with the exporting country W a VER limiting imports to $V_1 V_2$. The restricted supply in the market, $OV_2 = OV_1 + V_1 V_2$, drives the domestic price up to P_r, and this reduces the domestic demand to OV_2. The costs to the home economy from implementing the VER are the welfare losses $(a + b)$ and the rent transfer c from the domestic consumers to the exporting country W which administers the VER and takes full advantage of the price increase in the importing country to charge export price P_r. If instead of the VER the importing country had levied an equivalent

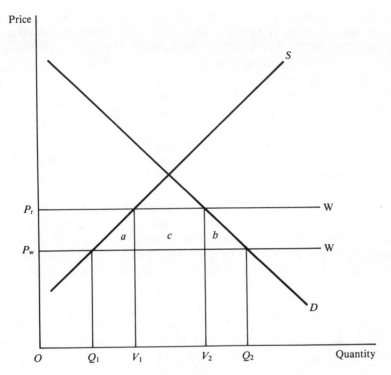

Figure 8.1 Voluntary export restraint.

tariff on its imports from W, area *c* would have remained in the country as tariff revenue. Therefore, the VER is even worse than the tariff for restricting trade in support of production by the domestic industry. But, since the foreign producers gain from VERs, they are more agreeable to the introduction of them rather than tariffs.

If the country is an exporter, it may attempt to alter the pattern of its domestic production and trade by resorting to export subsidies and other discriminatory policies, such as low-interest loans and preferential taxation, which reduce the producer cost of exports. Price discrimination in international markets is in general called 'dumping'. If the demand abroad is more elastic than the demand at home and the two markets are separate, dumping aims at profit maximisation by price discrimination, and it is beneficial to the consumers of the importing country but harmful to the consumers of the exporting country. However, many countries impose penalties against goods they believe are being dumped within their borders from abroad. These penalties are levied on imports to offset the competitive advantage gained by either price discrimination between exports and domestic sales of a given product (anti-dumping duties) or subsidies in the exporting country (countervailing duties). In general, the 'anti-dumping' argument for protection is valid if the dumping is 'predatory', that is, when it is designed to eliminate competition, after which prices are raised again. Otherwise, long-term export subsidisation by foreign suppliers improves the terms of trade of the importing country. If certain conditions are met, anti-dumping and countervailing duties are sanctioned by GATT under the International Anti-dumping Code signed in 1967.

Figure 8.2 illustrates the case of export subsidies and the imposition of countervailing duties. The demand for commodity X in country A is given by the curve D, and the domestic supply by the curve S. Country B's supply of exports to A is B, which is perfectly elastic. Under conditions of free trade, A's domestic price will be P_A, demand Q_3, domestic supply Q_2 and imports Q_2Q_3, supplied by country B. Next, B decides to increase its share in A's market by a subsidy s per unit price of exports, and this shifts its supply curve to B_s. If A does not retaliate, prices in

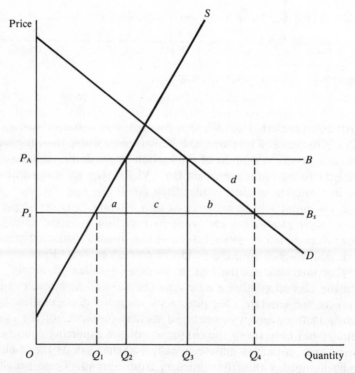

Figure 8.2 Dumping and countervailing duties.

its market will fall to P_s, demand will rise to Q_4, domestic production will become less competitive and fall to Q_1, and imports from B will rise to Q_1Q_4. The net welfare benefit to country A will be equal to $(a + b + c)$, which is a transfer from B to A, while the world (that is B and A together) will overall lose d from the operation of the subsidy policy. However, in an attempt to redress the 'injury', country A may react by imposing countervailing duties to restore the free-trade situation in its market. The necessary duty is a tariff rate equal to the subsidy rate s, which will shift the foreign supply back to B and raise A's domestic price to P_A. Imports will again be equal to Q_2Q_3, but they are now subject to the tariff. The net welfare effect of the two policies together, that is the subsidisation of B's exports and the taxation of A's imports, is a welfare gain for country A equal to the tariff revenue c, which actually is a net transfer from country B to country A. The basic results do not change if country B's export supply curve is assumed to be less than perfectly elastic: dumping and anti-dumping do not increase world welfare.

8.2 The Common Commercial Policy

As a rule, the EC is founded on the principles of free trade, but the exceptions are many and important. The Treaty of Rome stipulates that 'the Community shall be based upon a customs union' (Article 9), which would involve the gradual elimination of customs duties in trade between the member states, and the imposition of a common customs tariff on trade with third countries. These changes in customs duties were to be completed in three stages over a twelve-year period. In effect, the process was speeded up and the customs union was completed a year and a half ahead of the schedule set by the Treaty. By the middle of 1968 the six original members of the Community had (a) abolished all customs duties, charges of equivalent-discriminating effect and quantitative restrictions on trade between them, and (b) applied a common customs tariff (CCT, also called common external tariff, CET) on trade with non-member countries.

The three new members of the first enlargement (Denmark, Ireland and the United Kingdom) dismantled their tariffs on intra-Community trade and adopted the CET during a transitional period which ended on 1 July 1977. Greece, Portugal and Spain were given a seven-year transitional period, starting from the date of their entry, to phase out their tariffs and adopt the CET. By 1 January 1993 the process of tariff cuts and adoption of the CET will be completed and the Community will become a customs union of twelve full-member countries. Meanwhile,

Table 8.1 Community trade by partner countries, 1988 (per cent).

Country	EC-12	USA	Import origin Japan	ACP	Other	EC-12	USA	Export destination Japan	ACP	Other
B/L	70.4	5.4	3.4	2.6	18.2	74.2	5.0	1.2	1.1	18.5
DK	53.7	5.1	3.4	0.5	37.3	49.8	6.0	4.2	1.9	38.1
D	53.3	6.2	6.1	1.3	33.1	54.1	8.1	2.3	0.7	34.8
E	56.4	9.0	4.7	3.2	26.7	60.4	7.3	0.9	1.6	29.8
F	65.1	6.9	3.1	2.7	22.2	61.6	7.3	1.6	3.6	25.9
GR	62.4	3.8	5.7	1.6	26.5	64.3	6.3	1.4	1.0	27.0
IRL	71.2	14.5	3.9	0.8	11.4	74.1	7.7	1.9	1.0	15.3
I	57.5	5.6	2.5	1.3	33.1	57.1	8.9	1.9	1.6	30.5
NL	61.6	7.8	3.6	2.2	24.8	74.7	4.2	0.9	1.4	18.8
P	66.4	4.4	3.6	3.6	22.0	71.5	6.0	0.8	3.0	18.7
UK	49.2	11.0	6.1	1.4	32.3	49.8	12.9	2.2	2.2	32.9
EC	58.1	7.4	4.4	1.9	28.2	59.6	7.9	1.9	1.7	28.9

Source: Eurostat (1990) *Basic Statistics of the Community*, 27th ed., Luxembourg.

the Community is also attempting to reduce by harmonisation, and ultimately to eliminate, the existing national non-tariff barriers on internal trade and the internal frontier controls. Harmonisation of indirect taxes is also being pursued as discussed in Chapter 5. Table 8.1 presents the direction of EC internal and external trade. Trade between the members of the Community accounts for more than half of their total trade.

The Community has been expressly provided with powers by the EEC Treaty to conduct common external policy in the field of tariff and trade (Articles 11, 113), with regard to relations with international organisations (Article 229) and with regard to the conclusion of association agreements (Article 238). Article 3 of the Treaty states that the objectives of the Community require the establishment of 'a common commercial policy towards third countries'. Article 110 confirms that the member states 'aim to contribute, in the common interest, to the harmonious development of world trade, the progressive abolition of restrictions on international trade and the lowering of customs barriers'.

The Common Commercial Policy (CCP) began operating with the end of the transitional period in 1968, after the introduction of the CET, when the member states passed to the Community the power to enact foreign trade policy, that is to negotiate international trade agreements, fix customs procedures and determine export and import policies (including measures to be taken in cases of dumping or subsidies – Articles 91 and 113 – and countervailing duties – Article 99). However, the members retained some measure of autonomy in external-trade policy by operating, with Community authorisation under Article 115, their own lists of specific products subject to national import restrictions and originating from within or without the Community. In anticipation of the single European market, the EC Commission has issued a number of decisions making recourse to Article 115 more difficult. It will become obsolete by the end of 1992, when border customs checks are completely removed within the Community.

Article 116 specifies that the members shall act in common in respect of all matters of particular interest to the common market arising in international organisations 'of an economic character'. Decisions on Common Commercial Policy are taken by the Council, on proposals from the Commission, by qualified majority vote. Article 228 states that agreements between the Community and third states or international organisations are negotiated by the Commission and concluded by the Council by a unanimous decision. A similar procedure is followed in the case of application for membership in the Community by any European state (Article 237). Article 238 states that the Community may conclude with a third state, a union of states or an international organisation agreement 'creating association embodying reciprocal rights and obligations, joint actions and appropriate forms of procedure'. In 1984, the Community adopted under the CCP the New Commercial Policy Instrument to counter 'unfair' and 'unlawful trading practices', presumably those considered to be inconsistent with international agreements (such as GATT rules). Similar trade-policy tools are employed, or threaten to be employed, by other industrial nations to obtain a 'voluntary' export quota from another nation. Following the introduction of the Instrument, the EC has also broadened and updated its common legislation on anti-dumping and countervailing duties. The Community justified its action by invoking a general clause in GATT which allows countries to take action to prevent evasion of legally imposed measures. However, on this particular issue the Community has been accused of using anti-dumping measures as a means of protecting uncompetitive companies, especially in 'strategic' industries such as electronics, from their superior foreign rivals. Indeed, fears have been expressed regarding the possibility of using anti-dumping actions for tackling post-1992 adjustment problems and imposing the costs of adjustment on to the outside world.

The Treaty pays special attention to a group of non-European countries which are the subject of favourable trade and aid arrangements. These are 'countries and territories' which had dependency and colonial ties with some of the Six. Part VI of the Treaty (Articles 131–6) and subsequent agreements based upon it, granted to these now independent countries associate membership from the start for the purpose of promoting their economic development and establishing close economic relations between them and the Community as a whole. The association agreement involves rules regulating their trade with the Community and the supply of aid for their 'economic, social and cultural development to which they aspire' (Article 131).

On the basis of the relevant provisions of the Treaty of Rome, the Community has negotiated three enlargements and many association and trade agreements with third countries. As a result, the Community has become one of the most important trading blocs in the world and has affected both the volume and the direction of international trade. The EC is now the world's biggest exporter, accounting for 20 per cent of world trade, compared with the United States's 15 per cent and Japan's 9 per cent. Exports represent 10 per cent of the Community's GNP, compared with 5 per cent for the United States. In the process of developing, the Community faced criticisms from advocates of a more liberal economic order with regard to its position towards tariff preferences. Problems have also arisen in the Community's relations with other trading countries, some of which welcome the EC as a large trading partner predisposed towards trade liberalisation (for manufactures), while others saw in the EC the emergence of an adversary who does not always play the international trade game according to the rules, particularly so in the trade of agricultural commodities. Many countries also fear that in the process of establishing the single market, the EC may become more inward-looking by replacing existing bilateral quotas of some members by EC quotas (as, for example, quotas on imports of automobiles). This would mean extension of protection, since imports to all twelve member states would be covered. Thus the EC would turn into a highly protected and largely self-sufficient economic bloc, a 'Fortress Europe'.

This fear stems from the observation that intra-EC trade grows faster than total trade: its share on total trade rose from 49 to 60 per cent between 1970 and 1988. This has been taken as proof of rapid increase in self-sufficiency, indicating a trend for increasing reliance on intra-EC trade and a tendency to shift adjustment problems to non-member trading partners. In contrast, the EC has declared (Rhodes Summit 1988) that, as the largest exporter of the world, it 'has a fundamental stake in the existence of free and open international trade'. Therefore, 1992-Europe will be a partner, and the integrated market will be a decisive factor contributing to greater liberalisation in international trade on the basis of 'the GATT principles of reciprocal and mutually advantageous arrangements'. This has been interpreted by certain observers as an indication that extension of the benefits of the integrated market to third countries via further trade liberalisation will be conditional on reciprocity in market access.

In the following sections of this chapter we examine the relations between the GATT and the EC, and between the EC and non-member countries.

8.3 The General Agreement on Tariffs and Trade and the Community

The General Agreement on Tariffs and Trade (GATT) was signed in 1947. It has been updated since in order to adapt to major changes in the international economic order. The GATT is a voluntary agreement providing a code of rules for the conduct of world trade and a forum for the resolution of disputes and the reduction of trade barriers (Long, 1985). The Agreement is based on the free market, fair competition, free trade and specialisation according to comparative advantage. The contracting parties of the GATT have agreed to two main principles:

1. Trade liberalisation through the reduction of customs tariffs and the general elimination of quantitative restrictions and other non-tariff barriers to trade.
2. Non-discrimination in trade through the application of the most-favoured-nation (MFN) clause (GATT Article I), with the derogations and flexibility necessary to accommodate regional economic integration and special and more favourable treatment for developing countries.

Principle 1 aims at 'transparency' in the conditions in which world trade is conducted. Free trade is regarded as the best policy for the contracting parties, and trade liberalisation is the main objective of the GATT. However, given that free trade cannot be achieved in the short run, the tariff, which affects trade indirectly by its effects on prices, is considered as the least evil of the instruments of trade restrictions because it is transparent, easy to negotiate and fully compatible with the market (General Agreement on Tariffs and Trade, 1982).

Principle 2 specifies that any privilege or concession granted by one contracting party to a product of another contracting party will be unconditionally granted to the like products of all other contracting parties. Hence, this principle fosters a multilateral approach to trade liberalisation. However, three exceptions have been recognised. First, the less developed countries, which as a group may be subject to more favourable treatment. Second, trade preferences already in existence between countries before the formation of the GATT were excluded from the MFN extension, so that discrimination continued under the GATT. Third, by Article XXIV the GATT specifically allowed mutual preferences for free-trade areas, customs unions and interim agreements leading to economic integration provided that: (a) the tariffs of the customs union must not be higher than those of the member countries prior to union; (b) the arrangements must involve 'substantially all the trade' between the parties; and (c) the customs union or free-trade area must be completed 'within a reasonable length of time', that is within a relatively short period.

Article XXIV has been invoked and abused several times since the signing of the GATT owing to the growth of regional economic integration. As we have seen in Chapter 1, regional economic associations (REAs) combine trade liberalisation between the members with trade discrimination towards non-members. Therefore, they do not necessarily represent a move towards free trade and improvement in international efficiency. In effect, Article XXIV conflicts with the general principle of non-discrimination, since the abolition of tariff barriers between countries forming a customs union is necessarily regional and preferential and does not extend to all contracting parties of the GATT. The first two conditions attached to this exception attempt to direct countries to the formation of *trade-creating* customs unions which can be regarded as a step towards freer international trade. Nevertheless, even with a common external tariff limited to the level of the tariff prior to the formation of the customs union, some of the members could well experience trade diversion.

The EC's CET was set by the Treaty of Rome 'at the level of the arithmetical average of the duties applied in the four territories [Benelux (Belgium, Luxembourg, the Netherlands), France, FR Germany and Italy] comprised in the Community' (Article 19). The resulting average CET was approximately 11 per cent, much lower than the tariff of most of the important trade partners of the EC, such as the United States and Japan. However, the GATT considered that the method of calculation of the CET contravened the rule 'that the duties shall not on the whole be higher or more restrictive than the general incidence of the duties prior to the formation of such union' (Article XXIV). Despite representations by the GATT, the EC refused to discuss how it arrived at the CET, maintaining that Article XXIV did not demand any special method of calculation. Later, after enlargement of the EC to countries which were more protective than the original Six (such as Greece, Spain and Portugal) and had to adopt the CET, the GATT arguments became irrelevant. Moreover, under the GATT negotiations for tariff reduction of 1960–62 (Dillon Round), 1964–7 (Kennedy Round) and 1973–9 (Tokyo Round) in which the EC participated as a single unit (although not the Community as such, but its members, are contracting parties of the GATT), the CET was reduced further and it is today approximately 6 per cent. The Uruguay Round of trade liberalisation (September 1986–December 1990) is expected to promote further reductions of tariff and non-tariff barriers to international trade, not only on manufactures but also on services and perhaps on agricultural products, both of which are not bound in GATT.

Despite the repeatedly emphasised commitment of the Community to an open world trade system (EC, 1984b), the CET applies only to trade of manufactures. The CAP, which is based on high protection for the domestic market and on the granting of subsidies to exports, is clearly at odds with trade liberalisation. It is also at odds with Article XXIV which specifies that the internal barriers on 'substantially all' trade must be eliminated. Of course, the EC is not alone in this. The 1965 US–Canada automotive agreement, which provided for free trade in motor vehicles and parts at the manufacturer's level, was sector-specific and, therefore, an outright violation of the GATT.

Introduction of the CET and subsequent reductions in it do not mean that the EC has completely abstained from using other forms of protection. During the 1970s, world-wide economic recession and rising unemployment held back significant multilateral trade liberalisation, while protection by non-tariff trade barriers proliferated. The increase in protection was also prominent in the European Community. For example, in the steel industry, which is suffering from excess capacity, the EC operates volume controls in production and protection by voluntary export restraints (VERs). These are not controlled by the GATT which only prohibits discriminatory measures involving tariffs, duties and taxes, although they are applied on a discriminatory basis and against MFN principles.

Approximately three-quarters of all VERs known to exist world-wide in April 1988 originated from the EC and the United States. Under the Multi-Fibre Arrangement (MFA), which regulates trade in textiles (usually by limiting the imports of competitively priced textiles from developing to developed countries), the EC has negotiated VERs with twenty-five states. Similarly, in trade with Japan, which shows a large deficit for the EC countries, a mandate has been given to the Commission by the Council to negotiate VERs; meanwhile the member states have applied import ceilings bilaterally agreed with Japan or they even resort to unilateral implementation of non-tariff barriers. Both VERs and MFAs are formal derogations from the GATT, although MFAs are usually negotiated multilaterally under the auspices of the GATT. The EC has also introduced appropriate legislation for the use of anti-dumping and countervailing duties which, under certain limiting conditions, are consistent with the GATT (Article VI, the GATT Anti-dumping Code).

Another issue of contention and criticism by the GATT was the Association System of the EC. The preferences between France, Belgium, Italy, the Netherlands and their dependencies were permitted under the GATT rule, since they existed prior to 1947. Objections were raised when it was decided that association between the dependencies (listed in Annex IV of the Treaty of Rome) and the EC implies that preferences will extend to all the members of the Community, including those who had no historical ties with overseas territories. This was regarded as constituting the establishment of new preferences on a bilateral basis, thus contravening the spirit of the GATT which favours the multilateral approach to trade liberalisation. The EC maintained that its Association System constitutes an interim agreement for the formation of a customs union and therefore it is permitted under the GATT (Article XXIV). However, Article 133 of the Treaty of Rome stipulated that the associate overseas territories 'may levy such customs duties as are necessitated by their need for development and industrialisation', and this seemed to violate the GATT condition that the establishment of a free-trade area or customs union should include abolition of customs duties 'on substantially all the trade in products originating in such territories'. This issue was examined by a working party of GATT and EC representatives which concluded that, if at any time, contrary to their expectations, damage to the interest of third parties could be proved, the EC would take steps to mitigate it.

In 1965 the GATT enunciated a new rule, that 'the developed contracting parties do not expect reciprocity for commitments made by them in trade negotiations to reduce or remove tariffs and other trade barriers to the trade of less-developed contracting parties' (GATT, Appendix E, Article XXXVI, subsequently known as *Generalised System of Preferences*, GSP). This was also confirmed by a 1979 decision (*enabling clause*) waiving the most-favoured-nation provision to accord differential and more favoured treatment to developing countries, without according such treatment to other contracting parties. These rules imply that the EC's Association System, which is based on 'reciprocity' in tariff concessions, is in effect illegal and that the EC policy of 'reverse preferences' in its trade agreements with less developed countries (LDCs) constitutes an infringement of the GATT. The EC maintained that its trade agreements with LDCs are based on Article XXIV of the GATT which permits the establishment of free-trade areas based on the reciprocity of trade concessions. Therefore, if there is a problem, it clearly arises from contradictions between different GATT rules. The official view of the GATT has been that the free-trade areas between the EC and LDCs are more fictitious than real, and that 'the creation of preferential trade links between a few developed and one, or few, developing countries here and there through new discriminatory agreements for which no historical justification can be claimed' (General Agreement on Trade and Tariffs, 1972) violate the spirit of the GATT and should be deplored. Nevertheless, the association agreements between the EC and other developed and less developed countries have proliferated. Taking a pragmatic point of view, most members of the GATT have accepted that in all these agreements the EC has kept within the letter, even if not always within the spirit, of the GATT.

One can conclude that to the extent that the GATT objective is to help its less developed members, association with the EC is advantageous: the benefits received by the less developed associate members clearly outweigh those received by the EC. This has lately prompted some observers to claim that, with its network of preferential trading agreements, the EC has created a privileged group of client states with which it dominates the process of decision-making in the GATT, thus rendering the organisation a 'paper mouse'.

The growth of preferential trading arrangements is a cause for concern about the future of the international trading system, in particular after the EC's 1992 programme and the recently concluded (1989) Canada–United States Free Trade Agreement. The shares of these two blocs in global exports are 36.8 and 19.7 per cent, and in global GDP (excluding the countries of Eastern Europe) 26.6 and 34.9 per cent, respectively. This high degree of concentration is bound to have some effect on world trade.

8.4 The Lomé Convention

Under the Treaty of Rome, Part IV, Articles 131–6, the EC granted associate membership to certain overseas territories (listed in Annex IV of the Treaty) which were still dependencies of Community members. The association agreement entailed 'reciprocal rights and obligations' emanating from the establishment of a free-trade area with two-way free access for each other's products. It also included the granting of Community aid to the associate states by the European Development Fund (EDF), established for this purpose. Under the terms of the Treaty, this association system had to be reviewed after four years of operation. Soon after 1960, most of the EC associate overseas territories gained their national independence and started negotiations for a new agreement with the Community. This led in 1963 to the conclusion of the Yaoundé Convention, an agreement between the Community and eighteen African states. In contrast to the first agreement which provided for the abolition of customs duties between all the contracting parties, the Yaoundé Convention excluded the abolition of tariffs in inter-associate trade, establishing in effect eighteen free-trade areas, between the EC and each of the eighteen associates. The second Yaoundé Convention was signed in 1969. After the first enlargement which increased the full members of the EC to nine, it became necessary to reconsider the Community's Association System for possible inclusion of developing countries which had close ties with the United Kingdom through the Commonwealth. A new five-year association agreement, the Lomé Convention (1975–80), was signed in 1975 by the EC nine and forty-six African, Caribbean and Pacific (ACP) countries. This agreement was succeeded by the Lomé II Convention (1980–85) which was signed by sixty-three ACP countries. The Lomé III Convention (1985–90) was signed by sixty-six ACP countries in December 1984. The new ACP–EC Convention, Lomé IV, was signed by sixty-nine ACP countries in December 1989. The main innovations of the new agreement are that it is for a ten-year period and provides better trade and aid arrangements. As Table 8.1 shows, the share of the ACP group's trade with the EC is from the Community's point of view relatively small and decreasing.

Three institutions are involved in administering the Convention:

1. The Council of Ministers consists of the Community's Council, the Commission and a member of each ACP government.
2. The Committee of Ambassadors oversees the running of the Convention on a day-to-day basis.
3. The Joint Assembly is a consultative body which consists of equal numbers of members of the European Parliament and representatives elected or appointed by ACP states. It deals with and expresses opinions on matters related to the Convention.

The main provisions of the ACP–EC Convention are as follows:

1. *Tariff preferences*: almost all present ACP manufactures enter the Community at zero or very low tariffs. The Community, in return, gets 'most-favoured-nation' treatment from the ACP states and an undertaking that they will not discriminate between member states of the EC. The new Convention includes a chapter on trade in services, which provides for negotiations on more detailed provisions when the outcome of the Uruguay Round is known.
2. *Agricultural exports* from ACP countries competing with Community products are subject to CAP regulations. However, such products enjoy a preferential arrangement which includes levy rebate or exemption for out-of-season products. Special provisions exist for sugar, beef and rice which are subject to annual quotas. Agricultural exports which do not compete with Community products have preferences over third party supplies. In Lomé IV, the interaction between agricultural development and the preservation of ecological balances is also given particular attention.

3. *Aid*: under Lomé III and IV, in contrast to previous practice, aid is directed towards programmes rather than projects. The aid budget amounts to ECU 12 billion, the bulk of which is provided by the European Development Fund in the form of grants, soft loans and the financing of two institutions, the Stabex fund and the Sysmin scheme. The ACP countries also have access to funds from the European Investment Bank (EIB).

4. The *Stabex* fund provides EC financing for the stabilisation of earnings from the exports of certain, mainly agricultural, products. In order to qualify for a transfer from the fund, the product must account for 5 per cent of the country's total export earnings which must have fallen by more than 4.5 per cent below the reference level, which is 'the average of export earnings during the period of the six calendar years preceding each year of application less the two years with the highest and lowest figures'. In the case of least developed, landlocked and island states the activation thresholds are reduced to 1 per cent. Under Lomé IV the Stabex resources were increased by more than 60 per cent over those under the previous Convention.

5. The *Sysmin* scheme supports mineral production and provides financial assistance to ACP countries which are heavily dependent on mineral exports. The Sysmin is designed to help countries to cope with serious temporary disruptions affecting their export earnings from mining sectors. Lomé IV has extended the scheme's objectives to include investment for restoring a mining industry's viability or for economic diversification. The list of eligible products comprises copper, bauxite, iron ore, phosphates, manganese, tin, gold and uranium.

The European Community and its member states together constitute the world's leading source of official developing assistance, making up nearly one-third of all aid granted to developing countries. However, criticism against the Community's aid and Association Scheme have been raised by ACP members and third countries. ACP members argue that the aid provided by the EC is insufficient and non-increasing in real terms or per head of population (450 million people of the sixty-nine ACP states). On the other hand, the granting of preferences by the EC to the ACP countries has been looked upon with distrust and criticism by those countries, mostly Latin American, which were not included in the arrangements. They considered the Association Scheme discrim-inatory and divisive for the LDCs. Under pressure from them the United Nations Conference for Trade and Development instituted in 1968 (UNCTAD II) the Generalised System of Preferences (GSP) whereby developed countries provide non-reciprocal tariff concessions to exports of finished or semi-finished manufactures (other than those covered by the MFA) and selective processed agricultural products from developing nations. To its credit, the EC became the first major trading entity in the world to implement the GSP scheme. The beneficiaries of GSP are mostly Latin American and Asian countries which are not EC associates and therefore they would otherwise have to face the full CET. Still, the tariff preferences for the ACP under the Lomé Convention are more generous than the GSP for the outsiders.

8.5 Trade relations between the Community and other European countries

Besides the EC, two more integration schemes exist in Europe: the European Free Trade Area (EFTA) and the Council for Mutual Economic Assistance (CMEA or Comecon). In this section we examine the trade relations between the EC and other European countries, members of these organisations.

EFTA began life in 1960 by the Stockholm Convention. Its objective of trade liberalisation in industrial products between the members was virtually completed by December 1966. Agricultural products were excluded from tariff-free trade, and this raised questions about infringement of GATT's Article XXIV. The six EFTA countries are: Austria, Finland, Iceland, Norway, Sweden and Switzerland. From the original members of EFTA, Denmark and the United Kingdom left to join the EC in 1973, and Portugal in 1986.

Proximity and historical ties meant that the Community was by far the principal trade partner of EFTA. As members of the EFTA, Denmark and the United Kingdom had free trade in manufactures with the other member countries. Therefore, when they applied for membership in the EC, an opportunity was presented for negotiating the reduction of the barriers that divided Western European trade. Given that certain of the EFTA countries (e.g. Sweden, Switzerland, Austria) were against membership in the EC because of political neutrality, a merger of the two organisations was not considered. It was decided instead that negotiations should start over the future of their mutual trade arrangements. The bilateral agreements between the EC and each of the EFTA countries were concluded in the early 1970s and put into effect from the date of the first enlargement, 1 January 1973. Collectively, these agreements constituted the establishment of a free-trade area for industrial products throughout Western Europe. The elimination of tariffs on mutual trade was completed in July 1977. Rules of origin have been introduced to prevent *trade deflection* (imports from non-member countries entering the free-trade area through a low-tariff member and re-exported duty-free to the member with the higher external barrier), as well as safeguard arrangements permitting countries to introduce special protective measures in case of balance-of-payments crises. Each free-trade agreement is administered by a joint committee, consisting of representatives of the EC and the relevant EFTA country.

Further integration between the two organisations was envisaged by the Luxembourg Declaration of April 1984, which calls for the creation of a 'dynamic economic space in Western Europe'. The declaration included commitments to reduce non-tariff barriers to trade, such as border formalities, harmonisation of standards, improvement in the rules of origin and application of fair competition rules. Subsequent meetings expanded the scope of the cooperation agreement between the two organisations to increase the information about the distribution of state aids and opening up of government procurements. However, following the Single European act, the EFTA countries have become apprehensive that their access to the EC market will be reduced as a result of unification of the EC's internal market and the possibility of increased protectionism. Discussions on increased cooperation between the two organisations in economic, cultural and educational matters forged the outline (1990) of an eventual treaty, designed to draw EFTA fully into the EC's single market ahead of its completion, but without offering full membership in the Community. The deal is that EFTA will accept EC laws that govern the 'four freedoms': movement of goods, services, capital and people. Both sides are to start negotiations for the establishment of the so-called European Economic Space (EES) of eighteen states. The aim of negotiations is to implement EES by 31 December 1992, in parallel with the completion of the internal market. Meanwhile, Austria applied for full membership in the EC in 1988, but subject to its permanent neutral status (which resulted from the Second World War). There are also signs that other EFTA countries, dissatisfied with participation in the EES without having a say over EC policy-making, may apply for full membership in the EC. However, given that the EC has declared its intention to increase political cooperation between its members, the declared neutrality of some EFTA countries may be a major obstacle to membership.

The tendency towards closer economic cooperation in Western Europe did not receive an unqualified approval by the advocates of the multilateral, as opposed to the bilateral, approach to trade liberalisation, who accused the EC of violation of the GATT by treating the EFTA group of countries differently from the rest of non-EC industrialised world.

The CMEA was founded in 1949 with the objective of accelerating economic growth and establishing a more rational division of labour among its member countries. Its members are Mongolia, Cuba and Vietnam and the following 'state-trading' European countries: Czechoslovakia, Hungary, Poland and Romania, which are contracting members of the GATT, and Bulgaria and the USSR. The German Democratic Republic (GDR) was a member of CMEA before its unification with the Federal Republic of Germany in 1990.

Unlike the EC, CMEA has no supranational powers. It acts only as a broker and coordinator for its member countries, distributing production tasks to its members to avoid duplication efforts. Trade between the CMEA countries is conducted by a barter system in which the governments of the member states agree on the quantity of the goods to be exchanged, and then direct their respective firms to deliver them. They also agree on prices which normally bear no relation to production costs. Trade between CMEA countries and non-member countries is also conducted by a barter system on a balanced-trade basis. However, since perestroika this system of trade is under review. If it does not break down, CMEA plans to start trading at world-market prices (by 1991) and to replace its accounting system of unconvertible exchange rates to one based on a hard currency.

Until very recently no trade agreement existed between the EC and CMEA, among other reasons because the latter did not recognise the EC as a trading entity, while on the other hand the Community, which has the power to negotiate and conclude international trade agreements on behalf of its members, argued that the CMEA lacked the supranational character necessary for such an agreement. However, after unsuccessful attempts in the 1970s, the two organisations re-opened the dialogue to establish official relations in 1986. Two rounds of preliminary meetings brought progress in the process of *rapprochement* of their negotiating positions and 'The Joint Declaration on the Establishment of Official Relations between the EC and CMEA' was finally signed in June 1988. Agreements between the EC and individual members of the CMEA have already been concluded. These include trade treaties with Hungary and Poland which provide for an end to all quotas on manufactured imports into the Community by 1995. The treaty with Poland also breaks new ground by lowering customs duties on a small number of Polish farm products. Bilateral trade and cooperation agreements have also been concluded with Romania and Czechoslovakia while similar ones are being negotiated with the Soviet Union and Bulgaria. Formal accreditation has also come from the non-European members of CMEA. Finally, after the recent political developments in Central and Eastern Europe, the European Council declared its intention in 1989 to examine the question of an association with those countries which successfully and purposefully followed their chosen path of thorough economic and political reform.

Under the Treaty of Rome special arrangements applied to trade between the Federal Republic of Germany and the German Democratic Republic. The unification of the two Germanies in 1990 has transformed the German Democratic Republic from an independent state to a region of the European Community. With East Germany in the EC, would-be members such as Austria have a strong case for being let in too sooner or later. Czechoslovakia and Hungary have also announced that they intend pressing for eventual membership of the EC.

The first trade and cooperation agreement between the USSR and the EC was signed in November 1989. The ten-year accord is designed to promote trade and cooperation in a number of areas, including industry, science and technology, energy and the environment. The trade concessions granted by the Community refer to quotas which were directed specifically against USSR exports; they will be progressively dismantled by 1995 in return for better access to Soviet markets for EC firms. The fact that a formal agreement between the USSR and the EC did not exist before does not mean that trade between the two organisations did not take place in the past. The USSR for many years has been one of the top ten trade partners of the EC and one of its most important customers for agricultural surpluses, such as butter.

8.6   The Community and the Mediterranean countries

After the accession to the Community of Greece, Spain and Portugal, the term Mediterranean countries refers to the following non-member countries of the Mediterranean basin:

1. The Maghreb group: Algeria, Morocco and Tunisia.
2. The Mashreq group: Egypt, Jordan, Lebanon and Syria.
3. Turkey.
4. Israel, Cyprus, Malta and Yugoslavia.

Albania and Libya have no trade agreements with the EC.

For historical, strategic and economic reasons the EC countries have always had close relations with the countries bordering the Mediterranean. Today, approximately 10 per cent of EC exports are directed to these countries. They in turn sell more than 50 per cent of their exports to the EC.

Establishment of the EC, introduction of the CAP and restrictions on imports of agricultural commodities meant that many of the Mediterranean countries could lose their most important export markets. In an attempt to maintain access to these markets, they asked for special trade relations with the Community (Shlaim and Yannopoulos, 1976). The Community responded favourably, and from early on trade agreements were concluded with individual members of the Mediterranean basin. These agreements were different in legal structure from country to country, some taking the form of association under Article 238 with a view of eventual membership (Greece and Turkey), others aiming at establishment of free-trade areas (Tunisia, Morocco), and others offering only most-favoured-nation advantages (Israel, Lebanon).

Since the Mediterranean countries produce and export a broadly similar range of commodities, there was no economic rationale for this multitude of different trade agreements. Some of the countries concerned were in the past protectorates or dependencies of Community members and perhaps one reason for their preferential treatment could have been the historical and political ties (EC, 1985c). However, the most convincing explanation is that in its relations with neighbouring developing countries the EC had not developed coherent plans, the various agreements were uncoordinated and their terms were determined *ad hoc* as they came along with a view to current events and the lobbying activity of individual countries. The final outcome was a 'mosaic' of Mediterranean trade agreements openly contravening the MFN principle of the GATT.

The concept of EC's 'Global Mediterranean Policy' was developed in 1971–2, when the Community was preparing for its first enlargement, and the Tokyo Round of GATT negotiations for tariff cuts. The Commission proposals, which were presented in September 1972, were based on rational differentiation and envisaged the establishment of a free-trade area for industrial products by 1977, with exports of agricultural commodities to the Community based on specific quotas. However, with objections from the southern parts of the EC, who would have to carry the burden of concessions on the trade of agricultural commodities which they are producing themselves, the negotiations dragged on. Finally, a diluted 'Global Mediterranean Policy' was put into effect only by the end of 1978. The trade agreements are still bilateral between the EC and each of the Mediterranean countries, and differ substantially in their details. However, the following general principles can be discerned:

1. For the Arab Mediterranean countries and Yugoslavia the agreements are based on non-reciprocity, that is on MFN terms. For Turkey, Malta, Cyprus and Israel partial reciprocity applies.

2. Free access for exports of industrial commodities to the EC. Exceptions apply to certain sensitive commodities, such as textiles, clothing and refined petroleum for which exports are determined by quota allocation. In general terms the quotas for textiles and clothing are larger under the bilateral agreements then under the restrictions which the EC would have imposed on the basis of the Multi-Fibre Arrangements. For the Arab Mediterranean countries the benefit from free access for industrial exports is minimal because their industrial production of exportables is insignificant.

3. Agricultural commodities for which the EC is a producer but has not reached self-sufficiency are exported in quantities determined by licences, quota allocation or tariffs. Off-season supplies are treated more liberally. Agricultural commodities which are not produced on any scale in the EC are either subject to very low tariffs or have free access to the Community.

4. Aid in the form of loans from the EIB and technical cooperation agreement.

With the exception of the agreement with Yugoslavia, which is limited to five years, all other agreements are unlimited. The agreements with Cyprus and Malta provided for future negotiations for setting up a customs union. Both Malta and Cyprus are planning to apply before 1992 for full membership in the EC. Meanwhile, a new agreement with Cyprus came into effect on 1 January 1988. Under this agreement, Cyprus will remove customs duties on imports of industrial products from the EC and adopt the common external tariff over a ten-year period. Reciprocal concessions will apply on agricultural exports until complete liberalisation at some future date.

The trade and cooperation agreement with Israel provides for the establishment of an industrial free-trade area under Article 113 of the EEC Treaty. The agreement with Turkey established a customs union with potential full membership in the Community after the end of a lengthy association period. Turkey applied for full membership in April 1987, but the Community's reply in 1989 was that, although Turkey is eligible in principle to join the EC, the wide political, economic and social gaps between it and the EC mean that the country still has far to go before an application can be considered. Despite impressive growth in recent years, the Turkish economy was still only one-third of the EC average. Industry was heavily protected, and would be unable to face the blast of full competition. Inflation was running at 60 per cent, and unemployment was far higher than in any EC state. With half the country's workforce employed in agriculture, Turkey had as many farmers as the twelve EC countries together.

8.7 Trade agreements with other developing countries

The Community also has non-preferential agreements with Argentina, Brazil, Mexico, Colombia, Guatemala, Haiti, Uruguay, Bangladesh, India, Pakistan and Sri Lanka. Under the revised Multi-Figure Arrangements (extended to 31 July 1991) agreements concerning textiles have been concluded with India, Hong Kong, Korea, Pakistan, Thailand, Macao, Malaysia, Singapore, Philippines, Sri Lanka, Bangladesh and Indonesia. A second five-year (1985–90) trade and cooperation agreement has been negotiated with China. Cooperation agreements have also been concluded between the Community and Yemen AR, and the Andean group of countries (Bolivia, Colombia, Ecuador, Peru and Venezuela).

The first of a two-stage agreement with the Arab countries of the Gulf Cooperation Council (GCC – Bahrain, Kuwait, Oman, Qatar, Saudi Arabia and the United Arab Emirates), concluded on 15 June 1988, includes provisions for increased cooperation in the areas of industry, energy, science, technology and the environment. The second stage would include trade liberalisation with provisions concerning the exports of petrochemicals and oil from GCC and protection of their developing industrial structure on infant industry grounds.

8.8 Relations with the United States and Japan

The EC's trade relations with non-European industrial countries, that is Australia, New Zealand, Japan, South Africa, Canada and the United States, are supposed to be conducted under the GATT rules and regulations. But relations are frequently strained, mostly because of the effects of the CAP on world markets and the discriminate trade policies of the EC with non-member countries. Reforms introduced in the CAP since 1984 are perceived by many countries as having been motivated by the EC's budgetary problems rather than by any desire to open the market in agricultural products or reduce export subsidies. Consequently, trade disputes involving agricultural products occur frequently. After some period of strife, they are usually resolved by recourse to the multilateral GATT dispute settlement procedure.

The problems created by the impressive rise of Japanese exports to the Community are rather more complicated and more difficult to resolve. A number of industrial products imported from Japan to EC countries are subject to VERs (automobiles, electronic products, machine tools and steel; see also Chapter 12) and other tariff measures and administrative controls imposed at the national and Community levels. The removal of internal borders in 1992 implies that national restrictions on imports from third countries will no longer be enforceable. However, pressures exist within the EC to protect the integrated market by adopting as common policy the most restrictive of the national trade regimes. Although the Community has declared that it does not intend to build a 'Fortress Europe', it has also warned that access to the integrated market will be linked to reciprocal concessions granted by its trading partners, and Japan in particular.

The Community argues that Japan operates non-tariff barriers to trade while on the other hand its industrial policies provide its exporters, to some extent, with tax preferences and credit subsidies. In disputing the pricing of Japanese exports, the Community has in some cases resorted to the use of anti-dumping duties and administrative protection. Japanese exporting firms have reacted by foreign direct investment in the machine tool, electronics and automobile sectors in the protected markets of the EC and the United States. In certain instances, these investments amount to no more than the setting up of assembly plants. Hence, a new EC law was specifically introduced in June 1987 to stop these 'screwdriver' operations. Accordingly, if the assembly plants had been set up as a result of previous infringement in order to circumvent anti-dumping duties, and more than 60 per cent of the finished product consisted of components shipped from Japan, penal and anti-dumping duties were applied to the imported components. However, Japan appealed successfully to GATT against this legislation, which found that the EC measures were discriminatory since they cannot be applied to European companies conducting similar 'screwdriver' operations in the European market.

Since 1985, Japan has reduced tariffs and other 'visible' trade barriers and agreed to phase out quotas on imports of agricultural products. In addition to these trade liberalisation measures, it has also started bilateral discussions with the EC to ease barriers arising from standards, testing and certification procedures which restrict access to Japanese import markets. But, while there is no doubt that Japan has undertaken in recent years to stimulate domestic demand and to improve access to its markets, its competitors continue to complain about 'invisible' barriers to Japanese markets based on attitudes and traditions, irrational and unstated product standards that exclude foreign goods, and controls over the Japanese distribution system by domestic producers. There is also evidence that Japan protects its agriculture – mostly the rice producers – rather more than either the EC or the United States.

After several years of negotiations, the United States and Canada signed a free-trade agreement, which became a binding obligation for both countries on 1 January 1989. Since the two countries had already low average trade barriers against each other's manufactured goods, the expected welfare effects, trade creation or trade diversion, are not predicted to be large overall, but they may be substantial for certain sectors, such as textiles. The agreement incorporates several innovative provisions covering dispute settlement, foreign direct investment, services and some restrictions on the use of safeguard measures. Agricultural products, which are protected in both countries mostly by non-tariff barriers, are essentially excluded from the agreement.

Over recent years the trade relations between the Community and the United States have become very tense on a number of issues relating to imports and exports of both agricultural and industrial products. In general, the EC–US trade relations seem to be negatively correlated with the strength of the dollar in international money markets, improving when the competitiveness of the United States improves, and deteriorating when the deficit in the US balance of payments worsens. Growing external deficits over the last decade have also intensified protectionist pressures, led to the passing of new legislation extending the use of bilateral approaches to trade disputes (Omnibus Trade and Competitiveness Act, 1988) and multiplied the investigations for 'unfair' trade practices, anti-dumping and countervailing. Almost half of all anti-dumping investigations of the period 1980–87 was directed against the EC and Japan. A number of outstanding disputes with the EC concerned the following products.

Agricultural trade

Both the US and the EC agricultural policies are primarily oriented towards domestic problems. One of the main differences between the two areas is that the EC's agricultural policies (guaranteed farm prices) are relatively more transparent than those of the United States (top-up income payments to farmers). However, both policies have resulted in over-production which both the EC and the United States unload by increasing exports ('dumping') to the world markets of agricultural commodities. Hence, disputes about what constitutes 'fair' trade and over market shares are frequent. Until the mid-1970s the United States was the dominant producer and exporter of a number of key agricultural commodities such as grain, flour and animal feed, to the extent that the domestic US price level and the world price level were identical. But more recently, growing competition from other exporting countries, such as Argentina, Brazil, Australia, Canada and the EC, in conjunction with appreciation of the dollar have reduced the United States pre-eminence as world market leader. Thus, the US share of world wheat exports fell from 50 per cent in 1976 to 30 per cent in 1986. These developments, the elevation of the EC to the world's second largest food exporter and the United States' record trade deficits provided a prolific background for a number of disputes.

The United States objects to the EC's CAP on three issues:

1. Protection of the European market which affects US exports to the Community.
2. CAP policies of subsidised exports which compete with US production and exports in the markets of third countries.
3. Bilateral agreements of preferential trading with third countries and enlargement of the Community, both of which discriminate against US exports.

On these issues the United States has brought a number of 'lawsuits' against the EC under the GATT adjudication procedure, concerning many sectors (poultry in 1962, sugar, poultry meat and flour in 1981, citrus fruit and pasta in 1983, etc.). It has also retaliated by both levying protective taxes on its imports (countervailing duties) from the EC and underbidding EC export prices by increasing the subsidies to its exporters. The EC's response has been that its policy of subsidies is not different from the open and hidden subsidy policies which the US government has been following (EC Commission, 1984b), that the EC share in the export trade of agricultural commodities is, relative to that of the United States, very small, and that despite the CAP the EC is the biggest market in the world for imports of agricultural products (see also Chapter 7).

Although in certain cases GATT dispute panels ruled that the EC's CAP and preferential trade arrangements are indeed detrimental to US interests but do not contravene GATT rules, the GATT council (which takes decisions on the unanimity principle) rejected the call for further action. When in retaliation the United States set up the Domestic International Sales Corporation (Disc) and the Bonus Incentive Commodity Export Programme (Bicep) which provided subsidies to exports to help them compete with foreign suppliers, it was the turn of the Community to file a complaint with the GATT. A similar procedure was followed by the EC when the United States imposed restrictions on imports of wine from the Community. Similarly, when objecting to the Community's trade agreements with Mediterranean countries, the United States raised its customs duties on imports of pasta products from the EC by up to 40 per cent, the Community retaliated by taking counter-measures affecting imports of citrus fruit from the United States. This dispute was settled by an agreement, a key provision of which was that the United States accepted the consistency of EC's Mediterranean trade policies with Article XXIV of the GATT. On the whole, this hidden/open trade war is usually contained by mutual threats of actions and counter-actions which lead to a negotiated settlement rather than to escalation and economic sanctions. However, no permanent solution has been contemplated.

One of the most recent disputes concerned the effects of the latest enlargement of the EC to Portugal and Spain on US exports of agricultural and industrial products. Community preferences would have meant that intra-Community trade will displace competitive imports from non-members, such as the United States (Paarlberg, 1986). The problem was particularly important for US agricultural exports because, first, of a serious crisis in the domestic and export markets of agricultural commodities, and, second, the Iberian markets for cereals, particularly maize, and oilseeds prior to the enlargement had been dominated by US suppliers. The dispute reached a peak during 1986, with threats and counter-threats of retaliation and the publication by both the United States and the EC of hit lists of commodities which were to be subject to import tariffs of up to 200 per cent. Finally, the dispute was settled on 29 January 1987, again by a bilateral agreement which provides for four years a specific volume of cereals to be imported from non-member countries (and this in effect means the United States) in the markets of Portugal and Spain.

GATT's Uruguay Round of negotiations for tariff reductions, which will end in December 1990, has reached a deadlock regarding the liberalisation of agricultural trade. The United States proposed a 'double-zero' programme of eliminating export subsidies within five years and most other protection within ten, which is unacceptable to many countries and the EC. Equally unacceptable to many is the EC's proposed two-tier tariff, part fixed, but subject to negotiated reductions, and part variable to compensate for big shifts in prices or exchange rates. Japan also argues in favour of border restrictions on 'essential foodstuffs', i.e. rice. Without an agreement to reduce state support for agriculture and to open up domestic markets to farm imports from efficient producers, the whole round of negotiations for international trade liberalisation was in danger of collapse. Hence the summit of the leaders of the seven most industrialised countries, G-7, at Houston, Texas, in July 1990, called for 'substantial progressive' cuts in farm support, including export subsidies. The negotiations were 'suspended' in December 1990.

Steel

The effects of the current economic recession had particular repercussions on the world demand for steel. The US and EC steel industry also suffered additional blows from the onslaught of steel exports at competitive prices from Japan and newly industrialising countries, such as Korea, Mexico, India and Brazil. Under the Davignon Plan the Community introduced a policy which aimed at capacity reduction and modernisation of the steel industry (see Chapter 12). The Plan introduced voluntary agreements on production ceilings and minimum prices, supplemented by a code on state aid in the form of subsidies to producers who would agree to reduce capacity. Imports were also contained by voluntary restraint agreements and import levies. Under US law, firms that can sustain a claim that their products face competition from subsidised imports have recourse to automatic anti-dumping action in the form of countervailing import duties. These in effect act as import tariffs against users of export subsidies and in principle are equal to the foreign subsidy, as assessed by the US authorities. If the injured party can prove that the export subsidies paid have no adverse effect on the economy of the importing country, then the countervailing duties are lifted.

The procedure for levying countervailing duties was invoked in January 1982 by US steel manufacturers on imports of steel from the Community, which amount to approximately 6 per cent of total US consumption. The US official investigation estimated that in some EC member states certain steel producers received 20–40 per cent production subsidies and announced the introduction of appropriate countervailing duties. The Community's reaction was to object to the method used by the official US investigation which did not distinguish between operating subsidies and grants for modernisation. The two parties agreed to discuss their disputes in an attempt to resolve their differences. However, a problem appeared at the Community side: the Treaty of the European Coal and Steel Community (ECSC) specified that commercial policy for the products covered by it is exercised by the governments of the member states and not by the Community. Consequently, the ten Community governments first had to agree to joint negotiations with the United States. These negotiations led to the conclusion of a voluntary export restraint until the end of 1985. A similar dispute broke out in 1983 and 1984 when the United States announced restriction on imports of special steels. The Community respond by unilaterally adopting countervailing measures against certain US exports and filing a claim for compensated under GATT rules. An agreement was finally reached on 5 January 1985 which determined a market share of 7.6 per cent for Community products, excluding products the US industry cannot supply.

8.9 Conclusions

With the implementation of a Common Commercial Policy the Community has become a large economic unit with a unique, and potentially very strong, trading position *vis-à-vis* all other countries. In this capacity, the Community over the years has concluded a number of agreements with developed and less developed countries. A common characteristic of these agreements is the discrimination which the EC has introduced in its trade of different commodities and in its trade relations with different countries.

First, the CAP discriminates by restricting trade in agricultural commodities. The declarations of the Treaty of Rome regarding free trade and the frequently repeated commitment of the Community to an open world trading system apply only to industrial commodities. The CAP constitutes a serious departure from the principles of free trade, causing misallocation of resources in the Community and at a world-wide scale.

Second, the agreements which the Community has concluded with different countries are not based on the GATT principles of multilateral trade but on bilateral concessions which discriminate not only between developed and less developed countries but also within these groups between countries. These agreements have conferred privileges selectively, resulting in a ranking of countries according to their place in the Community's 'pyramid of preferences'. Among the less developed countries, the ACP associate states are placed higher than the Mediterranean countries which are placed above the non-associate countries of Asia and South America. Among the developed countries, the EFTA group are placed above the non-European industrial countries and the CMEA countries.

However, it can be argued that the lack of a consistent direction in the Common Commercial Policy of the Community was justifiable during a period of economic recession and turbulence in the world economy, when many developed and less developed countries have started to advocate the doctrine of 'new protectionism'. Moreover, after three enlargements the Community has become a common market of heterogeneous countries which are characterised by divergence in economic performance and domestic economic policies. Therefore, the incomplete state and the contradictions of the CCP should not be unexpected. However, opinions differ as to whether the European CCP will be more or less liberal in the future. The current economic recession has brought a number of problems to the economies of the EC countries which simultaneously face unemployment and contraction in their industries and loss of competitiveness in international markets.

An approach for solving these problems advocated by some members is to combine liberalisation of the internal market with a common industrial policy based on protection from foreign competition. The argument of the proponents of these measures is that European industry has fallen so far behind the US, Japanese and newly industrialising countries' industry that only some form of 'temporary' protection can revive it. It is also argued that protection is needed for the establishment of advanced technology industries on infant industry grounds (Richonnier, 1984). In this case, 'promotion' of the infant industry by production subsidies that do not discriminate between home and foreign trade are preferable to protecting by tariffs. Another variant of the argument for protection is based on recent theoretical models of trade policy, which suggest that government intervention can have an enduring effect on the competitive position of national firms in international competition, when such competition occurs in imperfectly competitive markets and involves research-intensive, high-technology products. These arguments have found more favour among experts and officials responsible for the industry rather than foreign trade, who argue that the international markets for high-technology products are indeed imperfect and that Japan is a good example of a country that has used strategic government policy (trade protection and export promotion) to gain a large share in world export markets.

Officially, the Community has declared its adherence to free-trade principles and its commitment to 'the progressive abolition of restrictions on international trade and the lowering of customs duties' (Article 110) under the auspices of the GATT. It has also stated that integration of the internal market should be regarded as a contributing factor to greater liberalisation of international trade, beneficial to both the EC and third countries. At the same time, the Community insists that it will extend the benefits of the single market to outsiders only on the basis of reciprocity, which is taken to mean that in the foreign markets EC firms should enjoy effective access and the same treatment as that accorded to domestic firms. However, decisions concerning the Community's post-1992 external regime have not yet been taken. Therefore, whether one day neo-protectionist arguments will prevail and the European Community will become generally or selectively more protective in international trade, is a matter for conjecture.

Further reading

On protectionism, old and new, see Bhagwati (1988). The Community's views on protectionism can be found in EC (1984c). Hine (1985) gives an overall view of Community trade policies. Issues in US–EC trade relations are examined in Baldwin *et al.* (1988). The post-1992 EC–Japan relations are discussed in Ishikawa (1990).

9

Regional policy

9.1　The nature of regional problems

Regional problems are the disparities in levels of income in rates of growth of output and employment, and in general in levels of economic inequality between the geographic regions of a country. They arise from unequal growth rates of economic activity. Higher income areas are invariably those where the centres of population, government and industry are to be found.

According to the neoclassical theory of regional development, free competition and factor mobility will tend to equalise factor returns across regions within a state and therefore regional differences in economic development cannot be sustained. However, in practice the conditions of the neoclassical theory are not always fulfilled. For instance, capital and labour might not be completely mobile and persistent disparities among regions may exist in production functions, economies and diseconomies of scale, and obstacles to the market mechanism. Consequently, it is possible that the process of development may tend to favour certain regions within a country by a cumulative gravitation mechanism. Thus, new industry and trade will be attracted where industry and trade already exist, and the necessary infrastructure, associated services and the market for selling output are relatively more readily available than in other areas.

This gravitation process leads to the phenomenon of intra-country polarisation, by which areas that are relatively developed continue to grow fast, while the relatively backward areas experience cumulative economic decline. Regional growth thus tends to be concentrated in 'poles of development', that is in geographic areas that provide new investment with economies of scale, thus making it possible for them to gain an initial headstart and to continue to grow at the expense of other regions of the economy. These scale economies are both external and internal, and are usually specified as economies of localisation and economies of urbanisation. Economies of localisation arise from the geographic concentration of plants in the same industry and the advantages gained by linkages between them and the potential for increased efficiency through specialisation. Urbanisation, or agglomeration, economies arise from the geographic concentration of a large number of economic activities served jointly by different facilities, such as transportation, availability of a skilled labour force, financial institutions and proximity of markets for their output. Polarisation causes a vicious spiral of economic growth which may assist the relatively more developed regions in a country to grow at the cost of the less developed regions. Hence, the regional problems are both causes and effects of the problems of unbalanced growth within the borders of a country.

Regional inequalities have economic and social implications and costs. The extensive trade and factor movement links between the regions of a country mean that the economic problems of the regions tend to be transmitted into other regions, and to affect the overall economic activity of the country. Regional unemployment, economic imbalances and inequity, and excessive concentration of residential, industrial and commercial activity in major conurbations cause severe costs to society. Hence, policies are introduced to deal with them.

Regional policy at the national level attempts to reduce the socio-economic disparities between regions. It is based on the principle that market forces cannot be relied upon to produce the necessary degrees of inter-regional balance in economic growth. This economic argument in support of regional policies is always supplemented by political and social considerations. The political argument asserts the importance of equity as an essential element in the cohesion between the regions of a country. The social argument stresses that, if the national economy grows, all citizens, wherever they happen to live and work within the country, should be provided with a reasonable share of the country's increasing prosperity.

9.2 Regional problems within economic unions

Once the process of economic integration is in progress, it is likely that already existing problems of regional disparities will intensify. There are two reasons for this. The first is that labour productivity and wage differentials between independent states are taken care of by adjustments in foreign exchange rates which restore export competitiveness. In effect, foreign exchange policies provide the depressed areas with a measure of protection by reducing domestic prices, and hence real wages, relative to foreign prices. But economic integration, free trade, enhanced competition and freer mobility of factors of production will tend to equalise commodity and factor prices (wages, rent of capital, etc.) between the participating states. However, productivity differentials will continue to exist and they will favour the technologically advanced firms of the developed areas within the economic union. With progressive integration of monetary policy and, at a later stage, monetary unification, the low-productivity regions will no longer be protected by exchange rate adjustments: they will be deprived of the option to devalue. At the same time, regional money wage differentials will tend to be eliminated and therefore the low-productivity regions will face progressive comparative disadvantage.

The second reason is that economic integration may encourage concentration of new industry and relocation of existing industry in certain areas of the economic union which give superior infrastructure, lower transport costs and availability of skilled labour. With enlargement of the market and enhanced competition, the most efficient enterprises will expand by the integration process, while the less efficient will contract or even be driven out of the market. It is not uncommon that the enterprises at the periphery are on the whole less efficient, with lower productivity than those at the developed centre. Therefore, economic activity at the periphery of the economic union will be affected negatively and disproportionately from the effects of integration.

In addition to these problems, there is always the possibility that common policies undertaken for the realisation of integration objectives, and later for the economic management of the integrated area, may have profound (and sometimes unforeseen) regional effects. Since the regions within and between countries are not homogeneous, the regional impact of a common policy may be positive for some and negative for others, so that the aggregate effect of any particular common policy may be beneficial for the economic union and detrimental for one or more of its regions.

As a consequence of these two reasons, the rates of growth in the developed centres will be higher than those in the less developed regions of the economic union. Different rates of growth will in turn induce a substantial degree of geographic relocation of industry and migration of capital and labour from the underdeveloped periphery to the developing centres. Peripheral regions, which before integration relied for their growth on small-scale production units, may become unable to reach the scale advantages of integration or to face the competition with large industry. Thus with progressing economic integration, the economic and social life of the underdeveloped regions will tend to lag behind the growth levels of the developed regions. This is not a remote theoretical possibility. Actual cases of the decline of regions after (economic and political) integration abound, as for example the economic decline of southern Italy after the unification of the Italian States in the 1860s.

The question then is, if economic integration tends to accentuate regional problems, whose task should it be to take appropriate policy measures to redress the decline of the regions?

During the process of integration regional economic problems undergo changes in dimensions and severity. Economic integration tends to exacerbate regional inequalities, to induce tendencies for polarisation at the larger scale of the economic union, and to create new problems by the different regional impacts of common policies. The process of economic integration internationalises the problem of regional divergence by adding to the already existing trends of national regional inequality the more powerful gravitation of the developed centres of the economic union which can very well be outside the borders of the country. Hence areas that were considered relatively prosperous before integration may turn into backward regions of the economic union. Obviously, this aspect of integration is not conducive to the furtherance of economic and political cohesion within the economic union. Therefore, under economic integration the purely national regional economic problem of the member states is transformed into a problem of the economic union. Regional inequality thus becomes the subject of a common regional policy.

This is necessary, among other reasons, because many of the policies which a member country will be advised to adopt for its regional problem may already be incompatible with the integration agreement or ineffective under the increased interdependence between the members of the economic union. For example, subsidisation, differential taxation, the granting of development aid, and other similar instruments of national regional policies operate in principle against the unification of the market and are incompatible with competition, the free market and the convergence of intra-union economic policy. National regional economic policies, which might have been effective for ameliorating regional disparities at the national level, may become ineffective within the integrating area, while at the same time the regional problems are exacerbated by structural changes brought about by the economic integration. A possible way out from this conundrum would be to respond collectively to the regional problems by integrating the regional economic policies. The effectiveness of national policies can be restored by coordination at the level of the economic union or by the inauguration of common regional policies aiming at a common objective. As a first step towards this direction, the regional economic policy of member states should be supplemented by union regional policies.

In conclusion, coordination and ultimately integration of regional economic policy at the level of the economic union is required in order to ensure the following:

1. The national regional economic problems of the member states are not aggravated by the dynamic process of integration.
2. The policies undertaken with regard to regional economic development are equitable between the members and compatible with the integration agreement.
3. The costs and benefits of integration are properly shared between the member countries and the regions of the economic union as a whole.

9.3 Regional problems in the Community

Regional disparities exist in every country of the EC, although the regional problem differs between countries in nature and intensity. In general, four main types of regional problems are found in the Community: rural underdevelopment, industrial decline, congested cities and frontier regions.

Underdeveloped rural areas

These depend primarily on agriculture for both employment and production. But farming in these areas is usually based on very small holdings of relatively infertile land, with low capitalisation and application of technology, low productivity, low participation rate and high incidence of disguised unemployment. Therefore these areas are in general decline, failing to achieve economic diversification and lagging behind the more prosperous areas in both income and employment. These features are common in many mountain and hill areas and certain islands which show evidence of progressive rural decline, depopulation and abandonment of land. Similar rural areas close to large towns and cities suffer instead from the effects of modern development associated with expansion of the urban centres, deterioration of the countryside and a worsening ecological balance.

Farming areas in developed countries also suffer from regional problems. But in contrast to the case of overdependence on uneconomic agriculture, the problems of these agricultural areas have come about from the application of modern technology, which led to fast increases in productivity causing rapid decline in the employment of labour. Over the post-war years the reduction of labour employment in agriculture has been pronounced in every European country, both developing and developed. This has forced rural labour to seek employment in other occupations and other locations. Large-scale migration has occurred from rural areas to developing industrial and urban centres, both domestic and foreign. However, the decline in agricultural employment has not spread evenly among the regions of every country, and has tended to encourage the migration of the relatively employable younger section of the population, with the consequence that those who were left behind were the older and the less productive. Moreover, in the less developed European countries, the expansion of employment in urban sectors and industrial regions has not been sufficient to offset the decline in agricultural employment nor has the released agricultural labour always had the necessary skills to be easily employable in other occupations. Hence, despite the outflow from the problem regions, surplus labour and chronic unemployment still exist.

Successive enlargements have added to the Community a number of peripheral countries which have substantially increased its regional problems. The accession of Greece, Spain and Portugal has increased Community GDP by 10 per cent, population by 22 per cent and employment in agriculture by 57 per cent. Hence, agricultural problem areas abound at the periphery of the European Community, the southern member countries, Portugal, Spain, Italy and Greece, and the west of Ireland. Similar but less severe problems are found in regions of the more developed member countries (north Netherlands, western France, south Belgium) but in most cases expanding alternative opportunities have kept the unemployment rate at bay. In general, over the 1960s the dispersion of income and unemployment among the regions of countries tended to decline by the migration of labour. But since the early 1970s the gap between the prosperous and declining regions has either increased (Italy, Spain) owing to the general economic recession and the upward shift in unemployment at the national level, or, at best, it has remained static. In certain areas the problem has recently been accentuated by the current recession which in some cases has caused reverse migration, the return of unemployed migrants from the urban centres to the rural areas of their origin where they swell the numbers of regional unemployment.

In general, the problem is not how to move resources out of the rural

economy, but how to preserve the rural society and economy by promoting balanced rural development which will ensure improvement
in the economic and social conditions of the rural population with
protection of the rural environment. This should be the objective
of coordinated action between the member states and the EC aimed at
strengthening the economic and social cohesion of the enlarged
Community.

Decline of existing basic industries

Basic industries located in certain areas within a country have declined,
while wage levels have remained relatively rigid. Hence problem areas
have emerged which are still predominantly industrial but face
increasing unemployment and deindustrialisation (southern and eastern
Belgium, Ruhr and Saar in Germany, northern and eastern France, and
in the United Kingdom, west-central Scotland, south Wales, north and
north-west England and Northern Ireland).

For historical and economic reasons certain industries (e.g. textiles,
steel, coal, shipyards) have been concentrated in the same area over long
periods of time. But, in recent years, shifts in technology, decreasing
demand for output and increasing international competition have led to
a declining demand for labour, and the emergence of severe regional
unemployment. These problems have been aggravated by the ongoing
recession. In a way, the problems of these industrial regions are structural. The existing industry is under threat because of rising costs associated with near exhaustion of stocks (such as coal), the emergence of
more competitive alternative sources of domestic supply and the
increasing competition from imports originating in low labour cost and
newly industrialising countries (NICs, such as Korea and Hong Kong).
Moreover, while in these declining regions the existing infrastructure
seems to be adequate for the development of alternative industry, the
new industry tends to be located nearer to demand centres and away
from traditional industrial poles. Therefore, industrial change and
renovation which would have kept these areas prosperous has not happened and it seems that it will never happen by market forces alone. The
uncontrolled expansion of the past and the current industrial decline
combined to produce only environmental degradation and desolation.
The introduction of labour-saving technology and the overall problem
of economic recession mean that the industrial decline of these regions
cannot be compensated by the growth of new industry, which is unable
to absorb the available labour surplus.

Congested areas

Regional imbalance means that within the same country regions of excess supply of labour may coexist with regions experiencing excess demand for labour. The latter, which are called 'pressured' or 'congested' regions, display the reverse characteristics of those found in backward rural areas and areas of industrial decline. In contrast to the underdeveloped regions, the congested areas offer a very high degree of agglomeration economies which are causing excess concentration of capital, labour and industrial production to the detriment of the declining areas. This concentration of economic activity is considered excessive because it combines the social benefit of increased economic activity with rising social costs associated with overpopulation, congestion, pollution, noise and other urban problems. These problems are a manifestation of market failure arising from interdependence, negative externalities and the divergence between private (firms) and social (public) optimums. Market failure due to externalities leads to misallocation of resources and welfare waste. A degree of optimality can be restored only by government intervention in the form of regional policy. In many cases, the benefits from high growth rates of income and employment in highly industrialised congested conurbations coexist with inner-city decay and pockets of poverty, general decline in the environment and deterioration of the quality of life.

Major conurbations in both the developed and the less developed members of the Community attract very large proportions of the population and of economic activity. The Paris region, which is just 2 per cent of French territory, contains 20 per cent of the population and 23 per cent of the total employment, and produces 30 per cent of the national output. The Randstad region in the Netherlands which has four major centres (Amsterdam−Utrecht−Rotterdam−The Hague) comprises 46 per cent of the national population. London and the south-east region of England are only 12 per cent of the national territory but contain 30 per cent of the population. Similar congested regions are the Rhine−Ruhr area of Germany, greater Copenhagen, Glasgow and Liverpool, and in the Mediterranean countries, Greater Athens, Naples, Barcelona and many more.

The regional problem of the congested areas consists of: (a) how to divert activity away from them in order to reduce congestion and stimulate growth through renewal of the existing industry; and (b) how to stimulate enough growth in other regions to attract economic activity from the congested regions.

Frontier areas

As a result of reduction of barriers to trade and factor movement, regions across the internal frontiers of the Community face a re-orientation of their economic activity arising from changes in their comparative advantage. They will develop closer economic links, trade and factor movement with regions of neighbouring member states and in the process some of them will benefit while others will lose. On the whole, regions across internal frontiers are handicapped by inadequate cross-border infrastructure associated with the historical separation of national states. In this case, regional policy is required to promote the necessary infrastructure and to encourage the border regions to exploit the opportunities offered by integration. In contrast to the internal border regions, a different kind of problem arises from the external border regions of member states, and therefore of the Community. These are the geographically peripheral regions for which economic integration may induce re-orientation of trade from their natural outlets in neighbouring states to other regions within the common market. Regional policy in this case attempts to protect and cushion the impact of integration on the economies of these border regions.

A different type of regional problem is created by the regional impact of common policies. For example, the CAP's price support system favours the richer agricultural areas of the relatively well off northern members of the Community rather than the poor agricultural lands of the Mediterranean countries. In turn, unless specific measures are undertaken to preserve the rural society and economy, the need for liberalisation of agricultural markets and adjustments in the CAP may result in serious economic and social divisions. Similarly, liberalisation of the transport sector, combined with abolition of national subsidies to rural transport would favour the most central and metropolitan regions. In this case, compensatory policies should be instituted in an attempt to neutralise the negative regional impact of actions which are considered necessary for the integration of markets and are, on balance, beneficial for the Community as a whole.

9.4   Regional economic policy of the Community

The Treaty of Rome does not specifically deal with regional economic problems, though in the Preamble it does mention the need to reduce regional disparities: the signatory nations expressed their endeavour '... to strengthen the unity of their economies and to ensure their harmonious development by reducing the differences existing between the various regions and by mitigating the backwardness of the less favoured'. References to regional problems are also found in the Articles dealing with the European Investment Bank (EIB) which is authorised to grant loans for 'projects for developing less developed regions' (Article 130), the Common Agricultural Policy (Article 49) and the European Social Fund (Article 125). In practice, the Community from early on recognised that the problem of regional disparities between the richest and the poorest areas threatened to disrupt the convergence of economic performance inside the EC and to delay the progress towards integration. Many areas, particularly in the south of Italy and France, lagged well behind the average level of European income and displayed the characteristics of rural unemployment and outward migration from subsistence farming. Other areas in the industrial north suffered inner city degradation and industrial decline.

From the start, it was acknowledged that the process of integration could itself accentuate the regional problems of some areas as the Community's competition rules promoted freer trade and factor mobility. During the 1960s the range of economic disparity between the regions of the Community narrowed somewhat. Hence, when in 1969 the Commission submitted its first set of proposals for the introduction of a common regional policy (EC Commission, 1969), the Council took no action. The regional problem was assumed to be a subject of national policy, and that growth and the positive impact of economic integration on the general prosperity of the Community would assist in bridging the gap between developed and less developed regions by national regional policy.

It was also expected that various Community funds and common policies which, though not exclusively regional, had been designed to function with regional problems among their objectives, would have a positive impact on the development of the regions. Institutions and funds, such as the European Coal and Steel Community (ECSC), the European Investment Bank (EIB) and the European Social Fund (ESF), finance regional projects for modernisation of the industry, investment for job-creation, and training and retraining schemes in problem regions. The Common Agricultural Policy also has regional implications, positive and negative: the guidance section of the European Agricultural Fund (EAGGF) aims at restructuring and modernising agriculture and can be considered as an instrument of regional policy; but on the other hand the guarantee section of the EAGGF (a) pays out vast amounts in support of agricultural production in rural areas which are not backward regions of subsistence agriculture, and (b) takes up the largest share out of the Community budget, so that there is not much left for use by other common policies, including the regional policy.

Regional policies usually take the following forms:

1. Government assistance for investment in new and existing industry which is expected to help solve problems such as regional unemployment, decentralisation, slow growth etc. The assistance provided consists of outright grants, special depreciation provisions, tax allowances, low-interest loans for investment, and so on.
2. Public expenditure on infrastructure, roads, ports, housing, etc.
3. General subsidies to reduce the cost of production, such as subsidies to the use of labour which encourage adoption of labour-intensive techniques contributing to the reduction of unemployment.
4. Negative inducements, such as controls over industrial location in an attempt to deter industry from concentrating in prosperous areas or areas of high congestion, etc.

Obviously, if the members of a common market follow different subsidy policies and in general have different degrees of government intervention in regional policy, the outcome will be unfair competition. In the EC, state aid which destroys competition is incompatible with the Treaty of Rome, but a special dispensation is provided for 'aid to promote the economic development of areas where the standard of living is abnormally low or where there is serious under-employment' (Article 92). This means that member states' plans for regional development require Community approval and, therefore, national regional policies are *a priori* subject to harmonisation.

After prolonged negotiations the Community moved, in October 1971, towards adopting a set of general principles which were to apply at the level of national regional aid schemes. These principles were that: (a) there should be an upper limit of permissive investment aid for the development of the regions; (b) all aid should be 'transparent', so that its extent could be easily ascertained; (c) regional aid should be region-specific and must not cover the entire national territory.

Although agreement on these issues provided some degree of uniformity among the members in the exercise of regional policies, it did not in itself constitute the inauguration of a common regional policy. But, from the beginning of the 1970s with the prospect of enlargement to nine members, two of which suffered from chronic regional disparities (the United Kingdom and Ireland), the problems of the regions could no longer be ignored. At the Paris Summit of 1972 it was agreed that the Commission should report on the regional problems of the Community, taking into account the forthcoming accession of three new members. It was also agreed that a special fund should be established, the European Regional Development Fund (ERDF), to give financial assistance to the development of the regions. The *Report on the Regional Problems in the Enlarged Community* was published in 1973 (EC, 1973b, the Thomson Report). Under the assumption that the Community regional problem is the aggregate of the regional problems of the member states, the Report recommended that the common policy should be one of coordination of the member states' national regional policies and of common policies with a regional impact, rather than of direct intervention by a Community regional policy.

Within a few months of the publication of the Report the first oil crisis necessitated revision of the members' and the Community's expectations of economic growth. With the recession deepening, unemployment started rising and the disparities among regions were aggravated. It then became clear that the recession will obstruct and delay the convergence of members' economic performance, and that under the prevailing conditions progress towards integration would require a different and more active regional policy at the level of the Community.

The ERDF was finally set up in March 1975 under Article 235 of the Treaty, and started operating in the same year with an initial budget substantially smaller than the one proposed to Council by the Commission. The Regional Policy Committee, a consultative body composed of senior policy officials of the member governments and the Commission, was also set up to advise the Commission on research programmes and general inter-country coordination in the regional development field.

From the start, problems were encountered with the definition of a region and the eligibility of regions for financial assistance and grants for development. Evidently, the relative terms 'developed region' and 'less developed region' are defined with reference to a single member state. In contrast, the Community regional problem has to be defined by inter-regional comparisons at the international setting of the EC, and therefore it is not identical with the sum of the regional problems of the member states. For example, within Germany there are more and less prosperous regions which give rise to a national regional problem, but in the Community context the less prosperous regions of Germany are actually better off than many of the prosperous areas in other member states. The 1973 Report used the regional subdivisions existing in each member state as the basis for analysing the Community regional problem. Two types of regions were recognised: level I are those regions which are subject to European regional policy; level II are smaller regions which constitute basic administrative areas within member states. The same classification of regions is in use today: the Community of twelve member states has sixty five level I regions (Table 9.1) subdivided into a number of level II regions (e.g. the United Kingdom had

Table 9.1 Main regional indicators.

Country	Level I Regions	Unemployment[1] per cent Total	Unemployment[1] per cent Highest	Unemployment[1] per cent Lowest	GDP per head index[2] Total	GDP per head index[2] Highest	GDP per head index[2] Lowest	Population[3]
B	3	9.2	12.7	7.0	101.0	154.7	83.6	68
DK	1	7.0	–	–	117.1	–	–	100
D	11	5.7	10.9	3.2	114.2	183.2	94.9	84
E	7	18.0	26.5	13.7	72.1	84.7	57.4	0
F	8	9.9	14.7	6.7	110.5	165.5	91.3	58
GR	4	7.7	10.0	4.3	55.3	59.0	50.5	0
IRL	1	17.2	–	–	63.8	–	–	0
I	11	10.9	21.8	4.1	103.2	137.2	67.0	54
L	1	1.8	–	–	124.7	–	–	100
NL	4	9.8	12.4	9.3	106.2	126.0	88.3	58
P	3	5.7	8.9	3.4	53.1	64.1	44.2	0
UK	11	7.0	16.7	4.0	104.8	125.5	80.3	34
EC-12	65	9.3	26.5	3.2	100	183.2	44.2	50

[1] Harmonised data: April, 1989.
[2] Purchasing power standard, 1986, EC-12 = 100.
[3] Percentage of total population in regions with GDP per head above EC average.

Sources: Eurostat (1990) *Basic Statistics of the Community*, 27th ed., Luxembourg.

eleven level I regions and no level II; the whole of Denmark constitutes one level I region, comprising three Level II regions).

Eventually, the member states settled for a political compromise rather than for radical solutions to the regional problem. The Fund was to function as an instrument of the Community designed to help the efforts of national governments to assist the development of their problem regions. It was decided that the following regions were eligible for assistance:

1. Where the GDP is consistently below the national average.
2. Where there is above-average dependence on agriculture or on a declining industry.
3. Where there is a consistently high rate of unemployment or net migration.
4. Where Community policies, in particular free trade, had an adverse effect.

It was also agreed that the disbursement of funds from the ERDF will be based on national quotas which would take account of the relative gravity of each country's regional problem. Although this arrangement was changed in 1979 by dividing the Fund in two sections, 95 per cent of it continued to operate under the national quota system. This meant that in effect the ERDF had no say in the choice of regions deserving financing; this was decided by the government of each member state. The Fund would finance expenditure directed towards improvements in transport and telecommunications, water and electricity supplies, the building of industrial estates and the development of social services. It is worth observing that from the amounts committed by the ERDF from 1975 to 1985 Italy received 37 per cent and the United Kingdom 24 per cent (*Bulletin EC*, **12**, 1985).

Under the original Regulation establishing the Fund, the Commission was required to review its activities and to produce proposals for the future of regional policy after the initial three-year period. Following proposals made by the Commission, in May 1984 the Council adopted a Regulation reforming the European regional policy and the Fund and introducing provisions for integrated operations and coordination of national regional policies. The Regulation specifies that the common regional policy will consist of three elements: periodic analysis of the socio-economic situation of the regions, coordination of national regional policies and assessment of the regional impact of all major policies. The Community shall support the achievement of the objectives of regional policy by the action it takes through the structural Funds. The ERDF in particular 'is intended to help redress the principal regional imbalances in the Community through participating in the development and structural adjustment of regions whose development is lagging and in reconversion of declining industrial regions' (*Bulletin EC*, **11**, 1985). Since 1985, all the resources of the 'new' European Regional Development Fund (new ERDF) are allocated on the basis of 'ranges', defined by a set minimum and maximum for each member state. In contrast to the old system of national 'quotas', which the member states effectively regarded as 'drawing rights' which they could use to replace sums they would otherwise have provided themselves to their regions, under the new system the requests for funding must conform to common specific criteria and are not satisfied automatically. Therefore, the lower limit of the 'range' is not a 'guaranteed' minimum of finance from the Fund. With the accession to the Community of Spain and Portugal, which has increased the number of poor agricultural regions located in the southern members, the new ERDF 'ranges' have been defined as follows:

Belgium	0.61– 0.82%	Ireland	3.81– 4.61%
Denmark	0.34– 0.46%	Italy	21.59–28.79%
Germany	2.55– 3.40%	Luxembourg	0.04– 0.06%
Spain	17.95–23.93%	Netherlands	0.68– 0.91%
Greece	8.35–10.64%	Portugal	10.65–14.20%
France	7.47– 9.96%	United Kingdom	14.48–19.31%

These 'ranges apply for a three-year period. The total of all the minima equals 88.5 per cent, which means that the Commission now has at its disposal a maximum 11.5 per cent of the ERDF finances available for regional 'Community programmes'. The Community element of such programmes is that they are initiated by a proposal from the Commission rather than from a member state, and their purpose is 'to provide a better link between the Community's regional development objectives and the objectives of other Community policies'. In general, the Regional Fund helps to finance Community programmes, national programmes of Community interest, projects and studies by providing supplementary aid to that allocated by a member state for the development of beneficiary regions. The rates of Regional Fund assistance are 50–55 per cent of the total expenditure. Community programmes concern the territory of more than one member state, e.g. inter-country infrastructure. The priority areas within a country are still nationally defined, but the member states undertake to communicate to the Commission their regional development programmes and to report on the progress of their implementation. National programmes are eligible for financial assistance from the Community if they serve national and Community objectives and policies. In principle, the aim of the ERDF is to make the sum available for investment in the regions larger by supplementing the regional development expenditures of the member states.

Along with the reform of the ERDF, the Council also considered the regional implications of the structural funds, and decided to improve their allocation by coordinating their activities in the form of integrated operations. These consist of a number of investment projects in a region of a member state which are financed on a complementary basis by national and local authorities and the Community. At the Community level, the criteria employed in ascertaining the need for regional policy measures include per capita income and the rate of unemployment. On the basis of these criteria, the EC Commission calculates a synthetic index of backwardness. Not surprisingly, the real problem areas turn out to be all regions of Greece, Spain, Portugal, southern Italy, the Irish Republic and Northern Ireland. A second group of regions with relatively severe economic problems includes six areas in the United Kingdom and two in Belgium.

Among the Community instruments for regional development are also included the Integrated Mediterranean Programmes (IMPs). These were limited-duration projects designed to assist the disadvantaged, agricultural and semi-industrial regions of Greece, southern France and Italy to adjust to the new competitive conditions which emerged in the EC as a consequence of the latest enlargement of the Community to include

Portugal and Spain. The IMPs were launched in 1985 for a six-year period. They aimed at investment in infrastructure, expenditure for the development and better use of human resources, and investment expenditure for conversion to alternative forms of production and new product lines. The financial resources 'integrated' in the IMPs were partly new, from the budget and the New Community Instrument (NCI), and partly old, redirected from existing Community funds. Non-infrastructural projects are usually financed from a combination of Community, private and national budget funds. Taking the funds as a whole, 50 per cent were reserved for Greece and 25 per cent each for Italy and France. The paradox is that the IMPs channel large flows of funds into the Mediterranean area of the 'old' Community, yet they exclude some of the poorest regions which are located in the 'new' members, Spain and Portugal. The Community intended originally to terminate the IMPs by the end of 1992, but the Commission has proposed that they should become a fourth 'structural fund' (in addition to ERDF, ESF and EAGGF), for advancing the development of the weaker regions of all the southern member states.

The problems of rural society worsened with the acceleration of the move towards the single market. The opening up of markets to wider competition and the restructuring of the economy in general had adverse effects on rural development which have widened the gap between the industrial centres and the periphery. The growth of rural areas has been impeded by 'distance (geographical and socio-cultural) from decision centres, a shortage of venture capital, a lack of easy access to information and technological innovation, a lack of appropriate services and the absence of an integrated economic fabric' (EC Commission, 1988i). Consequently, concern has been expressed in the Community which has led to proposals aiming at specific regional development programmes for the preservation of rural society. Rural development has been chosen as one of the priorities for assistance from the structural funds which, in addition to purely agriculture-related measures combined with protection of the rural environment, will also entail job-creation policies to provide additional and/or alternative employment outside farming.

9.5   Evaluation

Table 9.1 shows in very broad lines the extent of the regional problem of the EC-12 at the level I classification of the regions. In both the rate of unemployment and GDP per head (in purchasing power valuation), the disparities within and between countries are very substantial. Spain and Ireland have the worst incidence of unemployment in the Community, Luxembourg the best. Greece, Ireland, Portugal and Spain have no regions with GDP per head above the EC average. Denmark and Luxembourg, which are countries small enough to be just a level I region each, display GDP per head above the EC average. The remaining countries have national average GDP per head above the EC average, but some of their regions lag behind the EC average. The poorest member country is Portugal with average GDP per head 53.1 per cent of the EC average, nearly three-and-a-half times smaller than that of the most prosperous region in the Community (Hamburg in Germany with 183.2 per cent of EC average).

The Community's commitment to a more active regional policy as the means for promoting economic convergence for the development of the internal market has been repeated once again in the agreement reached at the Luxembourg Summit (December 1985) which states:

> In order to promote its harmonious development overall, the Community shall develop and pursue its actions leading to strengthening its economic and social cohesion. In particular, the Community shall aim at reducing disparities between the various regions and the backwardness of the least favoured regions.

But, despite all these very promising declarations, the Community's regional policy remains inefficient and weak. This results, first, from the fact that the Community regional policy has to function as a supplement of the national regional policies of the member states; and, second, from the relatively small financial resources allocated by the Community to the common regional policy. Under the national quota system, these resources were not only small but also widely dispersed, so that their impact was insignificant: in the first eleven years of its existence (1975–86) the ERDF committed the sum of ECU 14 billion, spread over some 25,000 projects in ten countries. With the limited resources available for an effective common policy for regional development, concentration of expenditure would have had a larger impact.

Completion of the single internal market renders inevitable that 'resources, both of people and materials, and of capital and investment, flow into areas of greatest economic advantage' (EC, 1985d). This means that, unless appropriate measures are taken at the national and Community levels, either the internal market will not be complete according to schedules or the regional problem will worsen. Unless the regional policy of the Community changes, the limited funds of the ERDF, as shared among twelve member countries, will not be sufficient even for alleviation of that component of the regional problem which has arisen from the process of integration, with the implication that the disparity between the richer and poorer regions of the EC will widen. This would mean that convergence of economic policy and performance, which is an essential adjunct to the development of the internal market, will not occur, to the detriment of European unity.

Increasing openness of product and factor markets will generate gains, but it is not certain that they will be distributed equally among the regions of the Community. On the basis of past experience at the member state and international level, the process of market integration would probably favour the centrally located urban agglomerations. The completion of the internal market would favour structural change in the organisation of production with a tendency for concentration in large enterprises enjoying economies of scale. Hence, medium-size firms in low-productivity areas, which to some extent depend for their existence on market impediments and subsidies, will face acute problems of competition in the enlarged market threatening their survival. There is also a strong possibility that firms and resources will be relocated to exploit the comparative advantage of different regions within the enlarged market. Consequently, the integration process may have adverse sectoral and regional effects on the problem regions of the Community. In contrast, certain of the policies for internal market opening may in fact be beneficial for the peripheral regions, as for example improvements in transport and communications. However, by operation of a 'cumulative causation' process, the increasing pace of market integration and the emergence or strengthening of agglomeration tendencies may make it more difficult for a backward economic region to catch up on the performance of leading economic regions.

The Single European Act (SEA) has envisaged this possibility and promises a considerable increase in the funds allocated to regional development (ERDF, ESF and the guidance section of the EAGGF), with particular emphasis on concentrating resources in the most deserving areas of the Community, those with per capita GDP of less than 75 per cent of the Community average. Thus, all of Portugal, Ireland and Greece, parts of Spain and Italy, and the French overseas departments are listed as first priority areas because of their structural backwardness. This entitles them to funding of up to 75 per cent from Community funds, which are to double by 1992, taking their share of the overall Community budget from 18 to 28 per cent. It is also planned that areas of declining industry, of long-term and youth unemployment, and of rural underdevelopment would receive additional finance in an attempt to direct more funds and effort towards alleviation of the regional problem of the Community (EC, 1988a).

Further reading

For a general introduction to regional economics and policies see Armstrong and Taylor (1985). The problems of EC regional policy are examined in Vanhove and Klaassen (1980) and Yuill *et al.* (1980). On the impact of EC policies on its regions see Molle and Capellin (1988). Armstrong (1985) discusses the reform of EC regional policy.

10

Social policy

10.1 Introduction

The Treaties of the three communities comprising the European Community refer to social policy. The ECSC Treaty includes provisions on wages and mobility of workers in the coal and steel industry. The Euratom Treaty deals with the health and safety of workers in the atomic energy industry. But the most comprehensive reference to social policy is provided in the EEC Treaty: besides general provisions (Articles 48–58), Part Three, Title III (Articles 117–28) of the Treaty of Rome is devoted exclusively to social provisions (EC, 1973a). Among the objectives outlined in the EEC Treaty are the following binding provisions:

1. Freedom of movement of workers (Articles 48–9).
2. Social security for migrant workers (Article 51).
3. Freedom of establishment, that is the right to take up and pursue activities as self-employed persons (Articles 52–8).
4. Equal pay for male and female workers (Article 119).
5. The establishment of a European Social Fund to promote employment opportunities and labour mobility between professions and countries of the Community (Articles 123–8).

The non-binding provisions cover the following:

6. The improvement in the living and working conditions (Article 117).
7. Close collaboration between the member states in matters relating to employment, labour law and working conditions, vocational

training, social security, prevention of occupational accidents and diseases, occupational hygiene and the rights of association and collective bargaining (Article 118).
8. Paid holiday schemes (Article 120).
9. A common vocational training policy (Article 128).

In addition to this specific section, Article 104 of the EEC Treaty states that the maintenance of a high level of employment is one of the prime economic objectives of the Community.

The references above show clearly that the relevant section of the EEC Treaty, 'without prejudice to other provisions of this Treaty', identifies social policy with issues mostly relating to the employment of labour. In practice, the Community coverage of social policy has been widened by subsequent legislation and policy action in a number of other fields, but it is still much narrower than the social policy of member states. Some observers define as Community social policy the work that is carried out by the Directorate-General for Employment, Social Affairs and Education (D-G V) which, in addition to the specifications of Article 118, includes among its terms of reference general social policy guidelines, migrant workers, the employment of handicapped persons and the ESF. Some of these areas have been regarded as marginal, and more appropriate for consideration by the social policy of the member countries, while others have received more attention by the Community.

The common social policy is part of a coordinated Community approach which also includes economic, industrial and regional policies. Since the member states have their own national social policies, the basic question is whether the Community needs a social policy at all. A common social policy can be based on the Treaty which confirms that the signatories are resolved to 'ensure the economic and social progress of their countries by common action to eliminate the barriers which divide Europe' (Preamble). In addition to the general common interest for improved social conditions which 'will ensue not only from the functioning of the common market ... but also from the procedures provided for in this Treaty' (Article 117), one objective of the Community is the harmonisation of social policy among the member states. Given that the member states for a number of ideological, political, economic and institutional reasons had set different priorities as to who and to what extent should be covered by social policy, and what share of the national expenditure should be directed to it, the differences among the members are very significant. If these differences have sharp external effects and remain unharmonised, they may cause serious distortions in the pattern of competition and resource allocation within the common market. Two answers have been provided to this problem:

1. The first argues that *ex ante* harmonisation is unnecessary, since it would happen by its own accord through market competition. This approach is based on the assumption that social systems reflect different preferences and capabilities of the various economies and cannot be smoothed without endangering other objectives of economic policy. Therefore it advocates market-oriented solutions.

2. The second argues that, left to the market, the differences in social provisions between the member states will converge but downwards. Accordingly, only *ex ante* harmonisation can safeguard the social rights won by workers in the economically more advanced members of the Community. Alternatively, countries with low social standards would gain 'unfair' competitive advantages.

Table 10.1 presents, as an example of the existing situation and problems, the social security expenditures as a ratio of national income (GDP) for the Community as a whole, and for each of the EC member countries. The figures reveal that over recent years these ratios have been rising. This increase was caused by expansion of both the coverage of state social security programmes and the eligible (beneficiary) population as a consequence of growth in state care and in the problems brought about by the contemporary economic recession. In 1985 and 1987 the

Table 10.1 Social security expenditures (as a percentage of GDP).

Country	1970	1975	1980	1985	1987
B	18.5	24.2	28.0	29.0	28.7
DK	19.6	26.9	28.7	27.8	27.7
D	21.4	29.7	28.6	28.1	28.2
E	–	–	–	18.0	17.7
F	19.2	22.9	25.5	28.8	28.3
IRL	13.2	19.7	20.6	24.0	23.6
I	18.4	22.6	19.8	22.5	22.9
L	16.4	22.4	26.4	25.4	26.4
NL	20.8	26.7	30.4	31.1	31.3
P	–	–	–	16.1	16.7
UK	15.9	20.1	21.6	24.5	23.6
EC (means)	(18.2)	(23.9)	(25.5)	(25.0)	(25.0)
(s.d.)[1]	(2.6)	(3.3)	(3.9)	(4.7)	(4.6)

[1] Standard deviation; no data available for Greece.

Sources: Eurostat (1980), *Social Protection Statistics*, 1970–80; Eurostat (1990) *Basic Statistics of the Community*, 27th ed., Luxembourg.

ratio of social security expenditure on GDP for the Community as a whole was 25.0 per cent, with the Netherlands at the top of the Table (more than 31 per cent), Portugal at the bottom (less than 17 per cent), and dispersion among the member states higher than in 1980 (standard deviation 4.7 and 4.6 against 3.9). One of the reasons for this overall deterioration is the inclusion in the 1985 and 1987 figures of Portugal and Spain which display the lowest social security expenditure ratios on GDP among the Community countries (data for Greece are not available).

Significant differences also exist among the members in the way social security programmes are financed. Table 10.2 shows the relative shares of contributions to current social security receipts by employers, employees and the government. While some countries mostly rely on earmarked taxation for the financing of social security, others depend on general government contributions. Thus, the lowest contribution of employers and employees is in Denmark (15.8 per cent) and the highest in France (79.2 per cent). The three countries with the largest government contribution, Denmark (77.5 per cent), Ireland (61.1 per cent) and the united Kingdom (43.4 per cent), are in fact those where the state maintains a basic social welfare system by financing directly (from general taxation) the major part of social security.

In general, the EC partners display many differences in national social policy but have also achieved some success in common. A major

Table 10.2 Contributors to social security receipts, 1988, (per cent).

Country	Employers	Employees	Government	Other
B[1]	41.0	19.7	27.5	10.8
DK	11.4	4.4	77.5	6.7
D	41.1	30.4	25.2	3.3
E[1]	52.2	19.4	26.0	2.4
F	51.8	27.4	18.2	2.6
IRL	23.1	14.9	61.1	0.9
I	52.4	14.9	29.9	2.8
L	33.3	23.2	37.2	6.3
NL	32.4	36.2	14.4	16.8
P	49.4	20.3	25.6	4.7
UK[1]	27.9	17.0	43.4	11.7
EC-9 (means)	(37.8)	(20.7)	(35.1)	(6.2)
(s.d.)[2]	(13.5)	(8.6)	(19.0)	(4.9)

[1] 1987; data for Greece are not available.
[2] Standard deviation.

Source: Eurostat (1990) *Basic Statistics of the Community*, 27th ed., Luxembourg.

driving force for the harmonisation of social policy in the Community is the differential social cost of production among the member states, and its implications on competition and the allocation of resources within the common market. Changes in the social security contributions, brought about, for example, by a policy of harmonisation, would lead to changes in the marginal cost of labour differentially across the member states of the Community. In principle, this would affect investment patterns between the members and cause capital (and perhaps labour) migration and capital substitution, leading to reallocation of productive resources within the economic union.

Although the national social policy programmes of the EC countries differ in scope and detail, their basic characteristics are substantially similar. All member countries to a greater or lesser extent use (payroll) tax contributions of the current year to finance current year benefits. These tax-transfer arrangements from taxpayers in the labour force to beneficiaries outside the labour force have income redistributional effects which affect labour supply decisions by changing the relative price between work and leisure. However, this particular issue, and the question of income redistribution in general, have created little interest at the level of the Community, do not constitute an activity area of D-G V, and will not be examined here.

In the following sections of this chapter we review the basics of the Community's social programme and the attempts for coordinated action in certain areas of social policy.

10.2 The European Social Fund

Article 123 of the EEC Treaty defines as an objective of the European Social Fund (ESF) 'to increase the possibilities of employment for workers in the Common Market and to contribute thereby to raising the standard of living' by 'rendering the employment of workers easier and increasing their geographical and occupational mobility within the Community'. For this purpose the Fund makes available financial assistance to training, retraining and job-creation projects for the unemployed, underemployed and handicapped persons.

However, the ESF had three major weaknesses:

1. The rule that the Fund would reimburse 50 per cent of the expenditure incurred by a member state's public authorities in providing vocational retraining to workers obliged to change jobs. The Fund resources, which from the beginning were small, proved increasingly

inadequate for fulfilling this objective as with the recession unemployment started to rise fast.

2. The Fund could only intervene retroactively, that is when the worker who had already received vocational training had been productively employed for six months.

3. By statute, intervention of the Fund in a particular country or region depended crucially on the scale of structures and funds available there for vocational retraining and resettlement (EC, 1983d).

A consequence of the latter provision was that, while the intention of the relevant clauses of the Treaty was to help eliminate unemployment in the least developed regions, such as southern Italy, the main beneficiary of the Fund was actually Germany.

The Treaty provided that after the transitional period the Council could 'unanimously determine the new tasks which may be entrusted to the Fund' (Article 126). Accordingly, a reform was implemented in 1971 which divided the Fund into two sections, one operating in response to current changes in employment and the other being used to help eliminate long-term unemployment and underemployment. The new Fund was endowed with a larger budget and become: (a) more flexible, by financing more projects directly chosen by the Community; (b) more effective, by deciding in advance how to allocate its own resources; and (c) more comprehensive, by opening up its operations not only to public bodies but also to private organisations and even business firms. For public projects the Fund would still provide up to 50 per cent of eligible expenditure, while in the case of private sector projects the amount of Fund assistance would be equal to whatever aid was contributed by the public authorities. More of the new Fund appropriations (90 per cent) continued to be directed towards training and retraining of workers in backward areas and regions where the predominant industry was in decline and to certain occupational (agriculture, textile and clothing industry, etc.) and social categories (migrant workers, handicapped persons, etc.).

However, despite the extensions, the ESF's statutory coverage limited its ability to aid the really needy regions, industries and population groups. During this time, the nature of the social problem had been changing with the effects of the recession, which had led to unprecedented levels of unemployment, particularly among the young. Hence a second reform of the Fund was adopted by Council and came into force in January 1978. Under the new regulations a larger share of the Fund's appropriations were designated for unemployment assistance to less developed areas of the Community (55 per cent). A further regulation was issued in December 1978 which introduced a new form of aid from the ESF to promote specifically the employment and the geographic and occupational mobility of young people. The next major reform of the Fund was approved by Council in October 1983 and the new provisions took effect from January 1984. The system of giving aid to public and private undertakings remained the same. The main changes are as follows:

1. The appropriations of the different operations of the Fund are entered under separate budgets for: aid for the under-25s; aid for the over-25s; less favoured regions and other regions of high unemployment; specific actions on pilot projects.
2. The major emphasis is in the financing of operations carried out by private or public operators, concerning the training and employment of young people. Approximately 75 per cent of all the Fund's appropriations in any one year are allocated to projects to help the young. The aid granted by the Fund to these groups amounts to 15 per cent of the gross average industrial wage.
3. Geographic concentration of assistance: 40 per cent of the total appropriations available for operations within the framework of labour market policies go to the least-favoured regions in the Community, i.e. Greece, the French overseas departments, Ireland, Northern Ireland and the Mezzogiorno. The proportion of these appropriations was raised to 44.5 per cent after accession to the EC of Spain and Portugal.
4. Up to 5 per cent of all the available appropriations are reserved for specific operations aiming at the implementation of innovatory projects, e.g. experimental training schemes. For specific operations carried out on the initiative of the Commission, the Fund covers the total of eligible expenditure.
5. The operations must concern the following target groups: young people under 25; the unemployed and the long-term unemployed in particular; women wishing to return to work; handicapped people; migrant workers; and the retraining of workers employed in small and medium-size firms.

However, with the economy in recession during the 1980s and less than 5 per cent of the Community budget allocated to social policy, applications to the Fund for assistance exceeded the available appropriations. Hence, new guidelines for the management of the Social Fund were adopted in 1985 which served to determine the types of operations regarded as reflecting Community priorities. These guidelines clarified the rules for ESF intervention and introduced stricter criteria for the assessment of applications for priority financing.

10.3 The Social Action Programme

The Social Action Programme (SAP) was drawn up by the Commission in 1973 in response to the declaration of the Paris Summit in October 1972, after the first enlargement, that the European Council 'attached as much importance to vigorous action in the social field as to the achievement of the economic and monetary union'. The form of the Programme finally adopted by Council in January 1974 included three main objectives (EC Commission, 1974): attainment of full and better employment; improvement and upward harmonisation of living and working conditions; and greater involvement of employer and employee organisations in the economic and social decisions of the Community, and of workers in the life of their firms. Although the economic and social conditions within and outside the Community have changed significantly since 1974, the SAP has continued to provide a reference point for a number of measures which the Community implemented in the field of social policy. The most important of these measures are described below.

Unemployment

Following the first oil crisis of 1973 the rate of unemployment in the Community started to rise. The ascent continued through the 1970s and early 1980s, with unemployment in 1985 reaching nearly three times the level of 1975. Certain of the member countries and regions within countries were particularly hard hit. As shown in Table 10.3, during the 1983–89 period, Spain and Ireland held the overall record of unemployment rate in the Community. Two groups of persons have faired significantly worse than any other population category: women, who display much higher unemployment rates than men in every member country, except the Untied Kingdom; and the young, who on average are twice as likely to be unemployed as the adults: nearly a quarter of the under-25s were unemployed in the Community in 1989.

These extremely bad figures do not reflect lack of concern or inefficiency of Community policy to combat the problem of unemployment. Instead, they demonstrate the confined role which has been assigned to the common policy for the unemployed. From necessity the function of Community social policy is limited to coordinating the work of various

Table 10.3 Unemployment rates: harmonised data (percentage of civilian working population).

Country	1983	1985	1987	1989	Total	April 1989 Men	April 1989 Women	Age < 25
B	12.6	11.8	11.5	9.6	9.2	6.1	14.2	15.4
DK	9.5	7.5	6.0	7.0	7.0	6.1	8.1	9.9
D	6.9	7.2	6.3	5.7	5.7	4.7	7.3	5.3
F	8.2	10.3	10.5	9.6	9.9	7.5	12.8	19.8
E	17.8	21.9	20.5	17.0	18.0	13.4	26.8	36.6
GR	9.0	8.8	8.1	7.7	7.7	4.9	12.5	25.8
IRL	15.2	18.4	18.1	17.2	17.2	16.6	18.6	23.8
I	9.0	9.5	10.2	11.0	10.9	7.4	17.0	32.9
L	3.6	2.9	2.7	1.9	1.8	1.4	2.6	3.6
NL	12.5	10.6	10.0	9.3	9.8	7.0	14.4	15.1
P	7.7	8.6	6.8	5.0	5.7	3.6	8.5	11.9
UK	11.2	11.5	10.5	6.5	7.0	7.5	6.3	9.1
EC	10.0	10.9	10.4	9.0	9.3	7.4	12.1	17.8

Source: Eurostat (1990) *Basic Statistics of the Community*, 27th ed., Luxembourg.

national employment services, rather than solving centrally the problems of unemployment. The Community decided from early on that the problems of recession and unemployment required active participation and shared responsibility of the two sides of the industry, management and labour. Accordingly, it set up a consultative body, the Standing Committee on Employment, whose main task is to facilitate joint appraisal by employers' and employees' representatives and by the members Ministries of Employment on current problems relating to employment and labour policy and measures contemplated by the Community. At the Community level, three areas of activity were pursued which aimed at: improvement of knowledge of the labour market; development and coordination of placement services; and concerted forward-looking management of the labour market. In May 1982, the Council adopted a resolution on Community action on unemployment and asked the Commission to submit proposals for an overall employment policy at the level of the Community. The Commission's proposals were published in 1983 and among other novelties they include the financing of small-scale local employment initiatives and schemes for the employment of women.

The Community has paid particular attention to the problems of the unemployment of the young, who were caught in a vicious circle: because they have no vocational training they cannot find a job, and because they have not got a job they cannot acquire in-job vocational training. Under the SAP, in 1975 the Council adopted a proposal of the Commission to set aside appropriations for the financing of the geographic and occupational mobility of persons under 25, with priority for first-time job-seekers. In 1976 a resolution was adopted concerning measures to improve vocational education and in 1977 general guidelines were issued for a common policy on vocational training. In the same year the Council established in Berlin the *European Centre for the Development of Vocational Training*, which was entrusted with the promotion of vocational education and planning for the harmonisation of national standards and training qualifications. In 1979 the Council adopted a resolution which advocated the development of closer links between work and training, and, for the first time, it directed the ESF to provide a financial contribution for the creation of new jobs. This was followed in 1983 by a resolution pledging support over the next five years for an active vocational training policy at member state and Community levels, including guarantee of training for a set period for unemployed school-leavers (this in the United Kingdom took the form of the Youth Training Scheme, YTS).

The equal treatment of men and women in matters of employment, according to Article 119, was dealt with in a number of directives during the period 1976–8. Accordingly, the member states were required to: (a) repeal all laws, regulations and administrative provisions incompatible with the principle of equal pay; (b) abolish all statutory provisions and terms of collective agreements prejudicial to the employment of women and implement the principle of equal treatment for men and women as regards access to employment, vocational training, promotion and working conditions; (c) extend progressively the principle of equal treatment for men and women in matters of social security, the obligation to pay contributions, and the calculation of benefits and allowances. The integration of these directives into national legislation is monitored by the Commission. If a member fails to act, the Commission can bring infringement proceedings before the Court of Justice. Private individuals may claim their rights by bringing action before their national courts, and as a last resort before the European Court of Justice. However, in practice disguised and open sex discrimination persists, in some instances becoming more acute in the adverse economic situation. Sex discrimination is not confined to the southern, less developed members of the Community: in 1985, Court proceedings were brought by the Commission under Article 169 of the EEC Treaty against Denmark, FR of Germany and the Netherlands.

In 1982 the Council adopted a new action programme (1982–5) on the promotion of equal opportunities for women, and in 1983 produced a communication on women's employment which contains suggestions for action on job creation and recruitment, vocational training, improvement in market opportunities, information campaigns and the adoption of measures to promote equal opportunities in practice. In 1986 the Council adopted recommendations presented by the Commission on equal treatment for women in self-employed occupations, including agriculture. Discussions have also started on a memorandum presented by the Commission on equal income tax treatment for men and women.

Working time

With the unemployment situation deteriorating, the Paris European Council in 1979 requested the Commission to consider the social and economic implications of a concerted reorganisation of working time. The Commission's proposals led to a 'Resolution on the adaptation of working time' which was adopted by Council in December 1979. This was followed by the Commission launching a number of initiatives which aimed at increasing the supply of jobs by a coordinated reduction and reorganisation of the current volume of working time, and by limiting systematic paid overtime. In 1982 the Council adopted a recommendation on the principles of a Community policy with regard to flexible retirement, that is a reduction in total working life with entitlement to retirement pension. The Council also adopted an amended version of the Commission's Directive on part-time and temporary work designed to give greater protection to and provide minimal guarantees for persons engaged in this sort of employment. Discussions were also initiated on memoranda dealing with a reduction in annual working time (entailing a cut in weekly working hours, longer annual holidays and more training leave), overtime and shift work.

In the 1950s the average working week was forty-eight hours in nearly every European country (except France which already had the shortest working week). By 1960 the working week had been reduced to forty-five hours or less in Belgium, Germany, Ireland, Luxembourg, the Netherlands and the United Kingdom. In 1975 the Council established by regulation the *European Foundation for the Improvement of Living and Working Conditions* which opened the following year in Dublin. Its objective is to research shift work and the organisation of working time, the impact of technological change on work organisation, and the psychological effects of work conditions. In the same year (1975) the Commission forwarded to the member states a recommendation for harmonisation advocating a forty-hour week with four-week paid holiday for all full-time workers. Accordingly, towards the end of the 1970s, the forty-hour week was applied to nearly all industrial workers of the Community. Greece, which joined the Community in 1981, agreed to comply with the recommendation, and to cut the working week to forty hours on 1 January 1983. In the same year, Denmark, France and Luxembourg followed Germany and extended the basic annual holiday to five weeks.

Industrial democracy

In most members of the Community industrial democracy, which means employee participation in the management of companies, is limited to consultation on matters relating to personnel, improvement of working conditions and safety standards. The Community has felt that industrial democracy has to expand, particularly under the current difficult conditions for both management and employees. Two Commission proposals have been issued to this effect. One concerns companies established under the proposed European Company Law. These companies will have a dualistic board structure, comprising a management and a supervisory board of which one-third of the members will be workers' representatives. Workers employed in establishments belonging to a European company will be able to enter into European collective agreements and will belong to a European works council. However, the European Company Statute has not as yet proceeded further than the draft stage (see Chapter 12).

The second proposal was included in a directive on approximation of member states' company law which was submitted by the Commission to the Council in July 1983, eleven years after it was first drafted (*Bulletin EC* Supplements 10/72 and 8/74). For companies with more than 500 employees, the proposal provided for a two-tier board structure with a management and a supervisory board; of the latter's members, one-third will be workers' representatives. Following lengthy discussions at the European Parliament and the Economic and Social Committee, this proposal was radically amended (EC Commission, 1989d). The new directive, which will now apply to firms employing more than 1,000 employees, recommends a more flexible board structure, allowing companies to choose either a dualistic or a unitary system, with a unitary board consisting of executive and non-executive members. Depending on the system chosen, four different structural forms of employee participation in the supervisory board are permitted.

Another proposal was the *Vredeling Directive* (submitted in 1980) which dealt with large national and multinational companies and the rights of workers to be consulted and informed on matters of the company they work for. The draft directive advocated consultation between management and employees on all major decisions (closures, dismissals, restructuring, etc.), and disclosure of comprehensive information concerning company operations, in particular transnational undertakings. The directive attracted strong opposition from employers on the grounds that its acceptance would increase costs, inhibit management, damage confidentiality and reduce foreign investment in the Community. After consultations and discussions in the European Parliament the Commission produced a watered-down, modified version of the directive in July 1983. This has been condemned by both the European Trades Union Confederation (ETUC), which supports the Commission's initiatives and the original version of the Vredeling Directive, and the European employers' organisation (UNICE), which opposes both versions of the Directive. Some member states also expressed concern at the possible disincentives offered by the Directive to investors from within and outside the Community. Finally the Commission decided in 1986 not to consider the proposal further, reserving the right to resurrect it at an appropriate time (EC Commission, 1988g). The issue of the form and extent of industrial democracy in the Community remains unresolved. However, developed systems of worker information and consultation already exist in some member states (Denmark, Germany, the Netherlands, etc.)

Handicapped persons

One of the priority tasks of the SAP was to help disabled people integrate into the life and work of the Community. To this effect, the ESF made financing available for pilot projects aiming at the rehabilitation of handicapped people, and the Commission prepared in 1981 an action programme for their employment in a free economy. The programme covers the following:

1. The establishment of a Community-wide network of *demonstration projects* aiming at improvement of the quality of vocational rehabilitation facilities currently in operation.
2. Improved exchanges of *information and experience* between rehabilitation and training bodies.
3. Studies and conferences aimed at drawing up *Community guidelines* for longer-term projects and policies.
4. More financial assistance for the existing Community network of *rehabilitation centres*.
5. Further development of the Community's scheme of *pilot housing actions* for the handicapped.

A Community network of model projects was set up, and later on the initial phase of a computerised Community database on the handicapped (Handynet project) was launched. A second Community action programme (Helios, 1988–91) has been adopted with two aims: to facilitate occupational rehabilitation and economic integration and to promote social integration and independent living of the disabled (EC Commission, 1986).

Migrant workers

There are 6 million migrant workers resident in the Community; with their families the figure is 12 million. Approximately 75 per cent of them come from countries outside the Community. In general the majority of the migrants are unskilled workers who take up rough, poorly paid jobs which the local workers refuse to do. In addition to poor housing and inadequate training and education facilities, the migrants face specific problems, such as linguistic difficulties and religious differences, which adversely affect their social integration in the community.

Community policies have been directed towards improving the social conditions for the migrant workers and their families as part of the overall social policy programme. The basic policy rules were outlined in a 1971 regulation on *social security for migrant workers* which specified that, under the Community arrangement for free movement of labour, workers who are nationals of one member state and work in another have total access to social security in the state of their work on the same basis as the nationals of that member state, and that they can accumulate employment insurance and pension rights in one state and export them to another. This scheme was extended to the self-employed from 1 July 1982. An *Action Programme for Migrant Workers and Their Families* was adopted by Council resolution on 9 February 1976. The Programme introduced specific measures relating to language teaching, vocational training, social security, housing, social services, schooling, and economic, political and trade union rights, all of which aim at obliteration of the discrimination against migrant workers and their dependants.

Poverty

Most national social policies include measures aiming at income maintenance of people living in poverty, especially the old, sick or disabled, unemployed, one-parent families, the homeless and vagrants. The policy objective is to bring these people up to some poverty line, expressed as a percentage of the national average income. The problem is that poverty is a relative term and no two states in the Community have similar poverty lines. Moreover, while in some countries poverty alleviation is pursued by a system of non-contributory supplementary benefits, either general (the United Kingdom, Ireland) or means-tested (Denmark, the Netherlands), most Community countries operate a contributory insurance system which leaves out those poor who have not contributed to the system. Therefore, it is not surprising that international studies, which used standardised data, have shown that even in developed countries, despite the existence of extensive welfare programmes, a large section of the population continue to live in poverty (OECD, 1976). A relevant example is Belgium, where approximately 20 per cent of the population were below the poverty line before welfare benefits, and 6.1 per cent remained there after welfare benefits.

The SAP did not include any reference to poverty. However, the Commission at a later stage did put forward a proposal making the fight against poverty a priority. Poverty was defined by reference to income where the unit of consumption was lower than half the average income per head in the country concerned. Hence, use was made of the concept of a poverty line at the national level by setting a particular variable of consumption per member state. An implication of this definition is that people with incomes below the poverty line in one country could be considerably better off than people above the line in another. The Community first anti-poverty programme consisted of twenty-nine pilot schemes and projects to be mounted in various member states, and two cross-national studies on the general issue of poverty. The proposal was adopted by Council in 1975 and ran until the end of 1980 with the cost shared on an equal basis between the Community and the participating member states. On the basis of these studies the Commission prepared an assessment report which was forwarded to the Council in 1981. The report confirmed that, despite the unprecedented growth in national incomes and in the welfare state since the mid-1950s, poverty had not declined and the gap between the standard of living and opportunities enjoyed by the average man and the poor had not closed: in the EC-9 approximately 30 million people were under the poverty line, about 11.4 per cent of households. However, the pilot studies had shown that action against poverty was possible and effective, and that at the national level the costs need not be high. The Commission's conclusion was that action against poverty needed to be given high priority and that a major strategy for combating poverty is to reduce unemployment by creating new jobs and sharing existing jobs. The Council noted this report on 10 December 1982, agreed that more action by the Community is necessary and laid down certain guidelines for such action. A second programme to combat poverty was authorised for the period 1985–8, taking into account the accession of Portugal and Spain. The aim of the new programme was, in addition to Community action in the fields of unemployment and related policies, to combat poverty by promoting or providing financial assistance for projects on long-term unemployment, young unemployed, elderly, single-parent families, migrants and refugees, marginals and underprivileged in urban and rural areas (EC Commission, 1989c).

The growth of unemployment, underemployment, single-parent families, etc., means that in many countries the number of poor has increased absolutely. Table 10.4 shows relative levels of poverty in the Community 1980–85, where the poverty line is set at 50 per cent below national average earnings. The data confirm that during the period under review poverty was reduced in four member states (Belgium, France, Greece and Spain), remained the same in one (Luxembourg),

Table 10.4 Relative levels of poverty in the Community: population share.

Country	Year	Population (per cent)	1985 ranking (1 = highest)	1980–85 rate change	Rate of change ranking (1 = highest)
B	1980	7.6	12	−5.26	12
	1985	7.2			
DK	1980	13.0	6	13.08	5
	1985	14.7			
D	1978	6.7	9	26.87	3
	1985	8.5			
E	1980	20.5	4	−2.43	11
	1985	20.0			
F	1979	17.7	5	−1.13	10
	1985	17.5			
GR	1981	24.2	2	−0.83	9
	1985	24.0			
IRL	1980	16.9	3	30.18	2
	1985	22.0			
I	1980	9.4	8	24.47	4
	1984	11.7			
L	1980	7.9	10	0.00	8
	1985	7.9			
NL	1981	7.0	11	5.71	6
	1985	7.4			
P	1981	27.8	1	0.72	7
	1985	28.0			
UK	1980	9.2	7	30.43	1
	1985	12.0			

Note: Poverty line = 50 per cent below average earnings in the country concerned.

Source: EC (1990) *Poverty in Europe: Estimates*, The Institute of Social Studies Advisory Service, Rotterdam University.

and increased in the rest (Denmark, Germany, Ireland, Italy, the Netherlands, Portugal, the United Kingdom), in some of them by a very high rate of growth. It has been estimated (1989) that in the Community of twelve member states, the number of poor is more than 38 million. Hence the dependence on social assistance systems has been rising substantially in most member states. In the three new members social protection systems are less developed than in the countries of the 'old' EC.

10.4 Evaluation

The Community social policy is supplementary to that pursued by the member states and its effects are rather marginal. Its main objective is harmonisation, if at all possible, in an upward direction. However, with the members at different levels of economic development and with unequal growth potential, the progress towards a uniform system of national social policies will necessarily be slow. The expectation that market integration and economic progress will automatically lead to (a probably downward) convergence of the social policies of the member states has not been realised. In recent years the social conditions have become even more difficult, since recession and slow growth have caused grave financial problems and, in an attempt to reduce inflation and large budgetary deficits, many countries have resorted to drastic cuts in public expenditure, including social services outlays. These measures, coupled with demographic changes, which have already reduced the birth rate and increased the number of pensioners, have had a regressive effect on social policy provisions. The prospect of the single internal market will generate a higher rate of economic growth, but unless the Community takes appropriate action and mobilises its resources more effectively, poverty will continue to exist (EC Commission, 1988e, 1988f).

In the EC, the countries which have the least developed social policy sectors are the less developed, the newest members of the Community (Greece, Portugal and Spain) which, with per capita income well below the EC average, cannot afford to raise their social policy expenditures to match the level of the most developed members. Hence, they will depend heavily on Community guidance and financial assistance to help them bring their national social legislation and policies in line with those of the developed member countries. Social policy harmonisation has thus become a larger issue for the Community after the latest enlargements. Under the prevailing conditions existing problems have become more intensive, and therefore Community action should be expected to continue in areas already pursued actively (unemployment, pay, working conditions, vocational training, migrant workers, industrial democracy, etc.). At the moment, the development of Community initiatives in other areas or the adoption of more radical solutions are severely constrained by the small amount of the budget devoted to social policy. Compared to the social policies expenditures of the national governments, the size of the Community social budget is minimal.

Financial constraints dictate that the Community can do very little on its own to solve social problems, such as youth unemployment, by direct social policy. What it can do well is organise coordinated action by the social services of the member states. In general, the Community can expand its operations in what it can do effectively within the financial means available to it, that is 'act in close contact with the member states through the promotion of studies, the giving of opinions, the organising of consultations both on problems arising at the national level and on those of concern to international organisations' (Article 118). In general, the Community can coordinate the search for a solution to social problems, which may differ in extent but otherwise are common in all countries, by guiding the member states towards harmonisation of social provisions and by showing the direction that social policy in the member states should take. A step towards this direction was taken by the Commission's proposal for a Social Charter.

10.5 The Social Charter

With the move towards 1992 and the single European market gathering momentum a sharp discussion began about its social consequences. The debate was initiated by trade union representatives who expressed the fear that competition in the single market would bring about a downward convergence of social standards as countries on the periphery of the EC with low social provisions would gain an unfair competitive advantage. Another argument in support of the need for increased harmonisation of social policy is the threat of 'social dumping': the danger that, with the free movement of capital after 1992, labour-intensive industries will migrate from countries of high standards of worker protection to countries where pay and working conditions are poor. Hence countries with relatively high social standards will be forced to lower them to woo companies back. Consequently, it has been proposed that the Community should be given greater powers over social policy to enable it to harmonise the multitude of national regulations on employment and social security in ways that would safeguard workers' employment and hard-won social rights in the more prosperous members of the

Community. Opponents of this proposal argued that as national differences in social standards are reflected in labour costs, they cannot be eliminated without parallel improvements in infrastructure, increases in labour productivity and adjustment in exchange rates. Accordingly, since national differences in labour costs exist already and have not caused significant difficulties to any of the peripheral member countries, the problem of divergence in social standards should be left to the market forces which would bring about any necessary adjustment. Therefore, the harmonisation of social standards to protect the 'high-standard countries is unnecessary.

As a compromise between the opposing views and under pressure by Parliament, the governments of member states and labour unions, the Commission proposed a 'Community Charter of Fundamental Social Rights', the aim of which is to set out the major outlines on which the European pattern of labour law and, more generally, the European concept of society and the place of labour in that society should be based. The Charter, which is a non-binding declaration of principles, will be followed by a work programme of action for its implementation. National laws and domestic deals between trade unions and employers are supposed to enshrine these principles.

The Charter, which to a large extent reaffirms and renews the provisions of the SAP, is intended to proclaim the major principles underlying the following rights and responsibilities:

1. *Improvement of living and working conditions*: the development of the Single European Market must result in an improvement of the living and working conditions of workers in the EC. This will be brought about by an upward approximation of those conditions and will concern the organisation and flexibility of working hours (working week, duration of employment, part-time work, temporary work, night shifts, etc.).

2. *Right to freedom of movement*: already provided for in the Treaty (Articles 48–50, 52–8), this right makes possible the exercise of any trade or occupation within the Community on the same terms as those applied to nationals of the host country in all fields.

3. *Employment and remuneration*: all employment (full-time, part-time, permanent, temporary, etc.) must be fairly remunerated. A fair wage should ensure workers of the means necessary for their own subsistence and that of their families.

4. *Right to social protection*: subject to the arrangements proper to each member state, any citizen of the EC is entitled to adequate social protection. This implies the necessity to establish a minimum wage and appropriate social assistance for those excluded from the

labour markets (elderly, unemployed, unable to be employed, etc.).

5. *Right to freedom and collective bargaining*: every employer and every worker in the EC has the right to belong freely to the professional and trade union organisation of his choice and to any legally constituted association.

6. *Right to vocational training:* every worker in the EC has the right to continue his vocational training throughout his working life. A machinery for continuing and permanent training must be set up to that end, enabling every citizen to undergo training, in particular through the granting of leave for training purposes.

7. *Right of men and women to equal treatment*: equal opportunities and equal treatment for men and women must be guaranteed and developed.

8. *Right to information, consultation and worker participation*: this must be developed along appropriate lines and in such a way as to take account of the legal provisions, contractual agreements and practices in force in the member countries of the Community. This will apply especially to companies or undertakings located in several member states.

9. *Right to health protection and safety at the workplace*: appropriate measures must be taken to guarantee this right and to continue upward harmonisation of conditions in this area.

10. *Protection of children and adolescents*: the minimum working age must be set at 16 years. All young people over 16 who are in gainful employment must be protected by labour rules arranged in their favour and must receive fair remuneration.

11. *Elderly persons*: every citizen of the community in receipt of a pension must have sufficient resources to enable him to maintain a decent standard of living. Those elderly persons who are not entitled to a pension and who have no other adequate resources should receive a minimum income and social and medical assistance adapted to their needs.

12. *Disabled persons*: specific measures must be taken to achieve the fullest integration of disabled persons into working life.

The European Charter was adopted by eleven of the twelve member states of the European Community at Strasbourg in December 1989. The United Kingdom, which had earlier in the year, at the Madrid summit meeting, given warning of its outright opposition to it, is the odd one out.

With the aim of completing the internal market, Articles 130 A–E have been inserted in the Treaty of Rome which instruct the Community to actively pursue policies that promote the economic and social development of the periphery. It is believed that balanced economic growth within the wide area of the common market will contribute to the upward convergence of social standards.

The existing inequality in social provisions among the EC countries, in particular the problem with the peripheral countries, is not that they are intrinsically against improvements in social standards, but that, with their present level of economic development and available financial resources, they simply cannot afford them. Therefore, without large inter-governmental transfers from the 'high social standard' countries to the peripheral 'low social standard' countries, the Social Charter will remain an empty political declaration.

Further reading

For the latest EC proposals on social aspects in the single market see EC (1990) and Venturini (1989). The Commission's views on the social dimension of the single market are in EC Commission (1988d).

11

Transport

11.1 The problem

The Treaty of Rome provides separate Titles, that is chapters, only for two economic sectors, agriculture and transport. In fact, with agriculture contributing 3.4 per cent and transport 7 per cent to the Community's GDP, transport is much more important than agriculture.

Transport is a service sector with many cross-links with other sectors. In the Community, expenditure on transport is estimated to represent 11 per cent of total private investment and 40 per cent of public investment. Many sectors of the industry (motor, aircraft, shipyards, road building, steel production, etc.) depend on transport. The sector accounts for 25 per cent of total energy consumption. Approximately 45 per cent of oil consumption is used by transport, 85 per cent of that by road transport alone. Expenditure on road, rail, waterways and transport infrastructure in general constitutes a major component of national expenditures on regional development. Transport is also a major sector of manpower employment: approximately one in ten of the working population work in transport.

Two of the most important problems of the sector are investment and resource allocation. Both of these problems are connected with the issue of 'regulation', that is government intervention in transport. In general, regulation is advised as a remedy for market failures causing misallocation of resources and welfare loss. Economic theory recognises three broad kinds of reason why unregulated markets may fail to allocate resources efficiently. These reasons and an additional fourth also apply to transport:

1. First, there is market power that allows firms to enjoy excessive rents by maintaining prices higher and volume of output lower than the competitive levels. In this case competitive solutions are desirable and feasible but are not achieved because of actions by incumbents. Market power has detrimental effects on static and dynamic economic efficiency. However, in transport this problem is frequently the cause (and effect) of economies of scale: in certain cases, carriers need to be large (railways, air-traffic control, airports and ports), and this creates barriers to entry. This case is similar to natural monopoly. Accordingly:
   (a) competitive solutions are not feasible and
   (b) regulation is preferable to competition.
2. Second, there are externalities that prevent private marginal costs and benefits from reaching equality with social marginal cost and benefits. This occurs when the welfare of one economic agent (person, firm) is directly affected by the actions of another. For example, when there is no explicit charge for the use of road space and one road-user imposes congestion costs on others. The externalities more frequently mentioned with regard to transport are congestion, noise and atmospheric pollution. Another form of externality is the transport's impact on the location of economic activity (housing, production, employment), the environment and land values.
3. Third, there is asymmetric information about product quality between the contracting parties (sellers/buyers) that prevents them from reaching optimum exchange. In this case competitive solutions are feasible but undesirable. Technical specifications, frequency and rigour of servicing, qualifications of carriers and similar issues associated with risk and safety (e.g. in air transport) are typical examples of this problem and are usually subject to regulation.
4. Fourth, there is 'excessive' competition that allegedly would destroy all except one or two firms, which would then set non-competitive prices. Price and entry regulation of airlines, trucking, shipping, etc., is frequently justified on this line of argument.

Government intervention in transport comprises market organisation (structural regulation) and market behaviour (conduct regulation). In general two kinds of broad attitudes exist with regard to regulation in transport which have resulted in two approaches, the 'commercial' and the 'social', each with different policy implications. The 'commercial' approach tends to regard transport as a service. The objective of government transport policy is to facilitate the market forces to operate efficiently. Government intervention aims at improvement of the structure and organisation of the market, so that supply matches the market demand in both quality and quantity, and at the lowest possible cost. The 'social' approach holds that transport does not only serve the existing centres of social and economic activity, but it also affects trade and industrial development, the distribution of employment, population and land use, as well as the quality of life of the community. Consequently, under the second approach transport policy is an instrument for pursuing wider economic and social goals, such as growth, allocation of production, energy conservation, quality of life, the environment and so on. Therefore government intervention is more widespread and active under the 'social' rather than the 'commercial' approach to transport policy. Clashes between advocates of the two different views occur frequently, whenever a major transport project comes under discussion, for example, the building of new motorways or airports, closure of rail lines, bus services, etc.

Whatever the approach, 'commercial' or 'social', an important characteristic of the sector is the pervasive presence of intervention. The government is omnipresent in transport, first as investor in infrastructure and then as provider of services directly to the public or indirectly by subsidising other carriers, as recipient of transport taxes, and as legislator of numerous regulations concerning the operations of the industry. In general, governments attempt to control the quality, quantity, organisation and resource allocation of the sector. The first three of these objectives are usually pursued by regulation and appropriate legislation, the last one by economic management. Quality controls are mostly regulations dealing with safety aspects (speed limits, minimum standards, working conditions, qualifications of operators, pollution, congestion, etc.). Quantity controls attempt to match the (usually public) supply with the requirements of the market. The organisation of the sector is concerned with the ownership of the industry, which in most countries is partly public enterprise, and the structure of the market (monopoly, oligopoly). Economic management for the objective of resource allocation aims to the attainment of efficiency.

Transport is characterised by high *indivisibilities* which are technical externalities that impinge on both pricing and investment. Many investments in the sector, which are usually large, have a long life-span and are infrequently made (such as infrastructure), are undertaken by the public sector. Therefore problems arise with the financing of transport projects and the allocation of costs. A far more complex problem is the pricing of the output of the sector, and the relationship between the prices of public and private transport services. In its turn, pricing directly affects the resource allocation and the efficiency of the sector. Efficiency is here taken to mean the benefit to the community derived from the goods and services that transport produces. Optimality implies the derivation of maximum benefit from transport at the least possible cost.

Additional complications arise from the multiplicity of forms of transport or *modes* that contribute to the total output of the sector. Production by different forms entails a multifarious sectoral output which is heterogeneous and cannot be easily aggregated, evaluated and compared between different modes. Therefore, it is also difficult to devise and implement comprehensive transport policies that would encourage fair competition between the different modes of transport.

11.2 Common transport policy

The reason customs unions require a common transport policy is that transport constitutes an important production input and thus transport costs fall on the pricing of output. It is estimated that on average 25 per cent of final costs are accounted for by transport costs. Therefore, transport directly affects the degree of competition in the market. Hence, a determined country can alter its comparative advantage and its trade flows by policy-induced changes (subsidies, taxation) of transport costs. Therefore, within a common market, trade liberalisation and a common transport policy should be implemented simultaneously.

However, the cross-links between transport and other sectors of the economy mean that common transport policies at the level of the Community will have implications on a number of other economic sectors. This characteristic, combined with the fact that a considerable section of the sector is not directly involved with inter-state trading and therefore it is considered to be exclusively in the domain of a state's domestic policy, implies that agreement on common transport policies cannot be reached easily. On the other hand, if a common transport policy is ever devised, it would constitute a major step towards the integration of a large section of the members' economies.

Transport cost is an important component of the final price and therefore transport affects relative prices and trade. Since a major object-ive of the Community was to liberalise and promote inter-state trade, transport was to be given an important role. It was therefore crucial to harmonise national transport policies with the view to advancing a coordinated and efficient Community transport system which would stimulate competition, help reduce costs and assist the development of inter-state trade on the basis of comparative advantage. For this reason the Commission endeavoured from the start to introduce a common transport policy in step with trade liberalisation. But the six original members of the Community had diverse interests and priorities in their national transport sectors which had developed by distinctly different national approaches to state intervention concerning regulation, conservation, land use and the environment. What all of them had in common was that for both economic and social reasons they exerted state quality and quantity controls over transport in the form of rates, quotas and licensing.

State intervention in individual member countries took the form of direct fixing of transport rates and control over entry in the industry by licensing, differential taxation or preferential granting of subsidies, and enactment of regulations to protect national carriers in general from foreign competition. A second source of important differences between the Community states was the preference which individual countries placed on the various modes of transport, some of them (France, Germany, Italy), departing from free-market principles, discriminated in favour of the railways, while others (the Netherlands) by a policy of impartiality created a competitive environment that actually assisted the development of road haulage. The inter-links between transport and other economic sectors were exploited by different countries at various degrees by using transport as an instrument of policy to further objectives in the fields of regional development, social policy, industrial policy, etc. Consequently, the quality of transport, the degree of government interference, and the objectives of government policies differed among the Community partners to a very large extent. Moreover, in some of the member countries, transport had been manipulated to serve external trade in a role similar to that of tariffs and subsidies, promoting exports and inhibiting imports. Since state intervention in transport was dissimilar between the members, trade liberalisation would bring forward cost distortions and price differentials emanating from different transport policies.

For all these reasons, the field where the common policies were to be applied was very uneven, had varying implications on the prices of traded goods and different social effects on the community at large. This made the search for common transport policies a difficult and lengthy enterprise. However, the importance of transport as a complement to the liberalisation of trade and integration of the market was recognised from early on. Transport is one of the three sectors specifically mentioned in Article 3 of the Treaty of Rome (external trade and agriculture are the other two) for which the Community intended to develop common policies. These policies were to serve a dual objective: first, to establish an integrated and efficient transport sector able to serve the integration of the market, regional development and economic growth; and, second, given the involvement of transport in every other economic sector, to use transport as an instrument designed to further the attainment of the general aims of the Treaty. The general framework of Community policy is presented under a separate Title of the Treaty, Articles 74–84. These Articles outline the basic principles for the development of a more detailed set of policies. The actual design and implementation of the common transport policy were left to the discretion of the Council and other Community institutions.

In Articles 74–5 the member states agree to pursue the objectives of the Treaty with regard to transport by a common transport policy and by a specified institutional procedure. Article 84 states that this common policy would apply to transport by rail, road and inland waterways, but also to shipping and aviation, provided this extension is decided by the Council 'acting by means of a unanimous vote', which was duly done. Among other general policy guidelines, Article 75 prescribes common rules for frontier-crossing traffic within the Community, and for opening up national transport markets to intra-Community competition. Agreement on these two issues constituted a fundamental prerequisite for achieving the short-term objective of the EC, establishment of the customs union. The remaining articles of the Title contain particular rules for removing the discriminatory practices of member states against carriers of other member states, for relating charges levied at frontier crossings to actual costs, and for regulating state financial assistance at the level of the Community. Article 83 sets up a consultative committee of experts, usually drawn from the transport ministries of the member states, to give the Commission advice (technical, financial, legal, etc.) on the formulation of common transport policy.

In fact, the formulation of a common transport policy proved to be a difficult and slow process. The first outlines for common action were presented by the Commission in the Schaus Memorandum (EC Commission, 1961). The purpose of this document was to initiate discussion on the principles that should guide the common transport policy (CTP) rather than a formal proposal for the formulation of such a policy. Accordingly, the main objective of the common transport policy was assumed to be the gradual replacement of national transport policies on the basis of gradual implementation of free-market competition subject to consistent Community rules in line with social and economic requirements. Transport in the Community was expected to be competitive and operator-oriented. Therefore the central aim of the common transport policy was to set free the transport operators from restrictive regulation, to eliminate discrimination and to coordinate investment, particularly on 'trunk routes of Community importance'. Consequently, more emphasis was placed on the 'commercial' rather than the 'social' approach to policy orientation: 'In particular, there seems to be no reason why goods transport should not, as a rule, operate on entirely commercial lines'.

The transport market was to be organised in accordance with the general principles of the market economy: free competition; free choice of means of transport by users; equality of treatment for modes of transport and for carriers as regards taxation, social charges and subsidies; financial and commercial independence for the operators; and coordination of transport infrastructure. Public intervention was not excluded *ad hoc*, but the understanding was that, whenever it would occur, it was expected to be minimal and discrete, having as its main function the supervision of the transport market for the attainment of operational efficiency. This principle continues to be the corner-stone of Community transport policy. The main objective of the CTP still is 'to allow free competition and only to create community rules where the proper functioning of the transport market makes them absolutely necessary' (EC, 1979b).

The Council of Ministers found the Schaus Memorandum too general and took no immediate action for implementation of its recommendations, except for a measure of harmonisation of national customs procedures, truck axle weights and drivers' working hours. However, in the general spirit of the Schaus Memorandum and in an attempt to refashion the transport services of the Six, the Commission produced in 1962 an ambitious action programme for the common transport policy. The Programme provided for the following:

1. Liberalisation of the national markets on the basis of commercial criteria as a prerequisite for the integration of members' transport sectors.
2. Organisation of the market with reference to competition and control of carriers charges.
3. Harmonisation of state intervention in the fields of fiscal, technical and operational measures as a step towards removal of discrepancies between the transport sectors of the Six (EC Commission, 1962).

However, these liberalisation proposals, which were not confined only to inter-state transport but extended over the national transport systems within the member countries, faced a hostile reception from early on. With some degree of justification, the member states considered the action programme an attempt to abolish national sovereignty in transport in the hope of establishing a competitive common market.

An area considered by the Community to be in need for change was the road haulage issue (Button, 1984). This is a private enterprise system in every country of the Community subject to national rules and regulations. Domestic road haulage is usually administered by licensing. The Community considered that this could continue to be subject to national rules which, however, should be harmonised between the members of the Community. Complications arise from inter-state road haulage which was governed by licensing and quotas agreed between states on a bilateral basis. The Commission took the view that, following the formation of the common market, inter-state trade would grow and inter-state transport should be subject to common policies. The first problem was that the quota system by which each state regulated the number and load capacity of foreign vehicles in its own territory would have to expand in conformity with the growth of trade. This could be done by progressively liberalising the existing system, first, by expanding the existing bilateral quotas and, later, by replacing the bilateral quotas by Community (multinational) quotas which would grow in pace with the growth in intra-Community trade.

Another important element in the Commission's plans for the liberalisation of transport was the proposal for immediate introduction of *forked tariffs*, that is establishment of a minimum (floor) and a maximum (ceiling) of charges determining the range within which carriers would be free to charge what they liked. The preference for forked tariffs rather than complete equalisation arose from necessity, that is from the fact that the national regimes for carriers' charges were widely different between the member states, and within each state between different modes of transport. The introduction of a common legal maximum charge was aimed at prevention of monopolistic exploitation of the market, while the common legal minimum charge was needed to prevent the development of destructive and socially detrimental competition. The idea behind this arrangement was that the characteristic inflexibilities of the short-term supply and the seasonal fluctuation in demand created price fluctuations in the sector. Hence, the forked tariffs proposal was seen as no more than a device to build some degree of stabilisation into the system. However, in reality the forked tariffs represented a sort of political compromise between the two extreme systems then in force in member countries, the fixed rates of Germany and the completely free pricing of the Netherlands.

Implementation of the CTP started with a Regulation issued in 1960 prohibiting discrimination in transport on ground of nationality (in accordance with Article 79). However, progress was slow. The Community quotas system was partially implemented by adapting the existing bilateral quotas, contrary to the Commission's proposal which envisaged complete elimination of bilateral quotas. Discussions on the forked tariffs proposal dominated the scene for more than five years, the issues raised being related to technical difficulties in the implementation of the proposal, the width of the fork, permitted exemptions, rules of enforcement, administrative costs, etc. Finally, the Six reached agreement on a watered down version of the forked tariffs, but owing to more general differences concerning the desirable degree of market regulation, the Council reached a stalemate and the forked tariffs proposals was not implemented.

In the end, under pressure from the governments of the member states, who repeatedly demonstrated their unwillingness to introduce changes in the status quo of their transport sectors, the Commission's action programme was abandoned as unrealistic. Instead of an all-embracing and general transport programme, a series of *ad hoc* policy measures were introduced (normalisation of railways accounts, Community quotas for road haulage, etc.), known collectively as the 'mini-programmes'. Among them, a mini-forked tariffs measure was introduced, imposing mandatory maximum and minimum of 11.5 per cent around the basic rate on frontier-crossing road haulage. This regulation was introduced in 1969 for an experimental period of three years. The Council also adopted a regulation in 1969 concerning the normalisation of railway accounts under common rules for granting state subsidies. Hence, in the 1970s, a certain degree of cooperation in transport was achieved, but not of the extent envisaged in the action programme. Meanwhile, the enlargement of the Community to include three new members (two of which were islands), which was expected to add more problems to the search for a comprehensive common transport policy, also contributed to the final demise of the action programme.

11.3 New directions

The functionalist school of thought believed that with the liberalisation of trade and the free exchange of goods, the transport system that carried these goods would be liberalised by the market process. However, this did not occur automatically or otherwise, among other reasons because of the unwillingness of the member states to cooperate in the search for, and the application of, an all-embracing CTP. At the same time, active state intervention in transport continued in every member state. With expansion of the Community to nine member states, some of which appeared to oppose the principles of the CTP plans of the 1960s, the need for a new approach became apparent. It was thus realised that CTP cannot start before harmonising the intervention policies of the member states. Thus from necessity, a change in direction took place. This change was manifested by the early 1970s, when the emphasis shifted from the attempt to regulate transport operations and pricing towards the development of a common infrastructural policy.

The idea behind this change in strategy seems to be that, if by common policies a compatible infrastructure of the appropriate level and type is achieved, then coordination of transport policies affecting the users will not be difficult. Long-term investment harmonisation coincided also with a change in attitudes towards transport in general and the role of transport policy in modern society. Contributing factors were the rapid increases in the cost of fuels and energy caused by the first oil crisis, and the greater awareness of the environmental and ecological implications of unrestrained transport growth. Unrestrained growth of transport and development of transport infrastructure have implications on energy consumption, transport safety, land use and environmental pollution.

The reorientation of Community policy towards the development and coordination of transport infrastructure was also prompted by the growth rate of traffic between member states, which was twice as rapid as that of the volume of purely national traffic. The problem was that the demand for international transport could not be satisfied with the existing networks, which were designed to cater mainly for domestic traffic.

With these ideas as background, and after the accession to the Community of three new members, the Commission presented in October 1973 an updated version of its 1971 plan for a CTP. The revised plan was based on the following basic principles:

1. Gradual implementation of the principles of market economy with free competition in the transport market and approximation of the starting conditions as between states.
2. Coordination with regard to national taxation of commercial vehicles.
3. Approximation of national provisions governing relations between the railways and the state.
4. Harmonisation of social legislation, improvement of working conditions, transport safety regulations, etc.
5. Coordination for the development of common transport infrastructure.

The Commission's transport policy programme was considered over the following two years by the European Parliament and the Economic and Social Committee, and was approved without substantial changes to its recommendations. However, the Council of Ministers did not commit itself by adopting the programme as a whole. The Commission was instead asked to define the priority problems for another working programme, covering the timetable for implementation of common transport policy over the next three years. At the end of 1977 the Commission presented a new document based on the fundamental ideas of the 1973 plan in which it listed the priorities for implementation of a CTP. The Council took note of these and agreed to act upon them when the situation should permit it. In October 1980 the Commission submitted its proposals to the European Parliament which approved in principle the transport programme (EC, 1984c). Finally in March 1981 the Council adopted the Commission's draft as a decision, laying down the new principal points for the 1981–3 programme, but it again refused to commit itself by adopting the Commission's list of priorities (Erdmenger, 1983). Thus, once again, we observe the fundamental difficulty of establishing and implementing a CTP: the Commission, either on its own initiative or sometimes after a request from the Council, presents proposals for the liberalisation of the market, but the Council does not take the necessary steps for the transformation of these proposals into active policy.

The slow progress towards the creation of a CTP urged the European Parliament in September 1982 to bring proceedings against the Council of Ministers in the Court of Justice for failing to carry out its obligations under the Treaty (Article 24). The Court held that the Council had indeed infringed the Treaty by 'failing to ensure freedom to provide services in the sphere of international transport and to lay down the conditions under which non-resident carriers may operate transport services in a member state'. However, since the Treaty does not define exactly what the CTP should consist of, the Court could only recommend the Council to work continuously towards the progressive attainment of such a policy. In the meantime, the enlargement of the Community to twelve members introduced new difficulties by widening the heterogeneity of the already diverse transport sector of the Community. Consequently, the introduction and implementation of common policies were again postponed until another day.

11.4   Recent developments

All these setbacks do not mean that nothing has happened in the field of common transport. By 1985, the Community had adopted some 200 pieces of transport legislation. Moreover, many member states, with assistance from the European Investment Bank and the European Regional Development Fund, undertook major national investments on transport infrastructure. But this record of legislation and infrastructure investment, which was approved piecemeal after many years of effort, made only a minor contribution towards establishing a Community transport policy. The failure to reach agreement on a common transport policy was considered by many as an example of the impossibility of proceeding with integration further than a customs union. All these changed with the Single European Act and the prospect for a common market, not only in commodities but also in services, and transport services in particular.

The Community transport programme can be divided into four areas:

1. Development of the infrastructural network.
2. Liberalisation of markets.
3. Facilitation of frontier crossings.
4. Standardisation of safety and operational regulations.

Investment in inter-state infrastructure is not subject to cost–benefit assessment on a completely national basis, because it does not provide benefits only to the country in which the investment is undertaken. The need for inter-state infrastructure thus becomes a supranational issue with benefits and costs accruing to the Community as a whole. However, Community action is not a substitute for the action of the member states which will continue to be responsible for the maintenance and development of the transport infrastructure within their frontiers. Hence, in this function the Community principally operates as the coordinator, who will guide the national authorities in such a way that the national transport networks combine to meet the Community's present and future needs. Infrastructure projects of importance to the Community as a whole receive Community financial support. In particular, the Community provides aid for transport infrastructure which aims specifically at: (a) elimination of notorious bottlenecks within the Community or straddling its external frontiers; (b) improvement of major traffic links between member states; and (c) integration of peripheral areas into the Community network. The financial support granted by the Community from this scheme is limited to a maximum of 25 per cent of the cost of the project, provided that the total contribution to this project by all Community sources does not exceed 50 per cent of its total cost.

Development of transport infrastructure will of course have implications, both economic and social. New investment will constitute additional expenditure, for which the required financing has to be raised. In turn, besides the availability of infrastructure ready to accept the increasing inter-state traffic, these investment expenditures will have positive effects on the rate of growth of the member countries (EC, 1979b). Positive and negative effects will also occur in the social field, in the effort for regional development, environmental protection, etc. For example, new transport infrastructure will induce changes in the location of housing and economic activity and, although these associated developments are expected to cause considerable beneficial effects on the organisation of production and distribution, they may also have negative social implications by inducing 'enforced mobility' of labour which may bring forward changes in the 'quality of life'. Increased infrastructural investment along the main axes of Community development also means that advanced regions will attract most of the additional expenditure, while peripheral regions, where current demand for transport is relatively low will again be left behind.

The prospect of a single market by 1993 has also opened up the possibility of liberalisation of the Community's heavily regulated road haulage, rail, shipping and air transport systems.

Road transport

The slow progress in reaching agreement for a common transport policy is explained by the intransigence of member states which feared that this would open their transport sectors to competition by firms of other member countries and will restrain their power to interfere in their national transport sectors. For example, it took nearly fifteen years of protracted negotiations to reach agreement on two long-running issues. In June 1983, the Council agreed on a maximum axle weight for trucks for continental Europe, and the United Kingdom and Ireland. It also decided to open up the road haulage market by issuing more Community quota licences permitting transport firms to pick up goods anywhere in the Community. The agreement provided that the system of Community quotas, which at the time were approximately 15 per cent of the total and were still arranged bilaterally between member states, would expand progressively by 40 per cent each year, so that by 1992 freight movement in the Community would be completely liberalised. Progress would also be made in harmonising the industry's operating conditions, taxation, drivers' terms of employment and transport taxes. A degree of harmonisation in the social field has been implemented, concerning periods of rest of those engaged in road transport, the introduction of tachographs and mutual recognition of qualifications. Finally a settlement regarding the deregulation of international transport was reached in December 1989. The system of Community quotas, bilateral quotas between member states and quotas for transit traffic to and from non-member countries will be eliminated by the end of 1992. From 1993 access to the market for transfrontier carriage of goods by road within the Community will be governed by a system of Community licences issued on the basis of qualitative criteria. This is expected to encourage competition. As more barriers to entry fall, haulage costs are expected to decrease substantially. Lower freight rates and fewer trade barriers may encourage companies to set plants further apart.

Railways

The Community has long been preoccupied with the problem of harmonising the subsidisation of railways, but has had little success in convincing the members that a common policy is required. The motivation of these subsidies comes from a different mix of transport, social, environmental and regional objectives in each member country and there is strong resistance to change. The CTP aims to make clear what kind of state subsidies are provided and for what particular purposes to railways, and to attain fairer competition with other modes of transport within the single market.

Rail transport has declined substantially in recent years but it still remains important in most countries of the EC. However, there is wide variation in conditions, performance and financial losses and diversity in the proportion of operating costs met from revenue. The high increase in road and air transport has led to excess rail capacity which potentially can be beneficially exploited to relieve congestion in other modes of transport. The application of new technologies, including high-speed trains and traffic management, can increase the competitiveness of the railways and help in the development of an integrated Community-wide rail-system. The Commission believes that the state monopoly of railways should be removed and that private transport operators should pay for track use on an equivalent basis to other modes of transport.

Shipping

Agreement on a common shipping policy narrowly failed to be reached in June 1986. Of the four questions considered, that of coastal shipping remained unresolved owing to the unwillingness of the Mediterranean member states to open their markets to intra-Community competition by admitting other members' boats to ply for trade in their coastal waters. However, with the exception of Greece and Spain, all other members agreed on the other three issues:

1. Common rules applying to competition in maritime transport.

2. Coordinated common response to third countries which reserve part of their trade to their own shipping.

3. Common response to unfair competition in maritime transport allowing the Community to impose anti-dumping levies against third countries whose shipping lines practise predatory pricing policies.

Since the Community is the world's biggest trading area, merchant shipping and maritime policy are important areas of the CTP. Since the accession of Greece, the Community has become the world's leading shipping power, controlling one-third of registered tonnage. Approximately 95 per cent of the tonnage of Community trade with non-member countries and 30 per cent of extra-Community traffic is carried by sea (Whitelegg, 1988). As in other areas of transport, the principle governing the EC maritime policy is that of free competition on world-wide scale, safety and environmental protection. Despite the decline in its fleet, the EC is a large merchant marine power with vast interests in this sector. The Community has for long been concerned with particular aspects of unfair practices, such as 'cargo-reservation' by which governments reserve a large proportion of the available trade for their own national carriers. The EC intervention in domestic shipping matters is pursued through its competition policy.

Inland waterways make up another important and long-standing mode of transport in Europe, handling about one-third of the total volume of traffic at comparatively low infrastructure cost. The CTP has aimed at harmonisation of national and international measures, improvement in competitive conditions and long-term balance of supply and demand.

Airways

Air transport is another area of contention. The rules governing the industry's conduct were originally intended to ensure a safe, reliable and inexpensive service. Regulation has sought to control entry and exit of carriers on routes and to set the prices, frequencies and capacity offered by those carriers. However, in recent years regulation has come under increasing criticism for being inflexible and over-protective, thus discriminating in favour of the existing carriers within a highly oligopolistic industry. Contrary to the scheduled markets, the charter industry, which accounts for roughly half the air transport in Europe, has been largely competitive: it is subject to a number of controls but entry and exit are largely unrestricted.

In general every member country agrees that the situation is chaotic regarding international air fares within the Community. The market is carved up among the state-owned European flag-carriers who fix fares and capacity by bilateral agreements and prevent any new airline from competing. Pooling arrangements, whereby scheduling and revenues are split 50:50, are typical, cushioning the most inefficient carriers and making Europe's air fares among the highest in the world. The airline lobby defends the status quo by claiming that deregulation would not be in the best interests of either the airlines or their passengers.

Ultimately, the aim of Community policy in air transport is to liberalise the industry by removing the plethora of bilateral and complex arrangements which maintain the high cost of inter-European air travel (EC Commission, 1981a). But repeated attempts by the Commission in the Council of Transport Ministers for a limited form of liberalisation by extending the application of existing Community rules to air transport did not succeed. Apart from the Commission and a few member states, all other member states and their national airlines favoured instead the status quo.

After many years of sterile discussions, the Commission finally initiated action by recourse to the interpretation of the Treaty's competition rules. Subsequently, the Court of Justice ruled in 1986 that the competition rules are applicable to air transport, and member states had an obligation under the Treaty of Rome not to approve fares if they know they result from an agreement or concerted practices between airlines. Under Articles 88 and 89 of the Treaty of Rome competent bodies for deciding whether violation of the competition rules has occurred are the Commission and the anti-trust authorities of member states. Hence, the Commission, through the competition or transport commissioners, can initiate legal proceedings to enforce competition in air transport. In June 1986, the Hague Summit also declared that the Council of Transport Ministers, which was in session at the same time, 'should without delay adopt the appropriate decisions on air tariffs, capacity and access to markets, in accordance with the rules of competition of the Treaty'. However, the Council again failed to reach agreement and the meeting ended in total disarray. The slow progress in the Council over liberalising civil aviation and growing criticism from consumer lobbies led some countries (Belgium, Germany, Italy, Ireland, the Netherlands, the United Kingdom) to make bilateral agreements, freeing market entry and prices on certain routes.

In an attempt to force a resolution, the Commission decided to act directly in the market by presenting cases of infringement of the competition rules by bilateral agreements on fare fixing and capacity sharing, fare structure and other restrictive practices, and asking the airlines to indicate how they proposed to comply with the competition rules. In the case of positive evidence of infringement and unsatisfactory reply, the Commission could declare such agreements null and void, making the airlines liable to prosecution. Moreover, under Article 169, a member state which abetted infringement of the competition rules by an airline could itself be brought by the Commission before the Court of Justice. In June 1987 the Commission reached agreement with the airline industry on a package of liberalisation measures sufficient to grant it a *block exemption* from direct application of the competition rules (see Chapter 3). This exemption, however, was only temporary and subject to conditions.

Another positive step for opening up air transport was taken in 1987 when the Council of Transport Ministers was set to agree on a fiercely bargained package involving four main components: fares, capacity, market access and application of the Community competition rules to air transport. This package was approved under the pressure for market integration emanating from the Single European Act. Finally, after years of timid liberalisation and following the example of deregulation in US air transport, which led to considerable increases in efficiency and capacity utilisation, substantial decreases in fares and a significant increase in the number of passengers, the Community transport ministers reached agreement on an air deregulation package in December 1989. Accordingly, capacity-sharing arrangements will be scrapped and access to European routes made freer. The Community will introduce a system of 'double disapproval' whereby airlines will be free to charge whatever economy fare they like on all routes, except where governments of the two countries at each end of the route lodge formal objections. This total fare freedom will come into effect on 1 January 1993; meanwhile fare zones will be introduced allowing airlines to cut their ticket prices to as low as 30 per cent of the standard economy tariff. The next step will be to liberalise the routes by 'multiple designation', whereby as many airlines as possible could compete on any intra-European service. Consequently, by breaking down frontier barriers and standardising regulation, Europe's rigidly controlled aviation network will be wide open to competition and the fares will be determined by the market. Deregulation will mean restructuring of the industry leading to winners and losers.

Transport and the environment

Concern about the environment has preoccupied the Community at least since the early 1970s, with the publication of the First Environmental

Action Programme (1973–7) which clarified the principles and objectives of community environmental policy. This was followed by the Second (1977–81), Third (1982–6) and Fourth (1987–92) Environmental Programmes which confirmed that the Community's objective of economic growth had to be linked with protection of the environment and natural resources. The transport sector is closely associated both with natural resources as a consumer of energy derived from fossil fuels (oil, coal, etc.) and user of land, and with the environment as one of the principal sources of air and noise pollution.

Besides the general reasons for Community involvement with the environment emanating from the Treaty of Rome and the objective of 'the constant improvement of the living and working conditions' of the peoples of Europe, different national standards regarding environmental issues implied the need for harmonisation and coordination. For example, in the field of transport exhaust emission curbs on motor vehicles that were more tight in one member country than in another would mean restrictions on inter-state transport, while different national standards, e.g. regarding passenger cars, constitute impediments to free trade. Moreover, the impact of pollution of inland waterways, the sea and air is not confined to any particular country. Transboundary pollution is an international problem requiring international solutions. On the other hand, some EC policies, such as agriculture and transport, can have serious impacts on the environment of each member of the Community.

In principle, the aim of the Community is to coordinate and harmonise the national environmental policies in an attempt to prevent, reduce and as far as possible eliminate pollution and nuisances by common action. In the field of transport the Community has concentrated its efforts to curb pollution on its own and at international level as a signatory to a number of international conventions for the protection of the environment. A number of directives issued by the Community have dealt with maximum permitted noise level and the emission of pollutants by different modes of transport; pollution at sea; land-use planning for road transport; air and noise pollution by heavy goods vehicles; and town traffic. The Commission's approach to the development of policies that respect the environment is based on the 'polluter pays' principle. Many observers find, however, that in many cases the Community's legal texts have not been matched by obvious improvements to the environment, because environmental directives either are frequently not implemented or are implemented late (Klatte, 1986). Indeed, increased awareness about the environmental implications of policies and mounting problems of congestion have convinced certain influential groups that what the Community needs is not deregulation, but increased regulation in transport.

11.5 Conclusions

The transport sector of the Community is not liberalised and a common transport policy does not as yet exist. The reasons for this lack of success are to be found in the intransigence of member states towards establishment of common policies which will open their transport sectors to competition by firms of other member countries and will restrain their power to interfere in their national transport sectors. However, the search for a common transport policy is reaching a crucial point with the Single European Act coming into force in 1992. The abolition of frontier controls means that the transport quotas will have to be progressively relaxed until they are abolished all together. This will require the adoption of common safety standards which will enable hauliers to operate freely throughout all the member states. There is more real chance for opening up the market and removing restrictions in every mode of transport, road, air, rail and marine. The consequences of this will include more traffic, increased demand for transport resources and space, and more pollution. Environmental considerations would have to be included in the balance between growth and improvement of living and working conditions in post-1992 Europe.

Further reading

Writers on transport matters usually criticise the CTP's lack of 'clear vision of transport as a process and an important determinant of economic and social justice, environmental quality and the quality of life'. For a comprehensive view of EC transport policy, past and present, see Despicht (1969), Bayliss (1979), Button (1979) Erdmenger (1983), Button (1984) and Whitelegg (1988). Swann (1988) gives a comprehensive summary of the transport problems and policies in the EC.

12

Industrial policy

12.1 Introduction

The focus of arguments for involvement of the government in industrial policy is, first, the issue of market failure, and, second, the competition between different sectors within a country and between similar sectors of different countries.

Economic analysis distinguishes between market failure caused by externalities, market power and asymmetric information. Externalities are usually expressed as divergences between private and social costs or benefits. Market power is detrimental to economic efficiency if, by distorting competition, it causes misallocation. Similarly, asymmetric information about prices and product qualities introduce imperfections causing allocative inefficiencies.

In almost every country there is a preference for industry over other sectors of the economy. In developed countries this preference arises from the fact that industry is already a high-priority sector of the economy for production, employment and growth. In less developed countries the preference for industry is often based on the alleged dynamic effects of industrialisation which are associated with technology and the capacity to raise productivity and the rate of growth of national income. Preference for industry usually implies some degree of government industrial policy, direct or indirect.

Since governments in different countries have different preferences for industry over other economic sectors or particular types of industry (capital intensive, advanced technology, etc.), and different views as to which market failures in which markets they ought to regulate, industrial policies are in principle multifarious and heterogeneous between

291

countries. By their implications on different sections of a country's population, regions and pressure groups (employers and employees, producers and consumers, government and voters, etc.), industrial policies always have both economic and political dimensions. For example, regional imbalances in the level of unemployment and the rate of growth would presumably be corrected by market forces. However, the social and economic implications of waiting long enough for the market forces to accomplish this objective may be politically unacceptable. Moreover, the issues of market power, rate of return, innovation and technological change are a subject of both domestic industrial policy and foreign trade policy. Similarly, aid to industry, protection from foreign competition and taxes on production and subsidies are policies that affect both industry and trade.

The advocates of activist government policy argue that, besides the issue of market failures and the general preference for industry, market forces provide inadequate incentives to invest in sectors essential for economic performance, such as high-risk, new-technology industries. The proponents of this line of argument claim that, without industrial policy, the country may end up with the wrong industrial mix. Hence the role of active industrial policy is to identify and promote the growth of those sectors that are of special importance for the development of the economy and society, as for example industries that generate substantial spillover benefits for other industries or individuals. Accordingly, if these strategic sectors face strong international competition, they should be protected and even subsidised to enable them to compete in the domestic and international markets. In contrast, the advocates of no intervention hold that governments need only remove all impediments to the smooth working of market forces and that any attempt to designate particular sectors of the economy as being especially strategic is unwarranted. Under conditions of perfect competition between firms within and between countries, absence of externalities and free entry and exit into and from industries, the market would allocate resources optimally by equalisation of factor returns across sectors and by specialisation of production and trade between countries according to comparative advantage.

In reality, competition within and between countries is not always perfect nor are private returns to factors of production always equal to social returns. Therefore, in principle there is scope for government policy designed to improve industrial performance in the domestic market. Moreover, if the industries concerned generate substantial positive externalities or display increasing returns to scale, trade policy may bring additional benefits to the country by shifting the terms of international competition in imperfect markets to domestic firms's advantage. The gains to one country are then clearly achieved at the expense of other countries. In general, if assistance to certain industries is to be provided, it is preferable that it takes forms other than protection by tariffs or quotas which discriminate between home and foreign sales.

12.2 European industrial policies

The Treaty of Rome advocates trade liberalisation and market integration based on competition across the whole of the Community. This will be implemented by specific measures to combat restrictive practices, control mergers, monitor state aid and eradicate dumping. These measures will create the environment where industry will function and develop. A common industrial policy would attempt to coordinate the abolition of barriers between the member states for opening up the market to competition by harmonising taxes and national standards, balancing the effects as between countries and regions and, if the case may arise, protecting the industry from unfair international policies.

In the European Community, the structure of labour employment and production differ considerably between the member countries. While on average in the Community of twelve, industry employs 32.7 per cent of the labour force and contributes 35.5 per cent of the GDP, the corresponding figures in Germany are 41.2 and 40.3 per cent, and in Greece 28 and 28.6 per cent (see Table 2.2). Where sectors of the industry are concerned, the disparities between different countries are even greater. These disparities are a consequence of differences among the member countries in the level of economic development, the degree of specialisation and other geographic, historical and economic reasons. Most of these reasons have been inherited from the past when the countries of the Community were separate and relatively small economic units. However, with the enlargement of the market within the Community new opportunities have emerged which favour changes in the structure and scale of production, specialisation according to comparative advantage and reallocation of production and employment in such a way that they could make the Community industry develop enough to compete effectively with that of its trade partners.

We remarked earlier that countries in general intervene in their industrial sectors for a variety of social, economic and political reasons. In the countries making up the EC, different attitudes towards the free market have led to different forms and degrees of government intervention, with the implication that the industrial policies at the national level of the Community members have been diverse. Many decentralised market economies, such as those of the EC countries, have followed mixed industrial policies, actively promoting structural change in some sectors and simultaneously submitting other sectors to free-market forces. In the latter case, responsibility for production, investment and technical innovation rests essentially with firms, while the role of the state is to supervise the orderly functioning of the free market. Some countries relied in the past on trade protection to insulate the industry from foreign competition. Most of the member states have from time to time made heavy use of assistance to industry through subsidies. These have taken the form of fiscal and financial incentives, such as tax and interest rate preferences, and contributions of funds to promote investment, research and development and labour employment at the national and regional level. In countries in which the government participated directly in industrial production through public enterprises, assistance has occasionally been provided to cover operating deficits.

Membership in the Community implies acceptance of the consequences of reallocation of production, and this means that many industries, which in the past were cushioned by interventionist policies, will be exposed to increasing competition through the enlarged market, and in the process some of them will perish. Under these circumstances it is likely that governments will attempt to protect threatened industries and jobs and to enlarge their country's share of high-return industries. Therefore, integration may itself induce a tendency for more intervention at the level of national industrial policy, or even to an industrial policy war between member states. This danger calls for coordination and harmonisation in the field of industrial policy during the process of market integration. A common industrial policy is also needed if the Community industry is to take advantage of the opportunities for rationalisation, specialisation and growth which the enlarged market presents. Improvements in the allocation of resources and reorganisation of the industry at EC-wide scale are expected to raise economic welfare by increasing the rate of growth of production, employment and income for the Community as a whole. This can take place at the same time as certain member states suffer adverse industrial shifts through market liberalisation and competition. The possibility of significant reallocation of industrial production adds another reason to the necessity for adjustment assistance by redistribution among the member states through the EC budget.

Under free-market principles and competition-oriented industrial policy there is no case for intervention in the industry by a common industrial policy. Nevertheless, the Community has to create the legal and competition environment in which the competitive industry will operate. Consequently, the Treaty of Rome entrusted the Commission with powers, independently of the Council of Ministers (but under the supervision of the Court of Justice), to dismantle restrictive practices by companies or governments which inhibit free trade between the member states and act against the interest of the consumers (EC, 1973a). But during the 1970s, when the plans for developing a competition and industrial policy were formulated, the economic climate changed by two dramatic increases in the price of oil and the subsequent rise in the prices of raw materials and the rate of inflation. Simultaneously, the combined pressure of rapidly increasing competition from newly industrialising countries (NICs) and rapid technological change had effects on both domestic production and international trade. Most of the developed and less developed economies found themselves unprepared for these events and unable to adapt fast enough to the changing economic conditions. Rigidities in the allocation of resources and the falling volume of demand and production led to rising unemployment. As in some countries the old and uneconomic industry became increasingly uncompetitive, a strong tendency developed towards contraction of the manufacturing sector and decrease in industrial employment (that is, de-industrialisation).

Against a background of halting economic growth, increasing international competition and rapid changes forced by technological progress, many countries altered their approach towards industrial policy by becoming more interventionist and by resorting to increased protectionism by non-tariff barriers to international trade. Change in favour of interventionist industrial policy was also observed among members of the Community.

In the following sections we examine how the Community, while aiming at enlargement, liberalisation and integration of the internal market, attempted to develop a common industrial base and to formulate a coherent common industrial policy.

12.3 Early attempts for a common industrial policy

The economic conditions of the 1950s and 1960s favoured the non-interventionist approach to industrial policy. Therefore it is not surprising that in the Treaty of Rome there is no specific reference to a need for comprehensive industrial policy. The Community's aims of integration could be served by opening up the market of the member states to competition and by facilitating the establishment of 'a single industrial base for the Community as a whole' (Paris Summit, 1972). Hence the Treaty deals only with the rules of competition and certain aspects of implicit industrial policy, such as the freedom of capital and labour movements, the right of establishment and the creation of a single market. Under the ideology of the neo-functionalist school of thought, it was expected that within the competitive environment of the Community's integrated market, industry would spontaneously transform itself to take advantage of the opportunities and facilities provided.

Competition-oriented industrial policy is based on the principle of non-intervention. The role of the central authority is limited to supervision of the process of market integration and the unimpeded functioning of the common market. Hence, in the highly optimistic times of the 1950s the Treaty of Rome entrusted the Commission to implement the rules of competition and to act only in case of excessive intervention by the governments of the member states. This was not the case with the other two Communities, the European Coal and Steel Community (ESCS) and the Euratom (EAEA), which were empowered to make use of interventionist policies. The ECSC aimed at a common strategy for modernisation of the coal and steel industry which suffered from over-manning, low productivity, excess supply and uncompetitiveness in the world market. Euratom's objectives were to promote atomic energy and to facilitate nuclear research in the member states.

Implicitly, industrial policy within the Community-wide market includes more than implementation and supervision of the rules of competition. The existing national industrial policies, which were based on different ideologies and objectives, and different power structures between the government, trade unions and employers in each member state, have to be harmonised in such a way that they would eventually converge to form the common industrial policy of a single market. Direct and indirect subsidies to industry have to be coordinated for those sectors of industry which show signs of growth and eliminated for sectors in decline and obsolescence. National industrial policies for regional development also have to be harmonised in order to remain compatible with the rules of competition within the common market. Similarly, at the level of the Community it has to be ensured that the existing structure of the industry is amenable to change and adaptation so that it can take advantage of the opportunities presented by the enlarged market to achieve maximum economies of scale. Research and development at the scale of the common market also have to be centrally facilitated in order to provide the momentum of industrial development and adaptation.

However, the Community policy of *laisser-faire*, free-for-all industrial market did not seem to work towards desired directions. With Germany continuing its policies of neo-liberalism and France and Italy intensifying their traditional policies of intervention, convergence of industrial policies did not occur. The industry of the member states did not seem to be able to adapt in the enlarged market or to attempt to gain from scale economies. In the period 1961–9 over half the foreign subsidiaries established within the Community were owned by non-members (primarily US firms); over half of mergers and take-overs were within the same member country, and two-thirds of the rest were accounted for by third countries; and only one-fifth of cooperative ventures were between firms of EC member countries. The events showed that the ideology of non-intervention and enhanced competition expatiated in the Rome Treaty had to be reconsidered in the light of increasing competition by US multinationals and Japanese firms. The first steps towards this direction were taken after the merger of the three Communities in 1967 and the establishment of a separate Directorate-General for Industrial Affairs to coordinate the work of the Commission in the areas of internal market, regional policy, industrial affairs, competition, transport and energy.

The first major task of the Commission was to draw up a profile of the Community's industrial structure and to put forward priorities for common action. The *Memorandum on Industrial Policy* (EC Commission, 1970, the Colonna Report) proposed the setting up of a common industrial policy of the Community aiming at economic expansion and technological development within a European industrial framework. The proposals put forward by the Memorandum dealt with five broad issues:

1. The creation of a single market based on the elimination of intra-Community barriers to trade.
2. Legal, fiscal and financial harmonisation to facilitate the right of establishment, and adoption of a European Company Statute to enable companies to be formed under Community rather than national law.
3. Active promotion of trans-EC mergers in order to enable European firms to adapt to the needs of the common market and to withstand increasing competition from outside firms.
4. Improvement in management techniques to ensure smooth adaptation to the changing industrial and employment conditions.
5. Common front and Community solidarity against competition from abroad, supplemented by the undertaking of research and development through Community financing on a trans-European basis.

However, with regard to the practical application of these principles, the Memorandum made rather general statements and recommendations which amounted to a formula for cooperation between the governments of the member states and the Commission rather than a supranational centrally administered industrial policy. At the same time it proclaimed a policy of intervention which according to many liberal-minded observers had no legal base on the Treaty of Rome, and therefore its implementation depended on the political ideology and will of the member states. The French reacted by submitting their own counter-proposals which, in the spirit of pluralism, stressed the need for coordination of members' national industrial policies but without an independent supranational role for the Commission. The Germans opposed on principle any form of intervention in the industry at the national and the Community level. The other members sided with the one or the other of these ideologies. Hence, with different members advocating different economic approaches and pursuing within their own frontiers different national industrial policies, there was no substantive consensus about what the objectives of a Community interventionist industrial policy should be. Therefore, the necessary political will for adopting and implementing the proposals of the Memorandum did not materialise.

The next major breakthrough in the attempt to lay the foundations for a common industrial policy was the communiqué of the 1972 Paris Summit which declared a commitment by the enlarged Community (of nine members) to adopt by January 1974 a programme of action for the establishment of 'a single industrial base for the Community as a whole'. Following this, the Commission submitted a *Memorandum on the Technological and Industrial Policy Programme* (EC Commission, 1973, the Spinelli Memorandum) in which it was emphasised that the industrial policy of the Community 'is , and will continue to be, based largely on free enterprise, on agreements freely concluded between workers' and employers' organizations, and on programmes carried out by regional public authorities'. In essence, the substance of this Memorandum was the introduction of a competition-oriented common industrial policy based on the following:

1. An accelerated but flexible approach towards elimination of technical obstacles to trade and harmonisation of national regulations.
2. Opening-up of national markets for purchasing by public sectors.
3. Encouragement of trans-EC enterprises.
4. Harmonisation of company law and liberalisation of capital markets.
5. Diffusion of information for the encouragement of cooperation and mergers between Community firms within the context of the competitive market.

Although with support from the European Parliament and the Social

Committee the programme outlined in the Memorandum was adopted by the Council in December 1973, the practical implications were minimal. What was missing again was consensus on the necessity of a common industrial policy, and also what such a policy should look like and how it would be implemented.

12.4 New directions

The two memoranda and the ensuing discussions highlighted the need for a strategy to improve the business environment by unification of the internal market and by implementing legal and institutional changes to alter the structure of the manufacturing sector. The Community's attempt to create the economic climate and the legal framework for the development of large European firms which would benefit from scale economies and be able to compete effectively in the world markets against the firms of the United States and Japan did not succeed. Despite numerous proposals put forward by the Commission since the 1970s and the lengthy discussions about them, the European Company Statute has yet to be adopted. The latest proposal (EC Commission, 1975a) is before the Council which stopped its examination in 1982 but returned to it in 1988. The aim of the retabled proposal is to relaunch the idea of the European Company concentrating on three key issues: the principle of an optional statute, the independence of this statute from national laws and the inclusion of specific alternative schemes to worker participation (EC Commission, 1989d).

The objective of the European Company Statute is to enable EC firms to choose an appropriate structure for cooperation on the scale required by the Community-wide market, thus helping them to be more competitive with their counterparts outside the Community. The European Company would be based on an independent legal order, separate from the national systems of rules, but alongside other types of companies set up under national laws. On the tax side, the company will be subject to the laws of the country where it has its head office. The proposal also recommends that workers should be consulted and kept informed about the firm's strategic decisions (EC Commission, 1988g).

However, these plans did not advance far during previous discussions, mainly because some members of the Community resisted the introduction of the European Company Statute on the grounds that it would interfere with national legal systems. Doubts were also expressed as to whether in large firms, as those envisaged in the proposal, the benefits of scale economies would exceed the cost of reduced ability to adapt to a rapidly changing economic climate.

Community multinational companies and industrial collaboration schemes exist, some at the company level and a few at the government level. The latter include collaborative schemes which are European but not Community projects, such as the Airbus (which involves companies backed by government financial support), the Joint European Torus (JET, which is a joint undertaking under the Euratom Treaty) and Ariane (which includes some non-EC participants). But although these collaborations are examples of remarkable initiatives, they are relatively few and have played only a minor role in the strategy for establishing a Community-wide industry and introducing a common industrial policy.

While the Community remained undecided about the necessity for changes in the industrial sector, the economic recession, which began in the second half of 1974, led to rising unemployment and falling output. At the same time, with increasing low-cost export supplies from Japan and NICs, the Community was experiencing loss of competitiveness in both the internal and the world markets. The member states, perhaps under pressure from their electorates, reacted individually to these events by resorting to inward-looking, defensive economic policies which gave priority to the short-term protection of industries, jobs and standards of living. These short-sighted policies intensified the fragmentation of the Community market where the economies of the member states started competing against each other; thus economic convergence suffered a setback and integration reached a stalemate. This situation compelled a reappraisal of both the objectives and the policies which would be required for a new drive towards European unity. The ensuing discussions showed clearly that for a solution to these problems three interdependent objectives must be pursued simultaneously: unification of the internal market, common industrial policy and improved competitiveness in international markets.

As a first step for renewing the impetus towards market unification and integration, the EMS was launched on 13 March 1979, after nearly two years of discussions and planning. More proposals for the elimination of barriers to internal trade were put forward which aimed at unification of the market as the means for invigorating the European industry. They included proposals for opening up public purchasing, setting up a wider system of common standards, increasing cooperation in research and promoting joint projects. Differences among the members emerged again when discussions started about the necessity for a common interventionist industrial policy. A solution advocated by some members and outside experts (Hager, 1982; Richonnier, 1984) was to combine liberalisation of the internal market with a certain degree of selective protectionism from external competition. This was justified on the ground that the domestic industry had fallen so far behind those of the United States, Japan and NICs that only protection of the domestic market could revive it. Protection against NICs was also advocated because of the lack of reciprocity and perceived undervaluation of their exchange rates.

The arguments in favour of activist industrial policy became more explicit during the Copenhagen Summit of December 1982, when it was proposed that industrial sectors whose existence was threatened by foreign competition must be protected by trade restrictions. Temporary protection on infant industry considerations was also envisaged for development of advanced technology industries which could not otherwise get a headstart in a market already dominated by US and Japanese firms. The Summit ended with agreement from all sides that the internal market should be strengthened, research related to industry should be speeded up, and more funds should be channelled to invest in industry, high technology and energy.

The Copenhagen discussions were followed by submission of memoranda to the European Council by interested members. The most comprehensive of these was the French memorandum (Richonnier, 1984) which emphasised the need for developing a European industry able to compete effectively against the duopoly of Japan and the United States. The memorandum argued that the investment required to achieve this objective is beyond the capabilities of any single European country and requires a market well in excess of the domestic markets of any single member state. A common industrial base would be accomplished by industrial cooperation at the level of the Community and by the adoption of a common industrial policy which would combine reduction of trade barriers within the Community with managed protection from external competition: this later became known as the 'Fortress Europe' approach. Detailed proposals were also included regarding harmonisation of company law, opening up of public procurement to intra-Community competition, pooling of research efforts and funds, introduction of common standards and granting of subsidies and other means of assistance to newly emerging industries or sectors in difficulty. Investments by foreign firms would be allowed but only if they create jobs and are directed to sectors which are not already in excess capacity.

The countries' memoranda present the views of particular countries but they do not constitute Community policy. The ideas aired in the French memorandum are opposed by Germany, Denmark and the Netherlands which advocate free trade and liberal economic policies. The United Kingdom and Luxembourg are rather closer to the liberal cause, although they would welcome the implementation of many of the French proposals. Italy and the three new members of the Community will rather support the French proposals. At the level of the private sector, some big companies, particularly in France and Italy, want the abolition of internal frontiers to be matched by stronger barriers against imports from the world outside, the 'Fortress Europe' pressure group. The proposals for more protection by countries and companies and the possibility that they may become Community policy have increased the lobbying activities of EFTA countries who seek to ensure that closer EC integration will not mean more obstacles for their goods and services. At the same time, some multinationals from the United States and Japan are concentrating more investment and production inside the Community, thus insuring against the possible introduction of restrictive trade policies.

In parallel with the countries' memoranda, programmes for a common industrial policy were also put forward in 1983 and 1987 by the Round Table of European Industrialists, a pressure group of chief executives, presidents and managing directors of big European companies. Their proposals aim at faster progress towards market integration, virtually free of government intervention. According to the group this sort of strategy will enable European industry to compete effectively against the industries of the United States and Japan. On the practical side, the group set up in the Netherlands a European venture-capital fund and continues to lobby European governments and the Commission for swifter action on implementation of the necessary legislation for completing the integration of the market by 1992. The group considers that completion of the single market is a step towards the right direction for developing a European industry.

Therefore, in conclusion, although each individual member of the Community will agree that the European industry as a whole is facing severe problems, there is no consensus on what should be done about it. Of the three interdependent objectives which have been considered as necessary for the establishment of a common industrial base and for the revival of the European industry only one is currently pursued. This is the objective of creating the single market by the end of 1992. The drive towards completion of the single market revived interest in the possibility of introducing the European Company Statute. To this effect, the Council adopted in 1985 a Regulation regarding the European Economic Interest Grouping (EEIG), which is an instrument designed to encourage links between independent companies on matters of common interest, such as joint research or joint sales. The European summit in Brussels on 29–30 June 1987 also declared that the Community's 'common economic area' necessitated 'swift progress with regard to the company law adjustments required for the creation of a European company'.

The market reacted to these developments rather swiftly. With the approach of 1992, companies started to become more aware of the realities of fiercer competition and of the opportunities presented by the single market and to use a variety of methods to meet the challenge of serving 325 million consumers. Many industrial and financial corporations entered into transnational alliances or joint ventures within the EC to pursue a clear post-1992 strategy. Cross-border mergers and acquisitions, which started to reach record levels in 1989, along with many joint ventures were spurred by the notion that market power and profitability require a large share in the single market. At the same time, mergers provide instant access to foreign suppliers, factories, sales-and-marketing networks and often cheaper labour. On the other hand, many medium- and small-scale companies have realised that the only way to survive the competition is to team up with larger companies. At last, the prospect of the single market is changing the shape and structure of European industry.

12.5   Problem industries

In addition to across-the-board measures relating to industry in general, the members of the Community have been taking specific measures to cope with particular problem industries. Further to action taken at the national level and approved by the Commission, the Community assists by providing financing in the form of grants and loans. For the modernisation and restructure of industry with specific regional or social objectives, financing is provided by the ERDF and the Social Fund. The ECSC provides loans, financed by ECSC borrowing, exclusively to coal and steel industries. For other projects, in particular those relating to small and medium industry, loans can be obtained from the EIB which supplies financial assistance under the powers conferred to it by the EEC Treaty or under the NCI. The latter provides loans specifically for investment projects which, through the dissemination of new technology and innovation, tend to reinforce the competitiveness of the Community economy.

For certain key industries, the 'crisis sectors', which are under threat from international competition or are facing problems over a long period of time, coordinated policies have been followed by the member states at the level of the Community. The more important of these industries are now discussed.

Steel

The steel industry was once one of the most important for the Community. But since 1974 it has been contracting in both output and employment. It currently employs only 0.6 per cent of the working population, or 1.5 per cent of all the Community's industrial workforce. Since the steel industry is traditionally concentrated in a few areas, the effects of its decline have created devastating regional problems.

The problems of the steel industry are not new: they were one of the two reasons for the establishment of the European Coal and Steel Community (ECSC) in 1951. But, while in the 1950s and 1960s the problem of the steel industry was how to respond fast to the rapidly expanding demand, since the 1970s it has been how to contract under the pressure of declining demand and rising foreign competition.

The present difficulties of the industry stem from the sudden change in demand from a long period of growth (6.6 per cent per annum during 1960–74) to a rapid collapse. The reasons for this change are, first, the generalised economic slow-down; second, the technological change in both production and utilisation techniques and the increased competition from plastics and other substitutes; and, third, the emergence of competition from non-traditional producers, Japan and the NICs.

The steady expansion of demand in the 1960s induced major capacity-increasing investment programmes which continued even after the first economic crisis of 1974, under the assumption that the difficulties of the industry were cyclical and temporary. But when the crisis started to bite, it led the European steel industry to massive underutilisation of capacity (62 per cent utilisation in 1980), substantial staff reductions (by 50 per cent between 1974 and 1986) and a slump in prices. Accumulating financial losses had adverse effects on new investment for modernisation. Thus the industry became out of date with low productivity, unable to compete effectively with technologically advanced foreign producers, such as Japan. Consequently, between 1974 and 1976 imports in the Community rose by 133 per cent, while exports fell by 32 per cent. In the meantime, the extra production capacity, which was laid down before the crisis, came into line and caused intensification of the competition for orders among the EC producers with further pressure on prices, which on average fell by 50 per cent within two years.

These conditions led in 1977 to a Community programme for steel (the Simonet Plan) which was based on reduction of domestic production by the introduction of voluntary sales quotas. But, with demand falling rapidly and import competition rising, the slump continued and new measures were urgently taken in an attempt to contain the crisis. The new package of proposals, the Davignon Plan, was agreed in May

1977 with the following provisions:

1. Voluntary restrictions of production.
2. Minimum and recommended prices at the Community level.
3. Import surveillance and conclusions of voluntary export restraint agreements with exporting countries.
4. Monitoring of investment programmes and national aids.

Although early results showed that these measures had a degree of success, the second massive rise of oil prices in 1979 intensified the crisis to the extent that in 1980 the Community was forced to declare the industry in 'manifest crisis' under Article 58 of the Treaty of Paris (ECSC). Under the 'Merger Treaty' the European Commission has executive authority for the ECSC and is invested by the ECSC treaty with powers to control production and prices of steel. Accordingly, in July 1981 the Commission introduced mandatory quotas on firms and imposed further restrictions on imports. Simultaneously, the efforts for restructuring the industry continued with the objectives of reducing excess capacity and increasing efficiency and productivity. State aid was allowed only if it was directed towards implementation of a restructuring programme leading to capacity reductions. The Community would also contribute aid directly to programmes for the alleviation of the consequences of restructuring the industry, as for example for redeployment of redundant workers, the financing of new jobs or early pensions, and for regional regeneration.

Although the code on state aids to steel, adopted in 1980, called for the termination of operating subsidies by the end of 1984 and of most aids by the end of 1985, these measures will now continue until the industry is restructured on an efficient basis and some form of long-term equality is established between demand and supply. The restructuring policy has already reduced the production capacity of the industry, thus raising the capacity utilisation rate from 50 to 70 per cent between 1982 and 1986. However, the capacity problem has not yet been resolved and more problems have been added by expansion of the policies to the new members, Portugal and Spain. Production quotas have recently been replaced by surveillance, while VERs on imports of certain finished products have been extended.

Textiles and clothing

Foreign competition and slow growth in demand have meant that this industry is in long-term decline which has recently accelerated with the slowdown in economic activity. In ten years (1975–85) production dropped by 6 per cent, consumption rose by 7 per cent, imports doubled and employment fell by 40 per cent, with a loss of 1 million jobs. But the textile industry is still very important for the Community as an employer of labour and significant contributor to value added (6 per cent and 10 per cent of total manufacturing) and as a supplier of exports.

The textile and clothing industry is characterised by a wide diversity of production with different problems from branch to branch. What all branches of the industry have in common are the stagnant or slightly rising demand, and the intense competition from low-cost producers, which are mainly low-wage NICs of the Third World. Between 1975 and 1985 the share of imports in EC consumption rose from 18 to 45 per cent.

With expectations of moderate rises in the domestic demand and fast rises in foreign competition, the future of the industry does not look promising. Therefore, for survival the industry requires substantial structural changes with reorientation towards branches in which the Community has a comparative advantage relative to its competitors, that is, capital-intensive production using advanced technology and highly skilled labour. However, these structural changes require the financing of vast new investment and have the undesirable effect that a substantial part of the present workforce will become redundant. The need for financing and the social and regional implications of policies for the renewal of the industry are the grounds on which public intervention is justified.

The policy at the Community level includes the reduction of over-capacity and the prevention of forms of government aid which tend to shift the textile industry's problems from one member state to another. Assistance granted by a member state to its industry must be linked to restructuring plans. In addition to measures taken at the national level, the Community is financing research and development programmes and provides limited aid through the ERDF to regions dependent on the textile industry which are affected by the crisis. Financial assistance is also provided by the Social Fund for the retraining of workers still employed by the industry, and of redundant workers, to help them find alternative employment.

The problems of international competition have been temporarily alleviated by the Multi-fibre Arrangement (MFA) which came into existence as a 'temporary' departure from normal GATT rules in 1974. In fact, under the auspices of the GATT, the MFA has been extended three times (MFA IV, August 1986–July 1991), the last time by thirty-nine participants, including the twelve members of the EC as a single entity. The MFA's initial intention was to help the Third World exporters in the short-term, without greatly diverting from the longer-term objective of eventually applying GATT rules to trade in textiles and clothing; but MFA IV does not specify a time limit for reaching this objective. A clause in MFA III, which stipulated that any 'mutually acceptable agreement' can be made between importers and their dominant suppliers, has been used by the contracting parties as the basis for negotiating VERs. In an attempt to help the domestic industry to recover its international competitiveness, the Community has also resorted extensively to signing VERs with most of the textile-exporting countries. Nevertheless, despite the MFA, exports of textiles from LDCs have increased significantly: during 1986–7, imports of textiles in the EC from MFA exporters rose by 54 per cent.

The presumption is that national quantitative restrictions on imports will be eliminated by the end of 1992. However, it has not yet been decided whether the national quotas on textiles allowed into the Community under the MFA will continue at EC-wide scale, and how they will be shared in the single market. A promising development is that, despite administrative barriers such as labelling and 'country of origin' requirements and different VAT rates, a good deal of integration between member states has already taken place in textiles and clothing.

Shipbuilding

Since shipowners are not in any way constrained to buy from domestic sources of production, shipbuilding is a pre-eminently world industry. The problems of this industry started well before the economic recession. International competition, which has always been intense in shipbuilding, changed in the 1950s and 1960s as a result of shifts in comparative advantage. Japan, Korea and other developing countries, new to shipbuilding, expanded their shipyards (mostly built with Japanese capital) and dominate world production. Characteristic of these shipyards was the extensive production subsidies they were receiving from state funds. In an attempt to offset the comparative disadvantage, other shipbuilding states supplied their industry with subsidies. Although at the time the high rate of growth of world trade sustained a rising demand for more shipbuilding, the subsidies to the industry at worldwide scale led to excess capacity. When the increase in the price of oil caused recession and a slump in international trade, the market for shipping collapsed and falling freight rates led to a world shipping surplus and hence to a fall in orders for new ships. The shipbuilding industry thus ended up with a vast structural imbalance between world capacity and world demand.

In countries with a tradition in shipbuilding, this situation, which is likely to continue for several years to come, resulted in more intervention in the form of state aid to shipyards, which were facing particular difficulties because many were old and therefore insufficiently competitive. These problems were particularly severe in the EC countries where most shipyards could neither operate on a large scale nor compete with the modern shipyards of Japan, Korea and other new suppliers from developing countries. Consequently, the EC's share in total world production has declined sharply, from about 31 per cent in 1976 to 19 per cent in 1987. Hence, despite cuts in production and workforce (by 50 and 40 per cent respectively between 1976 and 1980) the European Commission has estimated that a further reduction in capacity by one-third of its 1985 level is required. With increase in productivity through structural change and modernisation, this reduction in capacity is expected to cause a greater than commensurate decline in labour employment.

In an attempt to correct distortions in competition, the Community issued a series of directives for the harmonisation of members' state aid, by fixing a ceiling and limiting the eligibility for financial assistance to investments that improve productivity and competitiveness. Initially, the intention of the Community was to phase out state aid to the industry and liberalise the market between 1969 and 1975. But, following the oil crisis of 1974, it was decided that 'the continuation of the crisis has serious consequences for the Community shipbuilding industry which makes the immediate abolition of such aid impossible' (EC Commission, 1981b). Hence, the phasing out of state aid was indefinitely postponed and the aid ceiling was pushed up, reaching 28 per cent in December 1986. The state aid is now termed temporary or 'crisis aid' and is associated with an attempt to encourage undertakings to modernise and rationalise shipyards. The ceiling is to be reviewed annually, and is expected to be reduced over time as Community shipyards become internationally competitive. The long-term objective of the common policy is to restructure the industry by adjusting its capacity and activities to the Community's market, volume of maritime traffic and social and strategic interests. However, in the short term the outlook remains bleak, the recession continues, and so does the state aid to the industry. Lately, the Community started exploratory talks with Japan and Korea for a 'sectoral arrangement on production' aiming at stabilisation of the international market. This would involve agreements for capacity reduction, price policies and the subsidies provided to the shipbuilding sector.

The motor industry

The main car producers within the EC are France, Germany, Italy, Spain and the United Kingdom. The producers are state-owned or private firms, some mainly European and others multinational (mainly non-European). Collectively, the motor industry of the Community produces more vehicles than that of the United States or Japan, which is now the world's most highly automated manufacturer and the foremost exporter of vehicles. In the Community the industry uses 20 per cent of Community steel production and employs 2 million workers directly and 4 million indirectly, more than any other single manufacturing operation. However, with the exception of the German motor industry, which accounts for almost half the EC total value of car production, all other car industries in the Community have been in financial trouble in recent years, from which they were rescued by state intervention. At the national level support is provided by protection from foreign competition and state subsidies. In an attempt to integrate the market, the Community has in general made greater use of the competition rules to eliminate state aids that distort trade within the EC, although certain types of aid associated with restructuring the industry are still authorised.

The production side of the Community market is characterised by fragmentation, particularly in the components industry. Since the motor industry in general offers opportunities of sizeable economies of scale, there is scope for large-volume production and profitable cooperation among the European producers. Changes in production methods by the application of new technology and automation are expected to bring further economies of scale.

The fragmentation of production reflects the segmentation of the European market for motor vehicles. Levels of tax on sales, subsidies, protection from imports, technical and safety regulations, government subsidies to 'national champion' companies (Fiat in Italy, Renault in France and, formerly, and – after many changes of name – Rover in the United Kingdom), import restrictions on (Japanese) cars and many other devices have combined to distort or to limit competition, fragmenting the car market at the level of the domestic industry. All these make the prices of the same final product vary greatly among the partners of the common market (see Table 12.1). In fact, as the end-1992 single-market

Table 12.1   Motor industry: tax spread and pretax price of final product

Country	Pretax price for a new car[1]	Tax take on a pretax car[1] price of 100	Average pretax price[2] 1987	1989
B	100	25	121	123
DK	92	173	100	100
D	109	14	128	137
E	116	31	142	149
F	108	33	128	132
GR	112	156	n.a.	107
IRL			130	145
I	122	18	129	148
L	100	12	122	127
NL	92	50	122	130
P	107	39	127	140
UK	147	25	144	161

[1] 1.3 I Ford Escort at June 1985 prices, based on an index of 100 for the price in Belgium.
[2] Cheapest = 100.

Source: EC *Twelfth EEC Report on Competition Policy*; European Bureau of Consumer Organisations (BEUC) *Survey, 1989*.

deadline approaches, price gaps are growing, one of the reasons being that car-makers, and sometimes governments, continue to place illegal obstacles in the way of transnational bargain-hunters. Under existing EC rules, any individual can buy a car tax-free in the Community country of his choice and pay tax on it at home.

Research has shown that the technology employed in car manufacture implies unit cost reduction by 10 per cent with every doubling of volume, right up to 2 million cars. However, even the largest European producers fall short of this minimum cost scale (Owen, 1983). Market integration and increasing use of modern manufacturing methods, permitting both mass production and the production of differentiated output, can potentially lead to substantial economies of scale. Figure 12.1, which is based on the actual cost characteristics of car production (Rhys, 1977), illustrates the potential benefits from market integration and economies of scale. The domestic demand of one country before the formation of the customs union is *D*. The foreign supply in this market is *FF*, which is perfectly elastic at c.i.f. import price *OF*. The average cost of the actual or potential domestic production is *SS*, falling as the quantity of output rises. If the country follows free trade policies, market equilibrium will be reached at price *OF* and quantity 150,000 cars a year. In this case, domestic production is unable to compete with imports which will supply the entire volume of output. Assuming average cost pricing, the domestic industry requires total volume of production equal to 250,000 units per year to be able to compete with imports at the going market price. But this volume of output is 100,000

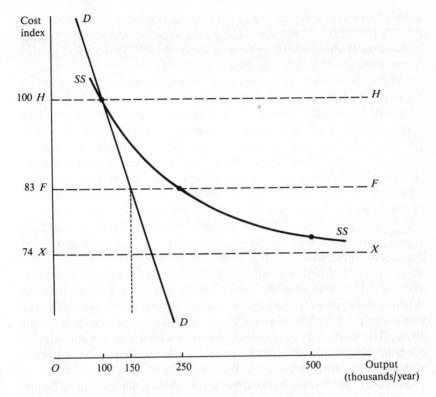

Figure 12.1 Economies of scale in the car industry.

units larger than the domestic demand. Facing insufficient domestic demand, the domestic car industry would consider exports to foreign markets as a possible outlet for the excess supply. However, exports would be possible only if the supply price falls below *OX*, the f.o.b. price realised by exporters. Alternatively, if the country does not follow free-trade policies, then the domestic demand for 100,000 cars is exactly matched by the domestic supply at the import-preventing price *OH*.

In the integrated market of a customs union, protection will be unnecessary if the combined demand of the partners is sufficient to support domestic production equal to at least 250,000 units. If the scale of production is sufficiently large, the industry will not only supply the market of the customs union; it will also be able to compete in the international market. The important point here is that increase in the industry's output through exporting to the union partners will reduce the cost of all its output, yielding benefits over and above those usually associated with free trade. This effect arises from cost reductions along a given (or potential) structure of production, and therefore it is dynamic only in a narrow sense. If market enlargement were to induce cost-reducing technological change leading to a downward shift of the average cost curve, then the effects would be genuinely dynamic.

When the market is fragmented, motor manufacturers react by adjusting the bulk of their production programme to the conditions prevailing on the markets where they sell the majority of their output. This practice in turn leads to resistance to market integration, since manufacturers will object to any sudden changes that will affect their market shares and require them to undertake vast investments on adjustment of their plants. In their turn, manufacturers also contribute to the fragmentation of the market by restrictive practices, such as exclusive dealerships, market sharing and price discrimination. Agreements on distribution and after-sales service in the automobile industry have been granted by the Commission *block exemption* of the competition rules prescribed in Article 83 of the Treaty until the end of 1995.

The present situation clearly is an obstacle to the development of a genuine EC motor industry which, with access to a large internal market, taking up almost 30 per cent of total world new registrations for private cars, should be able to modernise and compete with its main rivals. The Community's efforts towards reaching this end include the opening of the internal market by the harmonisation of technical standards, the development of a procedure for issuing Community certificates of conformity, approximation of motor taxation in different countries both on vehicle purchase and on fuel, and standardisation in safety specifications and pollution controls. Unresolved problems are those of common research and development, the monitoring of state aid, and the question of opening the internal market to foreign competition in conjunction with a more aggressive common external trade policy. However, despite the numerous Community directives relating to all these matters, the car market is by no means fully liberalised.

With increasing competition from foreign producers, most notably Japan whose share in the European market is around 10 per cent, the European motor industry is on the defensive. At the moment, imports of automobiles from Japan into member countries are restricted primarily at the individual member level, mostly by quotas imposed either unilaterally or bilaterally (in the form of VERs). Thus, the annual limits on imports of Japanese passenger cars in total sales are 0.2 per cent in Italy, 3 per cent in France and 11 per cent in the United Kingdom. Export restraints are also applied in Spain and Portugal. The fact that most members of the Community have taken the protection of their national market in their hand means that the Community protection policy is inadequate and in practice not very common. At the level of the Community, besides an 11 per cent common external tariff, there is surveillance on imports of cars from Japan and general restraint agreements.

A prominent feature of the international motor industry in recent years has been the strong and continuing expansion of foreign investment by Japanese motor companies, first in North America and in developing countries, and later in Europe, particularly in the United Kingdom. The reasons for this expansion are increasing protection of domestic motor industries and, in the case of the EC, the advantages of the single market and the possibility that further integration will raise import barriers. The removal of internal barriers in the EC by 1992 implies the removal of national quantitative restrictions against Japanese cars. This has raised concerns that the existing national barriers might be replaced by tighter EC-wide restrictions (Ishikawa, 1990). In this context, automobile producers in many EC countries have argued that any reduction in the restrictions should be conditional on a reciprocal increase in access for the EC automobile industry to the Japanese market.

The Commission's trade policy proposals, yet to be approved by Council, recommend the elimination of national import restrictions on Japanese cars during the period 1990–92. However, they allow for the possibility of introducing after 1993 a transitional period of controlled growth of imports at Community level in order to enable member states to adapt progressively to the total opening of the market. The proposal suggests that the growth rates for Japanese exports should be sufficient to allow increased access to the EC market, and in fact they would be 'monitored' by the Japanese themselves to prevent any surge in shipments, that is in the form of VERs. But this proposal is resisted by France, Italy and Spain who take a hard line against any rapid and unilateral liberalisation of their car markets, sometimes arguing instead that protection of the car industry should rise. Not surprisingly, member states with no major vested manufacturing interest in car production would resist such a policy. Although no formal agreement has been reached, it now seems certain that no additional external restraints will be imposed at the level of the Community. Higher protection has the adverse effect that consumers will pay more for their purchases and that restructure of the industry, which is a prerequisite for modernisation, cost reduction and increase in competitiveness, will be delayed.

Advanced technology industries

These are key industries which are expected to play an important part in the functioning and development of the economy now and in the future. Electronics, biology and genetic engineering, aerospace, nuclear energy and advanced engineering are sectors belonging to the category of industries which are marked by further developments obtained from intense research. Another reason for promoting these industries is their positive externalities, that is their large technological spillovers to the rest of the economy. It is in fact these externalities, in the form of generation of knowledge and innovation, which are unlikely to be rewarded at their marginal social benefit, that makes the high-technology industries fitting for industrial policy in the form of promotion and protection. If these sectors operate in an international environment of imperfect markets, then the arguments for intervention gain additional credence.

Collaboration in research, promotion and, if the case may be, protection should be a constituent part of the common policy for the development of these industries at the level of the Community. To this effect the Commission has made a number of proposals and has taken initiatives for the formulation of policy, as for example in the sector of information technology.

The market for information technology (computers, electronic components, databanks, modern telecommunications, etc.) is expanding rapidly world-wide. In the Community, the domestic industry is lagging behind its principal US and Japanese competitors, both in development and in market share: in 1982, US firms won more than 60 per cent of the world market for information technology, against 22 per cent for the Japanese and only 11 per cent for Community firms. To remedy this state of affairs the Community has taken a number of measures:

1. Policies towards market integration by harmonisation of standards and technical procedures, progressive opening up of public procurement markets to all Community firms, coordination of the research efforts of the member states and supplementary funding of technological development by means of Community funds.
2. Setting up of Euronet, the first major European network for long-distance transmission of computerised information.
3. Launching of the ten-year (1984–94) European Strategic Programme for Research and Development in Information Technology (Esprit). This is a joint Community and private sector programme (electronic industries, universities and research laboratories in EC member countries) to promote cooperation in research with potential industrial applications. Under this programme, projects undertaken by private companies which have joined the scheme receive half of the incurred cost from Community funds. The programme involves activity in advanced microelectronics, advanced information processing, office systems, computer-aided manufacture and

infrastructure activity for the promotion of co-operative research and development (R&D) at the level of the Community.

Esprit, which is Europe's largest single research programme, has three main aims: first, to provide the EC's information technology (IT) industry with the basic technologies it needs to remain competitive with the United States and Japan in the 1990s; second, to promote cooperation between EC companies in this field; and, third, to add momentum to the use of international standards. However, the goal of building up technologies with which the EC might fend off the United States and Japan has proved difficult to achieve. Although the Esprit has paved the way for international standards and Europe has made an appreciable gain in basic technology compared with the United States and Japan, its capital investment has proved inadequate for the goals it set out to achieve and is much smaller than the amount spent by the leading Japanese electronics companies in a single year. Esprit represents only 5 per cent of R&D expenditure of the IT industry. Therefore its greatest achievement perhaps is that it has helped to persuade EC's industrialists to tackle R&D projects that they would not otherwise have attempted.

At the private sector level, the industry is pressing governments to get the frontier-free programme moving faster. National markets, even in the larger member countries of the Community, are too small to enable firms to recover investment costs in new products, particularly for innovative high-technology firms. The Eureka programme aims at collaborative research which is led by the companies themselves with only a limited steering role from secretariat, based in Brussels. It currently comprises nearly 300 projects which involve about 1,000 companies and 500 research laboratories.

The Community has also initiated programmes for the development of a Community-wide market for telecommunications and for industrial applications of biotechnology, e.g. in pharmaceuticals, agrifoodstuffs and energy. Like Esprit, the research programmes for both sectors will receive half their funds from the Community.

12.6 Conclusions

Manufacturing industry is still the most important economic sector of the Community for production, trade and employment. In recent years the industry has operated against a background of economic recession, with slow growth of demand, rising unemployment, increasing international competition and rapid changes forced by technological progress. Although these are problems which to some extent are shared by all members of the Community, industrial policy still remains largely a national responsibility. The reasons for this are that, first, there is no consensus among the members of the Community that an industrial policy is necessary; and, second, the partners disagree about whether the common approach should be that of interventionist industrial policy. At the moment, the dominant opinion among the members of the Community is that industrial policy should not have a separate entity, but it should instead be developed as a part of the general strategy for integration which includes internal market unification and common policies for research and development, trade, monetary affairs and competition.

The Community's industrial strategy consists of policies aimed at improvement of the business environment, both by working towards the integration of the European market and promoting the necessary changes in the structure of manufacturing industry. The efforts towards completion of the single market continue and it now seems certain that the barrier-free European market will be realised according to schedule, in 1993. This has given a welcome boost to cross-border mergers, acquisitions and joint ventures which are shaping a new structure of production and distribution, and a new market of financial services in Europe. Similarly, a number of broad integrated programmes of research have been launched, but more are required at a scale comparable with those being undertaken in Japan and the United States to enable the Community to catch up with its rivals in modern technology, production and trade. The growth of European industrial output lags behind those of the United States and Japan. The level of productivity achieved by European countries is persistently below those reached in the United States and Japan: the best European performances still are about 65 per cent of the level in the United States, which on average is equal to that of Japan. An implication of these differences in performance is that on external markets the Community is rapidly losing ground, particularly in the case of high-technology industries, such as electrical and electronic equipment, office machinery and information technology. However, despite the fact that Europe's competitive position in international trade remains relatively weak, it seems more probable that the Community will neither become a free-trader overnight nor resort to increased protection as the means for industrial growth. At the moment, its efforts are concentrated in the completion of the single market which is expected to have a favourable impact on competitiveness and performance.

The attempts over the past few years for formulation of a consistent industrial policy have highlighted certain problem areas for which action must be taken at the level of the Community. Such problem areas are: (a) the lack of coordination and inconsistency of national measures, whether undertaken by private companies or by the government, and (b) the need for restructure and industrial renewal in the face of ongoing recession, increasing competition from foreign firms and rapid technological progress. These are problems which must be solved if the industry is to serve the Community of European peoples, and to contribute to the effort for reduction of unemployment and increase in growth and welfare. The industry will contribute towards this end by taking advantage of the large and integrating market of the Community to raise capital, to invest and to achieve efficiency via economies of scale and innovation, which will enable it to compete effectively within and without Europe.

Further reading

The Community's industrial strategy is summarised in EC (1982). Pearce and Sutton (1985) discuss the problem of protection and industrial policy, while Swann (1983) examines issues of competition and industrial policy. For a general review of the structure and problems of European industry see Geroski and Jacquemin (1985). For the problems in US–EC trade relations see Baldwin *et al.* (1988).

13

Europe 2000: progress and prospects

Economic integration has not been uniquely defined in the literature. Some writers define integration in terms of a process and a state of affairs. Others define integration in terms of objectives. As a process, economic integration brings about intensified application of the principle of international division of labour together with a greater degree of unity between states; economic integration thus encompasses measures designed to abolish discrimination between economic units belonging to different national states. As a state of affairs, economic integration is characterised by the absence of various forms of discrimination between national economies (Balassa, 1961). In terms of objectives, integration is the ideal of equal opportunity; it means a society whose members are treated equally and enjoy an equal degree of liberty to achieve whatever goals they may pursue (Myrdal, 1956).

The European Community has been on the road to economic integration for three and a half decades and it is just now attempting to form a common market. During the years its membership has doubled from six to twelve countries and hence disparity between the members on economic and social matters has increased. Nevertheless, the Community continues to pursue two principal objectives: in the medium term, to improve the living and working conditions of the member states; and, in the long term, to unite Europe. Both of these objectives require the members to reconcile their national policies and targets by abandoning the advocacy of purely nationalistic interests and objectives in such a way that they can work together on the building of economic union. This is not an easy task. The pattern of relationships between the states making up the European Community has roots in history both for and against European integration and cannot change easily from one day to the next. The common elements in the cultural and political heritage of Europe are intermingled with nationalism, conflict of interest and friction.

The procedure and the timetable for completion of the first phase of integration, that of customs union, had been defined in the Treaty. Actually, all customs duties of the six founder members were abolished a year and a half ahead of schedule. But the next steps of the process of integration were only lightly sketched in the Treaty. Insufficient Treaty provisions regarding both aims and timetables, and the volatile international economic environment of the 1970s and 1980s, meant that common policies for the creation of the common market were introduced piecemeal after protracted negotiations and over long intervals of inactivity. The requirement for unanimity in decisions of major importance for the participating states and the Community has been another factor retarding progress towards integration.

The Commission plays an active part in the policy-making process by both formulating and promoting the proposals on which decisions are based. But the final arbiter of what must be done is the Council, which still has the sole power of decision in all important matters. The Council of Ministers represents the governments of the member states and therefore the member states themselves through their governments are responsible for the degree of integration achieved in the Community at any point in time. We can criticise the Community for using suboptimal policies and indirect ways to reach its objectives or for being slow and ineffective, achieving too little in a very long time. But it would be unrealistic to subject the process of decision-making in the Community to optimality criteria. Decisions are reached by bargaining and compromise between (six, nine and now twelve) independent states who, having regard for their national interests, relinquish one aspect of national sovereignty after another every time a decision for more integration is taken. Given that political ideologies and the commitment to integration differ between governments and that in democratic countries governments are not monolithic and change rather frequently, it should not be surprising that Commission proposals take one form after another before they are finally approved by the Council and are transformed into policies. Therefore any attempt to devise welfare-maximising economic policies or to interpret actual economic policies by optimisation criteria is a rather futile exercise.

Integration is a dynamic process which involves the transfer of both economic and political power from the member states to the Community. Economic decisions at the level of the Community have political implications. Indeed for some observers economic integration is only the means for achieving the ultimate objective, that of political integration.

Conversely, politics, both domestic of the member states and inter-state, impinges on economic policy-making at the level of the Community. Membership in the Community widens the horizon of politics and reduces the degrees of freedom available to a government to design and execute domestic economic policies. Community policies may be opposed by member countries under pressure from interested parties, by Community-wide pressure groups or even by the Community institutions such as the Commission or the European Parliament. For the Community, a policy that conforms with its objectives, increases the cohesion between the members and contributes to the process of economic and political integration is a good policy. For each member state's government, Community policies are acceptable if they do not harm their standing in domestic politics and can be presented to their electorates as advantageous for the country or for specific influential groups of the population of the country (farmers, producers, consumers and so on). In general, there are limits to the extent governments can depart from the status quo by changing a given situation of domestic politics and economics in search for common policies in the Community. Given these constraints, we should consider the progress the Community has made during three decades as a qualified success.

Integration causes problems which affect the members in different degrees. When the need for solutions can no longer be delayed, coalitions of interests press the members to form alliances in order to force the adoption of common policies. Therefore, as integration causes increasing interdependence of the European economies, governments are forced to come to terms on their divergent and frequently purely national interests, to transform a collection of nation states to a rather more coherent entity, and to cooperate on the building of the union of peoples. It took the Community thirty years to reach this point with the enactment of the Single European Act (SEA, 1986).

Since the mid-1980s the European Community has made more progress towards integration than in any comparable period before. One of the most important contributing factors to this development has been the change in the rules of decision-making with greater use of majority voting. This has eased the process of reaching agreement by compelling even the less enthusiastic participants to keep pace with the frontrunners. The 1992 programme has provided the impetus for change. Its successful implementation has progressively convinced the people and the governments of the Community that the single market will actually happen. The EC's steady progress towards integration at a time of historical transformations in geo-political, economic and military structures has also changed the attitudes and the behaviour of outsiders towards the Community. Eastern Europe, EFTA, Japan and the United

States have realised that the Common Market at last has become firmly established and they have begun to upgrade their relationships with the EC and to form closer economic and political alliances.

The progress so far achieved has encouraged the Community to attempt even more ambitious projects. Economic and Monetary Union and Political Union are approved objectives, the details of which will be considered by two parallel inter-governmental conferences in December 1990. Although many of the goals still remain undefined, the directions are now clearer. However, this leaves a number of unresolved issues, the fate of which will be decided before the coming of the new century. Some of the most important EC domestic and international issues are the following:

(1) *The democratic deficit.* With accelerating progress towards European integration, many members of the EC are concerned about 'accountability' and 'democratic deficit', that national parliaments have little influence over Community legislation, while the European Parliament has only limited powers of amendment. The forthcoming inter-governmental conference on constitutional reform will consider how to reinforce the union's democratic legitimacy and make the European institutions more efficient. Any solution which will strengthen the European Parliament will move Europe towards a federal system of government, and it will be resisted by at least some national parliaments. The changing economic and political alliances in Europe may also require the formation of new EC-based security organisations and centralisation of foreign policy.

(2) *EMU.* Economic and Monetary Union is an objective which will be completed by the introduction of a single currency, issued by a new European Central Bank (ECB or Eurofed), and binding rules on national budgets. This development has been seen 'as the natural complement of the full realisation of the Single European Act and the realisation of the 1992 objective: the internal market without frontiers' (EC Commission, 1990). The basic question is not whether a single currency in Europe is necessary for realising fully the rewards of 1992, but what is the best way of getting there. Thus, it is now conceded that EMU will happen and the member countries will go along with the transfer of monetary sovereignty from national governments to the ECB. What will be crucial in the coming years is the speed adopted by the EC for reaching EMU, most countries and the Commission arguing that a rapid transition towards a complete monetary union will reduce the risks of monetary and financial instability, while others (especially the United Kingdom) maintain that the complexity of implementing EMU should

attest for a slow approach. Disagreements have also surfaced as to whether during the transition to EMU, national budgets should be limited by binding rules or only monitored centrally. These differences of opinion between the members do not imply that a two-speed Europe will be necessarily instituted: a divided approach to integration is contrary to the philosophy so far expounded by the Community, that every one should move forward together.

The latest proposal from the Commission (EC Commission, 1990) is to move forward with a faster timetable. Thus stage 2 of the process, during which the ECB will be established, should begin as early as possible and be 'as short as possible'. But this caused concern among member countries with weaker economies which could be left behind in too rapid a progression towards union. These countries fear that, unable to devalue in the single market, they will have to adjust through higher unemployment. Since this problem intensifies the possibility of a multi-speed Europe, the Commission has admitted in its plans a new element of flexibility, that the entry of weaker economies (Portugal and Greece) in the ERM 'will depend on the degree of convergence which they achieve. Rigorous economic policy programmes, supported by the large transfers of resources from which these countries benefit, could lead to entry before the second stage' (EC Commission, 1990).

During the transition to the single currency, the ECU will continue to be defined by its component currencies and 'should become an increasingly "hard" currency'. Following this proposal, the European Community summit at Rome (October, 1990), disregarding UK objections, agreed to begin the second stage of economic and monetary union in 1994 and to aim for a single European currency by the end of the decade.

The question about the speed and method for reaching EMU will be considered by the inter-governmental conference on economic and monetary union which will start work in December 1990. The same conference will also deal with the preparation of the necessary amendments to the Treaty of Rome which, according to decisions taken at the European Community summit (October, 1990), should be based on the following general principles:

1. Economic union is an open market system that combines price stability with growth, employment and environmental protection and is dedicated to sound and sustainable financial and budgetary conditions and to economic and social cohesion.
2. Monetary union will proceed by the creation of a new monetary institution comprising member states' central banks and a central organ, exercising full responsibility for monetary policy. The mon-

etary institution's prime task will be to maintain price stability. The monetary institution will be independent of instructions.

(3) *The EC budget*. The European Community countries have agreed the structure of revenues and expenditures of the European budget until 1992. After 1992, enhancement of competition in the unified market and the move towards EMU are expected to have profound effects on certain regions, population groups and even member states. 'As a consequence, the Community's own-resources system and the budgetary responsibilities of the Community institutions will have to be adapted to the needs of the economic union' (EC Commission, 1990). In the longer term, this will require the budget to evolve along federal finance lines.

The European budget will be called to play a more substantial role in the allocation of the cost and benefits of the common market because: first, this will be required for upward convergence, cohesion and growth in the whole of the Community, and, second, in the pursuit of common goals the member states will lose the use of some of their policy instruments, such as interest rates, money supply and exchange rates, and will have constraints imposed on the use of others, such as national budgets, so that a centrally directed common budget will be required to assist them reach their objectives during the process of integration. The issues relating to the European budget are economic, political and historical and involve a number of problems relating to national sovereignty and the delegation of power to supranational authorities. These problems lead to three interrelated questions, which have not been considered by the EC partners as yet:
(a) What are the proper functions of the European budget?
(b) What are the appropriate instruments for pursuing these functions?
(c) What are the proper sources and means of financing the European budget?
The answers to these questions require a decision on the principles which should govern the European budget in the single market of twelve sovereign member states which are becoming increasingly interdependent but constitute neither a proper political federation nor a homogeneous unified society with similar preferences.

(4) *Reform of the CAP*. Critics of the EC have long said that the Community is basically protectionist-minded and they point to the CAP to illustrate their position. The Community argues that most industrial countries protect their agriculture. The United States, for example, spent per farmer in 1987 'almost five times what the common

agricultural policy cost per farmer' (EC, 1989d). Although the liberalisation of international trade in agricultural commodities has been agreed in principle at the GATT Uruguay round of trade liberalisation, it is not yet clear how far it will go. The United States are pressing the EC to reduce its farm support by 70 per cent, including a 95 per cent cut in export subsidies over the next ten years. However, for a number of domestic economic and political reasons certain members of the Community (France, Germany) are at the moment reluctant to agree to such a radical change in the CAP. Nevertheless, after combined pressures by the GATT, domestic consumers and the international community, a first step towards liberalisation of agricultural commodity trade was taken in November 1990 when the EC decided a 30 per cent reduction in subsidies on most farm products. This reduction, however, fell short of the cuts demanded by the United States who, objecting to the fact that the Community had offered no guarantees on improving access to European markets or substantially reducing export prices, stated that 'Europe exports its problems and the rest of the world pays for it'. Divisions between the United States and the EC over how far to reduce farm export subsidies continue to imperil a successful conclusion of the latest GATT negotiations for world trade liberalisation.

It is now expected that the need for reaching a more liberal world trade regime, combined with domestic pressures for reform, will compel the European Community to rethink its agricultural policies, and it has already been recognised that 'in the 1990s the CAP should do more than simply continue the process of reorganisation' (EC, 1989d). Since farm subsidies still remain the biggest element in the redistribution of resources in the Community, the EC's budgetary finances are bound to exert additional pressure for a radical reform of the CAP in the not too-distant future.

(5) *Width or depth?* Many European countries have already applied (Turkey, Austria, Cyprus, Malta) or plan to apply for membership in the Community. However, the Commission and the Council have decided that no membership talks should start before completion of the single market. Meanwhile, the Community has launched a plan for the creation of an eighteen-member European Economic Space (EES) comprising the EEC and EFTA. Countries of Eastern Europe have welcomed the trade and cultural agreements offered by the EC, they expect that they will be elevated to 'association agreements' rather soon, and hope for 'eventual membership' in the Community some time in the near future. By that time there will be, not only clearer indications about, but probably significant progress in the implementation of Economic, Mon-

etary and Political Union. 'Deepening' before 'widening' is a strategy that will accelerate integration under the existing constitution of the Community, but at the same time it will make the admission of new full members more difficult. Hence federalists are especially hostile to a bigger EC, whose heterogeneity would threaten the goal of more political integration. Consequently, the system of concentric circles (a twelve-member EC surrounded by a first circle of EFTA and an outer circle of East European associate members), with the core moving faster towards a federal structure of government, might become a real possibility.

(6) *International trade.* Despite the assurances of the Community, the question of free trade versus protection still remains unresolved. In contrast to currently existing arrangements (Article 115 EEC Treaty), the internal market programme does not provide for differential treatment of imports from non-member countries in different member states. Therefore, the question is whether a uniform trade regime for the Community will tend towards higher or lower levels of protection. The Community insists that, unquestionably, its economic policy will not be that of 'Fortress Europe'. What Europe's trade partners fear is the tendency of any large area composed of diverse interests to attempt to reconcile conflicts over domestic difficulties by shifting as much of the burden of adjustment to outsiders as possible. They also suspect that powerful alliances between national pressure groups within the single market will attempt to stop, reverse or at least delay the planned application of liberal foreign trade policies, and that governments of the member states of the EC, mostly for political reasons, will go along with restrictive trade policies. A successful conclusion of the latest round of GATT negotiations would demonstrate that there is a world-wide consensus for freer trade.

The question of whether the EC will make a positive move towards a more liberal world trade order centres at the moment on the size of the cuts in farm support it will be prepared to make. However, in addition to agriculture, the GATT talks aim for the first time to set rules for world trade in services and intellectual property (patents and copyrights). This time, it is the United States that imperil a successful conclusion of these talks by arguing that for services it will grant MFN treatment only in those sectors it chooses. Without agreement in this area, the EC, which is the world's biggest services exporter, will have no qualms about refusing to make concessions on agricultural subsidies demanded by the United States. Under these conditions the Uruguay round of trade negotiations reached an impasse in December 1990.

Three months later they were resumed without a deadline for their completion. This would allow time for the EC to agree and implement its CAP reforms and to resolve its differences with the United States.

The formation of the European Community and the policies it has followed have affected the economic, political and security policies of all countries in Europe and the world. What will happen next will be decided during the remaining few years of the 20th century. What is hoped for is that: 'The natural attitude of a European Community based on the exercise by nations of common responsibilities will be to make these nations also aware of their responsibilities, as a Community, to the world' (Monnet, 1962).

References

Armstrong, H. W. (1985) 'The reform of the European Community regional policy', *Journal of Common Market Studies*, **23**, 319–43.

Armstrong, H. and J. Taylor (1985) *Regional Economics and Policy*, Philip Allan, Hemel Hempstead.

Artis, M. J. (1987) 'The European Monetary System: An evaluation', *Journal of Policy Modeling*, **9**, 175–98.

Artis, M. J. (1988) 'The EMS in the face of new challenges', in P. Arestis (ed.) *Contemporary Issues in Money and Banking*, Macmillan, London.

Artis, M. J. and M. P. Taylor (1988) 'Exchange rates, interest rates, capital controls and the European Monetary System: Assessing the track record', in F. Giavazzi, S. Micossi and M. Miller (eds) *The European Monetary System*, Cambridge University Press, Cambridge.

Balassa, B. (1961) *The Theory of Economic Integration*, Irwin, Homewoods, Illinois.

Baldwin, R. E., C. B. Hamilton and A. Sapir (eds) (1988) *Issues in US–EC Trade Relations*, National Bureau of Economic Research, Chicago University Press, Chicago.

Bayliss, B. T. (1979) 'Transport in the European Communities', *Journal of Transport Economics and Policy*, **13**, 28–43.

Berglas, E. (1981) 'Harmonisation of commodity taxes: Destination, origin and restricted origin principles', *Journal of Public Economics*, **16**, 377–87.

Bhagwati, J. (1988) *Protectionism*, MIT Press, Cambridge, Massachusetts.

Brooke, P. (1989) 'The Government's approach to the community: Some myths dispelled', in M. Gammie and B. Robinson (eds) *Beyond 1992: a European tax system*, IFS Commentary No. 13, Institute for Fiscal Studies, London.

Bryant, R. C., D. A. Currie, J. A. Frenkel, P. R. Masson and R. Portes (1989) *Macroeconomic Policies in an Interdependent World*, International Monetary Fund, Washington DC.

Buckwell, A., D. R. Harvey, K. J. Thomson and K. Parton (1982) *The Costs of the Common Agricultural Policy*, Croom Helm, London.

Button, K. J. (1979) 'Recent developments in EEC transport policy', *The Three Banks Review*, **123**, 52–73.

Button, K. J. (1984) *Road Haulage Licensing and EEC Transport Policy*, Gower, Aldershot.

Camps, M. (1965) *What Kind of Europe*, Chatham House Essays, London.

Cecchini, P. (1988) *The European Challenge: 1992: The benefit of a single market*, Wildwood House, Aldershot.

Cnossen, S. (ed.) (1987) *Tax Coordination in the European Community*, Kluwer, Deventer, Netherlands.

Cnossen, S. and C. S. Shoup (1987) 'Coordination of Value-Added Taxes', in S. Cnossen (ed.) *Tax Coordination in the European Community*, Kluwer, Deventer, Netherlands.

Cooper, C. A. and B. F. Massell (1965) 'Towards a general theory of customs unions for developing countries', *Journal of Political Economy*, **73**, 461–76.

Cooper, R. N. (1969) 'Macroeconomic policy adjustment in interdependent economies', *Quarterly Journal of Economics*, **83**, 1–26.

Cooper, R. N. (1985) 'Economic interdependence and coordination of economic policies' in R. W. Jones and P. B. Kenen (eds), *Handbook of International Economics*, vol. II, North-Holland, Amsterdam.

Corden, W. M. (1972) 'Economies of scale and customs union theory', *Journal of Political Economy*, **80**, 465–75.

Corden, W. M. (1979) *Inflation, Exchange Rates and the World Economy*, Lectures on International Monetary Economics, Clarendon Press, Oxford.

Corden, W. M. (1984) 'The normative theory of international trade', in R. W. Jones and P. B. Kenen (eds), *Handbook of International Economics*, vol. I, North-Holland, Amsterdam.

Denton, G. (1984) 'Re-structuring the EC budget: Implications of the Fontainebleau Agreement', *Journal of Common Market Studies*, **23**, 118–40.

Despicht, N. (1969) *The Transport Policy of the European Communities*, PEP, Chatham House, London.

Devereux, M. and M. Pearson (1990) 'Harmonising corporate taxes in Europe', *Fiscal Studies*, **11**, 21–35.

Dosser, D. (1967) 'The economic analysis of tax harmonisation', in C. S. Shoup (ed.) *Fiscal Harmonisation in Common Markets*, Columbia University Press, Columbia.

Dosser, D. (ed.) (1973) *British Taxation and the Common Market*, C. Knight, London.

EC (1967) 'First and second VAT Council Directives', *Official Journal*, 71.

EC (1973a) *Treaties Establishing the European Communities*, Luxembourg.

EC (1973b) *Report on the Regional Problems in the Enlarged Community*, (73) 550 (Thomson Report), Brussels.

EC (1979a) *25 Years of European Community External Relations*, European Documentation, Luxembourg.

EC (1979b) 'A transport network for Europe: Outline of a policy', *Bulletin EC*, Supplement 8.

EC (1980) 'Report on the scope for convergence of tax systems in the Community', *Bulletin EC*, Supplement 1.

EC (1981a) *The European Community's Legal System*, European Documentation, Luxembourg.

EC (1981b) 'Guidelines for European agriculture', *Bulletin EC*, Supplement 4.

EC (1982) *The European Community's Industrial Strategy*, European Documentation, Periodical 5, Luxembourg.

EC (1983a) *EEC Competition Rules*, European Documentation, Periodical, Luxembourg.
EC (1983b) 'Adjustment of the Common Agricultural Policy', *Bulletin EC*, Supplement 4.
EC (1983c) 'Further guidelines for the development of the CAP', *Bulletin EC* 6.
EC (1983d) *The Social Policy of the European Community*, 3rd ed., European Documentation, Luxembourg.
EC (1984a) 'The Budget', *Bulletin EC*, **6**.
EC (1984b) *Opinion to the Council and the Commission on the Issue of Protectionism*, Economic Policy Committee, No. 19.
EC (1984c) *The European Community's Transport Policy*, European Documentation, Periodical 3.
EC (1985a) 'Texts from the European Council' (Single European Act), *Bulletin EC*, **11**, 9–20.
EC (1985b) *The European Community's Fisheries Policy*, European Documentation, Luxembourg.
EC (1985c) *The European Community and the Mediterranean*, European Documentation, Luxembourg.
EC (1985d) *Grants and Loans from the European Community*, European Documentation, Luxembourg.
EC (1986) *The European Community's Budget*, 4th ed., European Documentation, Luxembourg.
EC (1987a) *The ECU*, 2nd ed., European Documentation, Luxembourg.
EC (1987b) *The Common Agricultural Policy and its Reform*, European Documentation, Luxembourg.
EC (1988a) 'Reform of the structural funds', *Bulletin EC*, **7/8**, 8–14.
EC (1988b) 'Interinstitutional Agreement on budgetary discipline and improvement of the budgetary procedure', Annex III, *Official Journal*, 185.
EC (1989a) *The European Commission and the Administration of the Community*, European Documentation, Luxembourg.
EC (1989b) *Europe Without Frontiers: Completing the internal market*, European Documentation, Luxembourg.
EC (1989c) *Completing the Internal Market*, Document, Luxembourg.
EC (1989d) *A Common Agricultural Policy for the 1990s*, European Documentation, Luxembourg.
EC (1990) *1992 – The Social Dimension*, European Documentation, Luxembourg.
EC Commission (1961) *Memorandum of the General Lines of a Common Transport Policy* (Schaus Memorandum), Brussels.
EC Commission (1962) *Action Programme of the Community for the Second Stage*, Brussels.
EC Commission (1963) *Report of the Fiscal and Financial Committee* (The Neumark Report), Brussels.
EC Commission (1969) *A Regional Policy for the Community*, Brussels.
EC Commission (1970) *Industrial Policy in the Community: Memorandum from the Commission to the Council* (the Colonna Report), Brussels.
EC Commission (1973) *Memorandum on the Technological and Industrial Policy Programme*, (the Spinelli Memorandum), Brussels.
EC Commission (1974) *Social Action Programme*, Luxembourg.
EC Commission (1975a) *Towards Economic Equilibrium and Monetary Unification in Europe*, Study Group on Optimum Currency Areas, Brussels.

EC Commission (1975b) *Stock-taking of the Common Agricultural Policy*, Brussels.

EC Commission (1976) *European Union* (Tindemans Report), *Bulletin EC*, Supplement.

EC Commission (1981a) *Civil Aviation Memorandum No. 2, Progress Towards the Development of a Community Air Transport Policy*, Brussels.

EC Commission (1981b) *General Report on Activities of the European Communities*, Luxembourg.

EC Commission (1984a) *Five Years of Monetary Co-operation in Europe*, COM(84) 125 Final, Brussels.

EC Commission (1984b) *Agriculture in the United States and the European Community: A comparison*, Agricultural Information Service of the Directorate-General of Information, No. 200.

EC Commission (1985a) *'Completing the Internal Market'*, White Paper from the Commission to the European Council, Document, Luxembourg.

EC Commission (1985b) *Perspectives for the CAP*, Green Paper, Brussels.

EC Commission (1986) 'The social integration of disabled people', *Social Europe*, Supplement.

EC Commission (1987a) *Completion of the Internal Market: Approximation of indirect tax rates and harmonisation of indirect tax structure*, Global Communications from the Commission COM(87)320, Brussels.

EC Commission (1987b) 'The Single Act: A new frontier', *Bulletin EC*, Supplement.

EC Commission (1988a) *The Elimination of Frontier Barriers and Fiscal Controls*, Completing the Internal Market, Luxembourg.

EC Commission (1988b) 'The Economics of 1992', *European Economy*, No. 35, Luxembourg.

EC Commission (1988c) *Studies on the Economics of Integration*, Volumes 1–3, Research on the 'cost of non-europe': Basic Findings, Document, Luxembourg.

EC Commission (1988d) *The social dimension of the internal market*, interim report, *Social Europe*, 7, Brussels.

EC Commission (1988e) 'The social aspects of the internal market', *Social Europe*, 7.

EC Commission (1988f) 'Social dimension of the internal market', *Social Europe*, special edition.

EC Commission (1988g) *Conditions for Industrial Cooperation*, Completing the Internal Market, Luxembourg.

EC Commission (1988h) *Common Agricultural Policy: 4 years of reform*, Spokesman's Service, Brussels.

EC Commission (1988i) *The Future of Rural Society*, Brussels.

EC Commission (1989a) *Report on Economic and Monetary Union in the European Community*, Committee for the Study of Economic and Monetary Union, Luxembourg.

EC Commission (1989b) *Eighteenth Report on Competition Policy*, Luxembourg.

EC Commission (1989c) 'The Fight Against Poverty', *Social Europe*, 8, Supplement 2.

EC Commission (1989d) Statute for a European company, *Bulletin EC*, Supplement 5.

EC Commission (1989e) *Harmonisation of Company Law in the European Community*, Completing the Internal Market, Luxembourg.

EC Commission (1990) *Economic and Monetary Union*, Communication of the Commission of 21 August 1990, Luxembourg.

Emerson, M., M. Augjean, M. Catinat, P. Goybet and A. Jacquemin (1988) *The Economics of 1992: The EC Commission's assessment of the economic effects of completing the internal market*, Oxford University Press, Oxford.

Erdmenger, J. (1983) *The European Community Transport Policy*, Gower, Aldershot.

Fennell, R. (1985) 'A reconsideration of the objectives of the Common Agricultural Policy', *Journal of Common Market Studies*, **23**, 257–76.

Gammie, M. and B. Robinson (eds) (1989) *Beyond 1992: A European Tax System*, IFS Commentary No. 13, Institute for Fiscal Studies, London.

General Agreement on Tariffs and Trade (1972) *GATT Activities in 1970/71*, Geneva.

General Agreement on Tariffs and Trade (1982) *GATT: What it is: What it does*, Geneva.

Geroski, A. P. and A. Jacquemin (1985) 'Industrial Change, Barriers to Mobility, and European Industrial Policy', *Economic Policy*, **1**, 170–218.

Giavazzi, F. and M. Pagano (1986) *'The Advantage of Tying One's Hand: EMS discipline and central bank credibility'*, Centre for Economic Policy Research Discussion Paper No. 135, London.

Giavazzi, F., S. Micossi and M. Miller (eds) (1988) *The European Monetary System*, Cambridge University Press, Cambridge.

Goodhart, C. (1990) 'An approach to European currency unification', in C. Johnson (ed.) *Changing Exchange Rate Systems*, Lloyds Bank Annual Review, Volume 3, 194–207, Pinter, London.

Gros, D. and N. Thygesen (1988) *The EMS: Achievements, current issues and directions for the future*, Centre for European Studies Paper No. 35, CEPS, Brussels.

Grossman, G. M. (1990) 'Review' of Emerson *et al.* (1988) in *Journal of International Economics*, **28**, 385–95.

Grubel, H. (1970) 'The theory of optimum currency areas', *Canadian Journal of Economics*, **3**, 318–24.

Hager, W. (1982) 'Protectionism and autonomy: How to preserve free trade in Europe', *International Affairs*, **58**, 413–28.

Harvey, D. R. and K. J. Thomson (1985) 'Costs, benefits and future of the Common Agricultural Policy', *Journal of Common Market Studies*, **24**, 1–20.

Henderson, D. (1989) *1992, The External Dimension*, Group of Thirty, New York and London.

Hine, R. C. (1985) *The Political Economy of European Trade*, Harvester Wheatsheaf, Hemel Hempstead.

Hitiris, T. (1982) 'Progressive interdependence and economic integration: a general case', in D. Dosser *et al.* (eds) *The Collaboration of Nations*, Martin Robertson, Oxford.

HM Treasury (1982) *The European Community Budget: Net contributions and receipts*, Economic Progress Report Supplement, October.

HM Treasury (1988) *Taxation in the Single Market: A market-based approach*, September.

HM Treasury (1989) *Economic and Monetary Union: An evolutionary approach*, Economic Progress Report (EPR), No. 205, pp. 1–3, London.

International Monetary Fund (1983) *The European Monetary System: The Experience 1979–82*, Occasional Paper No. 19, Washington, DC.

International Monetary Fund (1986) *The European Monetary System, Recent Developments*, International Monetary Fund, Occasional Paper No. 48, Washington, DC.

Ishikawa, K. (1990) *Japan and the Challenge of Europe 1992*, Royal Institute of International Affairs, Pinter, London.

Ishiyama, Y. (1975) 'The theory of optimum currency areas: A survey, *Staff Papers*, International Monetary Fund, **22**, 344–83.

Johnson, H. G. (1957) 'A Marshallian Analysis of Customs Unions', *Indian Journal of Economics*, **28**, 39–48; reprinted in Johnson, H. G. (1962), *Money, Trade and Economic Growth*, Unwin, London.

Johnson, H. G. (1958a) 'A Marshallian Analysis of Customs Unions', *Indian Journal of Economics*, **29**, 171–81; reprinted in Johnson, H. G. (1962), *Money, Trade and Economic Growth*, Unwin, London.

Johnson, H. G. (1958b) 'The gains from freer trade with Europe: An estimate, *Manchester School*, **26**, 247–55.

Johnson, H. G. (1962) *Money, Trade and Economic Growth*, ch. III, Unwin, London.

Johnson, H. G. (1965) 'An economic theory of protectionism, tariff bargaining and the formation of customs unions', *Journal of Political Economy*, **73**, 256–83.

Johnson, H. G. (1968) 'The implications of free or freer trade for the harmonization of other policies', in H. E. English (ed.) *World Trade and Trade Policies*, University of Toronto, Toronto.

Josling, T. E. (1979) 'Agricultural Policy' in P. Coffey (ed.) *Economic Policies of the Common Market*, Macmillan, London.

Kay, J. A. (1989) 'Myths and realities', in *1992: Myths and Realities*, 1–28, Centre for Business Strategy, London Business School, London.

Kemp, M. C. (1969) *A Contribution to the General Equilibrium Theory of Preferential Trading*, North-Holland, Amsterdam.

Kemp, M. C. and H. Y. Wan (1976) 'An elementary proposition concerning the formation of customs unions', *Journal of International Economics*, **6**, 95–8.

Kenen, P. B. (1969) 'The theory of optimum currency areas: An eclectic view', in R. A. Mundell and A. K. Swoboda (eds), *Monetary Problems of the International Economy*, Chicago University Press, Chicago.

Klatte, E. (1986) 'The past and the future of European environmental policy', *European Environment Review*, **1**, 32–4.

Krauss, M. B. (ed.) (1973) *The Economics of Integration*, Allen and Unwin, London.

Lipsey, R. G. (1970) *The Theory of Customs Unions: A general equilibrium analysis*, Weidenfeld and Nicolson, London.

Lloyd, P. J. (1982) '3 × 3 theory of customs unions', *Journal of International Economics*, **12**, 41–63.

Long, O. (1985) *Law and Its Limitations in the GATT Multilateral Trade System*, Martinus Nijhoff, Dordrecht.

Louis, J.-V. (1980) *The Community Legal Order*, EC Commission, Luxembourg.

McMillan, J. and E. McCann (1981) 'Welfare effects in customs unions', *Economic Journal*, **91**, 697–703.

Marsh, J. S. and P. J. Swanney (1980) *Agriculture and the European Community*, Allen and Unwin, London.

Meade, J. E. (1955) *The theory of customs unions*, North-Holland, Amsterdam.

Melitz, J. (1988) 'Monetary discipline and cooperation in the European Monetary System: A synthesis', in F. Giavazzi, S. Micossi and M. Miller (eds) *The European Monetary System*, Cambridge University Press, Cambridge.

Miller, M. H. and J. E. Spencer (1977) 'The static economic effects of the UK joining the EEC: a general equilibrium approach', *Review of Economic Studies*, **44**, 71–93.

Minford, P. (1990a) 'The Delors Plan or competing currencies?', *European Freedom Review*, **2**, 13–21.

Minford, P. (1990b) 'The path to financial integration in Europe', in H. Siebert (ed.) *The Completion of the Internal Market*, Mohr, Tübingen.

Molle, W. and R. Capellin (1988) *Regional Impact of Community Policies in Europe*, Avebury, Aldershot.

Monnet, J. (1962) 'A ferment of change', *Journal of Common Market Studies*, **1**, 203–11.

Morris, C. N. (1980) 'The Common Agricultural Policy', *Fiscal Studies*, **1**, 17–35.

Mundell, R. A. (1961) 'A theory of optimum currency areas', *American Economic Review*, **51**, 657–65.

Musgrave, R. (1969) *Fiscal Systems*, Yale University Press, New Haven and London.

Myrdal, G. (1956) *An International Economy: Problems and Prospects*, Harper, New York.

Neven, D. J. (1990) 'Gains and losses from 1992', *Economic Policy*, **10**, 14–62.

Noël, E. (1979) *The European Community: How it works*, Commission of the European Communities, Brussels.

Oates, W. E. (1972) *Fiscal Federalism*, Harcourt Brace Jovanovitch, New York.

OECD (1976) *Public Expenditure on Income Maintenance Programmes*, Studies in Resource Allocation, Paris.

Owen, N. (1983) *Economies of Scale, Competitiveness and Trade Patterns within the European Community*, Clarendon Press, Oxford.

Paarlberg, R. L. (1986) 'Responding to the CAP: Alternative strategies for the United States', *Food Policy*, 157–73.

Padoa-Schioppa, T. (1985) *Money, Economic Policy and Europe*, European Perspectives, EC Commission, Brussels.

Pearce, J. and J. Sutton (1985) *Protection and Industrial Policy in Europe*, The Royal Institute of International Affairs, Routledge and Kegan Paul, London.

Pearson, M. and S. Smith (1988) '1992: Issues in indirect taxation', *Fiscal Studies*, **9**, 25–34.

Peck, M. J. (1989) 'Industrial organization and the gains from Europe 1992', *Brookings Papers on Economic Activity*, part 2, 277–99.

Pentland, C. (1973) *International Theory and European Integration*, Faber, London.

Pomfret, R. (1986) 'The theory of preferential trading arrangements', *Weltwirtschaftliches Archiv*, **122**, 439–65.

Rhys, D. G. (1977) 'European mass-producing car makers and minimum efficient scale: A note', *The Journal of Industrial Economics*, **25**, 313–20.

Richonnier, M. (1984) 'Europe: Decline is not irreversible', *Journal of Common Market Studies*, **22**, 227–43.

Ritson, C. and S. Tangermann (1979) 'The economics and politics of Monetary Compensatory Amounts', *European Review of Agricultural Economics*, **6**, 119–164.

Robson, P. (1987) *The Economics of International Integration*, 3rd ed., Allen and Unwin, London.

Rollo, J. M. C. and K. S. Warwick (1979) *The CAP and Resource Flows Among EEC Member States*, Ministry of Agriculture, Fisheries and Food, London.

Rosenblatt, J., T. Mayer, D. Bartholdy, D. Demekas, S. Gupta and L. Lipschitz (1988) *The Common Agricultural Policy of the European Community: Principles and consequences*, Occasional Paper 62, IMF, Washington, DC.

Russo, M. and G. Tullio (1988) 'Monetary policy coordination within the European Monetary System: Is there a rule?', in F. Giavazzi, S. Micossi and M. Miller (eds) *The European Monetary System*, Cambridge University Press, Cambridge.

Schneider, K. (1973) 'Tax harmonisation policy from the point of view of the Commission', in D. Dosser (ed.) *British Taxation and the Common Market*, C. Knight, London.

Shackleton, M. (1982) 'The common fisheries policy', in H. Wallace, W. Wallace and C. Webb (eds) *Policy Making in the European Community*, John Wiley, London.

Shackleton, M. (1990) *Financing the European Community*, Chatham House Papers, The Royal Institute of International Affairs, Pinter, London.

Shlaim, A. and G. N. Yannopoulos (eds) (1976) *The EEC and the Mediterranean World*, Cambridge University Press, Cambridge.

Siebert, H. (ed.) (1990) *The Completion of the Internal Market*, Mohr, Tübingen.

Stoeckel, A. (1985) *Intersectoral Effects of the CAP: Growth, trade and unemployment*, Occasional Paper 95, Bureau of Agricultural Economics, Canberra.

Strasser, D. (1981) *The Finances of Europe*, revised ed., EC, Brussels.

Strauss, R. (1983) 'Economic effects of MCAs', *Journal of Common Market Studies*, 21, 261–81.

Swann, D. (1983) *Competition and Industrial Policy in the European Community*, Methuen, London.

Swann, D. (1988) *The Economics of the Common Market*, 6th ed., Penguin.

Swoboda, A. K. (1983) 'Exchange rate regimes and European–US policy interdependence', in A. W. Hooke (ed.) *Exchange Rate Regimes and Policy Interdependence*, IMF, Washington, DC.

Van den Tempel, A. J. (1970) *Company Tax and Income Tax of the European Communities*, EEC, Brussels.

Vanhove, N. and L. H. Klaassen (1980) *Regional Policy: A European Approach*, Gower, Farnborough.

Venturini, P. (1989) *1992: The European social dimension*, Document, Commission of the European Communities, Luxembourg.

Wallace, H. (1980) *Budgetary Politics: The finances of the European Communities*, Allen and Unwin, London.

Walters, A. (1988) 'A critical view of the EMS', *CATO Journal*, 8, part 2, 503–6.

Walters, A. (1990) *Sterling in Danger*, Fontana/Collins, IEA, London.

Werner Report (1970) 'Report to the Council and the Commission on the Realization by stages of Economic and Monetary Union in the Community', *Bulletin EC*, 11, Supplement.

Whitelegg, J. (1988) *Transport Policy in the EEC*, Routledge, London.

Wickens, M. (1990) 'European Monetary Union', *Economic Review*, 7, 27–30.

Winter, A. L. (1987) 'Britain in Europe: A survey of quantitative trade studies', *Journal of Common Market Studies*, 25, 315–35.

Yuill, D., K. Allen, and C. Hull (eds) (1980) *Regional Policy in the European Community*, Croom Helm, London.

Zis, G. (1988) 'The EMS: Performance and prospects', *Economic Review*, 6, 33–35.

Zis, G. (1989) 'Should Britain join the European Monetary System?', *Economic Review*, 6, 31–3.

Index

337